D1551504

ANTIQUES

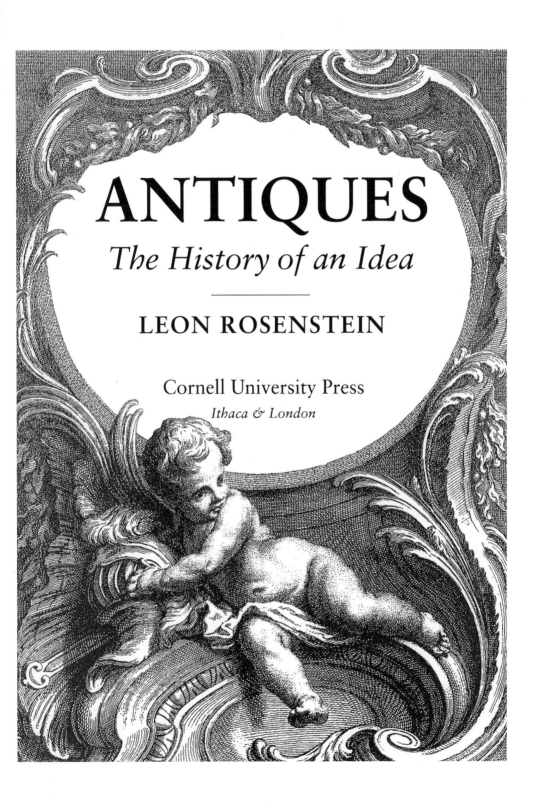

ANTIQUES
The History of an Idea

LEON ROSENSTEIN

Cornell University Press
Ithaca & London

First published 2009 by Cornell University Press

Printed in the United States of America

Library of Congress Cataloging-in-Publication data
Rosenstein, Leon, 1943-
   Antiques : the history of an idea / Leon Rosenstein.
      p. cm.
   Includes bibliographical references and index.
   ISBN 978-0-8014-4734-1 (cloth : alk. paper)
   1. Antiques—History.   2. Antiques business—History.   3 Collectors and
collecting—History.   4. Aesthetics—Philosophy.   I. Title.
   NK600.R67 2008
   745.1—dc22   2008029676

Cornell University Press strives to use environmentally responsible
suppliers and materials to the fullest extent possible in the publishing
of its books. Such materials include vegetable-based, low-VOC inks
and acid-free papers that are recycled, totally chlorine-free, or partly
composed of nonwood fibers. For further information, visit our
website at www.cornellpress.cornell.edu.

Cloth printing   10 9 8 7 6 5 4 3 2 1

For Sara,
who asks for nothing

Contents

Preface

This book represents in many respects a culmination of more than forty-five years' involvement with my subject. That is the period between my very first encounter with the philosophy of art (in a course called "History of Aesthetics" during my freshman year at Columbia University in 1961) and the present time. The book stems more directly from an article I published in the *Journal of Aesthetics and Art Criticism* several years ago entitled "The Aesthetic of the Antique." My academic involvement has been supplemented during the past twenty-five years by practical engagement with the antiques trade: my wife and I own an antiques business. Consequently, my personal experience has straddled the worlds of *praxis* and *theoria* with regard to art and antiques for some time. I hope that what follows also succeeds in some measure in bridging areas of knowledge and ways of thinking about antiques that are usually disparate: philosophical speculation, historical research, and everyday practice and experience in the antiques trade. This book is not insulated behind the walls of any one academic discipline; it is multidisciplinary and interdisciplinary. It is not consciously committed to any agenda—political, economic, social, or academic—and should be accessible to any educated reader.

My primary purpose is to provide an account of the *idea of antiques*, to explain what this idea has come to mean in the minds of those who hear this word when uttered by those who use it, or who themselves think of the idea when they encounter a certain type of object in their experience of the world. This account has a philosophical component and a historical one. These components may be taken separately, but it is my belief that the two approaches or modes of exposition and comprehension are inextricably intertwined, each reinforcing and confirming the other. This belief, moreover, can be confirmed in the everyday "world of antiques," the world of antiques collectors and dealers and connoisseurs, when, consciously or not, they apply an array of criteria in judging and evaluating antiques that is based on the history and meaning of this idea. This is not a "How to Identify and Evaluate Your Antiques" sort of book—very far from it. But if evidence of the idea's historical evolution and the associated philosophical issues surrounding antiques were not reflected in (not to say confirmed by) the daily practices of the contemporary "world of antiques," these matters would be of merely academic interest.

Because the idea of "antiques" itself has a history and has acquired this history in connection with a particular kind of aesthetic experience, my account entails an historical exposition not only of the idea of the antique per se but also of the sort of appreciation that antiques have come to acquire. As I will explain, I call this an "archeology" of the collecting and connoisseurship of antiques. This subject matter occupies the major portion of the book, and it is covered in the eight sections of chapter 2.

Based on this historical account, I derive general criteria for the evaluation and appraisal of antiques in chapter 3. There I attempt to reduce their common and universal traits to a set of ten criteria for the collecting and connoisseurship of antiques. Although the claims of chapter 3 are intended to be construed in connection with (indeed, can be justified by) the idea's history and the philosophical arguments I propose in the preceding two chapters, they can also be taken simply at face value, as practical parameters anyone may apply to any given object so as to determine its relative "antiqueness." That is, the ten criteria can be understood as indices or traits that the object must measure up to so as to be considered "an antique."

All philosophers like to explain things by carefully defining them, setting forth the conditions that make them possible, comparing and contrasting them with other things that they may resemble in some respects. I am by training and profession a philosopher, and so I attempt to do this in chapter 1. Even if I cannot construct an air-tight definition for all those things included in the category "antique" (in the sense of establishing the necessary and sufficient conditions for all such objects), still I hope there to have laid out the primary qualifying parameters for the idea of the antique so that some things are rightly considered "antiques" while others rightly ought to be excluded from this category. At the same time, I compare antiques to other things that are in one way or another like them—such as fine artworks and craft objects on the one hand, and collectibles, trophies, religious relics, souvenirs, and artifacts on the other. In making these comparisons I will necessarily also be saying something about what I understand "art" and understand "craft" to be, and something about the nature of the subjective experience that we have when we encounter an antique, explaining why our response to antiques differs from our responses (aesthetic and otherwise) to other sorts of objects. Readers who prefer their history straight and who are either unaccustomed or disinclined to engage in the rather philosophical discussions of this first chapter (especially discussions carried on in several of the lengthy notes that are almost independent appendices to some of the major issues in the philosophy of art) might therefore choose to skip it and proceed to chapter 2. They would probably enjoy my "case in point," however, the story of the *nef* with which chapter 1 begins.

I conclude the book with a final chapter that interprets the antique's role in civilization. This fourth chapter is admittedly speculative—not to say ruminative. Since I cannot provide either the philosophical arguments or historical evidence for a large portion of my interpretations of this relationship between antiques and civilization as a whole, I do not expect it to have the persuasive force of the earlier chapters. In recompense, the chapter is relatively brief. In particular, I try there to show how the antique serves to establish a civilization's self-consciousness by becoming a tangible locus for preserving a civilization's peculiar nature and historical character. On the one hand, antiques are a function of civilization because civilization "antiques" itself over time—not that civilization can itself *be* "an antique," but that civilization endures materially, sensuously, in artifacts that acquire ongoing significance for a civilization, and not necessarily the civilization that produced them originally. There can be no antiques where there is no civilization to "carry" them. And there I also argue that, conversely, civilization may be viewed as a function of antiques, for the antique "civilizes": that is, antiques enable a civilization to see itself as the product of a common humanity. This is because civilization is a human achievement—an achievement not merely in material terms, in institutions and technologies and the like, but in terms of "awareness" and "sensibility." And the development of the appreciation and connoisseurship of antiques in any civilization is one of the most prominent indicators that a real "civilization" has in fact been achieved.

LEON ROSENSTEIN

ANTIQUES

ONE

Preliminaries

Understanding Antiques

Why antiques? What is an antique?

At minimum, an antique is something that has endured over time: it carries some of the past into our present and has a story to tell. In fact, an antique usually has many stories to tell. Before saying anything definitive about antiques, let's begin by looking at one antique's story. It will serve as a case in point.

1.1
An Antique's Story: The *Nef*

In the October issue of two major antiques trade and collector-connoisseur publications, *The Magazine Antiques* (U.S.) and *The Antique Collector* (British), we find a display advertisement announcing the upcoming November sale in New York by Sotheby's auctioneers of "Important European Works of Art and *Objets de Vertu*." This advertisement is accompanied by a color photo of item #74 in the sale. Named the "Tornabuoni Jewel," lot #74 is described as follows:

A "*nef*" [Renaissance pendant in the form of a ship] in gold, crystal, cloisonné enamel and jewels. The body of the hull made of a huge baroque pearl, surmounted by triple masts with sails in diaper pattern white cloisonné enamel; a red enamel rampant griffon projects from the foremast; two upper decks set with alternating rows of rubies and white seed pearls; lower section of hull with scroll-engraved reserves representing waves in blue and green fish-scale cloisonné; three large tear-drop pearls pendant.

$^{7}/_{8}$ by $^{33}/_{8}$ in. (including pearl drops). Attributed to the Florentine gold-smith Bertoldo on the basis of a sketch by that master presently in the Bib-liothèque Nationale (Paris); and, according to a contemporary account by the 15th Century historian Politian, made as a gift for the wedding of Gio-vanna Tornabuoni in 1486. This is the earliest known historical instance and description of a "*nef*," a jewelry form that became popular in the later 16th and early 17th Centuries. The current piece may be the prototype of this form. This rare pendant does not appear to be recorded in the conven-tional literature; however, a small group of similar pieces are in major pub-lic and private collections (e.g., the Rothschild Collection in the British Museum, the Thyssen-Bornemisza Collection, the Hermitage Gold Room, and the Schatzkammer in Munich). A comparable (though later) *nef*, of form and materials similar to (and possibly based on) the present one, ap-peared in Sotheby's "Garga" sale (November, 1993) in Geneva as lot #90. The exceptionally fine workmanship, the unusually early date for the "*nef*" convention, its definitive attribution to Bertoldo (a pupil of the great Donatello) and its certain connection by Politian to the Tornabuoni family (a Florentine dynasty of distinction and renown comparable to the Medici) make this pendant a rare, if not unique, and highly important piece. Esti-mate: $45,000–$60,000.

What happened to this antique piece of jewelry in the roughly five-hundred-year span between its creation and its present status as lot #74 in the Sotheby sale?

It was consigned to Sotheby's by a private London collector of Renais-sance jewelry who had it in his possession for just a few months. He re-luctantly decided to part with it in order to help restore a country home he had recently inherited. He had purchased it from a highly respected London antiques dealer in the Burlington Arcade who had had "the eye" to recognize its quality while on a buying trip to New York and then the luck and expertise to uncover its Bertoldo-Tornabuoni provenance. Actu-ally, a nephew down from Cambridge completing his doctorate in Italian Renaissance history and seeing the pendant on his uncle's desk had made the connection with the account given by a Florentine historian he had recently been reading, Politian, of a "gioiello" that was owned by the Tornabuoni family and had been made by the sculptor-jeweler Bertoldo. Based on that contemporary account and description, the dealer himself had decided to travel to Paris and brave the archives of the old Biblio-thèque Nationale, where he knew a large collection of Bertoldo sketches was held. And there he uncovered a drawing exactly matching to the last detail the *nef* he had just purchased.

Prior to this identification, the *nef* had been passed along among three different upper-level (or "top end") dealers in New York and London who recognized only its Renaissance age and fine quality but were ignorant of its origin and provenance. During the previous several months, the trade had gone through one of its regular inward-turning cycles in which antiques pass back and forth through insider dealing, never finding their way out of the trade-maze to the public and private buyers. This sometimes occurs in "bust" or "flat" periods when antiques dealers, out of frustration, would rather sell to one another for a smaller profit than to the retail public for a larger one, and who in so doing are able at least to buy new things to refresh their inventories; and this seems better to them than doing no business at all.

In any case, the first of these New York dealers had purchased the *nef* on a buying trip to California, where she had discovered it at a three-day antiques show and sale in San Diego. The local San Diego dealer had recognized the quality of the workmanship and materials but had assumed it to be a Victorian (i.e., nineteenth century) Renaissance-Revival piece. He had purchased it three weeks before the antiques show from a dealer who rented a space in one of the local "antiques malls." And that mall dealer had it, in turn, from a "picker" (known as a "barker" in the U.K.) who had brought him several finds from that weekend's tour of a local "swap meet" ("flea market") and "garage" ("jumble," "boot," "tag," "yard") sales. This picker had been the third person to buy it that Sunday.

It had arrived at the Aero Drive-In Swap-Meet in El Cajon (a San Diego suburb) at 8 A.M. on Sunday in the back of a pickup truck driven by a young couple (brother and sister, as it turned out) and filled with "junk" from the garage of their recently deceased grandmother, a widow from Birmingham, England, who had immigrated to the United States in 1967. As soon as the truck pulled to a stop, many hopeful hands reached for the unknown contents of the packing boxes and cartons as they were unloaded. One box containing an assortment of paper goods and books was quickly snapped up by a used-books dealer. Recognizing a few nice-looking editions among the contents and fearing to look more carefully lest the exposed contents of the box reveal anything more desirable— either to its owners or, more dangerously, to a throng of competitor-buyers around him—he offered $10 for "a box of old books." The young sellers, glancing quickly through the partly opened lid, were delighted to accept; and the book dealer walked off to his own stall with his trove of books. As he examined the books—no first editions, but some nice (though rubbed) bindings and old (though "foxed") engravings—he uncovered two thick scrapbooks. Appearing to be a boy's collection of ship pictures, one of these scrapbooks contained primarily photos of modern warships and had a naval captain's brass insignia glued to the front cover; the other book contained cut-out pictures of sailing ships of various sorts, both real and fictional. And to the cover of this second scrapbook was glued our *nef*. It was certainly recognizable as a rather plump sailing ship—a lump of yellow metal stuck there in a mass of brown glue to the decaying, chased leather binding—but hardly recognizable as anything else.

Ten minutes later, a rather eccentric "regular" at these weekend sales, whom everyone knew as "Magnolia," appeared at the bookseller's booth and, after a bit of banter about the depressing lack of interesting finds that morning, she made an offer of $5 on "that old ship-looking thing." The book dealer, knowing that she collected costume jewelry, first countered with "It's worth at least $20," but settled for $10. That exactly covered his cost for the entire box. (The box was now "free.") And the offer accepted, the "ship-looking thing" encased in its mass of glue was pried from the leather backing and thus changed hands a second time that morning. Magnolia had not noticed the lanky young man in the red sweatpants who had stood by nonchalantly observing this transaction. He had very much wanted the "ship-looking thing" and would gladly have paid $20, probably more. But, coming on the transaction already in progress between Magnolia and the bookseller, he dutifully bit his tongue and observed the local etiquette of keeping silent and giving the appearance of disinterest during a transaction in progress, hoping their deal would collapse on a $5 difference of opinion. He now approached Magnolia and offered her $20. This was refused without a moment's hesitation by Magnolia, who walked on, searching for her next purchase; but when they encountered each other again about thirty minutes later, after an inconclusive argument as to whether it was really gold, $50 was accepted and the little "ship-looking thing" disappeared into the lanky young man's inside pocket.

Arriving home later than morning, he tried to clean the piece; but it was so encrusted with dirt and embedded in glue that he feared to harm the cloisonné enamel; and so he took it to a buddy more knowledgeable in such matters. He had liked its "classy" looks and obvious age and was especially delighted to discover on its being cleaned that the pin back (for it turned out to be a brooch) showed a gold mark of some kind and that, in fact, the whole thing tested apparently as gold of a reasonably high karat. At this point the picker called another friend who sold antique jewelry from a rented space at one of the local antiques malls and, assuring him that "no one else has seen it first" (meaning no other antiques mall dealer, i.e., no one at that level of the local trade), he brought it to him the next day. The mall dealer recognized the London assay mark on the pin; liked the subject, which he recognized as being in the form of a Renaissance *nef*; and, after some haggling about the stones, which were "real but small and of poor quality," and the "missing pieces" (apparently three pendant pearls were supposed to be hanging from the three tiny holes in the bottom rim of the hull), the mall dealer paid the picker $150. He checked his reference books and discovered that 1854 was the actual date of the London assay mark and thus was satisfied that he had a lovely Victorian Renaissance-Revival brooch.

When he sold it the following week for $375 to the local antiques dealer who had come into the mall looking for some new and interesting merchandise that he was scheduled to sell at the upcoming three-day Del Mar Antiques Show & Sale, they discussed the possibilities of obtaining three pearls to suspend from the holes at the bottom. And thus when the New York dealer saw the "*nef*-brooch" in the show and purchased it for $1,200, this amount included not merely the most recent profit but the cost of the triple pearl-drop "restoration" as well. The New York dealer was a bit suspicious of them when she bought the piece. But, apart from the beautiful detail of the *nef*, what had most aroused her attention were two inconsistencies that suggested the piece was "not right." The first of these was the enamel, for it was not consistent in technique with a piece of Victorian date. The second discrepancy was the slight difference in color (and thus, likely, in karat, and thus, likely, in origin and age) between the gold in the body of the *nef* compared with the gold of the pin clasp. She was delighted when chemical and other analyses back in New York confirmed her suspicion: it was a Renaissance *nef* (like those sixteenth-century examples she had seen in the Rothschild collection in the British Museum in London). A Victorian pin-clasp had evidently been added to its back in 1854, transforming it from a pendant to a more useful and fashionable brooch.

With its Victorian clasp now removed, the pendant passed among the several New York and London dealers who specialized in early European antiques, jewelry, and *objets de vertu* and then on to the London specialist who purchased it for $6,400 and discovered its maker and first owner. (On seeing the Bertoldo drawing, by the way, he decided to retain the three-pearl restoration, which he also recognized as recent, because of the pearls' almost perfect match with Bertoldo's original sketch.) He sold it to the collector for £18,000. And it was all of this that led, finally, to the *nef*'s placement as lot #74 in Sotheby's November sale with a sales estimate of $45,000 to $50,000.

What we have just recounted is the life of the *nef* "on the live market" over a two-year period and through the hands of ten different individuals whose primary interest in acquiring it (except perhaps for the English collector who put it up for auction) was economic, though we should not doubt that aesthetic pleasure was also part of the total response to the object by those who encountered it.

But this accounts for only the last ("market-lively") years of the *nef*'s life. What of the other five hundred-odd years? Presumably, during the vast majority of those years, its life was not circumscribed or driven by the vicissitudes of the antiques market. What of its full provenance and the larger stories it has to tell? The English grandmother had brought it to southern California in 1967. But how did it leave the possession of Giovanna Tornabuoni, for whom it was originally made in 1486? And what was its intervening fate?

For over a decade, Giovanna had much prized this wedding gift, which she thought quite original; but after seven children, the contemporary political instability in Florence, and her husband's own increasing mental instability, she had become preoccupied with more practical matters. Her husband, in fact, was now caught up in the Savonarola hysteria and, before Giovanna could stop him, had already contributed more than the family's share to the cleansing of his immortal soul by loading up the bonfire of the vanities with family tapestries and paintings of "obscene" pagan subjects, mirrors, musical instruments, dice, and other such worldly distractions. Thus, when her visiting cousin left for Mantua, Giovanna, at least in part to save it from destruction, presented her with a parting gift; and the *nef* made its way safely out of Florence to Mantua in 1497. Before long, it came into the possession of Mantua's ruling Gonzaga family and thence, when this noble line came to an end, into the collection of King Charles I of England in the late 1620s. When, in turn, this unsurpassed collector—one of the first genuine European "connoisseurs"—came to grief (well, lost his head, actually) in the English Revolution, the *nef* formed part of the great Commonwealth Sale of 1650. Purchased by Sir Cedric Wallingford, a Puritan partisan speculator, it then came to lose its costly three large pendant pearls; but, owing to its "lesser value in geld and jouels," it was saved from being otherwise dismantled and melted down and, rather, was given to his daughter on the occasion of her betrothal.

Its precise history is not entirely clear thereafter, but the *nef* appears to have done some sailing about the world. A granddaughter married to a Maryland governor brought it on its first trip to the New World in 1703 and, that tour of duty among colonists and savages being complete, she returned with it to London. The next century saw the piece leave for India (now with the Victorian clasp attached in order for it to be worn as a pin) with the wife of the aide-de-camp to General Dalhousie; but after the mutiny of 1857, his wife now deceased, the retired aide-de-camp carried the piece in 1844 to Birmingham, where he went to spend his remaining years at the home of his widowed sister. It was presumably from descendants of this family that the grandmother who later migrated to California had purchased the piece when she and her husband vacationed in Brighton in 1957. How it got to Brighton from Birmingham sometime during the preceding seventy years we leave open to further speculation. But it was her son (the father of the young pair of swap-meet sellers who opened our narrative) who, as a young boy, had rather messily glued the *nef* to the cover of his treasured album of sailing-ship pictures.

Thus we have rendered a skeletal historical account of the Tornabuoni Jewel—told the story of for whom and by whom it was made, of how it obtained and lost and then re-obtained its identity, of how its pearls and clasp and glue and grime came and went, and of its relations with the lives of those who owned it.

At this point I must confess to the reader that this historical account is purely an invention, as is the *nef* and the auction advertisement. In mollification of and compensation for any disappointment, however, I can promise the reader that this is the only fiction to be encountered in these pages. I think I also should now explain why I chose to open with such an extended falsehood. First of all, it is unlikely that anyone could actually reconstruct the narrative trail and circumstances of such an antique's ownership in such extensive detail over such an extended span of time and for an object that had, at least toward the end, almost lost its "value"—both aesthetic and commercial—because, having virtually fallen into the oblivion of trivial ordinariness, it had almost lost its noticeability, a fate that often occurs to antiques. This was partly because the materials of which it was made were unrecognized and its original form and design were perceptually obscured. But it was mainly because its historical character (its provenance) was unknown. This shows the prime importance of provenance in appreciating antiques; and we will observe later how important *what we know* about (or think we know about) an object when we see it determines *how we respond* to it aesthetically. Second, in the present case, to the extent that auction houses—like antiques dealers—are unlikely to divulge such recent particulars as the fact that within the preceding two years the antique object's history included a purchase price of a mere $10, had this fact been known to (or discovered by) the auctioneers, it would have been hardly credible to expect them to include this "detail" in the stated provenance of an item expected to sell for five thousand times that sum. I had to invent this "inconvenient truth." Thus, since a genuine *nef* example that incorporated all the historical particulars I have provided would not be a real possibility for a five-hundred-year-old object, and were all the facts of its past actually known, they would not have been advertised, I chose to create my own instance.

Above all, by constructing my own fictional instance I could introduce many genuine issues—beauty, restoration, subject matter, authenticity (and its documentary corroboration), rarity, style and fashion, signs of age, materials, "appreciation" (both monetary and aesthetic), technique and excellence of construction, accidents—that in my later account I will take up in detail but that might not all have been available in any given real case I could find. My fictional *nef*'s life is nevertheless constructed from genuine provenances of real *nefs*. Readers who would like to see actual accounts may consult the real examples in just about any Sotheby's or Christie's sales catalogues of "objets de vertu." Since similar instances of antiques with astounding provenances are serendipitously discovered weekly, if not daily, my case in point is certainly hypothetically plausible. Finally, it is a common fact in the antiques world that many fake—or shall we say "confabulated" or "conjectured"?—provenances are constructed for antiques that are genuine *as antiques* but that have "lost their history." One needs to be prepared to encounter this reality.

We have thus provided ourselves with an instance of an antique with a marvelous history—a pedigree, a provenance. It is this historicality that constitutes more than anything else the "aura" (to use Walter Benjamin's term) generated by an antique: how we subjectively experience it as an object from the past, for knowing its past in part determines how we see it. Its historicality objectively establishes its provenance, a provenance that would justify a goodly portion of the estimated $50,000 high market value in a Sotheby's sale catalogue for our imaginary *nef*.

Of course, just having a story to tell, even a five-hundred-year story, cannot constitute the whole of this antique's "value"—whether we understand this value in purely economic terms or in terms of its appeal to the connoisseur-collector of antiques. Let me point out a few of these particulars and thus further validate my employment of a fictional instance. First, our *nef*'s evident beauty is (and was always) part of its worth, its appeal. So was its subject matter: a square-rigged sailing ship is a theme that invariably evokes the delightful imagery of adventure. Then, too, there is its rarity, for in a world full of similar *nefs* our antique would pass as unnoticed as the "ship-looking-thing" stuck in glue or an old rusty nail. And there is the intrinsic value of the materials of its construction and the

appeal of the technical excellence of the metalsmith evident in its construction. And then there is not just the antique object's "age" in terms of
its provenance which gives us something to "know about" it, but the
"age" that we "see in" it (its style) and "see on" it (patina, wear, etc.). All
these latter qualities would—even if we knew nothing of the *nef*'s actual
history and provenance—contribute to its notable attractiveness, and
hence "value," in important ways.

As we will see in later chapters, we can more or less identify each of
these special attributes of an antique and locate (sometimes even explain)
their historical emergence and evolution (the task of chapter 2). We will
incorporate most of these attributes into our definition of an antique in
the following section. In fact, we will enumerate in chapter 3 all the important factors that determine an antique, establishing ten categories
that will become ten criteria of connoisseurship and collecting. All ten inform and influence the perceptions and images, the expectations and
concerns, of those who experience an antique for what it is. Discovering
or failing to find these qualities in the object in question, they will judge
the object more or less "an antique" or more or less desirable or valuable
"as an antique." These criteria would all be on the minds of the bidders
at our imagined auction sale—and more so at the auction preview, where
connoisseur-collectors could handle the object in person, for its physical
tangibility, its sensuous presence, is an especially relevant aspect of these
criteria, as we will see. In consequence, the object itself becomes more or
less competent to evoke the aesthetic response peculiar to antiques.

Hence, while of all ten criteria, what seems always to be particularly
important in the appreciation and recognition of any antique is its historicality (for, as we said at the outset, an antique is above all something
that has endured over time, carrying some part of the past into the present, and thus having a story to tell); "provenance" (understood as *who*
made it, *where*, and, if not obvious, *why* it was made, *when* it was
made—and even when we include in "provenance" a full narrative history of its life from its creation up through the present) is not the whole
of its historicality. And its historicality is not the whole of its *being an
antique*. After all, Shakespeare's plays exhibit their age in a unique historical style and an extra-ordinary language; rocks and old glass shards
and old wooden planks may exhibit patina and other signs of wear with
age; collectibles hold their appeal essentially on condition of their rarity
conjoined with provenance (by whom, where, and when they were made—
although where they may have been in the interval from their manufacture until now seems generally insignificant for collectibles, except for
confirming their authenticity). And yet none of these is quite an "antique."

In the example of the *nef*, we created an antique's provenance in the detailed narrative of its history. But by now, clearly, we see that there is more to its being an antique than we may at first have supposed. So let us attempt to arrive at the idea of the antique with greater precision.

I.2

A Definition of the Antique

Before we proceed further, it is necessary to suggest a definition of the antique per se.[1] This will be not a *formal* definition but a *working* definition. That is, it is not possible here to create an "air-tight" definition that includes both all the necessary and all the sufficient conditions for an object's being an antique. It will always turn out that some aspects of a given object's "antiqueness" may be a matter of "more or less"; and it may be that, even in the long run, only family resemblances can be discovered among the things we call "antiques." But this definition of the antique will help to focus the lengthy historical discussion in chapter 2 that follows. It will also provide an interpretive structure for the more detailed and specific analysis of the antique in terms of the ten criteria of collecting and connoisseurship in the subsequent chapter 3.

"The antique" (as a category or description) and "antiques" (as objects that embody this characteristic) have gained considerable attention in the modern world—on levels ranging from subjects of commerce and investment to items filling the glossy pages of home and decorator magazines. Not much serious thought has yet been given on a philosophical level, however, as to what sort of object an antique really is. That is our immediate concern. We ask, what is "*an* antique" and "the *antique*"? Why are antiques worthy of critical analysis? How does the idea of the antique differ from other things often associated with antiques—such as collectibles, artifacts, religious relics, trophies, and memorabilia? How are antiques to be understood in relation to similar things: crafts, in particular, of which they have traditionally appeared to be a subclass; and how does the antique compare with other things to which we also *respond aesthetically*: art, in particular?

If nothing else, the current broad popularity and appeal of antiques persuades and encourages us to come to a better understanding of what they are. Almost everyone has at least one acquaintance who pursues and collects them; books are published in the hundreds every year as identification and price guides to various categories of them; television shows are dedicated to them, and Web sites auction them. The source of this appeal, the functions antiques perform, are varied, to be sure. Economic investment as a hedge against inflation, acquisition of social status, and decorative service to fill the empty spaces of our home environment come to mind. But these functions are mainly extraneous to their aesthetic appeal proper.

There does seem to be a psychological function as well: escape from the reality of the present. That function has always been a large part of what fine art's purpose was thought to be, too—to provide us with a break from our daily round of needful dealings and create the enjoyable aesthetic experience of an imaginary alternative reality. But for many people, what passes for contemporary art no longer seems to serve that aesthetic function. Thus, there is no doubt that a large body of contemporary aesthetic experience devolves on the antique by default, as the only alternative to nature itself in the struggle against the void of the contemporary prefabricated environment on the one hand and the struggle to encounter contemporary art as an enjoyable aesthetic experience on the other. Here the antique becomes an antidote to the insipidity and vapidity of mass-produced furnishings as well as to contemporary "anomic" art, supported by attempts to elevate the "undone" (one cannot any longer employ the term "shocking" seriously) to the status of the highest criterion.[2] To be sure, the antique has this psycho-sociological function; but this can hardly be all that attracts us to antiques. Certainly it could not be a sufficient explanation of the category itself. Nor would it be the unique means of escape from the insufficiencies of our immediate reality: watching a televised sports event or reading a historical romance novel and/or having several stiff drinks would achieve approximately the same end, after all, if a temporary escape from the everyday present were all that mattered. There must be some special significance to the deliberate preference for the objects of a past reality that have physically endured into the present which the antique satisfies, something that requires the use of our imagination and our historical consciousness.

This fascination with the past and its objects is not a new phenomenon. Renaissances and revivals deliberately choose to re-create the past by fashioning new objects imitating the old, or by incorporating certain traits of old styles, or by collecting and analyzing actual old objects with appropriate appreciation or veneration. Western civilization has seen such recollections often enough and at regular intervals in the past—though in each instance with a difference.[3] A survey of revivals and renaissances may tell us where, when, and under what circumstances a preference for the past and its antique objects have become relevant to a civilization's taste, its artistic preferences, its historical consciousness, and its self-conception. But the concept "renaissance" cannot itself explain why and how antiques exert their special appeal; nor can it furnish appropriate criteria for distinguishing and establishing the antique as an aesthetic category, for showing how and why antiques are like (and not like) artworks or crafts or collectibles and so on. For that, we need a definition. And in order to make that definition fully meaningful, we need the following chapter's summary of the *history of the idea of the antique*, for this is an idea that has emerged and changed over time. Let me explain.

It is normally thought that what makes something *what* it is (the kind of thing it is) so that it is called by a certain name is a consequence of certain qualities or attributes it possesses or certain criteria or conditions it satisfies. Definitions of things generally try to specify as many important attributes or set out as many necessary and sufficient conditions as needed to clarify distinctions between and prevent confusions among the objects we encounter in the world. Thus, since we understand that the word "cat" names a species of small domesticated carnivorous mammal with claws on its paws that are useful for catching the mice it eats, should we come across a creature that looks and acts that way, we would assume it is a cat; whereas something that has scales, lays eggs, and prefers to eat vegetable matter rather than mice as its swims about is highly unlikely to be a cat. So it is with antiques. There must be certain criteria that these objects satisfy, a certain number of minimal attributes that antiques possess in common, or we would never think of applying the word "antiques" to any of them. But can we define antiques? One would like to stipulate necessary or sufficient conditions for a thing's being an antique. But the question regarding antiques seems especially difficult because although "cat" and "tree" seem always to have been understood in more or less the same way, the idea of "an antique" (like the idea of "human rights" or the idea of "art" itself) seems to have undergone enormous development and change over time. And this book is intended to show all the facets and vicissitudes of this emergence, of the idea's growth and its progress *as an idea*.

Interestingly enough, a similar situation, the question of definability or indefinability of art itself, is much in evidence in the contemporary "art scene," or at least among the theorists of that art scene. Here Brillo boxes and comic strips and can openers—not to mention "trash installations" and even "excremental events"—are currently proposed to us as art. It is instances such as these that have led many to despair of providing a satisfactory definition of "art" for all those contemporary productions that propose themselves for that status, for there seems to be nothing that could conceivably be excluded from that category.[4] Yet even if and when these productions can be presented as instances of "art" (i.e., they can be made to satisfy some idea of art), insofar as these artworks are accompanied by some contemporary art theory that may be able to provide some definition (however contorted or cryptic) for them and that may be able to explicate their idea by showing they belong within the class of things we can legitimately call "art" by the terms of that theory—even then this does not mean that we are thereby able to respond to them appropriately. What I am proposing here is that just "knowing that" they are art (understanding them intellectually) is not the same as "experiencing them aesthetically." In asserting this—that if it elicits no aesthetic response then it is not art—I admit a strong prejudice. I think that artworks *insofar as they are indeed art objects* are intended to provide us with responses different from those elicited by theories or ideas or descriptions of things. (And I think antiques need to do the same—as we will see, for example, with memorabilia and archeological artifacts that address not aesthetic response but cognition, thereby differentiating themselves from the category "antiques.") Consequently, if presumptive artworks are intended to elicit (or succeed only in eliciting) a purely cognitive response—in demonstrating some proposed truth or instantiating some theory or causing us to ponder the nature of something—then they are not (or are all the less) artworks. They are at best evidence for (or instances of) some assertion or set of *assertions about* art rather than *being* themselves art.[5]

And since we have been discussing art in relation to antiques, there are further important connections between definitions and expectations and between contemporary artworks and antiques. For it is perhaps precisely because of this deficiency in contemporary art, in default of these works being able to satisfy many of us aesthetically (even if and when we can "appreciate" the art theory intellectually which justifies them as art and then can "appreciate" them as confirmations or examples of that art theory), that we have come to seek the aesthetic satisfaction that used to be found in artworks in related objects: namely, in antiques, which, as we will see, share some similar traits.

Furthermore, although we cannot know the fate of most contemporary artworks in the future (will they remain great works of art—or even works of art at all? will they, in some way, themselves become antiques?), contemporary art and its supporting theories have called our attention to quotidian objects. The "quotidian object" is understood to mean any object of everyday use and encounter; it encompasses everything that is "entrenched" in our pragmatic use-world (a car, a shoe, a computer mouse) that is not a natural phenomenon (such as a rainstorm or an oak tree).[6] Contemporary art has conditioned us to appreciate everyday objects, if only because it has (at least since Marcel Duchamp's *Fountain*, which presented a urinal as an artwork one hundred years ago—and Warhol's *Soup Can* of fifty years ago) proffered and proposed to us at least the possibility of appreciating aesthetically everything and anything that anyone has made. Thus, whatever the ultimate consequences for "fine art" in general, twentieth-century art has had the inadvertent consequence of enabling us better to appreciate antiques aesthetically. This is because antiques are normally thought of as exactly such everyday kinds of object—furniture, dinnerware, oriental carpets, brass candelabra—rather than paintings, for instance. They are such things from the past that have now acquired age. Twentieth-century art has thereby enhanced the potential for quotidian objects to be considered "objects of aesthetic appreciation."

Just as beneficial has been the breakdown in the late twentieth century of the traditional distinction between the "fine arts" and those that were presumed to be "not so fine" (craft objects, or what were called "decorative" or "applied" arts), something we will look at in greater detail below.

In any case, because antiques are objects with provenances and perceptible properties that collectively constitute what has historically arisen as the "idea of the antique," they may be roughly defined in terms of these properties and provenances. The idea, the category, is now fairly well established so that when we encounter an object in our world that possesses a fair number of such properties we call it "an antique"; and we have a unique aesthetic experience in response to it. We might call this recognition of the object *together with* our aesthetic response to it "taste for the antique" if this word "taste" had not so fallen into disuse and gone out of fashion with the opprobrium of elitism, for "taste" on the one hand suggests the knowledge and discrimination of the connoisseur to evaluate and on the other (and equally) implies the ability to respond with the proper "sentiments" to certain objects, that is, to experience them aesthetically.

Let us therefore attempt to construct a working definition of the antique:

An antique is a primarily handcrafted object of rarity and beauty that, by means of its associated provenance and its agedness as recognized by means of its style and material endurance, has the capacity to generate and preserve for us the image of a world now past.

Next we will elucidate this definition by examining each of its components. Trying to get some handle on simply *what kind of thing* an antique is comes first. Then we turn to the *means* by which the antique achieves its effect on us, that is, *how* it produces our subjective response. And, as we engage in this analysis of *what* antiques are and the *means* whereby they produce that effect, we will simultaneously be presenting as well an extended account of the *end* antiques achieve for our sensibility, the unique aesthetic pleasure they provide, for none of these aspects of the antique is fully intelligible in isolation from the others.

1.2.1 Artworks, Crafts, and Antiques

We begin by continuing our comparison of the antique with the "art object" in general to get more clearly in mind *what kind of handcrafted article an antique is*, for, like art objects—or what one might call "artifactuals"—antiques are crafted by the hand of the artisan.

The being of an art object is unique. Art objects do not reside in the world like other objects but captivate our attention through the sensuous vehicles of their media. They "tear through" the extra-artistic world of everyday concern and attention; and they set up their own *worked worlds*, that is, "artistic," "artificial," "imaginary" worlds of meaning and reality. Such objects have ontological integrity (and thus are *genuine* "art objects") insofar as their corporeal nature (i.e., their sensuous vehicle or material medium) exhibits the special property that I have elsewhere called *translucence*.[7] To have this quality the art object must avoid two pitfalls: the opposite extremes of "transparency" and "opacity." If too transparent in its medium, the art object becomes merely an *instrument* for communication, because its corporeal nature (its sensuous physicality) dissolves and disappears from notice as we engage it: we "see" right *through* it, attending only to the end it serves, what it is "about"—like the pen we use to write with. This situation often occurs with didactic art, for example, where the medium is merely the means of delivery for the content or message and thus is finally superfluous. (Think of the "art-less" character of propagandistic art.) If too opaque, on the other hand, the art object becomes so enmeshed in the reality of its corporeality that it becomes a mere *curiosity, enigma, or potential instance of some as-yet-unelaborated art theory, at best, a "thing of fancy."* It inhabits the extra-artistic world and cannot construct or communicate any content, any worked world at all, because it is entirely a creature of this one like the lemon pie one has for dessert, a thing that has no message, no "aboutness" at all, but simply is what its physical properties are and is for the use of being eaten. This situation often occurs in contemporary nonrepresentational art and in art objects that are perceptually indistinguishable from everyday objects; or works whose media are incoherently blended into the material elements of the overall environment. That is, by not representing a "content" in the traditional manner, abstract nonrepresentational art objects of this sort may fail to provide sufficient "aboutness" or integrity (unity) for world-making to occur. (Think of the "art-less" character of a pile of rags on a floor.) But an art object that, on the contrary, *does* have ontological integrity is an object that is "translucent." Translucence of materiality occurs only insofar as we remain captivated by the unified corporeal structure and design of its medium (which is distinct from its environment) and, at the same time, are continuously attuned by this medium to the unique worked world that it generates as its content, a world with its own objective givens and its own values and interpretations. This is, then, the "illusion" of the art object as such: that it opens up its own world of space and time and "puts into play" there the creatures of its own reality. (Think here of great works of art that come to mind: while generating and communicating a world of meaningful content, they endlessly captivate our attention with their design, construction, and the perceptibly sensuous qualities of their media.)[8]

Certainly not all art objects are antiques. The question arises: Are all antiques "art objects"? To answer this question, now that we have briefly discussed the relation of antiques to art, we must introduce the subject of crafts. *World-reference* is a function of all meaningful objects, but *world-making* (or *world-generation*) is a function of all aesthetic experience and all art. A laundry basket, a teacup, a carpet—these objects are what they are, were made deliberately of the substances chosen, with their unique forms, having those specific characteristics they do, and thus have the meanings they acquire only because they *refer* to a world in which light portable air-permeable containers have a use, in which a hot caffeine-laden beverage is consumed in small leak-proof bowls, and in which hard and cold floors are best comfortably covered with warm, soft textiles. They refer to and are attached to and meaningful only in the context of the external world around them. Normally, when we hear the term "antique" in modern usage, we tend to confine its denotation, as we said earlier, to such craft objects, objects with world-reference but not world-generation. Indeed, before the machine age of mass production, all objects that weren't part of nature were crafted objects insofar as they were made individually by hand to perform some service; so in some respects this presumption is not entirely a false association. Nevertheless, this traditional distinction between fine art and craft—and the relegation of antiques to the latter category alone—rests in fact in part on historical and cultural accident; and it relies on two undisclosed assumptions that *are false*.

The first is the assumption that the distinction between "craft" and "fine" art is a hard and fast one and that "fine art" (rather than "decorative art" or "applied art") is a very special subclass of the crafted object (or the artifacted object), because "fine art" is "superior" to the lesser kind, which is "mere craft." Both the history of this distinction (and the particular arts that should be classified as "fine") and the arguments that have been advanced in support or criticism of this distinction have been made by others and would take us too far afield.[9] But insofar as crafts, as well as "fine arts," may succeed in world-generation and thus go beyond a mere functionality (world-reference) in the oblivion of the everyday use-world, any craft object may equally well be an object of aesthetic experience. And in the peculiar case of craft objects that are *also* antiques, such objects are *always world-generating*—even if and when we "put them to use." The world they generate is an image of a world now past. And even in their use in the present (their world-reference) we cannot fail to "notice" them, for they carry along with them (and in them) the image of a past world, the world they generate. That is why antiques are more like what we expect fine art to be than they are like new craft objects. Though craft objects per se *may generate* a world, they do not usually do so. Present-day, mass-produced, machined objects almost never do. These latter refer only to the contemporary world of their creation for their functionality. We may now answer our first question. No, not all antiques are art objects. But they are like art objects in this way: they generate a world. All art objects generate their own internally worked worlds. Antiques generate a world that *evokes and preserves for us the image of a world now past.* Art objects are deliberately created to generate a world. Antiques have "fallen into" this condition with the passage of time, for the world in which they were first made (and to which they once referred) no longer exists. Even when they can still be made to function for their original purposes—though often they cannot do so or must be modified to suit contemporary use—they generate and carry along with them the image of their past world. An artwork created in the past or an antique, whose world has long gone by, not only makes us (1) see the object for and as what it is; it likewise enables us (2) to see the totality of the past world that was the context in which it was what it was and had its intended assignments. And it also allows us (3) to conceive the endurance of the object from its past world into the present, that is, to apprehend the temporality of its "untimeliness," through the development of our historical consciousness. Finally, (4) because their past world can be found no longer in the present, antiques, like fine artworks, become an enticement to hold back, just look, and experience; they entice us to understand and appreciate them in terms of the world in which they had their work to do and to see what the world has worked upon them over time as they have endured, arrived, and now appear in our contemporary world.

Given these facts, there is no fundamental reason why *only* crafts should be called "antiques," for a fine art object may be an antique as well as a craft object. It need only meet the general terms of the definition. And hence a second (and related) erroneous assumption in this comparison of craft, antique, and fine art is that, in the experience of an art object that is admittedly *both fine and antique*, its "fineness" has priority over its "antiqueness." That is to say, because the world-generative capacities and reference of fine art (e.g., Delacroix's *Death of Sardanapalus*) are normally to an *internally* worked world (in this case the seventh-century B.C. Assyrian monarch besieged in Nineveh by the Medes) but the world-generative capacities and reference of the antique is to a world of the past (i.e., an *external* world—real or imagined—in this case the world of mid-nineteenth-century France in which Delacroix painted his Romantic visions), that these two are mutually exclusive alternatives requiring different aesthetic stances or attunements and that, further, in choosing between them, "fineness" has priority, these assumptions presume that eternal virginity is preferable to age and all the historical signs of usage, or that the imagined internal world that a work generates always takes precedence over the historical world in which it was created and has endured. These differences and the mistaken presumption of priority for "fineness" are worth pursuing.

Fine art objects set up their own internal, uniquely worked artistic world—a timed and spaced reality with its own arbitrary extra-artistic associations and its own interpretations, a virtual world. Thus, they remain forever at the center of their own stage, referring ultimately to themselves by means of their translucence.

Antiques set up (create/re-create) the image of a world of the past—a presumably real world in space and time with all the associations and interpretations appropriate to it (or at least as we best imagine it to have been) but a world that no longer exists.[10] And thus antiques are symbols for a context of past possibilities and are icons potent in transubstantiating the past reality's presence in the present by means of their style and an appeal to the duration of their materials. They do this (as we see below in greater detail) (1) by relying on certain constants in the interrelatedness of their forms and contents, which are art-historically isolable, namely, what we call their art-historical style, and (2) by relying in a certain fashion on the corporeality of their media, namely, their marks of agedness, such as wear and patina. And thus it is by both these means that they generate "an image of the past" (a past world), and this is the foundation of that special aesthetic pleasure that antiques deliver.

When one experiences a portrait of Charles V by Titian, for example, the life-world of the Holy Roman Emperor on whose domain the sun never set is generated. That is the world *of* the work, for here the work refers us to the historical facts of the past in which it was created. As I experience the work in this way—as an object crafted by Titian at the pleasure of Charles V for his use, for his commemoration and glorification and/or for his room decoration—it is a craft object. Insofar as it is *also* a *fine* artwork that I see, however—not a mere photographic regeneration or memorial image of the historical facts of the past world, but *fine art creation* by Titian—I find a generated world unique to this painting, one created by expression, position, posture and costume, interaction of objects and symbols represented, contrasts and combinations of precise colors, forms, volumes, of light and dark, intensity and hue, horizontal/vertical dispositions, surface texture, and so on. This is the world *in* the work. The world generated by and *in* the art object—which is what the work *is about* and which is constituted by the artfulness of the object, rendering aesthetic experience possible in the presence of this representational canvas—depends to some degree on the recognition of the prior historical world (the world *of* the work) which is the basis of the world represented in its contents. (Recognizing the famous Habsburg chin prevents me, for example, from thinking this representation of Charles a mere caricature or a technically artistic failing by Titian.) But the two worlds—the world generated by and *in* the work and the world *of* the past wherefrom it originated—mutually reinforce and sustain each other. One is not forced to "choose" between them. Rather, one is invited to "play" between them. They need not, and usually do not, conflict.[11]

Similarly with this work's antique-ness. "Pastness" (whether recognized in style or in material signs of agedness) is the invariable characteristic of the world generated by the antique. In this case "the past" encompasses Titian's life work (long and full enough to include several Charles V's portraits, each progressively more painterly and coloristic) and the art-historical world of his epoch (Venetian Renaissance) together with all the particular vagaries of accident and endurance that befell this painting in order to bring it into our historical present with its provenance and marks of wear and tear (a chip in the varnish, a stain in the lower left corner, etc.). But this recognition of the survival of the past in the present through the endurance of the work over time need not conflict with the internally worked world that the art object generates, any more than did the historical world in which Charles V lived. Rather, the work's "antiqueness" enriches and enhances the total aesthetic experience. To be sure, an antique, or the experience we have of it, differs from the experience of a "pure" (as in "virginal") art object, as we have said, for it is an "object with a past" that has shared a life-world with other objects (rather than appearing incorrupt and eternal in every experience). But this difference need not and *should not* create difficulties for us (as we noted above); rather, it can heighten and increase the totality of aesthetic experience possible. To lay to rest the second erroneous assumption regarding antiques, then: not only may fine art objects as well as crafts be antiques (assuming a precise distinction is even possible between craft and fine art), but the "antiqueness" in the experience of a fine art object need not be in conflict with, or be superseded in priority by, its "fineness." Indeed, with the passage of time, the antique fine art object generates two worked worlds: the world **in** the work as intended by (generated by) its original creator and the world **of** the past that its endurance into the present now enables it to imaginatively reconstruct for us. And thus to answer the basic question with which we began: yes, all antiques are objects of aesthetic experience insofar as they are world-generative; and because world-generation is a quality peculiar (if not unique) to art objects, antiques may also be thought of as being in this respect like art objects (either "craft" or "fine"). The worked world antiques generate for our imagination is not necessarily within the work but, as in the case of craft objects, the world of the work—the world of the past.[12]

That we in fact usually have in the past set aside "antique-ness" in favor of "fine-art-ness" is probably due, however, not merely to a sense of mistaken respect for the work's purely formal properties or its original intentions, both of which we have been taught to value solely (or primarily). It is due also to a genuine ambiguity regarding a presumed "correct" attitude. This occurs, as I have said, in great measure because of the apparent conflict arising between the respective worlds they evoke—fine art objects erecting a new world of their own through the *translucence* of their media, antiques re-evoking an image of past world generated through the style and materiality (the *agedness*) of their media. But I believe there is another relevant factor here to be considered. And it again involves the tenuous "fine" versus "craft" distinction insofar as it may be made at all. Crafts generally have less (or no) independent and self-subsistent ideational "contents." Thus, antique crafts are naturally more predisposed to the generation of the past world through the materiality of their media than are antique fine art objects. Crafts can "become antiques," then, more easily than can "fine art," for the world they generate is not an internally worked one. The internally worked world of a fine art object, on the other hand, might arise as an alternative in distinction to (if not actual opposition to) the world of the past. Though it is by no means certain that objects no longer useful *eo ipso* become fine art objects (i.e., crafts in default of use and in virtue of being aged do not necessarily, automatically, and merely *thereby* then become art objects), craft objects do come into being through their deliberate configuration toward some primary useful purpose in their world of *praxis*. Hence, antique crafts now out of their use-world have at least the *opportunity* of becoming objects of aesthetic experience and not just human detritus. Consequently, the criteria by which they came into being and were experienced initially are not necessarily the same ones by which they can live and have value when these objects have fallen "past use."

The crucial distinction to be noted here, however, is this: the world generated by antique crafts can *only* be the world of the past, whereas antique fine art objects may generate an internally worked world *in addition to* generating a world of the past. But both craft and fine art objects become antiques by displaying the appropriate modifications in the opacity of their media and by the peculiar modifications, coordinations, and combinations of their corporeal elements that we call "style."[13] Moreover, it is precisely because of the divergent "internally worked-world-generating" character of art objects on the one hand and the "past world-generating" characteristics of the antique on the other that antiques (as crafts invariably, and as fine art objects insofar as they are *generated* but not necessarily as they are themselves *generating*) affirm the values of the world they evoke and preserve. Antiques cannot critique that world and its values, as can fine art.[14] So, for example, we say that Goya's *The Third of May, 1808* critiques the extra-artistic world of its creator. Though perhaps it would be better to put it this way: this painting *as "fine art"* evokes ("generates") a worked world (the firing squad horror) that in turn subjects the contemporary real world of the subject it represents (revolutionary Spain in 1808) to criticism; but this painting *as "antique"* evokes ("generates") that past real world (Goya's life-world) and tends to preserve it as much as would, say, Goya's chamber pot.

We have developed some clearer notion of the "whatness" of the antique by comparison with crafts and artworks. Nevertheless, we must be wary of confusing a *tendency* with a necessity. Because (1) the distinction between "craft" and "fine" remains a relative one, because (2) we cannot ignore the genuine and impressive display of agedness appearing in the material media of fine artworks, and because (3) pastness *recognized as a property of the corporeal presence* of the fine art object need no more conflict with its total aesthetic experience than pastness *recognized as an essential ingredient in the subject represented*, but rather contributes to our experience (as in the example of Titian's *Charles V*)—for all these reasons fine art objects may be antiques just as well as crafts.

In general, we have been led to a discussion of crafts not only because antiques are usually thought of as being limited to this category of art-work (often called "decorative" or "applied" art) but also because craft objects, over time, often become like "fine art" objects because they become "translucent," that is, they develop a message (the image of the past world) consonant with (in fact resonant with) their medium (patina, for example); and this meant we had to begin this section with some discussion, some account, of what ("fine") art itself is as well as what craft is, insofar as these can genuinely be distinguished.

We need now to discuss the process—*how* the antique functions to evoke an image of past reality. We do so both by an examination of its *style* (the peculiar coordination of the object's corporeal and contextual elements that are constants which can be discriminated by art-historical analysis) and by an examination of its *material endurance* (a modification of opacity we call "agedness").

First, however, let us turn to two other issues mentioned in the definition of antique as already given. These are the references to "rarity" and "beauty."

1.2.2 Beautiful and Rare: Collectibles, Souvenirs, Trophies, Religious Relics, Artifacts

Although beauty is rare, not all rare things are beautiful. It is the quality of beauty above all others that *should* enable us to distinguish between the antique and other crafted articles that are often associated with it in practice—*artifacts, souvenirs, trophies, religious relics*, and *collectibles*—though, as we see below, there are other characteristics that also serve to distinguish the latter categories from the antique proper. I say "should enable us" because *beauty*, appearing as a formal property of the object, remains notoriously difficult to define as a quality. While I certainly would not attempt to do here what others have failed to do in much longer works, I nevertheless generally assert that any object of experience having the characteristics of *intensity, integrity*, and *transcendence* ought properly to be called "beautiful."[15] Since it must be admitted that a full account of "beauty" has not and will not be presented in this work, however, perhaps we may rely not on an exhaustive attempt to define a term but rather on the examination of these other objects often associated with antiques.

The antique is not a mere *artifact*. Objects encountered in archeological and art-historical contexts are "artifacts." They are seen as examples and evidence "among others such like." Such "demonstrative objects" have only antiquarian reality and a documentary and testimonial value. The stone doorjamb, the unglazed pot, or arrowhead as artifacts, moreover, are usually not sufficiently impressive, unique, or relevant to us to generate a *Lebenswelt* of the past—real or imagined. Normally (though not necessarily), they would fail to be beautiful for lack of intensity, transcendence, and integrity. On the other hand, to oppose documentary value to the aesthetic experience of the antique would be a false antinomy because, in the context of its appreciation, the past world it testifies to is indeed the artifact's most significant aspect. The only question is, is the object *merely* documentary and thus *merely* an artifact? The antique is always more than "merely" informative. The artifact may or may not be rare; often it is rare in the first instance (or several instances) of its documentary function. Further instances, once sufficient documentation is accomplished, are irrelevant no matter how many may later appear. Artifacts need not be beautiful, only genuine.

Neither is the antique a *souvenir*. The souvenir is an aide-memoir to personal experience. Natural objects, such as dried flowers pressed in books, may be souvenirs. A Metropolitan Opera program for a performance of *Il Trovatore* calls to mind a childhood event when, at six years of age, I had my first opera experience. This program, however, is not an antique, and my age alone has no bearing on that fact. Souvenirs have only subjective reality and autobiographical value. Souvenirs may *become* antiques—assuming they fulfill other requisite criteria—only if they obtain objective (not purely personal) recognition as icons of the past. But even apart from their private autobiographical limitations, in the examples above both dried flowers and the opera program still fail to meet the criteria set forth in the proposed definition: the first because it is a natural, not a crafted, object and the second because it is not "primarily handcrafted." Souvenirs need not be beautiful or rare—only successful in jogging my memory.

Nor is the antique a *trophy*. A trophy is like a souvenir, except that it is an object that has public (rather than merely private) status and that in some manner evokes fame. The trophy is the relic or memento of a world-historical event or of famous/infamous personalities which claims our attention by its association therewith. The trophy need not even be an artifact, but may be organic (a lock of Napoleon's hair) or a mass-produced piece of equipment (one of Hitler's shoelaces, the first baseball to have been tossed out in Yankee Stadium, Jimmy Hendrix's purple hat).

The trophy is, moreover, primarily a token of victory, whether as in booty seized by war (images of the gods of vanquished nations so as to possess their power, as were the idols stored by the Aztecs at the temple of Coacalo; or the great candelabrum looted from the Temple in Jerusalem and transported in triumph to Rome; or the four horses of San Marco, transplanted from Constantinople after the sack of 1204 and then carted off to Paris by Napoleon) or as a prize or medal awarded for achievement in competition or as a claim to shared fame by mutual ownership. Many venerable antiques often also have the status of trophies. "Trophy-hood" can attach to antiques by means of their *provenance* (about which we speak further later), for an object's fame would certify its authenticity; and, when the association is world-historical, it may guarantee the object's agedness as well. But clearly the antique and the trophy are distinct. Without its special public association with fame, the trophy object has no significance or aesthetic value in itself, but only the value that publicity imparts (and perhaps the pious hope that by some magic of contagion the owner or experiencer may extract from the object and preserve for himself a small portion of the glory contained therein). Certainly the trophy need not be beautiful. It may be rare and sometimes be unique.

Nor is the antique equivalent to the *religious relic*—though often enough some religious relics become antiques when their religious duties have disintegrated (usually through the collapse of the worshipful world in which they operated). Religious relics' original function was as equipment enabling a contact to occur between the human and the divine worlds (the secular and the sacred). Like antiques they seem to possess the magical power to convey us to another world by their presence or contagion. But of course many of these religious relics are organic— Buddha's tooth, a thorn from Jesus' crown—and that alone differentiates them from antiques. Other instances, such as icons, may certainly with the passage of time fall into the category of antiques when no longer used for worship, as may monstrances and reliquaries that were handcrafted to contain or display these relics.

Nor is the antique to be identified with the *collectible*. Collectibles seem to be much the rage these days and are often coupled with genuine antiques so that we frequently find advertisements for "antiques and collectibles." Collectibles are founded on a category of things whose forms and features are fully dictated by some practical function—for example, Coca-Cola signs, campaign buttons, bits of barbed wire, toys, beer cans— and that are invariably only one of the series of mass-produced like exemplars. But what especially differentiates them from antiques is that their value resides entirely in the fact of their collectibility. Last year's limited edition of numbered plates or commemorative medals by a recognized maker may be (though are usually not) instantly "collectible." They are not antiques. Once the authenticity of their issuance is established, their subsequent life and record of endurance into the present is generally irrelevant to their status. Unlike artifacts, which they may in some other respects resemble, collectibles need to demonstrate nothing and are válued above all for their collectibility—and vice versa. For these reasons they have a tautological reality and economic values established by the current peculiarities of their market or psychological values invested in them by the peculiar mentality of the accumulator or collector of that collecting category. Collectibles cannot by definition be unique: there must always be a significant though limited number of them, and they must all be *as alike in their series* and as *"like new"* (no signs of age) as possible. That is why having them in their original boxes, even unopened (with sales receipt, if possible), is most desirable for collectors.[16] Especially at the "lower end" of the collectible world and among the newest generation of collectible collectors, almost any category of durable goods evoking childhood nostalgia and having bright colors, interesting forms, and a wide variation within a series that has fairly ready availability becomes (indeed, has already become) a "collectible."[17] Within these parameters collectibles need to be rare; they need be not beautiful.

Thus, these other considerations, *in conjunction with beauty*, may serve to distinguish the *antique* from the *collectible*, the *artifact*, the *trophy*, the *religious relic*, and the *souvenir*. It is worth emphasizing in this context, however, that these quasi-antique categories, while they are to be distinguished from the idea of the antique proper, nevertheless share some family resemblances—though perhaps "tribal resemblances" would be a better phrase. This may be due to the specific features in their objective nature or the subjective conditions of the human imagination whereby we come to value them in their association with the past or their ability to generate and preserve a world. We will even note in the next chapter an evolutionary progression in the human valuation of certain types of associated objects: from the gold of the treasure (or trophy), to the wisdom of the words (or book), to the technical perfection of representational sculpture and painting, to the entirety of the artifactual world. Certainly, *historically* speaking, these five quasi-antique categories were not fully distinguishable (or at least not distinguished) from the antique itself until recent times, as we see in our archeology of the idea of the antique in the following chapter.

To return now to the terms of our definition of the antique—having left it at the quality of "beauty," which brought us to the quasi-antique categories—we note that in the antique, "rarity" is *not only* a function of beauty, for beauty is rare, as we have said. Rareness is, second, also a function of original "fewness" or "uniqueness." And this quality is itself normally a function of its handcraftedness. Third, rareness is a function of the durability of its medium. These last two factors—original limited fewness and durability of medium—are best understood in conjunction with "agedness."

Simply to define an "antique" legally as an "object over one hundred years of age" is about as meaningful and reliable as establishing the "maturity" of persons at twenty-one years of age. A somewhat more significant stipulation of time would be "pre-1830." This is because it places the antique object prior to the machine age and thus increases or guarantees both its rarity and its uniqueness, as well as its handcraftedness. Given the capacity of independent human labor, there will not be many exemplars; and given its variability, there will never be exact duplication. Furthermore, as the iconic embodiment of the objective spirit of its creator and an age now past, the antique must move us out of our present reality. A non-machined object reflecting a pre-machine world is an assurance of that move to the past. But "pre-1830" is still a false criterion because it remains arbitrary and artificial. The term "machine" is itself vague and arbitrary. A potter's wheel is "machine" of sorts. And there are many instances of objects we would call "antiques" without hesitation that are at least in part "machined." Moreover, the one-hundred-year dateline is far too restrictive in practice. An Art Deco bracelet by Cartier, for example, is certainly in today's antiques trade considered antique, although because it was made circa 1925, it would fail to meet either the 1830 dateline or the hundred-year criterion; moreover, Cartier, using machines, often made more than one bracelet of a given design.

More significant than a stipulation of their years and precise dates, so long as they show their age, it is the beauty and rarity of these examples that is important in our appreciation of antiques. This is so because they capture our attention and tell us this thing is uncommon, not everywhere to be encountered in the everyday world of the *present*, and therefore not *of this* world. Hence the importance of age—as an appeal both to the object's style and to the durability of its own materiality, components stated in our definition—is not simply to be reckoned in terms of an enumeration of years. And as we showed at the outset in our discussion of historicality in relation to provenance with our example of the *nef*, the age of the antique seems essential to its being antique. This brings us to a consideration of "agedness."

1.2.3 Agedness as Style and as Material Endurance

We must now come to terms with the *how* of the antique's nature. We must do so in conformity with our definition's stipulations of "style" and "material endurance"—both of which are indices of *agedness*. It is this quality of the antique that evokes and preserves an image of the past.

This agedness is first of all recognized in *style*.[18] We cannot here set forth a fully developed theory of style, but suffice it to affirm the following. First and foremost, style in art objects generally is a function of both form (the material vehicle) and content (the worked world erected by it). Style is the ensemble of distinguishable and distinctive characteristics of both form and content in a work, which ensemble—because of the relative stability and repetition of its characteristics—makes that work comparable with others and which has resulted from choices (deliberate or not) made by its creator from among possible strategies of construction available within (1) the laws (i.e., invariable parameters) of the genre and (2) the taste (i.e., variable cultural preferences) of his time and place. To illustrate (1) above, marble cannot be shaped by melting or blowing as can glass, and (2) the soft organic shapes favored by French Art Nouveau are created by the "whiplash curve" and "seed/pod forms," not the sharp right angle or the Doric column favored by classicism.

To offer a further example of the factors constituting style, we may consider the comparable case in literature. The Elizabethan style in tragedies is as much a creation of its vehicles of corporeal manifestation (i.e., the particular sounds and pronunciations of English words, sentence structure, method of acting, costumes and stage design, metaphors and imagery) as it is of its content (the structured, meaningful, worked world it generates for us, namely, a world of power-driven kings where tragic flaws and demonic forces work out their bloody plot solutions). Thus, the style of Elizabethan tragedy could not possibly be mistaken for Ancient Greek or French Neo-Classical or Modern tragedies. Similarly, Hippolyte, the "hero" in Racine's play *Phèdre*, is a virile suitor betrothed to the princess Aricie, but in Euripides' play *Hippolytus* he is a chaste devotee of Artemis. This change in the play's contents is not simply a divergence in plot and an alteration in the sexual persona of a character, but reflects an immense transformation in world-view (involving the very idea of what constitutes masculinity) and hence in taste between ancient Greek tragedy and French seventeenth-century Neo-classical tragedy.

Even if translated into ancient Greek with appropriate meter and music, with choral odes and performed on an ancient Greek stage with all the trappings of ancient Greek stagecraft, Racine's play would fail utterly to be ancient Greek in *style*. Similarly, in painting, the Impressionist style is as much a matter of subject (peaceful landscapes and domestic scenes of bourgeois or Bohemian daily affairs—no Old Testament patriarchs and prophets, or kings receiving peace terms from the conquered or ensconced in their seraglios) as it is of medium (spectrum palette, optical mixing, avoidance of black "holes," quick brushstrokes, mottled lighting effects, small easel canvases, etc.). One does not mistake such an Impressionist work for a Holbein, a Poussin, a Delacroix, or a Caravaggio. And similarly, *within* a given style one may distinguish the distinctive work of a master by these same two factors, more minutely discriminated. So, for example, van Gogh's heavy *impasto*, his bold, intense, contrasting colors, his gash-like brushstrokes, his brooding, interior subjects, and his crazed portraits and incendiary landscapes are not in the style of his Impressionist contemporaries Renoir and Monet.[19] Painters of the Spanish Baroque loved to paint saints in martyrdom perhaps more than any other subject; but any art history major can distinguish—between the anguished, tortured flesh of one such saint and the ecstatic, blissful radiance of another—the "brutalist" style of Ribera, on the one hand, from the "vaporized" style of Murillo, on the other.

Moreover, differences in style result from the unique fine-tuning of these two factors—the material elements and world elements—both within themselves and then each with the other. Thus, in itself, the material medium is composed of various sub-vehicles in painting (e.g., surface texture, disposition of shapes, clarity of line, contrast and intensity of color, thinness or type of paint), and these must each be adjusted to the other, some being more or less emphasized, actualized, balanced. Correspondingly, in itself the worked world is composed of sub-meanings or subjects in painting (e.g., social status of the persons depicted, expressions and intentions suggested by their dispositions and gestures, action or story being told, emotional atmosphere generated or themes communicated by symbolic objects, lighting, open spaces), and these must be harmonized too. And finally, the various contents or sub-meanings of the worked world and the various components or sub-vehicles of the material medium must each be coordinated to the other. Thus, clear line, realistic modeling, formal balance, glassy surface texture may (Raphael) or may not (Dali)—depending on the entire nexus of adjustments uniquely made on all levels and in all areas—generate a worked world of objective rationality and peaceful normality. Style is the result of the totality of these separate factors and the minute manner in which an artist in his epoch and in his medium coordinates each to each.

Again, noticing differences between the fine art object per se and the antique object proves helpful. Because the antique craft object exists primarily in the direction of the opacity of its medium, the appropriate modifications and coordinations in its corporeal elements surely determine the antique's particular style as well. But because antique craft objects are usually weak in generating an internally worked world of their own, but rather generate an image of the past world now gone by, we cannot usually speak here in the same sense of style as a function of an *interior* worked-world vision. However, in the case of an *antique* fine art object—that is, a painting—we certainly could and would characterize its style as a function of the worked-world vision coordinated with cognitive elements. We could, for example, speak of the blue "cloth of honor" placed behind the Virgin Mary as being the Early Renaissance stylistic convention for communicating her preciousness and her power as a vehicle of intercession for our heavenly salvation. Moreover, and at the same time, we would *also* be paying special attention to the character of its medium—the use of ground lapis lazuli mixed with egg tempera and the gilded punch work, for example, typically used in Early Renaissance painting and thus here to compose the Virgin's cloth, which is art-historically indicative of its style and period. Thus, the agedness of the work, the past world of the work, is generated both by the stylistic elements found in the interior worked world consistent with that age's style and by the material elements typical for the medium of that stylistic age.

We would say that we recognize a literary work's worked world as typical, for example, of the Elizabethan style when, in experiencing a Shakespearean tragedy, we find ghosts crying out for vengeance, just as we would recognize the style's *material* presence in corpses strewn about the stage or in its now "archaic" language. We recognize Botticelli's style, similarly, from both its Neo-Platonic images and the interrelative meanings of the idealized reality they construct (part pagan, part Christian, part Renaissance-humanist cognitive elements). We also recognize his style from the pure, clear, flowing, disembodied line that establishes itself in the sensuous vehicle through which this worked world shines, an element of its material medium. Taken together, these stylistic elements uniquely achieve the "Botticelli confection."

But what of the Meissen teapot, the bronze Ming dynasty temple bell, or the Georgian epergne? Surely one cannot speak in these instances of the unique and eternal internally worked world of meaning generated by the Georgian epergne. This craft object does not generate by imitation, by representing a fictive world that it was created "to be about." For just as this sort of object is tied ineluctably to the real world in its corporeality, so this very corporeality evokes an image of the real world, although it is the image of a real world of the *past*, because, as we have said, it has "fallen into" this role of representing the past in the present. And that past is the world that (in its age as betrayed by its style) it now generates, just as fine art objects generate their interior worked world at their inception.

Let us look, now, at agedness seen through the style of such antiques: where style demonstrates age and also where it may fail to. A bulbous-shaped teapot made from a hard-paste porcelain of an outstanding pure whiteness with hand-painted flowers and birds in a pattern fancifully suggestive of something Chinese but in shape and decoration entirely divorced from genuine Far Eastern productions indicates in its style and materials the great German manufactory of Meissen—before we even turn it over to check for the expected "crossed swords" mark in underglaze blue. Further investigation of its stylistic peculiarities, in conjunction with the knowledge of the world of its creation and the individual personalities of that time and place, indicate the probability that the piece was made by the factory's premier painter, Johann Herold, at the command of the factory's founder, Augustus the Strong of Saxony, either for his personal use or as a gift to a friend or another head of state. If so, we could confirm its period of creation to be between 1725 and 1740. A further associated history—perhaps a paper trail or a hypothetical reconstruction of successive owners, such as we imagined we could have in our introductory story of the *nef*—would simply authenticate by provenance what a physical examination of the unique characteristics of the teapot's style has already told us about its age, and therefore its agedness.

A Ming dynasty temple bell's style, its art-historically isolable peculiarities, similarly evokes and generates a world—an image of Imperial Ming China, of its long tradition of crafting in bronze, of its religious attitudes and ceremonial rituals. Because of this style recognition, moreover, we should immediately detect any "errors"—in our judgment of style or in the thing itself. So, for example, we might suddenly notice that the bell's metal is too thin ever to have been used for its presumed function or that the manner of stylizing the cloud patterns in its surface decoration is of nineteenth-century origin. In either such instance of "error" we would be noting *stylistic* contradictions—between its material structure and past world of its use or between material configuration of its design and its presumed age. So, too, in the instance of a Georgian epergne, the image of the opulence of the dinner tables where it performed its service is evoked: the guests, their clothes and conversations, the flowers and fruits and candies that the object held, and so on. But suppose, again, that we discover "errors" as we scrutinize it further: the unpolished bottoms of its cut-glass inserts are wrong for this period; the overall shape and design is exact for the period, however, and the sterling silver frame with its engraved and *repoussé* decoration is the correct material for that design; but the size of the whole object seems a bit diminutive for the kind of dinner service we would expect for the society using that material and that design for that object; still, the hallmarks on the silver are absolutely correct. We breathe lightly on the hallmarked area to test, and a resulting line of condensation indicates that solder has been used to "let in" a genuine hallmark cut from a Georgian spoon. Thus, we conclude it is a deliberate forgery. We have done all this precisely by combining and contrasting the material elements in themselves and then these with its style and also with elements discovered (or not discovered) in the image of the past world it generates. In this process we have pursued a dialectic of agedness, of its *style and medium and past world*, part of the appraisal process that we develop in greater detail in chapter 3, where we introduce the ten criteria of antiques connoisseurship.

Style is something we can (and that antique dealers, connoisseur-collectors, and museum curators *must*) become keenly, even subconsciously, attuned to. Seeing the past in the antique through its style, through its consistencies and inconsistencies, is the prime technique of the appraiser/authenticator. Thus, it is often noted as a truism in the field that deliberate fakes of antiques, hard to spot when they are new, become easy to detect after "agedness" has set in (a generation or more). Because the style of the immediate present is always too transparent for us to notice, we can detect clearly only after that passage of time the incongruity of *two* past styles "in collision" in the object.[20] (We shall deal with authenticity and authentication of antiques more fully in chapter 3.)

In these various ways, then, style enables us to recognize agedness; for style, as we now see, is the result of a nexus of interrelated elements, of forms and contents, which are art-historically isolable and sufficiently constant for us to recognize congruity and incongruity. The antique in its style shows its age and thereby evokes the image of a historical world.[21]

There remains now the second consideration in the recognition of the antique's agedness: *material endurance*. Agedness here relates to the modifications in the materiality of the sensuous vehicle. It explains how, through this mode other than style, the antique becomes an icon for the image of a past reality. It also explains how antiques differ from certain artworks that may also be historical (or, better, that "exist historically").

Hence musical art objects (as opposed to their books or scores) cannot be antiques. My hearing of the art object called *Le Nozze di Figaro*, an event of great "rarity" and "beauty," can certainly by its *style* evoke and preserve an image of a world now gone by. My reading of *War and Peace* re-creates Russia at the beginning and at the end of the nineteenth century and makes those worlds alive again for me. But the literary masterpiece, the novel itself, like the musical masterpiece, the opera performance, cannot be an antique. These works *can* generate a past world by means of their style. They *cannot* evoke a past world by appealing to the durability of their own materiality because their media cannot display that sort of material modification we call "agedness."[22]

All antiques, we say, should show their age. Agedness appears not merely in style, however, so that we recognize an object's beauty as not presently in vogue, as "old-fashioned," of "another time and place." Style is, here, a *formal* indicator of the object's age. But there remains also the *material* or *corporeal* aspect of agedness experienced in the antique. This appears as dirt, wear, damage, discoloration, patina, and the like. The recognition of this materially present agedness has two aesthetic effects. First, it may increase or decrease the object's *formal* aesthetic appeal per se (i.e., making it more or less beautiful). Second, it increases the object's *material* aesthetic appeal (i.e., demonstrating its perseverance through time makes us experience it as antique).

In the first instance, the purely formal aesthetic response may increase through the effects of agedness. This can occur in two ways. First, agedness enables the object's present appearance to coincide with current expectations or preferences so that, for example, the colorlessness of Classical Greek marble statues now appeals to present taste as tasteful (beautiful), whereas their original bright pigmentation would appear garish and non-conformative to our past-world expectations (for brightly painted they would appear ugly, or at least not beautiful, and certainly un-Greek). Second, agedness improves surface qualities: sometimes it makes objects simpler, as when, for example, wear smooths and obscures initial irregularities or patina blends and softens original sharp incongruities—hence Ruskin: "whatever faults it may have are rapidly disguised . . . whatever virtue it has still shines and steals out in the mellow light."[23] Or, more often, agedness improves surface qualities through the contrary effect, making these aged objects more complex, as when, for example, stains, small chips, tiny cracks, or the disappearance of very minor parts creates irregularities and asymmetries that are, in their visual and tactile conditions, more interesting and stimulating to the imagination than uniform regularity—hence Kant: "all stiff regularity . . . has something in it repugnant to taste; for our entertainment in the contemplation of it lasts for no length of time, but it rather . . . produces weariness."[24]

But materially present (as opposed to formal, i.e., stylistically present) agedness—such as patina—has the second effect of increasing the object's *material* (as opposed to purely formal) aesthetic appeal. Materially present agedness denotes the object's historicality and stimulates the aesthetic response of "antiqueness" by awakening our historical consciousness. Patina here becomes the peculiar modification of the object's corporeal structure in which we recognize the duration of the object's persistent existence through its *material endurance*. This objective manifestation of endurance in time—agedness—becomes an Ariadne's thread conducting the mind to the image of a past world, an icon invoking a past reality, inducting it into the present, and preserving the past in a transubstantial entity that stands before us. Thus, for example, an Ancient Greek play or a Renaissance madrigal may evoke for us the spirit of its age, but they cannot *sensuously materialize* a realized embodiment of that time past which can exist for us now encapsulated in "this thing" because it has endured the continuum of existence. The play, the tune, are abstractions and can enjoy only the "intervality" of existence. The antique wears time like a trophy—like Ahab's White Whale, bearing the scars of experience, accounts of deeds done and endured, and the weight of history.

Hence, if it is true (and I think it is), as Trilling claims regarding *literature* of the past, that "its historicity is a fact in our aesthetic experience,"[25] then, a fortiori, antiques, as physically enduring *objects that sensuously display their history in agedness*, contribute a unique element in the totality of our aesthetic response.[26] It is one thing to *know* the age of the work—what we call its provenance and what we illustrated in our opening case in point—but another to *see* and *feel* its palpable presence. In antiques, historicality is patently tactile: we feel, we can hold and caress, the age. The persistence of its material endurance, which marks of agedness prove, objectifies the duration of the antique's reality and so its "right" to speak for the past. This characteristic of the antique—its patina and such materially present signs of agedness—has great bearing on the issue of "restoration," about which we will have much to say in chapter 3.

Hence, it is at least as much in the duration of its materiality, noted by physical signs of agedness we can "touch," as in style, noted by formal coordinations of material elements we recognize, as in provenance that attaches to the object by way of narrative association that we experience the aesthetic enjoyment of the antique. It is primarily in this corporeal

and sensuous mode—in its historicality rather than in its mere history—
that we appreciate *authenticity* in the antique. Authenticity, as Benjamin
has noted, is not merely a matter of who made it and when and where; it
is a function of the object's entire existence in the world. Authenticity, he
writes, is "the essence of all that is transmissible from its beginning,
ranging from its substantive duration to its testimony to the history
which it has experienced"; and we will have more to say about it later. In
the age of mechanical reproduction, therefore, an object's own "time and
place" become irrelevant; and the "aura" (as he calls it) of the object is
eliminated, and consequently it loses its "authority."[27] Thus, to be told
of a pocket watch that it was "made for Napoleon" serves not merely to
verify its antiqueness as to date and "provenance," but to ascribe to the
object a life-world that it has *lived through* and *lived from* into the present and that has consequently earned it the right to speak for and evoke
an image of the past.

This brings us to our last consideration: What function does the antique serve, and what do we mean by "evoke and preserve the image of a
world now past"?

1.2.4 The Evocation and Preservation
of the Past World

In addition to the pleasure deriving from any object of beauty, it is the
evocation (or generation) and preservation of a world now past that is
the chief delight for lovers of antiques. One might wonder here whether
the image or conception of the world now past is one that is "correctly"
evoked and preserved, that is, whether or not it is *a* world (some world)
or *the* world, and whether it is *the* image or *an* image. Ultimately, I
think—and without entering into Post-modernist debates in the philosophy of history—it makes little difference to the aesthetic experience
whether the image or world evoked is singular or accurate. We have an
historical consciousness; and we set it to work imaginatively when encountering antiques—consonant with and to the degree delimited by the
perceived properties of the object, by the attention we direct toward it,
and by the extent and accuracy of our historical knowledge.

In some respects this seems to be a human experience of relatively recent origin, perhaps only one hundred fifty or two hundred years. However, we will see in detail in the next chapter that the ancient Romans
already appreciated and coveted Greek statues as antiques, that the taste
for both Greek and Roman manuscripts, statuary, and cameos was revived by the Italians of the early Renaissance (so that by the late 1400s it
was already a fashion, not to say craze, manipulated by dealers), that the

seventeenth century universalized the quest for the antique when "the past became a foreign country," and that by the eighteenth century "furnishings"—*objets de vertu*, decorative arts, glassware and porcelains, tables and chairs, and so on, as opposed to paintings and statues—were actively pursued by those who could otherwise have afforded new things. It was the European Enlightenment of that century that created the new awareness of the historicality of world civilization and of the individual's own self-consciousness as historical—an awareness first inspired by such eighteenth-century thinkers as Vico, Winckelmann, Lessing, and Rousseau, but finalized by the likes of Hegel in the first quarter of the nineteenth century—and that thereby established the ground for this new type of aesthetic experience.[28] (These are merely samplings, a quick overview, of a few of the variations of how the evocation and preservation of the world now past has evolved vis-à-vis the appreciation of the antique.)

If we would seek a material or objective equivalent (perhaps a causative principle) for the creation of this new subjective historical spirit (as Hegel would describe it), then, as the subsequent chapter will show, the spatial correlative of temporal recollection became *empire*—the world empires recently constructed in the economic and political spheres by the English, Dutch, French (and later other power centers of Western civilization). In order to view themselves as legitimate possessors and due inheritors of the greater world and its past, these empire builders found it necessary to possess the objects materially embodying that world so as to be able to identify (or at least empathize) authentically with the image thus evoked, and to see themselves world-historically as the legitimate focus and purpose of a world-historical evolutionary process. For such a "seeing," the mere de facto ownership of spoils and trophies is not enough; but rather, imagination coupled with understanding and a new sensibility and connoisseurship is required; and thus antiques became a trigger and touchstone for the engagement of that imagination's reconstruction of the exotic past. The antique becomes our "wormhole" to an accommodation within this universal past; reciprocally, this past finds its present presence by our accommodation of its "remains" in our own world. Consequently, it was in the eighteenth century that politically (as empire) and intellectually (as historical consciousness) the ground for a new type of aesthetic experience was formalized.

It took only two further steps along the road to historical and world-heritage awareness for antiques to become appreciated as they currently are. The first step was Romanticism, with its "cult of the ruin" and nostalgia for the past, the exotic, and the lost. The second step—the "tail" of

Romanticism (as Rococo is sometimes construed as the "tail" of the Baroque)—was Romanticism's extension and dissipation in the *L'art pour l'art* and *Décadence* movements in the last third of the nineteenth century. To the proponents of these two movements, the contemporary utilitarianism, positivism, socialism, and the like of the bourgeoisie, with its optimistic fanaticism for the progressive future, was anathema. The Decadents opposed such bourgeois sentiments and ideals with nihilism, yearning for the distant and past, and uselessness. (Baudelaire railed against the good bourgeois as "an enemy of art, of perfume, a fanatic of utensils.")[29] For such mentalities as these, art and artifact were not useful equipment to manipulate the world of practical reality but hallucinogenic touchstones of escape for the imagination. Hence, their appreciation of the antique as a decontextualized ("worldless") utensil without a function, the object that is un-at-home in the present—just as they saw themselves—that is, as a contradiction of the present, one with no serviceable implications for the future, but a cherished reminder of the past and stimulus for fancy—indeed, as an "art object." Meanwhile, the detested bourgeoisie, the popular culture, took the opposite road to the same result. Imbued with materialism, it took to the antique not as a symbol of unreality and vanity but as a fetish of self-aggrandizement: it became for the masses the materialization and certification of a heritage otherwise unimaginable—of culture and class, of taste and status. We will examine these matters, this evolution, in great detail in the next chapter.

What was the—*is* the—aesthetic reward of such a new awareness? It is to locate, to define, ourselves within the entirety of human civilization and its achievements. What was the—*is* the—reason that the antique arouses our interest and the special delight it affords? It is to expand *objectively and materially* (beyond the immediate givens in the actually perceived everyday world of the present) what *subjectively and intellectually* we have already assimilated—or wish to assimilate—as our own. Thus, it is not *merely* the present reality's inauthenticity or blandness that one wishes to "escape" by means of the antique (a possibility we suggested above). It is not merely its "triviality" or "bad taste." It is its limitations. It is its incompleteness and insufficiency for a consciousness sufficiently historical, sufficiently worldly—and sufficiently *imaginative*.

As possibility is freer than actuality, so imagination provides a more expansive world than perception. This is true for all art objects in general. Art objects open up new relations of possibility in imitation of the limited orders of reality and create new substantive worlds, like quasars glowing within the known and given sphere. Antiques are symbols for a context of past possibilities and are icons potent in transubstantiating past reality in an image evoked by an object "yet present" from that time. It is because we want to own and assimilate ourselves in the multiplicity—or some portion of the universality—of human civilization and its achievements that we can be attuned to the appeal of the antique. By surrounding myself with antiques I can also live in their worlds. I can do so as these antiques serve my imagination, and it is from the operations of my imagination that the antiques please.[30]

If the aesthetic experience is based on the transformation of actuality into possibility by the imagination's generating a more expansive world than the mere faculty of perception can provide, then we may add that the historicality of certain objects of our experience (namely, antiques) may establish a context in which the imagination can entertain us with images reflective of past possibilities. And this would be a claim entirely consistent with any aesthetic theory that can admit of diverse sources for varied aspects to the totality of the aesthetic experience.

The antique preserves an image of the past encapsulated *in nuce* in the present.[31] The antique's form—its style and aged, enduring corporeality—enables our imagination to fancy in it the subjective spirit hibernating there. To live among the handmade is to live among the human. And particularly, to live perceptively and sensitively among the great creations of the past is to live among the historicality and universality of the human, for antiques are the materially immanent indicators of universal human historicality.

In affirming this we have concluded our attempt at a working definition of the antique together with an analysis of its primary components. But a definition, here or anywhere else, is merely a point of departure, a bare skeleton. It remains to elucidate and develop some of the major claims made in the process of explicating the definition of the antique in this chapter. Chapter 2 will arrive more or less at the same place by putting flesh on the skeletal definition presented here. It re-presents the components of the idea of the antique and its appreciation as *archés* within the historical evolution of antiques collecting and connoisseurship in Western civilization. And it attempts to show how and when and where and why "the antique" as we now understand it came to be that way, came to be conceived as it is and appreciated as it is.

TWO

An Archeology of Antiques

*A History of Antique Collecting
and Connoisseurship*

**How did the idea of antiques and the aesthetic response
to them emerge over time?**

The eyes must also eat.
— SICILIAN PROVERB

Oh, my poor friend, I must leave all this! Farewell dear paintings
that I have loved so much and that have cost me so much.
— CARDINAL MAZARIN

I know not how it is, but I never sent a gentleman in public capacity
to Italy, but he came back a picture dealer.
— KING GEORGE III

T he idea of antiques and the development of the ability to regard
them as objects of a unique aesthetic appreciation are bound up
with the history of connoisseurship and development of a "taste"
for them. The idea of antiques is also bound up with the history of the
idea of art in general, with the advent of historical consciousness, and
with the historical emergence of theories of art and beauty called "aesthetics."

It is not my intention in these historical chapters to present an encyclopedic history of collecting, connoisseurship, and taste. Much of that has
already been done admirably by other authors—F. H. Taylor and Joseph
Alsop, to mention only two—and I quote extensively from them.[1] But for
the purpose of my inquiry here, these works are deficient in two respects.
First, they do not specifically focus on (and do not show the development
of) the idea of *antiques* and the evolution of the accompanying aesthetic

response that is unique to these peculiar objects. These works provide a history of connoisseurship and collecting in general—primarily of "fine arts" but of other sorts of objects as well—and not a history of the connoisseurship and collecting, expressly and explicitly, of "objects with a past." Their second shortcoming, from our point of view, is that they are simply informational chronicles (anecdotal records) without interpretation. Even when some of these authors claim to see a pattern recurring within different periods or art traditions, they do not show how the idea of what "art" is—much less what "antiques" are—emerges progressively and developmentally over time. They fail, moreover, to provide an explanatory theory for the categories and criteria that have arisen over time, categories and criteria in terms of which we comprehend art and antiques. Thus, for our purpose here, they are unsatisfactory not only in scope but in theoretical structure and explanatory force.

This explanatory structure would be the kind of theory some philosophers call an "archeology," and that is why I use the term for this chapter rather than simply a "history." An archeology should enable us to see the real developments and connections, repetitions and permutations of patterns over time and place, to see how connoisseurship and collecting in the area of art and antiques came into being, grew, decayed, reemerged, and were transformed. Without this archeology, we could not come to understand why the working definition we proposed in the preceding chapter actually works when we think about antiques nowadays, why it is not an arbitrary definition, why and how the traditional distinction between crafts (decorative or applied arts) and fine arts came about (and may or may not be a useful distinction), and why the five types of objects I named "quasi-antiques" (the souvenir, collectible, religious relic, artifact, trophy) are not "antiques" in the fullest sense of the word. Likewise, the ten criteria of connoisseurship and collecting that I propose and explain in the next chapter would seem to be a subjective preference and capricious choice without this archeology. Abstracted from the factual past in which they are embedded and from which they arose and evolved, they would be arbitrary categories or criteria, giving us no sense of the times, the cultural "ambiance"—much less the particularities of cause and effect in evolution—that brought them into being. Moreover, such a skeletal schema—"the ten criteria"—could not inform us regarding the real "passions of the soul" that the antique object bestirs, for the passions of the connoisseur (the aesthetic response to the antique) are always better understood in terms of the particulars of history. Thus, in the lengthy historical account we begin here, I have chosen individuals,

sources, anecdotes, periods, and movements in collecting, connoisseurship, and taste, not for completeness of historical record or for panorama
but as the means by which to demonstrate and elucidate the combined
development (often in recurrent patterns) of our criteria of antiques.
They show how the idea of something being an "antique" has emerged
historically and can be grounded in an archeology.

In this archeology, therefore, we will find that each stage or epoch
adds a progressive facet to the total vision we currently have of our
world and the place antiques have in it. This is because in each stage we
will encounter one or more new *archés* with which to interpret the connoisseurship of and aesthetic response to the antique.[2] Since this connoisseurship of the antique is a self-conscious activity, it is carried on
within a world of meaning that is delimited by the "historical sight" or
vision of its own time. To explain the activity is to interpret the vision,
the historical consciousness of the era. This vision in our own time is
composed of a complex of culturally inherited visions or sightings. And
if so, then, like a white light whose wholeness is composed of many colors each of which is "bent" at a different layer and each of which illumi-
nates its object in a different hue, in what follows we will be refracting
the path of our present and complex vision of "the antique" through diverse moments in history, each of which carries a different "density" of
particular facts and forms, perceptions and preferences. As we pass
through this historical survey, therefore, we will be locating the *archés*
that will make our current interpretation of the antique possible. It is
in this sense that this chapter is an "archeology." It is an archeology of
culture that seeks discovery through the mutations and evolutions in the
cultural responses of civilization to the products of its past and the past
of other civilizations. It is an archeology that seeks the explanatory reasons, the *principles* (these are the "*archés*" in the primary sense in
"archeology"), in accordance with which the theory of the antique for-
mulates its interpretation. And it is an archeology that moreover views
these principles as reasons originating from efficacious events in the
course of history, that is, as *causes* (a secondary sense of "*arché*") for the
present view of the antique and its appreciation.[3]

In this way, the insight obtained by the historical analysis of our subject of inquiry is continuously modified and enriched with new details as
this archeology moves through the epochal periods selected, one moment
evolving from, contrasting with, or recapitulating another. Thus, as our attention is drawn back and forth between the parts and the whole (the particulars and the context, between the example and the world of meaning

that makes it meaningful), the intended outcome of this process becomes a deeper and more self-conscious understanding both of the whole and of the particular details that compose it.

2.1
Collecting and Connoisseurship
in the Greco-Roman World

There is no evidence for widespread antiques appreciation and collecting per se before Roman times, but there were precursors certainly before Alexander in the Hellenistic period.

It is even possible that this activity may have existed as early as late dynastic Egypt, where archaism in art reflected a general nostalgia for the golden age of the Old Kingdom.[4] But there is no solid evidence for it. According to the written account given by Howard Carter, Tutankhamen's tomb contained "a dynastic museum" of "art of various periods and even of various nations,"[5] but no doubt this was an "accumulation" of dynastic treasures and gifts of foreign embassies, possibly trophies (as we have distinguished this concept from antiques in the preceding chapter), and not an *art*—much less *antiques*—collection deliberately acquired by a connoisseur. Neither can we call the later Library and Serapion of Alexandria, which was partly modeled on Aristotle's *mouseion* in Athens, a real "museum collection," even though it was open to public use and contained not only books but also "pictures, statues, silver, and gold" (as we are told by Philo of Alexandria in *On the Seven Wonders*). It probably resembled more a Late Renaissance or Early Baroque *Wunder-* or *Schatzkammer* (as we explain later).[6]

In Greece, however, already in the third century B.C., there was apparently a taste for revival and deliberate archaism. According to Pierre Grimal, "Athenian workshops produced copies of classical works, or perpetuated an archaic style whose commercial success was due not to an increase in the aesthetic sense but to the desire to maintain artificially customs that would otherwise disappear."[7] As these were new works *in an old style*—they were not themselves antiques—their archaism may just as probably have been sociopolitically inspired as aesthetically motivated. Nevertheless, the third century, the post-Alexandrian or Hellenistic period, is, as we will see shortly, a turning point.

Evidently there was not much *theorizing about art* either—much less about "antiques"—even as late as the High Classical or Golden Age of Greece.[8] We use such terms as "antiques," "the arts," "crafts," "beauty," "aesthetics," "connoisseurship" as if current usage were quite definite and historically invariant—as if the things themselves, and the terms used to describe and categorize such things, and the theories, conceptions, and modes of appreciation that are "about" them have always existed, and as if it were just a matter of translating the ancient words with modern English equivalents. This is false, of course. Presumably, "in the beginning"—either with the emergence of *Homo sapiens* or with the appearance of Adam and Eve—there were no art objects as such, much less the "old" ones we now call "antiques," nor was there the conception of the "arts" or of "aesthetics" and the like. In fact, even after the emergence of civilization, such things as would later be called "arts" or "crafts" and perhaps such responses to them and thoughts about them that might in some other universe of experience be called "aesthetic appreciation" or "aesthetic theorizing"—such things, or rather, *such ideas*—did not exist for the people who made and possessed such objects. At least there is no evidence for such ideas and such experiences until late classical times. And if no "aesthetic experience" or "art" per se, then certainly no aesthetic encounters with "antiques" in anything like the modern sense of the word.

Of course, we do not need a theory of numbers to get "4" out of "2 + 2" if we are packing a lunch basket; we don't have to know the meaning of "prose" to speak in it. Likewise, just because there is no indication that the *ideas* of (much less "theories of") either art or antiques as special kinds of things existed at that time does not mean that such things as we would now describe by those words did not then exist or were never given some special consideration. The presence of signatures on some of the sculpture and painted vases of archaic period Greece (sixth century B.C.) indicates that their makers probably believed that their achievement was in some way unique or distinguishable from a more or less routine labor or production such as digging a trench for irrigation.[9] Classical sources record that one Theodoros of Samos cast a bronze self-portrait and wrote an architectural treatise on a temple of Hera on that island as early as the mid-sixth century B.C.[10] By the time of Pericles it was not at all unusual for architects, sculptors, and painters to write treatises regarding the nature of their art and advocating some particular method for achieving beauty in their respective media. The sculptor Polyclitus of Argos (maker of the great chryselephantine statue of Hera for the Heraeum at Argos) in the late fifth century wrote a canon on rhythm and proportion in sculpture and embodied these theories in his famous sculpture, "Doryphoros" ("The Spear Carrier"). Pliny writes that Polyclitus' treatise was "called *The Canon* by artists, who draw from it the rudiments of art as from a code (so that Polyclitus is held to be the only man who has embodied art itself in a work of art)."[11] In mid-fifth-century Athens, Ictinus, architect of both the Parthenon and the temple of Apollo at Bassae, and the painter Parrhasius, famous for the subtlety of his outline, both wrote treatises on their arts. The late-fourth-century painter Apelles of Colophon (whose portraits of Alexander the Great and Philip of Macedon were famous in his time) was said to have argued in his discourse on painting for a theory of style wherein he contrasted his pictures against those of his painter contemporaries Protogenes and Melanthius. The latter showed superiority in composition, he admitted, but with a certain "stubborn harshness"; the former displayed "excessive elaborateness," he said, while his own works were superior to those of both rivals in displaying a greater "charm" (χαριζ).

We have a good number of whole art objects from the classical age of Greece (almost all of which "show their age") and a lot of fragments; and we have many more Roman copies of Greek works. But though they too existed once, none of the Greek literary texts noted above are known to us now except second- and third-hand in fragmentary citations—many from (the Roman) Pliny the Elder's first-century A.D. *Historia naturalis*. This is primarily because none of the great classical Greek philosophers, orators, historians, poets, or dramatists of the Golden Age whom we (and their contemporaries) most admire and whose works have therefore survived to us by repeated copying ever showed much interest in the systematic cataloguing or description (much less the preservation of reflections on) the artworks of their time. There is the exception of Duris of Samos (a late-fourth-century B.C. pupil of Theophrastus), who, very much like Vasari in the Renaissance, wrote about the *lives* of noted painters and sculptors and apparently held that the creation of realistic illusion was the criterion of artistic excellence; but only a few fragmentary pages of this work survive. There is also one Xenocrates ("of Athens," some sources say, but more likely from Sicyon, in the latter half of the third century), who claimed that artistic excellence depended, rather, on mathematical proportions and supposedly wrote an "art history" of sorts in which art "ends" at the time of Lysippus and Apelles, and thus probably sounded somewhat like Aristotle's account of the evolution of tragedy in *The Poetics* (where he claims that poetry in the form of tragic drama had now, after Sophocles and Euripides, "stopped on its attaining to its natural form").[12] Nothing of Xenocrates' treatise on art survives (except again through the incorporation of fragments in Pliny's *Historia naturalis*, e.g., book 34, 53–70). Although we thus may suppose with the great art historian Rudolf Wittkower that many of these written works "showed the artists' attempt to grapple with their problems on a

theoretical level, to discuss matters of principle, to regard art as an intellectual profession divorced from the old tradition according to which art
was just one craft among others,"[13] we certainly can doubt this claim.
We can doubt it because there is simply no concrete evidence that these
written works were anything more than self-promotions, technical manuals, catalogues, chronicles, or biographies. And even if they dealt with
theoretical issues on the nature and appreciation of painting or sculpture,
they were precisely that—genre-specific, and not theories of art or theories of the aesthetic experience per se and in general—and there is no account of any sort dealing with "antiques."

Since we have already made reference to "beauty" in our tentative definition of the antique, and will discuss beauty in the next chapter in our
account of the ten criteria for the aesthetic appreciation of antiques, it
might be worthwhile to mention here the first usages of this term. If we
look at the use of Greek and Roman words, the Greek καλος and its Latin
equivalent *pulchrum*, which are translated by our "beauty,"[14] we find
that they were never clearly or consistently distinguished from the moral
and practical conceptions of "good" or "useful." Beauty was not, in fact,
thus "separated out" from the moral and epistemological spheres until
post-Renaissance times, and as we will see later in this archeology, it was
not specifically defined so as to distinguish it this way until the eighteenth
century. In addition, beauty was not conceived of as *primarily* relevant
to *art* at all.

Plato's most famous discussions of the idea of beauty in the *Phaedrus*
(249) and *Symposium* (216) occur in reference to human bodies, to
ideas, patterns of behavior, and conditions of soul, but *not in relation to
art*.[15] For him, beauty is a property in some manner ingredient in things,
which may be identified with or by (or be concomitantly present together
with) certain other properties such as symmetry, order, proportion, fitness, measure, precision, and a harmony of parts in relation to a whole.
Strictly speaking, for Plato, Beauty per se is really beyond sensual perception. Only its symptoms, indicators, or reflections are encountered in
material form; and these are sufficient manifestations of Beauty's power
to move us to progress beyond our sensuous everyday condition—both
by education (literally leading us out of it as from a dark cave) and by
love, which inspires the soul with desire. For Plato, Beauty is the object
of love in two senses: (1) it is what love pursues and (2) it is what love
creates. In this way, Beauty inspires love, and love inspires Beauty. However great this Platonic scheme is, it is too broad to have much relevance
to aesthetics or theory of art or theory of antiques as presently understood, though clearly, it is not irrelevant, since the contemporary antiques

connoisseur would happily admit that he loves and his "soul is inspired by" these objects of desire. Still, in Plato's own "theory of art" in its most severe moments,[16] art is allotted no independent epistemic or ontological value whatsoever, since art can neither depict reality nor convey truth, since it is a "mere appearance, a shadow of reality." Thus, a theory of art per se—vis-à-vis interpretation, evaluation, relation of medium to content, and the like—would be a trivial pursuit. Certainly there is no such thing as, for example, "disinterestedness" or "aesthetic distance" in Plato's account of Beauty. There is no connoisseurship, no "l'art pour l'art," no "historical consciousness," much less "antiques" appreciation. And yet by presenting in whatever context and for whatever purpose the *classical* conception of beauty for his time, Plato created *the* conception that was to dominate thinking about beauty until the eighteenth century and that was to predominate in all aesthetic/artistic theories up to the twentieth century.

Meanwhile, the Greek term τέχνη and its Latin equivalent *ars* meant not "art" in the modern sense (i.e., either "painting" in the generic sense or the "fine arts" generally and as distinct from the "crafts"), but a whole range of practical activities requiring "skill," from medicine to statesmanship to pastry making. Although we would probably associate the visual arts of painting and sculpture most with the specific concept of "fine" (as in "fine arts" and with its implication of "high class"), the Greeks and Romans would have associated these arts with manual labor (with its attendant social stigma).[17] Poetry was "high class," but it was associated with rhetoric and philosophy, never with the visual and plastic arts.

In fine, we hardly find in ancient Greek civilization anything at all like a modern conception of "beauty" or "the arts" or a philosophical system for interpreting them. It is true that Aristotle distinguishes the skills of "doing" (a practical science) and "making" (a productive science); and he separates the latter (as we noted in the preceding chapter) into arts that complete nature (what we would probably call "craft") and those that both complete and imitate (what we would probably call "fine"). His *Poetics* begins with a subgroup of the latter, namely, the aural/oral arts (the arts of speaking and hearing, or what we would call literature and music); and in functional terms on the basis of their various causes—their material media, their efficient manner of production, their subject matters—Aristotle proceeds to systematize the subclasses of the aural/oral arts into tragedy, comedy, epic, and so on.[18] Furthermore, he suggests that there are varying purposes to the arts and different pleasures and different beauties appropriate to different arts.[19] But these ideas and suggestions occurring primarily within the context of a literary theory are nowhere followed up in his surviving corpus so as to account for the rest of what we would nowadays include in the category of *art*; nor, insofar as I am aware, are such possibilities discussed by any of his immediate followers or interpreters. And regarding the universal concept "beauty" itself, Aristotle has precious little to say that wasn't already said by Plato. On these bases, perhaps, Aristotle *could* have laid groundwork or created a framework for a general theory of art and/or aesthetics. But in point of fact, there is nothing that specifically sets out "aesthetics" as a science of feeling or perception or experience of the beautiful; and there is nothing like a system of fine arts (including painting, sculpture, architecture) on which to impose a comprehensive "philosophy of art," not by Aristotle or any other classical Greek or Roman author. Thus, as Oskar Kristeller remarks,

> we have to admit the conclusion . . . that ancient writers and thinkers, though confronted with excellent works of art and quite susceptible to their charm, were neither able nor eager to detach the aesthetic quality of these works of art from their intellectual, moral, religious, and practical function or content, or to use such an aesthetic quality as a standard for grouping the fine arts together or for making them the subject of a comprehensive philosophical interpretation.[20]

And if there was for that time no idea quite in the modern sense of "art" and no aesthetic theory accounting for it, there was certainly no idea of "antique," much less an aesthetic theory accounting for its special appreciation.

If not among the ancient Greeks of the classical period (pre-Alexander), then when did this taste and appreciation for "art" in the modern sense, and especially for art and artifacts that have endured over time ("antiques") and that requires a special conception of the past in its relation to the present, first appear? As Taylor writes, it was

> the Hellenistic monarchs [who] began systematically and reverently to collect ruins and fragments of the classical age; and Sicyon [an ancient city just west of Corinth which became famous as an art center in the fourth century B.C.] became the gathering place for the art dealers of the empire. . . . No king or satrap of Alexander's empire . . . would overlook the fashionable necessity of having works of art. . . . It was indeed here that the vogue of art collecting, as it was to be carried on in Roman times, had its origin.[21]

Probably the first such collector was Attalos I of Pergamon (269–197 B.C.), third ruler of a historically surprising (for its time and place) state that was founded on the embezzlement of Lysimachus's treasure. Noting this connection with Alexander's heirs is not frivolous, because with the advent of Alexander we find for the first time a relatively benign mixture of a multitude of civilizations forged into a political empire such that while one, the Greek, was dominant, the necessity of toleration and consequent valorization of cultural diversity led to the desire on the part of rulers to conceive of themselves as at the unified center of a new inheritance of civilization.[22] (And as we will see, the same situation on a grander scale, with greater aesthetic sensibility and keener awareness that the greatest artworks were primarily to be obtained from the *past* of *other* civilizations, was to occur in the following century in Rome itself.) Attalos I imitated Ptolemy's Alexandrian Library, and seeking to make his provincial kingdom a center of Greek culture, he enriched Pergamon with as many examples of past and present Greek art as possible. For example, he not only bid 30 talents (a huge sum, equal to about 824 kilos, or 26,580 troy ounces, of silver) for a painting by the great third-century Athenian painter Nicias, but commissioned copies of any famous works he could not obtain. He even purchased the entire island of Aegina so as to acquire its portable art.[23] In the following century, Attalos II, richer and more acquisitive than his forebear, bid 100 talents for a painting of Dionysos by the mid-fourth-century Theban master Aristides, who was renowned as the first to "capture the affections of the soul" in paint. The painting had become available through the auction of goods looted in the sack of Corinth, one of the oldest and most luxuriant of ancient Greek cities, by the Roman general Mummius in 146 B.C. Apparently this painting was being used by Roman soldiers at the time as a flat surface on which to play a dice game. According to Pliny's account of the incident, when General Mummius heard of Attalos's bid, he was so astonished at the huge sum that he immediately withdrew the item from the sale for a dedication in Rome.

The sack of Corinth may have been the first spark to later Roman collecting voraciousness and connoisseurship. More likely it was a good second. The first was probably the sack of Syracuse by M. Claudius Marcellus in 212 B.C., which led to the earliest flood of Greek antiques into Rome. In fact, Plutarch in the first century A.D. laments not so much the immorality of Rome's being filled with art at the expense of other nations' treasures but the consequent aestheticization (read "corruption") of the public when he recounts the art-looting of Syracuse. He holds Marcellus responsible for encouraging in the Roman people "a taste for leisure and idle talk, affecting urbane opinions about art and artists, even to the point of wasting the better part of a day on such things."[24] Plutarch is probably the first—hardly the last—instance of the culture critic who laments the moral degeneracy of a society that has fallen into effete aestheticism.

Gaius Verres was the most rapacious and obsessive collector of his time. Securing in 80 B.C. the Roman governorship of Sicily, he scoured this veritable treasure trove for the Greek art of earlier times. The despoiled Sicilian owners hired Cicero as a lawyer to bring suit for recovery, and Cicero's Verrine Orations provide us with all the details. Verres, found guilty of malfeasance, escaped with much of his loot to Marseilles, but later, proscribed by Mark Anthony, who required him to return a famous set of Corinthian bronzes (not to Sicily, apparently, but to Anthony himself), he came to die for his collection: he drank poison sent by Anthony in a splendid antique vase whose beauty comforted his last moments. (Pliny claims that Anthony similarly proscribed the senator Nonius in order to obtain a great gem in his possession.)[25] The significance of "Corinthian bronze" in this story above should not be passed over. The term "Corinthian" denoted not merely a place of origin or even a style of object but a very specific quality of "antiqueness," and this already indicates a sophisticated appreciation for rarity and the *agedness displayed in patination*. According to the contemporary belief of many Roman collectors, the prized surface color and texture found on Corinthian bronzes was produced by a secret technique lost in antiquity. A more probable explanation is that the bronzes' rich patination was the direct result of the burning of Corinth by Mummius.[26] This explanation seems to have been appreciated by at least some Roman connoisseurs at the time. Apparently certain Corinthian bronzes were cast of a metal alloy already rich in gold content and were then gilded (and perhaps also coated with bitumen to enhance the relief); the heat of the conflagration must have caused a curious fusion of these elements on the oxidizing surface. Thus, the patina of these bronzes may not have been a "secret" but was accidentally and uniquely acquired by the rare pieces that had survived the city's destruction. The richly colored patina gave distinction to any Roman collection, and according to Seneca, "through the insanity of a few," rapidly caused examples to command astronomical prices.[27] In this account, we have here already, then, many of the features implicit in the developed idea of the antique: age, patina, rarity, beauty, high price, and an association with an important historical event and/or a supposed "secret technique" of the past now in the present time "lost."

The general public was not immune to the pleasures of art. Marcus Vipsanius Agrippa built public baths filled with painting and sculpture. The sculpture garden of Sallust—embellished primarily with loot he had acquired while governor of Numidia and from which grounds in the nineteenth century the famed "Ludovisi Throne" (if indeed it is genuine) is said to have been excavated—was open to visitors, who applied for entry. And later, when the emperor Tiberius became so infatuated with Lysippus's "Apoxyomenos" that he had the beautiful bronze nude removed from its public place in these baths to his private bedroom (perhaps as much for erotic as aesthetic enjoyment), the citizens of Rome raised such a clamor that he had to return it, "in spite of the passion he had conceived for the statue."[28] We find in these instances from history already, then, the idea that the greatest artworks of the past (especially the art of the Greeks) belong to the people of Rome and that great collectors have an obligation to make their collections available—if not to the public in general, then at least to other connoisseurs, so that a kind of fraternity of like-minded individuals sharing similar tastes was established.

Victorious armies have a way of bringing to market many great masterpieces. Sulla did some extensive looting in Athens on his way to get Mithradates in 86 B.C. Titus's sack of Jerusalem in 70 A.D. provides us with the famous image (still to be seen stamped on his coins and carved on his Arch in Rome) of the great menorah carried away from the Jewish Temple. For those who were not victorious generals or governors of artistically rich provinces, the best was still available for purchase at a sufficiently high sum. Of course, one then was not doing one's own "harvesting fresh from native soil," as it were, but had to rely on middlemen, the dealers, who were often inventive in the quality and provenance of their antiquities. Cicero, in his *Epistolae ad familiares*,[29] notes one such art dealer, the Greek Damasippus, who sold Greek "old masters" to new Roman millionaires, a custom that was later the subject of a Horace satire. Maurice Rheims observes that "as early as the 1st century [A.D.] charming statuettes in ancient styles were being fabricated for Roman patricians."[30] The emperor Caracalla collected supposed souvenirs of Alexander the Great. When Petronius refers sarcastically to "those silly little Greeks, Apelles and Phidias," he is only throwing into high relief for the purpose of ridicule the esteem in which they were held and the prices to be paid for their works (or supposed works). High prices did not necessarily mean high *aesthetic* appreciation, however, any more than they do in our own time. Pliny again: "It is extraordinary that when the price given for works of art has risen so enormously, art itself should have lost its claim to our respect."[31] And, as in our own time, once the empire acquired these antique art treasures, it was concerned not to lose them. Consequently, in the first century A.D., Rome promulgated a plan to nationalize certain objects to keep them from being exported to the colonies.[32] Thus, we find in Imperial Rome yet more features associated with the contemporary idea of antiques: social status in their ownership, specialized dealers providing antiques at high prices and specialized techniques of imitating (and/or forging) them, questions of provenance and prestige associated with owning the works that famous artists of the past had made or famous persons in the past had owned, and laws prohibiting the export of masterpieces (and for Rome this generally meant ancient Greek masterpieces).

By the second century B.C., therefore, Romans had evidently developed a taste for things that belonged to cultures of the past, and by the first century this became a fashion and passion among the upper classes and an obsession among a few. Pliny observed that Romans of his day "took thousands of Greek statues in silver, countless numbers in bronze and marble, and inconceivable numbers of Greek paintings, including murals detached from their walls and brought to Rome in wooden frames."[33] Where it could be contrived with some plausibility, this looting took the form of "payments" or "reparations." It was in this way that in the first century B.C. there arrived in Rome Sycion's entire public art gallery (the first of its kind). All the art went "to liquidate the public debt."[34] Even ancient sites within Italy were ravaged. Pliny again tells us that at Lanuvium "are two nude figures [by Ekphantos] of Helen and Atalanta. . . . They [have] sustained no injury though the temple is in ruins. The Emperor Caligula, who was fired by a passion for these figures, would undoubtedly have removed them if the composition of the stucco had allowed it."[35]

Italy certainly had its own ruins and remains (Greek, Etruscan, and others), but travel abroad was considered best. "Young Roman citizens went to Greece, to Africa, and to Asia Minor in much the same spirit in which the whig aristocrats of the 18th century took the *Grand Tour* to Italy."[36]

As Averil Cameron has noted, "whatever the Roman Empire was, it was never nationalistic."[37] Apart from an occasional senatorial or literary outburst in republican times (or in a later anti-imperial hankering after republican times), Rome was rarely culturally chauvinistic. Given its wholesale usurpation of things Greek, it could hardly pretend to be. After advancing from the conquest of Greece to the conquest of the remaining Mediterranean lands, and after the purges of the senatorial class by successive Julio-Claudians, family background was no longer a guarantee of social standing. Racial, religious, national, or ethnic origins were no obstacle to advancement in the political or social hierarchy. Anyone in the empire with the wealth and desire to do so "could readily acquire the appropriate degree of elite education . . . since he could buy classical culture, the entrance ticket to the system."[38] And if the actual education was not possible or desired by the newly wealthy or suddenly powerful person, then its mere appearance—the material trappings of educated culture, namely and especially, classical Greek objects—would suffice.

Given Rome's earlier complete absorption of (and with) ancient Greece, it was to be expected that when the empire expanded, so did its taste. After Actium, when Egypt became the personal property of the emperor, a vogue for things *à l'égyptienne* soon emerged in Italy. Of course Rome had had contacts with Egypt and its art from earliest times (as had classical Greece, for which Egypt represented—to Homer and Plato, among others—a font of ancient wisdom), and an impressively grand temple of Isis had long stood near the Forum. But around 12 B.C. Caius Cestius had built for his tomb the small, steep, marble-cased pyramid that still stands just outside the Porta Ostia in Rome. There is no evidence that Cestius was anything but an ethnic Roman or that he was a worshiper of Isis, Ra, Serapis, or any other Egyptian deity; so presumably he built the edifice as a matter of taste—and perhaps some of his contemporaries thought it about as garish as some of ours would view a similar choice of a pyramid at the Louvre or for a Las Vegas casino hotel. It was Augustus who imported the first of many a subsequent Egyptian obelisk—to stand as the gnomon of his gigantic sundial. Two additional obelisks that Augustus ordered to be shipped to Rome from the great temple of Re at Heliopolis—all that survived when the temple was razed to the ground by Cambyses five centuries earlier in punishment for that city's rebellion—remained stuck in Alexandria until the nineteenth century, when one went to New York and the other to London.[39] The obelisk still standing in the Piazza of St. Peter (with a ball on top believed from Medieval times to contain Julius Caesar's ashes) was imported by Caligula and later stood in Nero's Circus (presumed site of St. Peter's martyrdom). Eighteenth-century excavations at Tivoli unearthed several sculptural portraits of Hadrian's favorite, Antinoös, dressed in Egyptian costume. (True, he was drowned in the Nile, but the choice of this apparel had to be a matter of taste associated with his "romance.") There can be no doubt that the vogue for things Egyptian extended to smaller objects as well, since these have been unearthed throughout the Roman Empire. Even Chinese pieces have been found. That the surviving *literary* evidence does not discuss much collecting and connoisseurship with regard to these smaller objects of *non*-Greco-Roman origin—except for an occasional reference (e.g., to a Nilometer stone, carved with the Nile god and surrounded with sixteen playing children)[40]—has simply to do with the greater number of (and prestige of and connoisseurship attaching to) things Greek as opposed to objects available from other cultures.

In the first century A.D. the area of Rome known as the Saepta Julia was a bazaar for Rome's dealers in luxury goods, including art and antiquities. At least as early as Augustus these goods included works falsely signed by Praxiteles and Myron. They even incorporated phony restorations. Antiquities could also be had at auctions—often rigged—in the quarter of the Villa Publica that was devoted to art dealers, booksellers, and antiquarians.[41] Pliny the Younger, in a letter to his friend Annius Severus, gives some indication of what one might call—then as well as now—not really "buyer's remorse" but "post-purchase-panic" as he describes a bronze he had just acquired:

> I have lately purchased with a legacy that was left me a statue of Corinthian bronze. It is small, but pleasing, and finely executed, at least, if I have any taste; which most certainly in matters of this sort, as perhaps in all others, is extremely defective. However, I think even I have enough to discover the beauties of this figure; as it is naked, the faults, if there be any, as well as the perfections, are more observable. It represents an old man in standing posture. The bones, the muscles, the veins, and wrinkles are so strongly expressed, that you would imagine the figure to be animated. The hair is thin and failing, the forehead broad, the face shriveled, and the throat lank, the arms languid, the breast fallen, and the belly sunk; and the back view gives the same impression of old age. It appears to be a genuine antique, alike from its tarnish and from what remains of the original color of the bronze. In short, it is a performance so highly finished as to fix the attention of artists, and delight the least knowing observer; and this induced me, who am a mere novice in this art, to buy it.[42]

From these examples, it is evident that the appreciation of the antique and of "antiques"—if not precisely in the modern sense of the term, then with very close approximation—was fairly well developed in ancient Rome. It needs to be emphasized that it was primarily Greek works (with some Egyptian, Etruscan, and Asia Minor examples) that were pursued by Romans, and that they were required to be old, to show signs of agedness, and if at all possible to show the mark of an "old master." If they had a known history or provenance, so much the better. A friend of Martial's, one Novius Vindex, who was said to have been a great enough connoisseur to tell a genuine work of Apelles' by his line "even at a distance," owned a statue of Heracles that had successively belonged—it was claimed—to Alexander the Great, Hannibal, and Sulla.[43]

Contemporary *native Roman* sculptors and their works barely existed at all, and no one bothers to name them anyway. New commissions were usually executed by Greeks or Greek-trained slaves who spent their time copying actual ancient works or imitating by imposing ancient styles on original creations. Pliny remarks that in the art of bronze casting no one "for generations" has matched the ancient (i.e., Greek) masters.[44] The Roman aesthetic preference, therefore, was not an indication of cultural chauvinism or pride in a Roman *artistic* achievement equal to its successes in the *political* sphere, but the contrary: Roman taste admitted the inferiority of its own art and of its own time in the production of art.

Moreover, it is not to be thought that the works Romans collected and appreciated were conceived of merely as treasures or trophies. One could understand the inherent material value of gold, silver, gems, and bronze, but even "old furniture" was appreciated. Cicero laments not having obtained a certain old "citron wood" table as a gift; and since the materials and craftsmanship evidently were available to him for making a new one, it is most likely to have been the nonreproducible *age* of the object which he valued and could not replace.[45] For further confirmation that agedness was a quality to be admired even in nonrepresentational (i.e., "craft") objects, we have again Pliny's testimony regarding Greek silver cups: "Nowadays we only value wrought silver for its age, and reckon its merit established when the chasing is so worn that the very design can no longer be made out."[46] Martial talks about the counterfeiting of antique silver in his *Epigrams*. In one instance he mocks a host whose dinner table was covered with antique cups and goblets of great beauty, of high technical quality, and great age—this he admits was impressive—except the wine they contained was too young![47]

We even find in Roman connoisseurship a precedent for the phenomenon that occurred again only in the earliest decades of the twentieth century when *High* Renaissance masters like Raphael were snubbed for *Early* Renaissance masters like Piero della Francesca, Mantegna, Lorenzetti, and Giotto.[48] There developed after a while a similar ancient Roman preference for the Greek "severe Attic" style, even for the earlier archaic style, over the previously preferred and "easier" Hellenistic realism of Lysippus. It became a mark of class distinction and cultural refinement to prefer older, "more difficult" works. Thus Alsop quotes Quintilian: "Of the 'enthusiastic admirers' of the 'almost primitive works' of [the severe style masters] . . . he remarked crisply that 'their motive' struck him as being 'an ostentatious desire' to seem persons of superior taste."[49] Again, we find a contemporary counterpart in antiques collecting and appreciation—a pride (some might call it arrogance) in the most esoteric connoisseurship regarding "difficult" categories of antiques—for example, Japanese samurai swords of the Yamashiro school or mid-sixteenth-century Iznik ceramics or Mameluke carpets or Benin bronzes.

It is impossible to estimate the range, quantity, or value of these great Roman collections. The contents of even the best of them can often only be surmised. (There is, for example, no certain surviving example of the famed "Corinthian bronzes.") But some conception of their worth can be conjectured from the fact that the later emperor Marcus Aurelius could finance the entire cost of the Marcomannic Wars by selling off—at an auction that lasted for many days in the Forum of Trajan—part (only a part) of the Imperial collection of art, clothes, jewels, and the like.

Toward the end, many great works were taken from Rome to Constantinople by Constantine to ornament his new capital, and he and his immediate successors continued to import works from sources throughout the Eastern Empire. Meanwhile, in the West, with the barbarian invasions and the rise of Christianity, the old order and its support for the connoisseurship of antiques went into decline. When Emperor Theodosius II (misnamed "the Great") suppressed with all the zeal of the religious fanatic every pagan place of worship in 385, the cult images and temple furnishings were required to be removed or destroyed. Good Christians here happily played the role of the barbarian. Not everyone in the empire was affected by religious scruples about such pagan idols, however. Consequently, there were those who knew how to take advantage of the new situation. The Byzantine eunuch Larsus—himself a connoisseur and overseer of the Sacred Bedchamber, and therefore a court insider—sent his agents throughout the empire to offer to buy these newly suppressed pagan goods, preserving them (at least for a while) from destruction. If the historical accounts are to be believed, Larsus thereby acquired for his personal collection not only the archaic period "Emerald Athena" of Lindos and the Praxitelean "Aphrodite of Cnidus" but the Phidian "Zeus of Olympia"—all of which were presumably destroyed by the great fire of Constantinople in the late fifth century A.D.[50]

What we find, then, in our survey of the taste, connoisseurship, and collecting preferences of ancient Rome is a situation remarkably similar to our own times vis-à-vis art and antiques. The connoisseurship and collecting of antiques among the Romans was clearly well developed (in some respects not equaled until the nineteenth century) and far surpassed anything to be seen among the Greeks. But when it came to theorizing about them (e.g., defining the antique itself and developing a theory to explain their unique status as objects of taste and appreciation), the

Romans did nothing beyond the Greeks—and that, as we saw, was very little about art in general and nothing about "antiques."

With the collapse of that classical civilization, such taste (connoisseurship) and such practices (collecting) and any theorizing there may have been about these matters necessarily went into decline. Whether they existed at all in Europe in the Medieval period is a matter of some speculation. Perhaps Edith Wharton was correct in believing that "since the Roman Empire, there has probably been no period when a taste for the best of all ages did not exist,"[51] yet finding it again in the Middle Ages and seeing it emerge again in the Renaissance is an intricate affair, one to which we will shortly turn our attention.

2.2
The Chinese Analogue

With the demise of Rome and the classical world, probably for all those reasons that have ever been advanced since the Renaissance—from barbarian invasion to Christianity to lead contamination—"civilization" in the largest sense of the word came to an end. This was only in Europe, of course, for there is always "elsewhere." It is not my intention to archeologize the globe; but it should be noted—what Alsop and others have already touched on—that there were and are other "rare art traditions" besides the West's.[52]

In China by the time of the Han dynasty (206 B.C. to A.D. 220), calligraphy, whether as writing (primarily) or as painting (secondarily)—although, given the identical nature of the medium and techniques of production and the pictographic nature of the script, these are not as distinguishable as in the West—was appreciated and collected as the highest art(s) of that culture.[53] Chinese aesthetic theory has in fact always construed the greatest work of art as a unity of "the three perfections": poetry, painting, and calligraphy. Properly, these arts produced the unified art object, the "calligraphic-poem-painting." Nevertheless, antique bronze objects were also collected as early as the second century B.C. They are listed among the objects in the collection of Western Han emperor Wu-ti (reigned 146 B.C.–87 B.C.), "who constructed a royal storehouse for works of calligraphy, paintings, and bronzes," according to one recent authority.[54] Certainly by the fourth century A.D. (the Three Kingdoms Period) *antique paintings as such*—that is, as distinct from a written text—were already collected; and in the fifth century the first Chinese book (by Xie He) to name individual ancient painting masters appeared, covering the art of the preceding three centuries. In the Liang dynasty (500–563) the imperial collection is known to have contained more than 250,000 works of calligraphy and painting. By the Tang dynasty (600–900), naturally, these ancient scrolls were already being faked in some quantity. Alsop reports that even in the fifth century, the Liu Song dynasty emperor Xiao Wu having died, his collection of calligraphy was found to contain many fakes of ancient masters (according to Yu He).[55] That it was the *physical medium* of the scroll per se and not merely the message it contained which had come to appeal to the aesthete is evident from a work by the Tang calligraphy and painting dealer Zhang Yanyuan. In *The Calligraphy Dealer* he states: "It is an inner necessity for collectors to feel scrolls in their hands and to determine their value by discussions . . . [and] regard keeping them in their chests and boxes as the only important thing."[56] It was especially in the Song dynasty (960–1279) that ancient jades, inkstones, and bronzes began to be appreciated—though it was additionally any inscriptions *on* the jades and bronzes that connoisseurs found made them most attractive.[57] During the Song, the emperors T'ai-tsung and Hui-tsung amassed thousands of art objects, especially ancient ones, for the imperial collections.[58]

There is also possible evidence of an early Chinese appreciation even for foreign antiquities. In the Soshin Treasury at Nara, Japan, there exists a Sassanian (sixth-century Persian) blue glass vessel which is mounted in silver so as to transform it into a goblet and which was presented as a gift from a Tang emperor to the ruler of Japan. Of all the Chinese dynasties up until the Tang, none was more deliberately "international" and culturally open to foreign influence, especially during the roughly hundred years from A.D. 650 to 750, when Persian Zoroastrians, Manicheans, and Nestorian Christians as well as Indian Buddhists brought their native religions and art styles into a culturally receptive and expanded China. Nevertheless, this instance is more likely an indication on the Chinese side not of an aesthetic appreciation of this glass vessel *as an ancient work of Persian art* but rather of Chinese marveling at and fascination with an exotic rarity. And likely its preservation by the Japanese in the Soshin Treasury is due to similar motives, perhaps combined with an appreciation for the craftsmanship of the Chinese silversmiths who encased the vessel.

It was not until the early Ming that antiqueness per se and in a wide variety of objects came to be appreciated clearly, as can been seen in the fourteenth-century connoisseur's manual, *Ko Ku Yao Lum.* In this work we find discussions of patina and agedness in various types of objects, and specific categories of collection-worthy objects (e.g., Song dynasty

fish pendant-medals) come to be established. Such antiques manuals
were written and read by the literati, who, apart from the imperial court
itself, were also the collectors, the connoisseurs, and the taste makers.
Regarding the particular attributes of ancient Ting ware, for example,
the manual's author clarifies terminology: "dealers call faults in a piece
mao; a cracked pot is called *mieh* and the lack of glaze shrinking, *ku-
ch'u*. These are just terms the antique dealers use."[59] Ming dynasty collections of the fine porcelains of previous dynasties have also been
recently confirmed by archeological discoveries in Ming tombs.[60] Living
in a time when "culture had reached a point where pure enjoyment of the
arts could become an end in itself," Ming dynasty literati "were learned
scholars who loved antiques and rare objects and who had the ability to
serve at court if they were needed," though most literati preferred to be
"free of all worldly obligations."[61] Li Rihua, a scholar-connoisseur of the
late Ming, had an "encyclopedic interest in every kind of fine object." In
his diary, *Zitaoxuan Zazahui* (*Miscellanea from the Peach Studio*), he
writes down a "ranking of antique objects." The first ten are all forms of
writing and painting; number 11 lists "brilliant examples of bronze vessels and red jades before the Han and Qin"; 12, ancient jades of the *xun*
and *lin* types; 13, Tang inkstones; 14, ancient *qin* [zithers] and world-
famous swords." These are followed by examples of rare natural objects,
and the list ends with "number 23, shiny white fine porcelain and mysterious colored pottery."[62] This connoisseurship is confirmed by a marvelous Ming dynasty hanging scroll painting, *Enjoying Antiquities*, by
Tu Chin (fl. 1388–1462)—a treasure of the Imperial Collection in the
National Palace Museum, Taipei—that shows two such connoisseurs on
either side of a long table examining more than twenty different types of
what appear to be bronze, ceramic, and jade vessels.[63] Hence, the contemporary scholar Chu-Tsing Li concludes, "Although the literati clearly
valued calligraphy and painting more than the various kinds of objects
they collected, whether cultural relics or examples of the decorative arts,
the artistic status of such [decorative arts] objects definitely rose during the
late Ming."[64] It should be noted that these enumerations of collection-
worthy objects did not include furniture or *sancai*- or *wucai*-glazed clay
figures from tombs. These remaining antiques genres were neglected by
Chinese connoisseurs until they began to be collected by Westerners in
the nineteenth century.

From this brief summary, we can see that the Chinese pattern follows
to a marked degree the mentality and pattern of the Greco-Roman world
we detailed previously. We will find it again in the Western periods to
come. Although China seems to have had the most consistent and

comprehensive tradition of antiques and art collecting outside the West, there are other instances of connoisseurship in the history of civilizations. In sixteenth-century Savafid Persia, for example, Sultan Ibrahim Mirza owned three thousand volumes of calligraphy and miniature painting, all presided over by their own art historian. In India, Akbar, who became the third Mughal emperor in 1556, had such a tremendous collection of jewelry, manuscripts, and other objets d'art that the whole lot was divided by its curators into 360 parts so he could relish a different portion of his collection each day of the year.[65] Alsop tells us of a Fatimid caliph of Egypt who, a collector like Caracalla, was sold the "authentic" saddle of Alexander the Great.[66] And at Begram or Bagram (the ancient city of Kapisa, near Kabul in Afghanistan) there was recently unearthed a cache of "bronzes probably of Alexandrian manufacture cheek by jowl with *emblemata* (plaster discs, almost certainly meant as models for local silversmiths) bearing reliefs in the purest classical vein, Chinese lacquers, and Roman glass. The hoard was probably sealed up in the mid-3rd century [A.D.], when some of the objects may have been as much as 200 years old, *i.e.*, 'antiques', and often themselves copies of classical Greek objects."[67]

2.3
Medieval Survival

Returning to the West in the Middle Ages, we find that the various conditions—socioeconomic and political, as well as religious and cultural—were not generally conducive to the connoisseurship and collecting of art and antiques. The practice recurred at rare times among a privileged few but was severely limited in scope and often did not clearly distinguish aged artifactual objects from other kinds of things that might be accumulated, such as relics, natural objects, and objects without age.

The Middle Ages, at least the late Middle Ages, was in a curious position vis-à-vis the past and its remains. In one way, at least, it had a unique mentality for appreciating the arts of the defunct Greco-Roman civilization. This was a consequence in part of the Christian's faith. Since one had nothing to fear from their now innocuous pagan origins, classical statues could be enjoyed for their aesthetic value—provided that they demonstrated in some way the ruination of the civilization that had produced them. Historically decontextualized, *déraciné*, and drained of their original function, they had the potential of becoming objects of contemplation and of instruction—and hence, at least potentially, they could be objects of beauty, as most antiques are today. They evoked the image of a world now long past.

On the other hand, to be a good Christian, one had *also* to approve the more recent past's deliberate despoliation of these pagan idols and the palaces and temples in which they were housed. Thus, the thirteenth- and fourteenth-century chroniclers tell us approvingly (and probably with some exaggeration) how Pope Gregory the Great (540–604) had burned the ancient libraries and "caused the heads and limbs of the statues of demons everywhere to be truncated, so that the root of heretical depravity would be ripped out and the palm of ecclesiastical truth more fully raised."[68] Moreover, in the religious eschatology of the time, the approach of heavenly splendor required the collapse of all earthly splendors. Hildebert of Lavardin (d. 1133), in the second part of his *Elegy*, tells us that "Rome's monuments, symbolizing by their deplorable state of dilapidation the irresistible decline of the realm, had ceased to be things the aspect of which would provoke a desire for '*renewal*.' "[69]

To be sure, the attitude of the vandal is not well suited to the aesthetic appreciation of the connoisseur, who must desire the *preservation* of the object. However, another religiously motivated attitude arose which at least pointed in that direction. This was the mentality of the pilgrim traveler. Twelfth-century Rome, which first saw a huge influx of such pilgrims, no longer resembled the sixth-century Rome of Gregory the Great. The glory and wealth of late Medieval Rome was its pilgrims. Of course they came ostensibly to visit shrines of Christian martyrdom. But these shrines were inextricably bound up with the pagan universe. Indeed, in some instances the priority relation was reversed. As early in the late Medieval period as 1140, a guidebook—the *Mirabilla urbis Romae*, by one Benedict, canon of St. Peter's Basilica—centers its attention almost exclusively on ancient Rome. Thus, holy places are noted solely for the purpose of locating the presumed site of an ancient building or sanctuary and not the other way around! One might construe this as a humanly perverse fascination with evil, just as Milton's Satan in *Paradise Lost* and the damned characters of Dante's *Inferno* have always been more satisfying to readers than their godly opposites. But Benedict's book ends: "These and many more temples of emperors, consuls, senators, and prefects were in pagan times in the city of Rome, as we read in the old annals, and see with our own eyes and have heard from our elders. How beautiful they shone in gold and silver, bronze, ivory and precious stones we have taken care to sum up as best we could for the remembrance of future generations."[70] Clearly there is an appeal to aesthetic splendor and to the imagination in these words (and therefore to temporality) that goes beyond the "let's-see-the-ruination-of-the-evildoers" mentality. Indeed, we find two factors essential to the later development of connoisseurship in antiques: (1) the attempt to evoke imaginatively a reconstruction of the world past and (2) concern for preservation of the image of the historical past into the future. It should be noted, however, that this passage also appeals to its contemporaries in terms of a vision of a "restored gem-like perfection."

What this suggests is that, in addition, and despite Christianity's break with paganism and the consequent outright contempt for things pagan (as we noted in Gregory the Great, or find in the writings of such early Christian Fathers as Tertullian [d. ca. 220], or observed in Hildebert), there was a somewhat contravening strain of thought in many Medievals. Not conceiving of antiquity as a discrete and terminated period of history, they sometimes thought of themselves rather as "still citizens of the empire which had been founded by Augustus."[71] What the Medievals most earnestly desired, after all, was peace, which St. Augustine had identified with the *summum bonum*.[72] The emperor Augustus, pagan though he was, had brought peace to ancient Rome. And thus they were likely to conceive of their own times as being a *continuation* of the "Fourth Monarchy," the "final realm."[73] As W. S. Heckscher puts it, "it is in the light of this '*principium unitatis*' that we must understand the Medieval attempts to restore Antiquity which goes under the name of '*renovatio*.'"[74]

Roman citizens (when not in a quarrying mode for building materials) had often shown a fondness for "renovating" the antiquities of their own city. There still exists today, for example, among the few remaining instances of Medieval architecture in Rome, a brick tower near the Ponte Rotto—the "Casa dei Crescenzi"—which has antique friezes embedded in its walls and whose builder, one Nicholas, tells us in an inscription that this was done "Romae veterem renovare" (to renew the town of Rome).[75]

Many a visitor was not content merely to look at the ruins, using Benedict's *Mirabilla* as his Baedecker. He also wished to take some home. Richard Krautheimer tells us:

> Between 1145 and 1150, Henry, Bishop of Winchester and brother of English King Henry II, on a business trip to Rome, was buying up ancient sculpture to take home with him. So set on his quest was he as to go about the city seriously, his beard unkempt, like many an avid collector. He was ridiculed for this whim of his by native Romans. But John of Salisbury, who tells the story, saw clearly that the pieces he bought were "produced by the subtle and diligent, rather than intentional, error of the heathen";

their pagan content, though damnable, was separable from their aesthetic qualities. There was most likely no regular dealing in antiques. But if a stonecutter had a good piece around, as did the one in whose workshop a well-preserved statue of Antinous was found among column shafts and other spoils ninety years ago, he would part with it, were a mad Englishman willing to pay.[76]

The "Grand Tour" collector was many centuries yet in coming, but we find a progenitor in Henry.

And he was not entirely alone in his epoch in his passion for collecting relics of the past. His French contemporary, Suger (1081–1151), abbot of St. Denis, was also a great collector. Suger generally adopts St. Augustine's Neoplatonic view of beauty as "that for which my soul sighs day and night," and he speaks of its efficacy in calling him away from mundane concerns to reflect on that which is ultimately immaterial so that "by the grace of God I can be transformed from this inferior to that higher world in an analogical manner."[77] This mentality recalls our earlier discussion distinguishing between the antique and the religious relic. Here is a splendid instance of the conflation of the religious relic with the antique proper. For Suger had in mind not merely a spiritual transport from the current mundane world in which he lived. He also had in mind a vehicle for transport of the artistic achievement of the past. As the abbot recounts in his *Liber de consecratione*, while erecting the cathedral of St. Denis and being in need of building materials, he considered the beautiful columns he had seen in Rome in the Baths (he says "palace") of Diocletian. He would gladly have removed them, for their beauty was reusable, had not the cost and effort of transporting them to France been so great, he says. Suger especially searched after rare and antique Roman gems, intaglios, and cameos. These he usually had remounted in gold or silver-gilt for reuse in new frames, vessels, casements, boxes, and the like.[78] In this remounting we find Suger's idea of the "renovation" of Antiquity through the reuse of its objects. Heckscher comments:

> The most impressive example is the famous "eagle vase" of Sugerius, abbot of St. Denis, which is now preserved in the Louvre. It is inscribed around the lip with a dedication of Sugerius to his Church, and there can be no doubt that it was made under his supervision. The wings, claws, neck and head, of gilded silver, enshrine the antique (in this case probably Egyptian) [porphyry] core which is treated as a delicate treasure. We may take this as a typical instance of a purely "additive" procedure which clearly expresses the reverence for the antique unit by leaving it intact; *adaptavimus* is the term used by Suger himself, while the creative act proper is described by him as a transposition ("*transferre*") of the

amphora "in aquilae formam" [in the shape of an eagle]. Needless to say, the eagle, thus superimposed upon the antique relic, is meant as a symbol of Christ.[79]

Another of the greatest surviving examples of such workmanship— from the time of Suger but not actually commissioned by him—is the twenty-inch, gold "Cross of Lothair" that currently resides in the Aachen Cathedral Treasury. Dominated by a great ancient Roman cameo at the crossing of its arms, it is set in the *opus inclusorium* fashion typical of Medieval metalwork with various antique (i.e., Classical-era) gems.

The use of these gems for this aspect of the Medieval vision of Antiquity is significant. The Church admitted the inherent power of pagan gems, even though some of the very early Church Fathers (such as Clement of Alexandria [d. ca. 215]) explicitly inveighed against the use or reuse of pagan images. Thus, before setting ancient gems and cameos in ecclesiastical objects, the Church "found it advisable to exorcise the evil forces residing in them" so that now "all the ancient stones which we find in Christian objects of cult have undergone some form of sanctification" and "a pagan image could thus assume a new power as a magical charm by means, not in spite, of its Christian adaptation."[80] An additional ideological justification for the reuse by adaptation of such classical pagan objects in religious or ecclesiastical context was the theory of "adumbration," the symbolic foreshadowing of Christ and Christianity in pre-Christian images and figures. All these gems were supplied by the *gemmari*, Medieval dealers in gems and cameos, who appear to have been well established as early as Carolingian times.[81]

Although this collection and reuse of classical antiquities certainly indicates an appreciation and valuation of such gems, it is not proof of a connoisseurship of antiques *as antiques* or even a "purely aesthetic" appreciation of these objects *as old*. It was never agedness per se that the Medievals preferred. Heckscher notes, in connection with such reused cameos and gems:

The flawless appearance of ancient stones, their transparency, their stern resistance to corrosion or *patina*, which secures the permanence of the shape once assigned to them, fully responded to medieval ideas of the beautiful. In the medieval conception of the hierarchies of perfection a complete thing automatically ranks above an incomplete one. To a modern spectator a structure fallen to pieces may reveal a tragic contrast or an idyllic union between the efforts of man and the impersonal forces of nature. The mediaeval view will not allow of such pleasant mingling of opposites. It conceives the universe as a static order in which each thing is well established and ranked, according to the divine plan. Such a system rejects anything that has forsaken the form originally assigned to it. A palace, to the mediaeval mind, is beautiful only as a palace; as a ruin it ceases to be so. The various stages of decay can only mean a diminishing and slackening of a once flaw-less form. Never can stages of decay engender another stage of existence in which the object concerned might claim a new significance and beauty of its own. To my knowledge there is in mediaeval literature no collective noun that has the range of our term "ruin." . . . [Thus] St. Thomas says in his famous definition of the beautiful . . . "*quae enim diminuta sunt, hoc ipso turpa sunt*" [things impaired are ugly for that very reason].[82]

In fact, the medieval artist could not (or would not) bring himself "ac-curately" to represent the decay or ruination of objects, buildings, or cities in contexts that obviously required such representation. Ruination and de-cay is shown through the separation of the object into "perfect pieces." Heckscher notes that in the *Bamberg Apocalypse* "the city of Babylon, shown in the usual way as an abbreviated conglomeration of buildings en-closed in a wall, one gate standing open, is turned upside down, but other-wise quite intact. . . . Destruction was depicted as 'integrity' with an inverted sign."[83] Hence, the logical progression of this particular train of Medieval thought with respect to the objects of Antiquity was restoration, wholeness, perfection, beauty, and useful functionality.

Finally, as we review the range of Medieval *archés* in our archeology of the idea of the antique we must add that the Medieval sensibility was not generally able to discriminate between the trophy and treasure, be-tween artifact, souvenir, memento, relic, and magical amulet or charm, between curiosity and natural wonder. As Umberto Eco notes in *Art and Beauty in the Middle Ages*: "The predominant sentiment is one of amazement, a sense of the Kolossal, rather than of beauty. [Abbot] Suger is thus like the other collectors of the Middle Ages, who filled their houses not just with art works, but also with absurd oddities."[84] Even two centuries later, as the dawn of the Renaissance was about to break, there was little change in this aspect of the vision. In the collection of Jean, duc de Berry (1340–1416), greatest French collector of his time, and "possessed by an insatiable curiosity and the desire to own every-thing that caught his fancy,"[85] we find just such a mixture, comprising "about three thousand items. Seven hundred were paintings, but it also contained an embalmed elephant, a hydra, a basilisk, and an egg which an abbot had found inside another egg, and manna which had fallen dur-ing a famine. So we are justified in doubting the purity of the Medieval taste, their ability to distinguish between art and teratology, the beautiful and the curious."[86]

Similarly we may see in what appear to be early prototypes of world-wide art collectors—in the Venetians Marco Polo (1254–1324) and Doge Enrico Dandolo, for example—merely a quantitative (rather than qualitative) advance on the early Medieval practice of accumulating the valuable, exotic, curious, and fascinating. With the sack of Constantinople in 1204 by the Fourth Crusade, the Venetians under Dandolo literally "made out like bandits." Indeed, a tour of San Marco today suggests in its myriad adornments (of which the four bronze horses and Pala d'Oro are merely the most spectacular) the souvenir trunk of "La Serenissima, The Tourist," or even more aptly, a trophy case for her spoils of trade and war. In any case, as Taylor notes, "it is safe to assume that no patrician sent a ship out from Venice to the Levant without its returning laden with antique marbles, fragments of inscriptions, and works of art of every kind, which also served as ballast to the comparatively light but precious cargo of silks and spices which she carried."[87] When extensive trade with China developed later on, the same shipping techniques applied: ceramics (heaviest and impervious to saltwater seepage) were packed on the lowest levels, teas (more fragile and valuable) above, and silk (the most precious commodity) on the top.

In medieval times it was always a mark of the highest distinction to possess a "Saracen" sword or "Turkey" carpet, an Oriental vase or Chinese silk embroidery. It was the Crusades above all that had brought the taste for the exotic luxuries of the East to Europe: in Jerusalem, pilgrims were already taking back with them the "souvenirs" plied on them by native craftsmen, made to order and also ready-made, just as later British nobility (as we will see) brought back to their country estates their Canalettos from the Grand Tour of Venice. And we know that genuine Chinese porcelain began to trickle into Europe from the Far East at this time, although it remained so rare that the material itself was unfamiliar. Thus, for example, in the 1380 inventory of the art collection of the duc d'Anjou (brother of Charles V of France) we find item #714: "une écuelle d'une pierre appellé pourcelaine" (a bowl of a stone called porcelain), which was mounted like a great jewel or exotic curiosity in silver-gilt and enameled with the duke's coat of arms[88]—an instance not unlike the Sassanian cobalt glass vessel at Nara mounted by Chinese silversmiths noted above.

Hence, in Late Medieval and Early Renaissance Venice and other wealthy culture centers of Europe, collecting was primarily a reflection of unselfconscious aggrandizement and love of the visually astonishing and extraordinary made possible by new prosperity—*not* part of a program of inquiry, leading to scholarship, taste, and connoisseurship. There was no idea of the antique as we currently conceive it and no special aesthetic experience of the antique *as antique*, for the medieval collector's vision did not necessarily include appreciation of the *age of the object*; and it generally forbid exhibition of *the effects of age on the object*. For *these* developments to happen—for a revival in the appreciation of agedness and patination of the sort we found in ancient Rome—we must turn to the Renaissance.

2.4
Renaissance

Change from the Medieval to Renaissance vision first occurred in humanists such as Petrarca. This required an alteration in the attitude toward Antiquity. Only once Antiquity was clearly and finally construed as *over* could its world be "lost." Only once it had been lost could it be retrieved. Only once it could be forgiven its sin of paganism (or once that issue became irrelevant altogether) could it be seen aesthetically for its beauty independent of its moral evil. Hence, whereas the Medieval mind might consider restoring or more often *adapting* its relics ("renovation"), the Renaissance thought more of copying or more often *re-creating* and *recapturing* the classical spirit ("imitation") and of *retrieving* and *preserving* Antiquity's actual objects from the rubble of the past for objective contemplation. Thus, in the Renaissance we rarely find the Medieval reuse of Classical objects—their incorporation into the usages of the present by a reworking of their medium and a reinterpretation of their meaning. Rather, we find an appreciation of the *fact* of their integrity and their worthiness to stand alone with their original meanings undiminished, and an appreciation of their pastness for its own sake and an enjoyment of (aesthetic pleasure in) the signs of their agedness as the very badges of their worth. In the Renaissance, under the "spell of historical sentiment," the "fall of great cities began to assume the glamour of an individual destiny."[89]

In this way "antiques" as they are understood today began properly to come into being (or, better, to come into being again, after their demise with the Ancient Roman Empire). They would not "arrive" until the Romantic vision of the nineteenth century, however, for it is only then that all their *archés* can be said to have run their course of development and the criteria for what counts as an "antique" to have taken on their final form. And it is really only in the latter part of the twentieth century that through the impact of modern art (and art theory), a *purely aesthetic*

response to antiques has come to be understood and antiques appreciated as having "aesthetic values" at least equal to those previously reserved to "fine art" objects.

Many have credited Coluccio Salutati, chancellor of Florence in the
late fourteenth century, with being one of the primary stimuli to the Renaissance mentality. He was the first to launch a serious and scholarly investigation of the classical past in its own terms and for its own sake.
Thus, he prevailed on the banker Palla Strozzi to invite (at Strozzi's expense) the Greek scholar Emmanuel Chrysorlas to come from Constantinople in 1397 to teach Greek in Florence. In addition to the knowledge
of Greek texts, we find in Chrysorlas the fascination with and passion for
ancient Greek art objects *as aged* objects. He came, after all, from
the more sophisticated Byzantine Empire, now in its last remaining decades before the Ottoman conquest. Visiting Rome in 1411, Chrysorlas
wrote in a letter home to Constantinople that he found in this venerable
city

> beauty not in living bodies but in stones, marble, and images. . . . We do
> not concern ourselves with whether the beak of a live bird or the hoof of a
> live horse is properly curved or not, but we do with whether the mane of a
> bronze lion spreads beautifully . . . or whether the sinews and veins are
> shown in the stone leg of a statue. These are the things that men take plea-
> sure in. Many people would willingly have given many living and faultless
> horses to have one stone horse by Phidias or Praxiteles, even if this hap-
> pened to be broken or mutilated. . . . [This preference] indicates a certain
> nobility in the intellect that admires them. . . . [for the reason] that we ad-
> mire not so much the beauties of the bodies in statues and paintings as the
> beauty of the mind of their maker.[90]

The use of "we" suggests that Chrysorlas was unique in his outlook in
contemporary Rome but that he shared this vision and appreciation of
the antique with like-minded connoisseur-collectors in Constantinople.
Yet we should not be too hasty in crediting the origin and cause of this
new antiquarian sensibility in Early Renaissance Italy *solely* in effects of
the residence of this foreign visitor. In the earlier part of the century there
was also one Oliviero Forzetta (1300–1372), a successful moneylender in
Treviso who purchased ancient objects "not because their shapes were
unusual or their materials uncommon but simply because they were
old."[91] Nevertheless, Forzetta was unique in his time in the West, and
Treviso, unlike Florence, was not the center of the early Renaissance. Unlike Chrysorlas, therefore, his taste for "old things" had no direct disci-
ples or cultural consequences.

In the humanist circle of Salutati in Florence was also one Niccolò Niccoli (b. 1364), who, though not wealthy himself, had a passion for collecting antiques. He is described by his contemporary, Vespatiano da Bisticci, as an eccentric dandy who liked to wear long red robes and to drink his "wine from beautiful old dishes and crystal or other precious vessels from his art collection."[92] Niccolò made many enemies of contemporary humanists by his criticism of their errors in classical Latin, but he was a lively enough companion for Cosimo de' Medici to enjoy his company and even pay for the satisfaction of his acquisitive passions when Niccolò's own inheritance was exhausted. Niccolò's collection "even served as a kind of public art museum" during his lifetime; and on his death, one way or another, his library of more than eight hundred codices and his collections of crystal and hardstone vessels, medals, bronzes, and early coins all wound up in the Medici collection.[93]

It must be remembered, however, that in the late fifteenth century a reverence for the antique was not primarily directed toward objects. Even for most humanists, it was *literature* of the past—the words of wisdom mainly and the manuscript as physical text only by extension—that was valued.[94] It took the full Renaissance to extend this reverence to *art objects*, and this meant essentially sculpture (since there was no surviving classical painting to speak of)—sculpture in marble (usually) and bronze (rarely). And much of this new appreciation of physical objects had to do with contemporary artists like Michelangelo and with the change in the collector-connoisseur's perception of the sculptor and painter. This was a change from the view of the painter and sculptor as a sort of skilled day laborer to the view of him as a creative genius.[95]

We see, then, in our brief account of the transition from Late Medieval to Early Renaissance an evolving pattern of preference in appreciation and collection of the works of the past, a pattern prefigured in our investigation of similar processes in the classical Roman world and in China. This pattern of progression in appreciation begins with the religious relic, then advances to trophy of war or other historically significant event or person, to treasure (of gems and precious metals) or rare and astonishing artifact, to literature and books, and then to sculpture (and painting).

It was in Rome (especially) in the late fifteenth century that the real craze for the connoisseurship and collecting of such sculptural works of art occurred. As noted above, artists such as Michelangelo can be seen as both the causes and the effects of this change. During his life and largely as a consequence of his example, the artist (at least the best among them) ceased being a laborer and was elevated to the status of the intellectual—just as he was liberated as an individual from the group, the guild, which was the "closed union shop" of the Medieval era.[96] The painter or sculptor was even—when he was a Michelangelo or a Titian—permitted the prerogatives of nobility and granted the titles "genius" and "divine" whereas before these appellations would have been bestowed only on eminent literary men such as Petrarca and Dante.[97] The often-recounted anecdote of Titian being handed his dropped paintbrush by his sitter, Holy Roman Emperor Charles V, who stooped to pick it up for the painter, is ample evidence of this change in attitude, as is the entire mature career of Rubens, who in the next generation regularly served as an ambassador for the governors of the Netherlands.

Michelangelo's specific relation with the world of antiques and antiquity is to be found not only in the "classical" style of his new (i.e., commissioned) works. The story of his fraud—the sleeping cupid made and aged as if an antique and sold as such to Cardinal Riario—has often been recounted. (The essentials are as follows: Michelangelo, while still at the Medici court, carved a sleeping cupid of marble; seeing it, Pierfrancesco de' Medici commented to him, "If you buried it, I am convinced it would pass as an ancient work, and if you sent it to Rome treated so that it appeared old, you would earn much more than by selling it here." It was subsequently taken to Rome by Baldassare del Milanese, who had first called Pierfrancesco's attention to the work, and, aged either by Michelangelo himself [Vasari says "he had the genius to do this and more"] or by Milanese in his Roman vineyard, the cupid was sold to Cardinal Riario as an original antique [the cardinal paid 200 scudi, but Michelangelo was given only 30]. The cardinal soon discovered the forgery for what it was, however, and returned the cupid, recovering his money but not his reputation—not just for having failed to detect its genuineness, but for then, according to Vasari's judgment, failing to appreciate its greatness as a work of Michelangelo despite the misrepresentation: "[he] did not recognize the value of the work, which consists in its perfection, for modern works are just as good as ancient ones when they are excellent and it is a greater vanity to pursue things more for their reputation than for what they really are.")[98]

There is also the matter of his *use* of genuine antiques from ancient Rome. Vasari tells us in his account of the life of Verrocchio in Rome about the "high value that was put on the many statues and other antiquities being discovered there and the way the Pope [Sixtus IV, 1471–1484] had [an antique] bronze horse set up in St. John Lateran as well as the attention given to even the bits and pieces, let alone the complete works of sculpture that were being unearthed every day."[99] This Sixtus, once a friend of the Medici but later behind the Pazzi conspiracy, had also been the first—but hardly the last—pope to forbid the export of classical antiques from Rome. (A prohibition that had not happened since Imperial Roman times, as we saw.) The equestrian bronze that Vasari speaks of—really a statue of Marcus Aurelius, but thought in the Middle Ages to have been of Constantine (and therefore saved from the predation of religious fanatics)—was moved by Michelangelo a half-century later from its position in front of the cathedral of Rome to its place as the very centerpiece of Michelangelo's newly composed Campidoglio (the piazza at the top of the Capitoline Hill), where it stands today.[100] In its liberation from an ecclesiastical context, the incident symbolically demonstrates how the classical object came to represent for the public of Rome the new secular *civitas* founded in imitation *and preservation* of the classical past. Rome had a long imperial memory.[101]

In Italy, therefore, we find three stages of Early Renaissance antiquities collecting: from a few unique and exemplary individuals (1300–1360), to an elite group of like-minded connoisseur-collectors (1360–1420), to a popular activity, indeed, a public vogue and craze (1420–90).[102] And so the public appreciation for the works of antiquity, already present in Rome when Michelangelo arrived there in 1496—Rome after all necessarily had a greater number of objects to be unearthed—only confirmed what he had already experienced among the Medici in Florence. And he, in turn, simply became the most renowned of contemporary artists who reinforced that appreciation. By the time of his death during the High Renaissance (1490–1570), the connoisseurship of antiquities was a social and political sign of grace, so much so that Donato Bramante's mock heroic poem on Roman antiquaries studying the ruins of Nero's Golden House caricatures these men who "crawl along the dirt upon [their] bellies, with bread, *prosciutto*, apples, and some *vino*," becoming more bizarre than the *grottesche* they saw painted on its walls. Moreover, Roman society had developed its way of transforming such antiquarianism into life through art by dressing in classical costumes and reviving pagan feast days (in Christian guise) in pageants and lavish dinner parties surrounded by fragments of classical statues where social gossip blended with classical scholarship. In this way a new culture took shape in which "prelates and scholars alike set out to live ancient lives in their *vigne*."[103]

Popes did not exclude themselves from this life. Paul II (pope 1464–71), Sixtus IV's predecessor in Vasari's account noted above, had also been a "collector in the truest sense," as Taylor comments:

> He had the most voracious appetite for works of art of any of the early Renaissance Popes and was chief competitor in the salesroom of his contem-

porary Lorenzo de' Medici. As a Venetian cardinal . . . he created the Palazzo Venetia . . . and filled it with what was at that time considered the foremost museum of Classical and Byzantine antiquities in Italy. . . . A link between the Proconsul Verres and 57th St. [New York] . . . he would have been equally at home in a villa in Pompeii or in the showroom of Lord Du-veen. Paul II's collection, which was later sold to Pope Sixtus, only to be purchased in large part by the Medici Cardinal, Giuliano (later Pope Clement VII), and thus passed on with his property to Florence, was rich-est in Byzantine objects in gold and ivory, particularly in diptyches.[104]

Indeed, most of the Renaissance popes were collectors of antiques. Martin V, who led the papacy back to Rome from its "Babylonian cap-tivity" in Avignon, and his successor, Eugenius IV, both attempted to rebuild and restore Rome from its ruins. There was already the strong awareness among natives and some visitors of the beauties surviving from Rome's past. We have noted the report by John of Salisbury of the doings of Henry, bishop of Winchester. In a letter of Alberto Alberti (dated March 1444), we find an even stronger appeal to our imagina-tion to relate the present ruins to the men and age that made them. He writes of

edifices in infinite number, but all in ruins. There is much porphyry and marble from ancient buildings, but every day these marbles are destroyed by being burnt for lime in scandalous fashion. What is modern is poor stuff, that is to say the new buildings; the beauty of Rome lies in what is in ruins. The men of the present day, who call themselves Romans, are very different in bearing and conduct from the ancient inhabitants. *Breviter lo-quendo*, they all look like cowherds.[105]

Eugenius IV had ordered the clearing of trash from around the Pan-theon and "forbade the extraction of masonry from the Coliseum and other ancient monuments under the severest penalties."[106] His successor, Nicholas V (1447–55), re-erected ancient walls and monuments, but in rebuilding St. Peter's Basilica and constructing a new Vatican Palace to house a new Vatican Library, "in violation of his predecessor's prohibi-tion, he had no less than 2,500 wagonloads of materials from the Coli-seum carted across the Ponte Sant'Angelo,"[107] so that *his* successor, Pius II (1458–64), had once again to forbid the practice of quarrying from old buildings. These contradictory processes of quarrying and restoring fur-thered the discovery of statues and fragments from antiquity. The con-noisseurship wherewith to appreciate these finds was bolstered by the appearance in Rome of additional Byzantine scholar-refugees arriving af-ter the fall of Constantinople to the Ottomans in 1453. Meanwhile,

Nicholas declared 1450 a Universal Jubilee year with plenary indulgences for all pilgrims who came to Rome. This incentive brought tens of thousands from throughout the European continent to see all this and disperse the new taste on returning to their homes. And it brought a nice profit to the Church of 100,000 florins, which was promptly deposited by Pope Nicholas in his account with the Medici bank.[108]

Mention of the Medici again—and their wealth—recalls to mind Cosimo (*Pater Patriae*, 1389–1464), to whom we referred earlier. It is significant to note that these Renaissance connoisseur-collectors—whether pope, duke, or banker—were not motivated in their taste or attachment to antiques by financial, political, or religious goals, but rather by antiquarian and aesthetic ones. Thus, while Cosimo in fact augmented his own collections through his purchase of Niccolò Niccoli's estate when in 1433 the latter died 500 ducats in debt to the Medici bank, he apparently did not view this as a financial coup—as a normal investment banker would a good return on a savvy investment. He was an aesthete and connoisseur, and was encouraged more by the Florentine artists of his day, who stimulated his taste, than by his fellow financiers counseling asset appreciation. In his *On Painting* (1436), Alberti notes that an artwork's raw materials are of no consequence; the work of the greatest antique masters is beyond price even if made of lead. Vasari tells us that Cosimo was encouraged to agree with such views by Donatello, who told him to collect antiques for their aesthetic pleasure alone.[109] Indeed, we have Cosimo's own testament, a reflection on himself as collector: "For fifty years I have done nothing else but earn money and spend money; and it became clear to me in the end that spending money provided greater pleasure to me than earning it (*ed accorgomi che ancora sia maggoir dolcezza lo spendere che il guadagnare*), [for] all those things have given me the greatest contentment and satisfaction (*grandissima contentamento e grandissimi dolcezza*)."[110]

Filarete's *Treatise on Architecture* offers us a similar eyewitness account of Cosimo's son, Piero, who succeeded him briefly (1464–69). Stricken with gout (and called "Il Giottoso"), he is carried to his study to delight in his collection of antiques, "for the noble mastery of those ancient angelic intellects who made such things as bronze, marble, and such materials acquire such great price. . . . They have made it worth more than gold by means of their skill."[111]

Piero's son, Lorenzo the Magnificent (ruled 1469–92), though both a collector of Classical works and a patron of contemporary Italian masters, was more of the former than the latter (especially if we include the noncommissioned works he often purchased from non-Italian masters

such as van Eyck and Rogier van der Weyden), so that as Galeazzo
Sforza remarked, he had obtained "the noblest objects from the entire
universe."[112] Lorenzo also purchased in 1471 the only other rival fabulous collection in Italy at that time—that of Pope Paul II (d. 1464), formerly cardinal of St. Mark's—from the then reigning pope Sixtus IV after
his predecessor had bankrupted the papal treasury in his collecting passion.[113]

Pope Leo X, a younger son of Lorenzo's, later followed well in the
family tradition. Upon receiving the triple crown, he uttered the famous
quip: "Now that God hath seen fit to grant Us the Papacy, let Us enjoy
it." To enjoy for Leo meant to collect art. Taylor describes him thus:

> Leo was a collector in the grand manner . . . a man of taste and instanta-
> neous decision, he was always ready to pay the asking price for an object
> even if he had to lie awake at night contriving ways and means of getting
> even with the man who had sold it to him. . . . The Pope's income
> amounted to between 500,000 and 600,000 ducats [per annum]. The pa-
> pal household alone, which Julius II had maintained on 48,000 ducats,
> now cost double that sum. In all, Leo spent about 4,500,000 ducats. On
> his unexpected death his creditors faced financial ruin.[114]

Not only popes but also great Roman patrician families became
connoisseur-collectors. Prospero Colonna's palace at Santi Apostoli contained the "Apollo Belvedere," the "Three Graces," a giant Hercules, and
two statues of barbarian warriors.[115] Paul III, elected in 1534, was the
first pope to be selected from a Roman family—the Farnese—in 104
years. While still a mere cardinal (created at the tender age of twenty-
five), Alexander Farnese showed rapacious collecting skills. Having been
granted by the Borgia pope, Alexander VI, the rights to all the ruins
around the Church of San Lorenzo Fuori le Mura to use for the com-
mencement of his new Palazzo Farnese (now the French Embassy in
Rome), the future Paul III found twenty-two splendid portrait busts of
Roman emperors among the rubble-filled bulwark from the eighth century (hastily thrown together there against invading barbarians). He subsequently obtained from Pope Alexander a further concession: all the
materials from the ruined sites throughout the city that he could carry off
in one night. The cardinal hired seven hundred oxcarts with drivers. In
one stroke he thereby obtained everything necessary for the completion
of the Palazzo Farnese *and* the assembly of a fabulous collection of antiquities to fill it as well, all of which were bequeathed by his grandson to
the city of Rome.[116] This collection did not remain in Rome, however,
but was transferred to Naples in 1788 against a Bourbon claim through

the House of Parma (because of the marriage of Paul III's nephew to Holy Roman Emperor Charles V's daughter Mary of Austria, who later became Mary of Parma). Apart from this instance, and the Medici collection that went to Florence with Ferdinand, by the mid-seventeenth century many of the noble and princely Roman collections—and there were more than one hundred of them—wound up in the Vatican.

Before we move on to the next epoch, the seventeenth and eighteenth centuries, we must pause and assess all this collecting in terms of the historical vision and aesthetic sensibilities that evidently arose along with it by the end of the High Renaissance (roughly 1470–1550). Four considerations occur, which collectively constitute the Renaissance *archés* for the idea of the antique and the aesthetic response to antiques that they entail.

1. There was an overall "raising up" of the plastic arts—whether of the near or distant past—to a status equivalent to literary works. This raising up occurred in two senses: (A) the change in the social status of artists themselves from laborer to genius and consequently their works from artifact to masterpiece; and (B) the literal digging up of classical art objects so that their true character did not need to be inferred from classical literary accounts alone but could be seen and owned in the actual things themselves. Thus, paintings, sculpture, and architectural works (as genres of art) were viewed as objects of the highest aesthetic appreciation, equal to literary works.

2. There is the glorification of the past per se. The past became the most powerful force in the aesthetic consciousness, and works of the present were measured in its terms. This, in turn, is manifest in three forms.

(A) The past was not something merely studied with the antiseptic rigor of the historian and antiquary in the modern sense of pure scholarship. And this had two consequences. First, the past was to be *used*—not merely imitated—but reawakened in the life of the present. And the very *process* of discovery of the past and innovative ways to incorporate the past and its discovery process into the life of the present became a large part of the activity of daily life, or at least a fashion among those who had the money and leisure to pursue it. Second, the absence of rigorous and antiseptic scholarship had the consequence of encouraging forgeries. We cited Michelangelo's sleeping cupid made for Cardinal Riario. That was far from an isolated case; Dossena's productions are the most famous examples. But this was also a time in which the distinctions between copy, stylistic imitation, and forgery were not clearly drawn. In fact, the first work known to make a systematic distinction between forgeries, copies, and originals was the book *Discorsi di M. Enea Vico sopra le medaglie degli antichi* (1555), in which Benvenuto Cellini is listed among the forgers of antique coins. And where taste and the aesthetic imagination are aroused, much historical fantasizing and the willing suspension of disbelief are sure to surface,[117] especially in a culture that appreciates bravura, daring, and panache as the highest virtues and in which the joyous glory of the affective moment must always transcend objective truth. That is why even though the "realism" of a painting was much admired, a work's greatness was judged not merely on the precision with which it imitated nature, but also on the great technical difficulty in achieving this effect and the invention and inspiration required to work the material to achieve the semblance of the real while revealing the brilliant ingenuity and panache of the individual artist (what the Italians called *sprezzatura*).

(B) By the start of the Early Renaissance (1420) connoisseurs were already conscious of the connection between the history of *art* and the history of *civilization*. They understood that through the remains of the art of the past we can see the genius of the men and the civilization that made them—even if this awareness was not quite conceptualized through the same modern categories we would now use. Thus, it has been noted that the collectors and connoisseurs of the Early and High Renaissance did not clearly conceive of the works of ancient Greece and Rome as each exhibiting its own unique "classical style" and that "the first attempt to define the stylistic characteristics of ancient sculpture appeared [in the Late Renaissance] in Francisco d'Ollanda's *Da pintura antiga* of 1548, a work that even today is available only in the original Portuguese or in a Spanish translation of 1565."[118] This placement of the advent of the stylistic consciousness per se in the Late Renaissance (roughly 1550–1620, the period referred to art-historically as "Mannerist") is to be expected, because Mannerism was the first art style that deliberately and consciously took as its subject matter not "nature" (whether understood as the physical environment, portraits of persons, or subjects religious, mythological, or historical) but "art" itself. Mannerism had therefore an appreciation and understanding of historical style *as artifice*, something that was variable over time and not eternally fixed by natural laws or the requirements of the craft, but the result of human effort and choice and thus open to evaluation.[119] This stylistic categorization in terms of historical styles was the consequence, in turn, of the genuine development of historical consciousness, though it was in fact not made explicit until the seventeenth century (in the "Battle of the Ancients and the Moderns," as we note below). It was not really stated in formal terms until the eighteenth century (Winckelmann) and was not theoretically universalized until the nineteenth century (Hegel).

Finally, (C) in relation to the revival of the past, in addition to this connection between art and civilization, by the end of the High Renaissance (1550–75) there seemed to be a further genuine consensus among art connoisseurs that—given the exemplary achievements of Michelangelo and Raphael and their like in the preceding generation—art had now come to its fruition by having reached its "natural perfection." This was not just the invention of Vasari.[120] It was, rather, a recapitulation of the same intellectual processes we observed earlier when Xenocrates of Athens said, in the third century B.C., that art had "stopped" in the generation of Lysippus and Apelles. However ill-conceived and unprescient this view turned out to be—Caravaggio and Bernini, Bronzino, El Greco, Rubens, Rembrandt and Vermeer were just over the horizon—this sense of "art already completed" turned art connoisseurs from potential patrons into collectors. If Michelangelo is as good as Lysippus, then Lysippus is as good as Michelangelo; and nothing that could still be newly commissioned could be as good as either. Hence, the connoisseur's attitude toward the works of the recently deceased masters of the prior generation or two was that they deserved the same respect as the works of the ancients, that art had reached its own perfection in imitation of them. Their own time (the Late Renaissance) could not equal the past, recent or distant. Why commission a new sculpture that cannot be as good as *either* a Michelangelo or Lysippus (or presumed Lysippus)? In 1601, just as the popes had repeatedly and without success forbidden the export of *classical* works from Rome, so Ferdinand I, Grand Duke of Tuscany, now forbade export from Florence of any work by the hand of eighteen listed new "old masters." Most of those on that list were Florentines. Some (like Raphael and Titian) were not; and some Florentines (notably Cimabue, Giotto, Botticelli—all too "medievalist" and thus "imperfect" by the canons of the time)—were also not listed. At first it was, perhaps, the simple fact that obvious reserves of classical examples of great art had become exhausted after two hundred years of intense excavation. This scarcity translated into the requirement to find *new* (i.e., Renaissance) "old masters." Thus, in the *Ricordi* of Fra Sabba da Castiglione (1549) we find the observation: "Since beautiful antiques are rare and cannot be obtained without the greatest difficulty and expense, others [i.e., collectors] choose works by Donato [Donatello] who can be compared with any sculptor of antiquity in sculptural design and workmanship. . . . Still others have chosen the works of Michelangelo, the glory of our century in both painting and sculpture."[121] But by the end of the sixteenth century, the art connoisseur-collector pursued the Michelangelo and the Praxiteles with equal fervor; and the glories of Michelangelo, Titian, and Raphael were appreciated in their own right, both because of their intrinsic worth and because now their *time was also past.*

3. Another aspect of the Renaissance vision of antiques was only nascent in sixteenth-century Italy. The Renaissance was appreciative of works in only two time periods: it valued only the Classical works of ancient Greece and Rome (indeed, seeing little difference between them) at first, and then, at its end, the works of the masters of its own high point (the High Renaissance)—but not Archaic Greek art (as some ancient Romans of the late empire did) and certainly not Medieval art, and not even its own Early Renaissance masters to 1450.[122] In like manner, the Renaissance appreciation of antiques was geographically and culturally circumscribed: great art was to be found in Italy and Greece. True, Renaissance collector-connoisseurs like Lorenzo the Magnificent or Francis I sent agents abroad to non-European locations to look for treasures.[123] But it was Classical works, and especially manuscripts, that they pursued there. That civilizations the world over could be scoured for their indigenous objects of aesthetic pleasure, ones unique to themselves, and that they provided an illumination of the life-world of their creators, was a conception only dimly perceived (if at all) in the Italian Renaissance. Whereas the peculiar Italian Renaissance vision of art was inspired by the discovery of the Classical *past,* it would be the northern and western European pursuit and discovery of the corners of the *world at large* that inspired a new element: a fascination with the exotic and a passion for the extraordinary object. This expanded conception arrives in the ages succeeding the late Renaissance, the Baroque and Rococo eras.[124] Thus, the passion for the exotic and fascination with the extraordinary (even monstrous), the desire to possess and incorporate into one's world the entire globe (and the past of the world) really takes its form in the *Wunderkammer* of the Habsburgs and their like; and we follow its development in the next historical section.

4. The final consideration in our assessment of the historical consciousness and aesthetic sensibilities available to Renaissance connoisseurs of the antique—one that will complete our Renaissance *archés*—concerns the possible appreciation of *objects of the past in general* as antiques worthy of aesthetic experience. That art objects in general, that is, that decorative arts, the "crafts" (and not merely paintings and works of sculpture), might provide a similar pleasure to objects classified as "fine arts," and that they might do so, moreover, in the context of their past just as "antiques" in the

modern sense do, was not part of the Renaissance vision. There were some exceptions,[125] but by and large, for a more inclusive appreciation of the decorative arts as "antiques" we must wait until the eighteenth century, a yet further stage, which will add a new layer and a new collection of *archés* to this archeology of the connoisseurship of the antique.

Now that we have detailed and analyzed the Renaissance mentality vis-à-vis its idea and appreciation of antiques, detailing its limitations as well as elucidating its achievements, let us briefly prefigure and survey what *archés* are yet to come in the remainder of this lengthy chapter's archeology of the antique. In this way we can keep better track of where we have been and where we must yet go. The next moment of this saga, the seventeenth and eighteenth centuries, begins as Austro-Germanic (and is primarily, though not exclusively, Habsburg), in the main because this vision produced the beginnings of this archeology's universalist aspect. Here, as Descartes will remark, the past itself becomes a foreign country. Following that, we briefly look at France in the age of *le Roi Soleil*, and then, after considering the circle of Charles I of England, the situation of Holland, the mentality and consequences of the Grand Tour, the Augustan neo-classicism of England, and the antidotic effects of Gothic revival and of chinoiserie on this neo-classicism, we will move back to France and ponder the consequences of the French Revolution, followed by the effects both there and in England of the Industrial Revolution.

The predominance of France and England in the archeology of the antique that follows is indicated by several factors. At the outset of the eighteenth century, France was the arbiter of taste and theory for Europe; furthermore, the effects of the French Revolution both on Western consciousness and on the sheer availability of antiques "on the market" at the end of that century inaugurated a profound modification of Western civilization's conception of and sensibility toward the antique. Meanwhile, England was just emerging from its condition as a backwater of Western civilization at the outset of the seventeenth century, and yet at the end of the eighteenth century it had already become the empire on which the sun never set.[126] The "Grand Tour" was both a cause and effect of this process; it verified the dictum "the past is another country." Passing through the intellectual consequences of the era of the Enlightenment and the effects of Romanticism and the Industrial Revolution, we will pause to collect these *archés* in the Victorian age. This finally brings us to the United States, as our contemporary center and focus, closing the archeology of the antique with a discussion of the connoisseurship and collecting of antiques in the early years of the twentieth century and touching on the impact of modern (twentieth-century) art and art theory on the contemporary aesthetic appreciation of antiques. We end the archeology with archeological conclusions that will bring us to the following chapter's ten criteria for the idea of the antique and the aesthetic response to it.

2.5
The Seventeenth and Eighteenth Centuries

To clarify the nature of connoisseurship and collecting and to observe some of the changes of vision that occurred in the seventeenth and eighteenth centuries, we may look first simply at the different terminology used for the Italian and German rooms that housed these collections. The Italian term *guardaroba* is a general name for that section of a princely palace where collections were stored. The collection was never available (i.e., "out in the open," as it were) in its entirety. Paintings and sculptures that were set up for decorative use and display to guests were located in a large hall or salon called the *galleria*; and the personal study of the master, where he spent his days with his papers and his most intimate and cherished objects, was the *studio* (dim. *studiolo*). These various rooms and chambers contained sculpture and painting (Classical and High Renaissance) as well as newly commissioned work; certainly silver and gold *objets de vertu*, medals and gems (ancient Greek and Roman cameos were highly prized), and usually a few exotic rarities of the natural world—a narwhal horn (thought to be from a unicorn), a silver-mounted and gem-encrusted coconut, an ostrich egg, a nautilus shell, and the like. But for the far-flung exotic and strange, the bizarre and grotesque, one must look to the north of Italy. There the primary term for the room of the collection is *Wunderkammer*—literally, a "wonder chamber." Out of this generic specification grew specific collection rooms (*-kämmern*), each with its specified purpose. According to the rather pedantic discussion of Caspar Friedrich Neikel in his *Museographie* (1727), the *Schatzkammer* was a treasury for gold and gems; the *Naturalienkammer* contained rocks, shells, fossils, and the like in their natural (i.e., unmodified) condition; a special *Antiquitätenkabinett* did not contain "antiquities" in the modern sense but tomb furnishings and "heathen" items associated especially with death and burial. All these *kämmern* were held distinct from the *Kunstkammer*, which contained those items we would now include among both the fine and decorative arts—all of which, Neikel stipulated, must be "originals and not copies, they must have been created by the most famous masters, and they must reflect in some way the fancy of the person who collects them."[127]

The greatest of all Habsburgs, who presided over the first empire on which the sun never set, Holy Roman Emperor Charles V, was himself a man too much engaged with the world of the moment to enjoy the pleasures of connoisseurship and collecting. Nevertheless, his mere position (as the focus of the centripetal force generated by dynastic world empire) guaranteed that even without deliberate effort on his part, art treasures would accumulate around him. On his death in 1558, almost all of them were auctioned off. It was his brother, Ferdinand I (1503–64), to whom Charles V bequeathed his German Empire, who was the first Habsburg to make a concerted effort to collect and preserve the Habsburg art and antiques patrimony.

Ferdinand's cousin and namesake, Habsburg archduke Ferdinand II of Tyrol (1529–95), had a fabulous *Wunderkammer*. Not in that early period precisely distinguished from the *Schatz-* and *Kunstkammer*, it contained not only art and treasure but any object of rarity that would spark amazement (*Wunder*), whether by its exotic origins or material or rarity or association with glory or famous personality. One such object—which caused wonder no doubt in virtue of all these characteristics—was Montezuma's quetzal-feather headdress, which the Aztec emperor had given to Cortez. Cortez gave it to Charles V; then he, to his brother Ferdinand I of Austria; and thus it came into the collection of his son Ferdinand II of Tyrol. It was much admired by Albrecht Dürer for its "ingenia" when he saw it in Brussels, where it was temporarily held at the court of the young emperor's aunt, Margaret of Austria. Dürer records the experience in his travel diary (June 7, 1521), making it thereby the first aesthetically motivated reference known to a particular pre-Columbian artifact by a European. He says that it was "more beautiful to behold than prodigies. . . . All the days of my life I have seen nothing that had gladdened my heart so much as these things, for I saw amongst them wonderful works of art."[128] If this was a genuine aesthetic response, it was indeed rare. For as a category of objects susceptible to such response, the idea "pre-Columbian art"—as well as the ethnographical concept "pre-Columbian *artifact*"—is a twentieth-century phenomenon. In any case, such New World objects began to appear in other Germanic *Kunstkämmern*. Albrecht V, Duke of Bavaria (1550–79), who first established Munich as a south German capital of art and culture, had a *Kunstkammer* built in 1563. Filled with stuffed animals, seashells, and games, even exotic foods, all acquired by his own agents, given by Cardinal Francesco de' Medici, or by his father, Emperor Ferdinand I, it contained an "idol in human form . . . from Mexico" (*ain abgott von allerlai . . . von Mexico*).[129] Holy Roman Emperor Ferdinand's grandson, Emperor Rudolph II (1552–1612), was a zealous connoisseur and collector. Taylor remarks that he was

> closest in spirit and in taste to his great uncle Philip II at whose Spanish court he had spent his boyhood. Whereas Philip's religious zeal expressed itself in a fanatical personal austerity, Rudolph abandoned himself to a life of scholarship and to the extension of his medieval *Wunderkammer*. He had a sure eye for pictures, developed largely through his admiration for Titian, and he was an enthusiastic collector of the works of Dürer and Hieronymus Bosch. Rudolph was to be the link between the Vienna Museum and the Prado and he seemed to unite in himself several complex strains of the ancient Hapsburg heritage. Leaving Spain at nineteen, he retired to Prague, where he closed himself up in the Hradschin [castle], refusing to attend to affairs of state and spending his time and fortune on his collections. He lived among his scientists and astrologers, who included Tycho de Brahe and Kepler, his women, his painters, his adventurers and wild animals. There he employed the best goldsmiths and artisans in Europe to create the most complicated instruments imaginable, taking a profound and daily interest in their progress and ingenuity.[130]

Further north, Augustus II ("the Strong" 1670–1733), Elector of Saxony and king of Poland and one of the last but hardly the least of these great collectors, established an incredible collection in Dresden (where most of it still remains).[131] It was he who first clearly distinguished the *Schatz-* and *Wunderkammer* from the *Kunstkammer*,[132] and it is on this example that Neikel's 1727 book was based.

The Baroque love of the multiplicity of times and worlds and its delight in the possibilities for their miniaturization, encapsulation as it were, in the *Kammer*, was quite self-conscious. Indeed, it was expressed with prodigious bravura in Baroque art. A 1998 exhibit at the National Gallery in Washington, D.C., titled "A Collector's Cabinet," epitomized this self-consciousness in two extraordinary paintings, displayed on opposite walls of a gallery.[133] The first was *The Archduke Albert and Archduchess Isabella in a Collector's Cabinet,* by Jan Bruegel the Elder and Adriaen Stalbemt. Here the duke and duchess stand in the center of a room while paintings fill the space behind and sculptures, medals, and musical instruments surround them. In the foreground, couples inspect individual objects in a state of leisure and peace, while through an open door we see soldiers in preparation for war. At the center of the painting, a small painting propped up against a chair depicts the destruction of the artistic achievements of civilization (paintings, musical instruments,

furniture) by creatures with animal bodies and human heads (perhaps referring to the destruction of Catholic ecclesiastical art by rabid Protestants earlier in the century). All this creates a fascinating stew of
contraries—of art and life, war and peace, past and present, animal and
human. The second painting was by Jan Bruegel the Younger, titled
Venus and Cupid in a Collector's Cabinet. Here there are no people, but
rather playing monkeys and statues of Venus and Cupid dominate the
central stage. The statues are painted in the pink tones of living human
flesh, however; and the various objects displayed incite the imagination
to wonder at the complex imagery scattered everywhere about the cabinet and to muse on the relations between past and present civilizations,
between art and nature, Europe and the rest of the known world, myth
and reality, the impermanent softness of human flesh and the durable
materiality of stone. One of the most distinctive characteristics of
Baroque art itself was its ability to astonish by confusion, to visually
amalgamate: both diverse media (painting, sculpture, architecture,
stucco, bronze, lacquer, water, stone) and the diverse and incompatible
worlds that the art represented in fusion (past and present, the divine and
human, the public and private, the fictive world of the painting and the
real world of the viewer). This aesthetic ideal and artistic technique of
the art of the time was reinforced by the optimism of the age, the belief
that man through science, reason, and craft could transform one reality
into another, one nature into another, just as the exotica of ostrich eggs
and coconuts were transformed by metal encasements into decoratively
useful ewers and goblets for the titillation of European sensibilities. This
optimism was itself partly a product of the New Science of Bacon and
Descartes.

Thus, we find in Francis Bacon's account of a scientific utopia, the
New Atlantis (1627), a description of the holdings of "Solomon's
House" in accordance with his new ideal of the inductive method in philosophy, wherein diverse collections of objects are arrayed so as to reveal
encyclopedic knowledge of the "Causes and secret motions of things,
and the enlarging of the bounds of Human Empire, to the effecting of all
things possible."[134] Descartes himself made the connection between
travel to experience the wonders of the world and the investigations of
ages past in his remark in the *Discourse on Method* (1637): "for to hold
converse with those of other ages and to travel are almost the same
thing."[135]

Arthur Wheelock, author of the exhibit catalogue for "A Collector's
Cabinet," argues that Baroque collectors had as a self-conscious aim to
experience the totality of the universe in all its diversity, all compressed

in the comprehensive collection, which provided tangible sensuous evidence for the sense it all made, a sense to which the curiosity (the monster and irregularity) formed the exception that added spice.[136]

Except for grand salons and galleries (which correspond more to the Italian than Germanic model), the French seem to have eschewed "chambered" collections and, again like the Italians, generally preferred to devote their connoisseurship rather more to the arts (fine and decorative) than to natural wonders and curiosities gathered from around the globe.

The greatest French collection outside the royal one itself in the first half of the seventeenth century was that of Cardinal Richelieu (1585–1642). This founder of the French Academy and power behind the throne of Louis XIII filled his Palais Cardinal (now the Palais Royal in Paris) with an inventory of five hundred pictures (including works by Raphael, Titian, Leonardo, Bellini, Romano, and Rubens), antique marble and bronze statues, Florentine *pietra dura* furniture, tapestries, Persian carpets, and Chinese lacquers and ceramics.[137] He even owned a huge collection of pipes (though he never smoked them himself) and an assemblage of twelve Poussins (until he lost them to young King Louis XIV in a tennis match).

His successor as the power behind the throne of the young Louis XIV was Cardinal Mazarin (1602–61), a collector and connoisseur of yet more astonishing proportions. Between 1640 and 1648 Mazarin built his palace (now the old Bibliothèque Nationale in Paris, just a few blocks farther north of Richelieu's palace) on the rue de Richelieu to house his collections. He engaged in at least as much effort and intrigue to acquire them as he did to govern France.[138] He collected only what was beautiful, having no interest whatever in the "curiosities" of the *Wunderkammer*. In January of the year following the completion of his grand palace, Mazarin had to flee Paris temporarily because of the first of the Fronde uprisings.[139] But even during his self-imposed exile in Cologne, he had his agents scurrying to London to buy the art objects of the deposed Charles I, then being auctioned off by order of Cromwell's Parliament. (And what he couldn't acquire there he instructed his agent in Holland to buy for him when it arrived on the Dutch market.)[140] Immediately on Mazarin's departure from Paris, the entire contents of his own new palace were ordered sold by decree of the Paris Parlement, then dominated by his sworn enemies. But the sale never came to pass. Although the decree was reissued in 1651 and again in 1652, it was repeatedly sidetracked by the young Louis XIV, Mazarin's protégé. When the Fronde finally collapsed in February 1653, Mazarin returned to his collections and his palace—together with many additions he had acquired in his exile abroad—and recommitted himself to the consolidation of political power on behalf of the king and to the continued aggrandizement of his collections, which became the envy of all Europe.[141]

Collecting on the grand scale always requires a fair amount of intrigue and manipulation. Mazarin, who had managed to pry loose Correggio's *Sposalizio* from Cardinal Barberini only by getting Queen Anne of Austria to pretend that *she* wanted it, was later himself in terror of having his collection fall into the ravenous hands of Queen Christina of Sweden. Another great connoisseur and collector, Christina had come to see Mazarin's collections once during his absence from Paris. He wrote home fretfully to a retainer: "I am not clear if the Queen has seen my apartments in the Louvre; but in any case, should she ask to see them, I beg you to ensure that this madwoman keeps away from my cabinets, because otherwise some of my miniatures [*petits tableaux*] might be taken."[142]

Though he bequeathed his entire estate to Louis XIV, the young king asked only for eighteen precious stones—which some believe to have become the eighteen diamonds in the French crown. (Colbert later made some purchases on behalf of the king, but most went to Mazarin's heirs.) This chapter began with a quotation from Mazarin's poignant farewell to his collection. Actually, the text continues a bit further: "Que j'ai eu de peine à acquerier ces choses! Puis-je les abandonner sans regret? Je ne les verrai plus où je vais!" (Oh, but I had such trouble acquiring these things! Can I leave them without regret? I will no longer see them where I am going!)

Louis XIV took little interest in the connoisseurship of artworks himself, leaving such matters (along with the formation of his economic policies) to Colbert to arrange. Colbert, with the assistance of Le Brun, brought together on the king's behalf the fabulous collections in the various galleries of the Louvre, using the Grande Galerie for the most important paintings. An account of its opening, for which occasion the king arrived from Versailles, is preserved for us in a contemporary issue of the *Mercure de France*.[143] Unlike Mazarin, Louis thought himself only minimally deprived on being separated from his art treasures. He sold them whenever he required ready cash to finance his wars (and there were many wars)—although he preferred to melt down his silver plate. (One of the ornamental silver railings of a garden path in Versailles which he had melted down for this reason produced 2,788 kilos of silver.) The death of Louis XIV (1715) followed shortly on the War of the Spanish Succession. Its outcome brought half the French Royal Collection to the Prado when the Bourbons came to inherit the Spanish throne in the person of Philip V, Louis XIV's grandson. This fortuity kept that portion of the French Royal Collection from being dispersed at the end of the century when the contents of Versailles were ordered to be auctioned off by the Revolution.[144]

We will come to the consequences of this momentous event shortly. First, it is worth noting that although connoisseurship and collecting on a grand scale in the latter half of the seventeenth century was primarily limited to the two cardinal–prime ministers of the king, by the mid-eighteenth century France was home to a community of like-minded collector-connoisseurs not part of the royal court. These included wealthy businessmen like Crozat as well as members of nobility like the duc de Chartres. The latter's "parc Monceau" in the 1770s included "tartar tents, Dutch windmills, and a carefully ruined temple of Mars with a desolate obelisk. The whole thing was designed deliberately to resemble a series of stage-flats at the opera, so that one might move imaginatively through space and time across the scale of world history."[145] Rheims, observing that already in the seventeenth century there were some connoisseurs in France who collected for the purpose of living imaginatively outside their place and time, quotes the contemporary D'Allemagne, who "recorded that when they came as amateura/dilletanti to one another's homes to admire their collections of [American] Indian artifacts 'it was considered good taste that he himself should put on the clothes and weapons of an American savage.' "[146] As early as 1603 in England, James I's queen asked Ben Jonson to

> write a masque, an entertainment-cum-drama-cum–court ball, to be performed in Whitehall on Twelfth Night, and to be called the Masque of Blackness. The queen and ten of her beautiful young aristocratic companions were to appear as blackamoors, an Aethiop Queen and the Daughters of Niger. Their azure and silver dresses designed by Inigo Jones, all lit by glimmering lantern light, were excitingly transparent, their breasts visible beneath the gauze, "their hayre thicke, and curled upright in tresses, lyke Pyramids."[147]

Such world-encapsulating spectacles we saw earlier, in our account of Renaissance Rome. There it was limited primarily to the world of the classical past. Now in the Baroque (1621–1720) and Rococo (1720–1770) eras, society's haute monde performs a conspicuous and capacious consumption of the entire world, both past and present. The "same things" are simply *conceived* of and *used* in a different way. For example, in the

Medieval period spices were imported from the East primarily for their pleasant taste, or for food preservation, or to disguise the taste of rotten foods. In the later eras their use became for some a conspicuous consumption (a sociopolitical matter) and for others an aesthetic event, inspiring by their taste and aroma the very image of a *paradis terrestre*, of exotic or ancient gardens filled with saints or lovers depicted in the tapestries and paintings on their walls and in the fables recounted in their poetry. In the Baroque era, as Wolfgang Schivelbusch details in his *Tastes of Paradise*, tea and chocolate and coffee (all oriental imports) were generally served in exotic, oriental surroundings (i.e., *à la turque*) with appropriate (or what was believed to be appropriate) utensils such as imported porcelains (until Europeans discovered the porcelain secret in 1715—and began by reproducing oriental-like wares) and with participants often wearing exotic costumes.[148] These imaginative reconstructions of reality had a basis in the new conception of a psychology. As Gordon S. Wood points out: "Lockean psychology presumed a world that could be fashioned and made over, if only the impressions and sensations that besieged the senses could be controlled. People became aware, as never before in history, that they might be able to create their own culture."[149]

Thus, by the eighteenth century, if not earlier, art and antiques collecting was in full swing on much wider territory than in the Italian Renaissance. Collection of exotica and the imaginary universes they inspired were a passion of European society. And the trade of antiquities and exotica was international in scope and scale. The consciousness of the collector could move "imaginatively through space and time across the scale of world history" because there was now an international, indeed a global, market to supply connoisseur-collectors who were developing a keen historical and cultural sensibility. What was only now being formed in this consciousness and sensibility (this *mentalité* or vision) was a conjunction of the sensibility toward the past with a sensibility toward the global (universal) that would ultimately find its locus in the appreciation of the *quotidian object as an antique*. This consciousness and sensibility would underlie the eventual ability, for example, to appreciate a Ming dynasty bronze temple bell for what it imaginatively evokes of its own past civilization and for the role it plays in the life-world of the connoisseur who aesthetically engages it in his contemporary world.

Meanwhile, the groundwork for another *arché* in the sensibility for the antique had also come into being by the end of the eighteenth century—and this by way of the "Battle of the Ancients and the Moderns" that was mentioned at the end of our discussion of the Renaissance. It was the optimism of the Age of Reason, its presumption to embrace all the truths of the universe in an unshakably rational system (think of Descartes, Spinoza, Leibniz) and its hope to possess in miniature specimens the whole world in all its variety, that is reflected in this great debate of the century, the *Querelle*, as the French called it.[150] We saw a precursor of this debate in the conclusion of the preceding section. It was implicit in the late Renaissance view that on the one hand, if Michelangelo was as good as Lysippus then Lysippus was as good as Michelangelo, and on the other, if art had indeed finally reached its "completion" or "perfection" (evidently twice—in ancient Greece and in Renaissance Italy), then no new work by a living artist could be as good as the great "antiques" from either of these historical periods. But in the following centuries—the seventeenth and eighteenth—this view, insofar as it applied to man's general progress in civilization as a whole, came into dispute, for that put it in opposition to the general optimism of the age.

Rémy Saisselin, for example, claims that it was early French eighteenth-century aesthetic thought, stemming from the famous *Querelle* that had begun in the seventeenth century, regarding the superiority of the ancients versus the moderns, that "could be taken as the starting point for the modern aesthetics."[151] He cites Tatarkiewicz's remark that whereas Germanic thought regarding art and beauty was *philosophical* in nature and British thought was *psychological*, French thinking was *artistic*.[152] This last term Saisselin takes to mean something like "bound to cultural preoccupations with the taste, based upon historical awareness." The *Querelle* grew out of flattery of and praise for Louis XIV's taste and patronage on the one hand (resulting in his being favorably compared with such classical ideals of rulers as Pericles, Alexander the Great, and Caesar, and even with Apollo as ruler of the arts). On the other hand, the *Querelle* stemmed from the legitimate recognition of genuine progress in the new natural science that had liberated itself from the ancients. Saisselin argues that this debate regarding the superiority of the moderns over the ancients gave rise to the idea that the arts, too, needed a separate and independent system of comprehension, with its own categories and laws, something new and free from that of the ancients—and from Christianity and any other (even Cartesian) system as well. Because the arts produce works of the ever-mutable imagination, the basis for such a system could not be found in nature (the realm of science), which is constant, but only in the culturally and historically conditioned (hence mutable) taste of those who experience such works.

Consequently such a system for understanding the arts required the development of the "connoisseur." And Saisselin concludes that

> modern aesthetics did not only grow out of speculations on perception, but also from serious considerations of historical questions, the meaning of civilization, and a historical consciousness. The peculiarity of French aesthetics lies in that. . . . Aesthetic perception or taste may thus be possible only to the man of taste who is himself a product of civilization—which is not to say that there was no sense of beauty, or enjoyment of it, before 1700, but merely that certain men were not *conscious* of the implications of this type of pleasure and enjoyment. It seems to us then that aesthetics and the rise of historical consciousness are closely linked.[153]

I might note here that some historians of philosophy push the origins of aesthetics back yet further, to the *sixteenth* century. Richard Woodfield claims that it was the appearance of Protestantism in England and Germany and the reactions of the Council of Trent to these events in the latter half of the sixteenth century that initiated the creation of aesthetics and philosophy of art in the modern sense. Sharp distinctions had now to be made for the first time between *religious* art, for which a precise didactic function and rules were prescribed by the Church, and purely *secular* art, which was for sheer enjoyment. This latter purpose had come to full flower in the taste of the "sophisticated art lover" that Mannerist art with its complex iconography and conceits had recently created in Catholic countries, a taste and a pleasure that the strictures of the Council of Trent were meant to restrain within doctrinal grounds. Dutch art satisfied the same enjoyments in secular landscapes and still-life easel paintings, and the Protestant Englishman preferred family portraits. That art should have a purely secular purpose led thinkers to consider the possibility of an unfettered and independent "aesthetic" theory, one free from religious (and perhaps even moral) preoccupations.[154]

Both the *Querelle* (which linked the origin of aesthetics to the rise of historical consciousness and understood this new science as developed and overseen by connoisseurs whose experienced taste determined its rules) and the distinction between the art created by the rules of religion for the propagation of faith and the art created purely for pleasure (which ultimately became *ars gratia artis*) meshed conveniently with the Lockean psychology we noted earlier, which suggested that people could create their own worlds, refashioning them to taste. Religious works are bound by doctrine, and Nature is bound by its eternal laws of time and place; culture and its arts are bound only by human imagination and taste.

It should be noted regarding the possible origins of aesthetic theorizing that very likely little (if any) of this speculation would have occurred at all were it not for the example of the ancients, of Greece and Rome, to begin with (Aristotle at least attempted an independent theory of art in general and as noted earlier came close to establishing a theory of tragic drama in *The Poetics*)—and had not the Renaissance "resurrected" their conceptions of art and beauty as eternal verities and had not the Medievals forgotten, misconstrued, and deliberately turned away from them.

As for the *Querelle* itself, it is generally accepted that the moderns won. Their view entailed belief not only in the evolution of civilization but in its *progress*. The idea of the antique in the modern sense then became possible against the backdrop of the idea of the progress of civilization. If the moderns are in some sense "better" than the ancients (because they have progressed beyond their achievements), then there is no reason why that past *should* in any way be revived. On the other hand, this conclusion reaffirmed an idea only partly realized in its full implications at the end of the Medieval period and beginning of the Renaissance, namely, that the *past really was over*. Being over, history leaves a residue that cannot ever be assimilated into the present in such a way as to be *freed from its pastness*. Thus, apart from the question whether or not it *should*, the past really *could* not be revived *as it was* and *in* the present. At best, it could be *preserved as past* and *for* the world of the present; and those of its objects that had endured through time into the present could enable our imaginations to evoke through them an image of a world gone by. On this account, in a curious way, then, the ancients had "won" too. The contemporary world could never again produce works "equal" to those of the past because their pastness itself could not be equaled; objects could not be detached from their history and freed from time. In some respects the achievements of the past could be surpassed in the sense of "improved on"—in philosophy and science there was no doubt. It could never be "regained" in its virgin purity. Objects of the past increased their value by becoming "rare"; and they were rare not merely in the sense of being in short supply, but because each one was unique and each had a unique origin and history. After all, there would be no need to value any particular thing that *was*, if "what was" is merely another instance of what could always be again. It was this historical consciousness that established the basis for later aesthetic appreciation of such features of antiques as provenance and patina; for while provenance is the known pedigree, patina (and related observable characteristics) is the physical evidence whereby the past is displayed as an ineradicable endurance into the present. In this mode "patina" not merely is proof of age but enters directly into the aesthetic experience. Hence, from the past's "being over," which enabled the Renaissance to believe it could "revive" it, we have now moved to the past's irretrievability *in* the present. The past can be only *for* the present. This conception give rise to a new and essential *arché* in the evolution of the idea of the antique, since for the antiques connoisseur the past lives *in* and *through* the object that displays its agedness—a past that has endured *as past* in the object.[155]

But before we leave the eighteenth century with the French Revolution, and in order to uncover a new facet in the total vision behind connoisseurship and collecting that arose in that century, we must turn briefly to England. It has often been noted that three of England's kings have been famous art collectors and connoisseurs. One (George IV) was generally disliked, and the other two, Richard II and Charles I, were put to death. This fact did not dissuade other British aristocratic connoisseur-collectors from their prodigious pursuit of aesthetic pleasure through art and antiques—as easily attested by the present existence of great British estates with their collections still intact.

Of Richard II's collection we know little, for the details are not preserved, but we may presume its equivalence in taste to his near contemporary the duc de Berry. After him in England only Cardinal Wolsey was a significant collector of artworks, as distinct from books and treasure.

In 1611 we find from a contemporary report that James I's heir, Prince Henry, had a "gallery of very fine pictures, ancient and modern, the larger part bought out of Venice."[156] These artworks were inherited by his younger brother, Charles I, when he came to the throne instead of Prince Henry, who died before his coronation. James I was no collector-connoisseur, but several of his favorites were. And more appeared—along with his son Charles I—in the next generation. Let us look in greater detail at some of the case histories to see *what* they collected, *how* they did so (and at what cost), and to some degree *why*. This will reveal further *archés* of the connoisseurship of antiques as they arise in the English Baroque (1620–1715).

One of James's favorites, Robert Carr, the Earl of Somerset, relied especially on a British dealer, Daniel Nys, who had a palazzo in Venice. In one instance, Nys received an order from Somerset through the British ambassador, Sir Dudley Carleton, for an assemblage of five Tintorettos, three Veroneses, and a large quantity of Greco-Roman sculpture.[157] Another of James's handsome young favorites was George Villiers, 1st Duke of Buckingham, who arrived at court just as James was tiring of Somerset's arrogance (followed shortly by his being found guilty of murder). Buckingham rapidly rose to the rank of Lord High Admiral and soon essentially controlled the king's dispensation of patronage. He was sent by James to accompany the future Charles I—who now himself became enamored of Buckingham—to arrange for Charles's marriage to the Spanish infanta, María. This project was a disaster for two reasons. First, it failed in its mission, a marriage. (On the other hand, though Charles returned without a bride, he brought back many antiques and art treasures, which he purchased through Buckingham's loan to him of £12,000 from a small fortune Buckingham received from James I.) Second, the trip was a political failure because it earned Buckingham the hatred of the strong Protestant faction in Parliament, which dreaded the thought of a Catholic queen. But on his return, Buckingham suggested war with Spain instead. That was more to Parliament's liking—if not a marriage, why not a war? Yet then, in the following year, Buckingham went to France to arrange for Prince Charles's marriage to another Catholic princess, Henrietta Maria, sister of Louis XIII. While it was at least rumored that Buckingham had in the interim seduced the French queen, Anne of Austria, certainly he gained not only a bride for Charles but the enmity of Richelieu and, again, of the English Parliament. On the other hand, others were more impressed. Mme de Motteville described Buckingham as beautiful and rich with a penchant for lavish purchases: "He was handsome, well put-together, and high-spirited . . . he had all these treasures to expend, and all the gems of the English Crown with which to adorn himself."[158] He did some serious acquisitioning, evidently. In the next year Buckingham was impeached by Parliament (1626), but Charles, having become king in 1625, dissolved Parliament to prevent his trial. (It was the beginning of Charles's long battle with Parliament, ultimately leading to the Civil War and Charles's beheading in 1649.)

In 1627 the Gonzaga (Dukes of Mantua) collection came up for sale. (What did not sell was seized by the invading French three years later and wound up in the Louvre.) Charles commissioned his father's former dealer, Nys, to purchase it for a price of £80,000, thus establishing some of the finest works in the king's collection. Though Buckingham could not compete directly for the Gonzaga collection against his sovereign, he managed in that year to acquire the major portion of Rubens's collection of antiques.

Another "friendly rival" of both Charles and Buckingham in the collection of art and antiques of the period was Thomas Howard

(1586–1646), 2nd Earl of Arundel, from the older generation. Apart from Charles I himself, he had acquired the most wide-ranging collection in England, sending agents not only to Italy but to the Levant as well. Henry Peacham's characterization of Arundel in *Compleat Gentleman* (1634) suggests that he was the first Englishman to recognize the necessary connection between collecting and connoisseurship on the one hand and art and archeological scholarship on the other. He made several trips to Italy in person, the first in 1606, bringing back many newly excavated statues from Rome. But when he returned to Rome in 1612–13, with Inigo Jones as companion, he was forbidden to either excavate or export from there. He therefore turned farther East, as Peacham explains:

> In Greece and other parts of the Grand Signor's Dominions[159] (where sometimes there were more Statues than men living, so much had art outstripped nature in those days) they may be had for digging and carrying. For by this reason of the barbarous religion of the Turks, which alloweth not the likeness or representation of any living thing, they have been for the most part buryed in ruins or broken to pieces; so that it is a hard matter to light on any there that are not headlesse or lame, yet most of them venerable for antiquity and elegancy.[160]

A curious example of how competition in his collecting turned to collaboration occurred in Constantinople in 1625–26. Arundel prevailed on Sir Thomas Roe, ambassador to the Sublime Porte, to act as his agent for antiquities in Ottoman domains. When Buckingham, having discovered this fact, required the ambassador to send half these finds to him, Arundel responded by sending out one William Petty—"a Cambridge scholar whose knowledge and appreciation of classical works of art was exceeded only by the subtlety of his wit and his indifference to ordinary ethics"[161]—to bypass Roe. But when Petty met Roe they decided to collaborate on an audacious scheme that would satisfy the wildest dreams of both their patrons: they sought to obtain six of the twelve reliefs that adorned the finest gates of the city: the Porta Aurea, erected by Theodosius the Great in the fourth century A.D., but now completely inaccessible, having been enclosed since the Turkish conquest of 1453 in fortifications known as the Seven Towers. Unfortunately, they could not gain the consent of the sultan, could not find anyone with sufficient authority to bribe, and though they tried, could not find anyone with adequate resources to enable them to steal them, so neither Buckingham nor Arundel managed to acquire these architectural antiques.

Nevertheless, on Arundel's death in 1646, the inventory of his collection included nearly eight hundred objects, of which two hundred were objets d'art and nearly six hundred were paintings (among which, although more than two hundred were without signature, many were by masters). His classical sculpture now forms the core of Oxford's Ashmolean collection. An album he purchased in Spain in the 1620s of Leonardo's drawings (now part of the British Royal Collection) is still the greatest assemblage of that master's works. Arundel also managed to acquire through Nys in Venice a collection of Old Master drawings that Nys had held back for himself from the Gonzaga purchase he had made for Charles I.[162] As for Buckingham, after his impeachment in 1625, though saved from trial by Charles, he lived only another three years, being assassinated at age thirty-six by a disgruntled sailor while making preparations for a military expedition to relieve the Huguenots at La Rochelle. Charles, meanwhile, continued to acquire.

From his inauguration as Prince of Wales in his late teens in 1616 until his fatal confrontation with Parliament in 1640, Charles managed to amass the greatest collection of art and antiques since the Medici—and, together with all his other hereditary possessions, probably the greatest collection in the Western world. It was ordered sold by Parliament in the Commonwealth Sale of October 1651. It contained many classical Greek and Roman works (more than four hundred sculptures were at least so attributed).[163] It also contained fourteen hundred paintings, by choice as well as default the more recent "antique" paintings from the preceding century of Renaissance masters. Naturally, the Commonwealth Sale (which dragged on until 1663) was a great opportunity for other European collectors; and the works that were most avidly competed for were in fact not the classical (or pseudo-classical) sculptures but rather paintings by the giants of the High Renaissance. That we have no record of any piece of Charles's classical sculpture collection entering any other great contemporary collection—but a great deal of information about the paintings—shows how far collecting and connoisseurship had changed from the taste of the preceding century.[164] The Spanish ambassador bought so many paintings for his king that when they were unloaded at Coruña on the Spanish coast, eighteen mules were required to take them to Madrid. His purchase of "la Perla," originally from the Gonzaga collection and supposed to be by Raphael, for £2,000 was the highest price paid for any single item, though Charles's sets of tapestries were the most valuable collectively, one set selling for over £8,000. Mantegna's *Triumph of Caesar* went for £1,000, and Titian's set of *Twelve Caesars* (now lost) went for £1,200. But Titian's *Doge Andrea Gritti* sold for only £40, and none of Charles's Rembrandts sold for more than £5! (Charles's taste for Rembrandt and his purchase of Medieval works such as the *Wilton Diptych* are evidence of his connoisseurship and advanced taste.) Queen Christina of Sweden (whom we have already mentioned in connection with Mazarin) purchased medals and jewelry for her collection, which she had recently much augmented through the fortunes of war by the addition of the collection of Holy Roman Emperor Rudolf II. Mazarin's own agent, Jarbach, acquired many paintings, tapestries, objects d'art, and antiques, which later came to the Louvre.

The total value of the sale was £118,000 (with £36,000 for paintings and £18,000 for sculpture), an unheard-of sum for a collection—and double the original estimate. But considering what was up for sale, one could well understand the judgment of the Venetian ambassador in London, who reported to his doge that masterpieces could be had for "prezzi vilissimi."[165] One must also agree with the assessment of Charles made by Horace Walpole one hundred years later in his *Anecdotes*: "If Charles . . . had shewn as much discernment in life as he had taste in the arts, he might have figured among the greatest of princes. . . . He was skilled in things of antiquity and could judge of medals whether they had the number of years they pretended unto. . . . The art of reigning was the only art of which he was ignorant."[166]

We should at this point review and summarize some of the peculiar features (some of the *archés*) of English collecting in the seventeenth century. First of all, there was a broadening of scope in the sources for antiques to the territory of the Ottoman Empire. This included the territory of modern-day Greece proper and those portions of the ancient Greek world located in Anatolia. (Since Ottoman rulers were generally indifferent to antiquities of any kind, the conditions for the future purchase of such antiquities as the Elgin Marbles from the Parthenon were established by good precedent.) In part this was because Italy was already well excavated (if not exhausted) and in part because the Italian states (except under the duress of war or financial hardship) had no intention of parting with their antiques—whether classical or works of Renaissance masters. True, the Habsburgs and other Germanic princes, as we noted above, acquired objects from around the world, but these were primarily in the form of booty, homages, trophies, and curiosities. The location of more or less permanent agents stationed abroad and on the lookout for objets d'art was, if not a novelty, becoming much more an established practice. (In the Renaissance this would have been done only for the acquisition of ancient manuscripts.) There was also the increasing importance of art and antiques not just for status and personal aesthetic satisfaction but also for their use as a basis of serious scholarship,

stimulating research into authentication and attribution. Not that collecting and connoisseurship ceased to be related to social status. On the
contrary, taking only Buckingham as the first of many youngbloods who
were to be all the more in evidence in the next century of the Grand
Tour, although it was far from the case that the sword (and the danger-
ous adventure it implied) was merely a sartorial decoration, it was now
becoming a world in which men displayed their virility and prowess not
merely in their arms (as displayed in the hard-body muscles or automatic
weapons of today's movie poster stars) but also by their taste. And the
exhibition of this taste in their collections was a mark not only of social
rank and political power but of their virility as well.[167]

Reviewing the European political scene at the end of the seventeenth
century, we find further changes with significant consequences for the
collecting and connoisseurship of art and antiques. With the slow disintegration of Spain's empire, the weakening in Italy of the city-states,
dukedoms, and especially Rome and the Venetian Republic, with England still working through the Restoration, with all France under the
thrall and patronage of Louis XIV (and more often than not drained for
various wars), and most of central Europe still destitute after the Thirty
Years' War, the art and collecting market moved to Holland. First
Antwerp and then Amsterdam, which lacked a royal court but possessed
a large merchant class, became the economic hub for the liquidation of
Europe's princely collections that were glutting the market in the latter
half of the century. As in London after the French Revolution and New
York between and after the two world wars of the twentieth century, the
nature of art and antiques collecting of necessity was transformed in the
hands of Dutch burghers and mercantile tycoons. Like gilt-edged securi-
ties in an age of economic uncertainty and tangible goods in an age of
inflation—and with a crisis in uninvested gold (amassed from the preceding generation) saturating the market—art objects were considered a safe
investment by the middle class. It was not unusual to find a burgher with
a hundred-odd paintings adorning the walls of his otherwise modest
home. And apparently not just burghers. John Evelyn reported while visiting Holland in 1641, "The peasants were so rich that they were looking
for investments and often spent 2000 to 3000 florins for pictures."[168] It is
no surprise, then, that Charles's collection was sold again in this environment. Buckingham's collection, also ordered sold by Parliament, likewise wound up in Amsterdam's salesrooms. But Arundel's collection was
wisely moved to the Netherlands in 1643—not for sale but for safekeep-
ing, to avoid confiscation by Parliament—evincing another important
role of the Netherlands in those days vis-à-vis art and antiques collecting:

its function as a safe haven, just as Switzerland often functions today in the art and antiques trade. Contemporary Dutch artists were not immune to this new supply and new bourgeois taste: Rembrandt's passion for fine imported textiles and antique busts as well as weapons and specimens from the Orient and New World rendered him bankrupt in the end.

Not only paintings and antique marbles were collected in this hothouse environment. New objects were collected, too, especially imported ones. Rheims notes that in 1684 a flotilla of eleven ships from the East Indies arrived in Holland and unloaded 45,000 pieces of Japanese porcelain and 101 pieces of gold lacquerware; another cargo manifest that same year lists 16,500 pieces of porcelain and 12 lacquerware panels.[169] The average yearly importation of Oriental ceramics to Holland seems to have been about 100,000 pieces in the last quarter of the seventeenth century.

Thus, Holland had another important historical role in establishing the *archés* of our inquiry into antiques, even though these imports from the Orient were new and not antique. The Dutch were the first to turn to the world of the Orient and import that world's material goods to the Occident in quantities huge enough to have an impact on their nation's entire public.

On the one hand, the Dutch vastly disseminated the conditions for a new aesthetic sensibility; this was just one implication and consequence of the past being a foreign country. Like the world of the past, the foreign is also a strange world. Things arriving from these worlds—worlds not here and not now—appeal to our conscious attention. Both the thing and their original meaning in the world in which they were created are to some degree beyond our pragmatic grasp and are alien to our immediate purposes. Even when they are usable, imported into our "home turf" from the past or from foreign soil, their sheer appearance makes us attune our attention to them imaginatively, hypothetically, aesthetically, so that they are not just the everyday pieces of equipment with which we engage ourselves routinely (almost unaware) in our everyday lives.[170] Thus, the quotidian object—the Chinese vase—became a candidate for aesthetic appreciation.

On the other hand, these imported Chinese ceramics were to become over time an important category of antiques connoisseurship and collecting in the modern sense. Holland provided the first *mass* entry port for oriental antiques to the Western world. Chinese blue and white porcelains themselves then became the impetus for the establishment of the native Dutch majolica manufacture of the Delftware type, creating a yet further class of future antiques much prized by collectors today. When a generation or so later the discovery of true porcelain was made in Europe in 1715, all the major manufacturers until the 1750s—Sèvres, Meissen, Vienna, and Venice (some of which even had their own branches in China)—more or less imitated these oriental motifs, sometimes accessorizing them with European variations or placing them on traditional European shapes.[171] In addition, the consequences of this trade for instigating the European taste for orientalizing motifs—the so-called chinoiserie and japonism of the next century—were enormous. (The influence first traveled abroad to France, where the first Trianon, *le Trianon de Porcelain* [of which nothing now remains], was erected in the 1670s; and within two decades had crossed the Channel, the Dutch influence being reinforced by the accession of William of Orange to the English throne in 1689.) But probably the most novel and noteworthy characteristic of Dutch collecting in this period was its move from the narrow class of reigning dukes, princes, and kings to the vastly broader class of *haute* (and even not-so-*haute*) *bourgeoisie*. This characteristic was to expand vastly in the next centuries in England, France, and the United States.

It is not yet the "middle class" but rather the aristocratic, wandering collectors and connoisseurs of the eighteenth century to whom we now turn our attention, the "Grand Tourists." Dr. Johnson put it simply in 1766: "A man who had not been in Italy is always conscious of an inferiority from his not having seen what is expected a man should see."[172] Where should he go? Certainly Italy. France, since it was on the way and worthy in its own right; and Holland too; and if time and money permitted, to Greece (and the Balkans) and possibly even a stay in Istanbul. And what should he see? All artworks and sites made famous in history and literature. And what do? Meet important people (he usually came prepared with letters of introduction) and enjoy the local "color" (this meant everything from the weather—which was bound to be better than England's—to food and other entertainments, sometimes intellectual, sometimes sensual). And of course much time was devoted to searching out small pieces of the foreign and the past to purchase and send back home, for now the past was seen in terms of a "foreign country" by the English Grand Tourist as never before. In the Italian Renaissance the past was at least literally, if not figuratively, still at home. And when, in section 2.3 above, we mentioned Medieval guidebooks to Rome that sometimes called the tourist's attention to the glorious history of classical sites and remains (as opposed to Christian ones), the referenced past in question was still the classical past. Now these Grand Tourists were referred to the remains of a more recent foreign past. There were guidebooks to Florence (which has no classical remains) as early as 1510. By the next century, according to R. W. B. Lewis, these "guidebooks were being written in several languages."[173]

In the first decade or two of the eighteenth century there was still some minor reluctance and suspicion of this kind of touring activity from certain portions of the English aristocracy, especially those portions that had overthrown or replaced the Stuart supporters of the prior century. In general, collectors and connoisseurs were considered a bit dull and eccentric (this especially by the "sporting set," who took their sensuous delights, apart from sex, only from the hunting of assorted wild creatures). Worse, they could be considered "subversive," according to Louise Lippincott's *Selling Art in Georgian London*, "as being Catholics, atheists, Jacobites, spies, or homosexuals."[174] (To view the persons on whom such suspicions fell, one need only look at Anthony van Dyck's famous 1638 painting of Lords John and Bernard Stuart, sons of the 3rd Duke of Lennox and cousins of Charles I. They pose for their portraits just before their departure on a three-year Grand Tour of the continent. Though their clothes and posture may to us seem foppish in the extreme, in fact they are dressed for their long journey, and according to a contemporary account, Lord John "was no delighted with the softness of the Court, but had dedicated himself to the profession of arms."[175] In any event, the young dukes both perished "manfully" in the Civil War fighting for the Stuart cause shortly after their return to England.)

However, several patriotic, Protestant Englishmen began to collect paintings while fighting or traveling abroad; Colonel (later General) Guise and James Brydges (the future Duke of Chandos) come to mind. Their example, coupled with increasing familiarity with foreign collections through the Grand Tour, did much to calm traditional suspicions and spark a positive fashion for collecting. "The 1720s and 1730s can be characterized as a time of enthusiastic importation of Continental art, encouraged by theoretical publication, acts of Parliament, and foreign tourism."[176] Soon books appeared which defended, encouraged, and instructed the Grand Tourist in such activities. Jonathan Richardson published the first English guide to the art treasures of Italy in 1722 and in 1719 had published his *Two Discourses*. Here he advances several arguments in favor of a gentleman's taking up collecting and connoisseurship and undertaking the Grand Tour as the best means toward this end. First, it enables one to understand the principles of artistic creation as a whole, beyond expertise in a particular artist. Second, it not only serves to improve the understanding but also fills one's leisure time pleasantly without leading one into behavior "Criminal, Scandalous, and Mischievous." Third, native English artists and craftsman could improve their work by seeing examples of what was acquired abroad. Fourth, one's connoisseurship and collection would itself attract interesting visitors to one's own estate. And last, in the long run one could reap financial benefits from the fineness and rarity of one's collection:

> many Summs of money which are now lavish'd away, and consum'd in Luxury . . . [could better be spent on] an Improving Estate: Since as Time and Accidents must continually waste and diminish the Number of those Curiosities, and no New Supply (Equal in Goodness to those we have) is to be hoped for, as the appearances of things at present are, the Value of such as are preserv'd with Care must necessarily encrease more and more.[177]

If this practical side of antiques collecting and connoisseurship took the form of the Grand Tour, a more philosophical approach to connoisseurship in England was offered by the 3rd Earl of Shaftsbury's *Letter Concerning Design* (1732), which "gave a lead to those, consciously discerning, who wished to explore the principles on which their discernment was based; and critical discrimination, or taste, became a fashion and almost a habit with a small but important class of society at the top."[178] More important, Shaftesbury's earlier work, *Characteristics* (1711), became the first British philosophical work to devote considerable and separate attention to beauty and the arts.[179] Despite its lack of system, *Characteristics* did introduce the principle of "disinterestedness" in the aesthetic judgment.[180] The idea that beauty had nothing whatsoever to do with *use* was perhaps an overreaction to the previous conceptions of art as in some way always bound up with and subservient to sociopolitical ends, or religious or moral purposes, or even philosophical ones. It was Shaftesbury's disciple, Francis Hutcheson (*Inquiry into the Original of Our Ideas of Beauty and Virtue*, 1725), who proposed that beauty was the perception of "uniformity amidst variety" and who was among the first in England to make a serious and clear attempt to free a philosophy of art or aesthetics from its moral and religious subservience. And this last point is worth emphasizing again, though we have already alluded to it often, especially vis-à-vis the *Querelle* and the Council of Trent. It is the idea of the "freedom" or "independence" of aesthetics from extraneous moral or epistemological concerns and consequently the "disinterestedness" of the aesthetic experience itself in the sense of its independence from extraneous pragmatic concerns (knowledge, usefulness, goodness) which is often singled out as essential to (if not the beginning of) modern aesthetics. Although some have seen it in Shaftesbury's own writings, a full-fledged and systematic philosophical exposition of such an aesthetic theory appears for the first time at the end of the eighteenth century in the German philosopher Kant in his *Critique of Judgment*. The point to be made is that the *explicit* elimination of "usefulness" and "moral/religious/political" preoccupations when experiencing an object aesthetically—even if not always a complete or consistent exclusion—was a crucial event in the creation of aesthetics and philosophy of art in the eighteenth century. It enabled this area of philosophical speculation, to be called "aesthetics," to set up its own territory with independent criteria.[181]

Now that the question of the historical origin of aesthetics and the idea of art and of craft has been explicitly raised in this chapter, it might be worthwhile to consider their relationship again. It has been claimed by Larry Shiner in *The Invention of Art* that art—the *idea* of art—entered the consciousness of Western society for the first time in the eighteenth century, particularly in and through German philosophical thought, and he means primarily such philosophers as Baumgarten, Lessing, and above all, Kant.[182] As we have seen, the particular theoretical consequence of the eighteenth-century theorizing about art was the proposal of a new mental faculty called "taste" to account for the subjective process that made the special encounter with "fine art" possible. And two novel consequences of this proposal were questions concerning (1) whether (and to what degree) this taste was culturally relative and (2) the role played by historical awareness in art interpretation.[183] Not until (and precisely when) "art" arose, Shiner says, so too did a theory of it. And then, for the first time, a "fateful division occurred in the traditional concept of art," he adds, so that *craft* was to be distinguished from *fine art* such that only the latter, as works of inspiration and genius, were "meant to be enjoyed for themselves in moments of refined pleasure."[184] He quotes M. H. Abrams's characterization of this change as a "Copernican revolution" in the concept of art, insofar as "in the course of a single century . . . the construction model . . . was replaced by the contemplation model, which treated the products of all the fine arts as . . . objects of rapt attention."[185]

As we noted earlier, however, the distinction between "fine art" and "craft" was not new. Aristotle made it in *The Physics*—on the basis of "imitation"—though the explicit theoretical consequences of his distinction were left, if not unnoticed, then undeveloped.[186] Indeed, Aristotle (at least in *The Poetics*) could well have been on his way to separating aesthetic theory and the principles and criteria for judging artworks from the domination of ethical and metaphysical preoccupations and principles.[187] In any case, the early-eighteenth-century psychological speculations of Shaftesbury and Hutcheson vis-à-vis "disinterestedness" in the object of aesthetic experience, and the consequences of the *Querelle* and Council of Trent that inspired a new science of taste already in the seventeenth century, hardly make "art" or "aesthetics" the child of the German philosophers of the eighteenth century alone.[188] Though without a formal theory to systematize and explain them, as we saw at the beginning of this archeology, the ancient Romans must have had in their minds independent principles and criteria for connoisseurship and collecting of not only art (both fine art and craft) but antiques as well; and the written and physical evidence that remains certainly suggests they had the taste to appreciate these works with aesthetic disinterestedness.

Furthermore, though Shiner and Abrams claim that the demarcation between fine art and craft was for "first time established" with Kant, for craft objects could be claimed to be objects of use and thus incapable of disinterested aesthetic appreciation whereas fine arts could only be contemplated, this was not in fact the case—and for several reasons. First, in his own discussion and classification of the "fine arts" Kant makes no such claim for the distinction, and he includes among the "fine arts" that he discusses both "landscape gardening" and "interior decoration."[189] Second, as early as the late sixteenth century there were several Italian authors who, basing their speculations mainly on interpolations of Aristotle's *Poetics*, began to regroup "the arts." Vasari's *Lives* coined the phrase "arti del disegno" (arts of design) as its guiding principle, and from this idea the French phrase "beaux arts" was probably derived.[190] Moreover, it was the Abbé Batteux, in *Les beaux arts réduits à un même principe* (1746), who was really the first to distinguish the fine arts from craft with the principle "usefulness for some other end" (hence denoting a "mechanical" art) versus "pleasure as an end in itself" (hence a fine, or *beau*, art), thus freeing the fine arts from their subservience as a mere means to some higher practical (i.e., moral or religious) end. (At the same time, however, in deference to the ancients, the Abbé Batteux also tried to include the older Aristotelian principle of "imitation of beauty in nature" as a common requirement for all *beaux arts*.)[191] In any case and more to our particular concern, third, in the practical realm of connoisseurship and collecting at the time, the reverse had been in fact occurring: now, at least in the area of antiques collecting and connoisseurship, for the first time (assuming we can exempt the instance mentioned earlier—the "old citron wood" table that Cicero failed to obtain), connoisseurs of antiques collected "decorative arts" (i.e., crafts), and in their contemplation received the same "disinterested satisfaction" supposedly available only from the "fine arts."

England's Neo-classical, or "Augustan," age was established by the prosperity ushered in by the prime ministry of Robert Walpole in the first half of the eighteenth century. As John Steegman puts it in *The Rule of Taste*:

> Certainly until about the middle of the reign of George III [1790] it was necessary for a gentleman of quality to acquire a familiarity with the fine arts, to learn at least the names and particularities of those Italian painters most in demand or to master the rules of Palladian architecture. . . . [And therefore] when collecting became a fashionable pursuit about the middle of the 18th century the great majority of those who bought pictures did so in obedience to the commands of authority, defying the vituperations of Hogarth.[192] First Italy, then the Low Countries, were ransacked by the collectors and dealers; France too was thoroughly searched. . . . Before long the Fine Arts came to be regarded as the only intellectual activity for which enthusiasm was not only permissible but desirable. It is not intended to suggest that the whole governing class suddenly became devoted to The Arts, but an important section of it (not only in London) did. . . . Evidence of this is seen in the foundation, about 1732 or 1733, of the Society of Dilletanti . . . most [of whose members] were young men . . . which gave the Society so great an influence on the taste of so many successive generations. . . . For 100 years every enterprise of artistic or antiquarian importance, at home, in Greece, in Italy, or in the Near East, was either undertaken or supported by the Society, as a whole or acting through individual members; more particularly its activities were devoted to the study of classical antiquities, and it was the money of the Dilettanti that made possible the surveys of Gavin Hamilton or Stuart and Revett. . . . There was certainly, after about 1740, a widespread interest among educated people in archeology, and an interest in the past became a fashionable affectation.[193]

In 1719, one early Grand Tourist, Lord Burlington (Richard Boyle), bringing William Kent back with him from Italy, began building his own villa in Chiswick in accordance with the Palladian and classical models they had seen abroad, filling it with his various Continental acquisitions, antique household furnishings of every sort. Moreover, he became an adviser for many friends who also were building a home to be "the physical expression of the standing of their family and the tangible repository of its traditions."[194] The Grand Tour was becoming part of this family tradition. But now this collection of the foreign and past was not limited to paintings, sculpture, and architectural fragments but included furniture as well. This was a "new" development, for as Alsop notes, "old furniture was never collected before the 18th century."[195]

The manner of travel was, though much more difficult, also much more luxurious than today. In 1780 the young British aesthete William Beckford set off in three carriages (for retainers and luggage) of such richness and style that he was mistaken for the Habsburg emperor. Once in Italy (having stopped in France briefly), Beckford, like the typical young English aristocrat, would naturally be introduced to the likes of Joseph Smith, who was then serving as consul to the Republic of Venice and whom Horace Walpole once baptized "the Merchant of Venice." Visiting his sumptuous palazzo, such tourists would "happen upon" Canalettos and other *vedute* (which recorded in such glowing canvasses the splendid sights of the ancient city). These the good consul could obligingly be induced to part with for a certain compensation. No surprise that young Beckford returned to England with 878 pieces of baggage.

Horace Walpole himself, son of Prime Minister Robert Walpole, while in Rome in 1740 at the age of twenty-three, wrote home: "I am so far gone in medals, lamps, idols, prints &c . . . I would buy the Coliseum if I could."[196] One contemporary English traveler reported that so famous were these tourists that Romans joked, "Were our amphitheater portable, the English would carry it off."[197] Not all natives had so sanguine a view of the rapacious English; one proverb deriving from their huge presence ran: "Inglese italianato e un diavolo incarnato" (An Italianized Englishman is a devil incarnate).[198]

Roman antiquities and paintings by the great masters of the Renaissance were most sought, but they were also (except for forgeries) not generally available. Coins, collections of antique hardstone cameos, terracottas, bronzes, micromosaic pictures, and jewelry were more easily obtained. But more recent works, made especially for these *milordis* as souvenirs, were substituted as required. They were the cityscape picture postcards of their day. Canaletto's paintings of Venice are now generally considered the greatest of these, having themselves become "old masters." In 1703 Luca Carlevaris (1663–1730) published *Fabriche e vedute di Venita*, probably the earliest collection of these Venetian "views," to make "knowledge of the magnificent treasures of Venice more widespread in foreign countries."[199] Also popular were miniature versions carved in marble of famous buildings or portions of them (such as pediments, porticoes, or columns, often in sets of assorted orders); these could serve not only as souvenirs but also as study tools for students.

Besides playing the tourist, an alternative for the more educationally minded was to enroll in a university. Paris and Padua were favorites. For the more politically connected, one could become an ambassador or

consul from the Court of St. James. Joseph Smith (1674–1770), mentioned above, began his career as a merchant; later becoming British
consul to Venice, he simply continued this occupation in a different category of merchandise and on a different scale. He himself acquired the
greatest collection of contemporary Venetian artworks (as well as
gems, illuminated manuscripts, etc.). They were later sold (1762) to
George III.

But perhaps the greatest of these consul-cum-connoisseur-cum-
collectors was Sir William Hamilton, British plenipotentiary to Naples
for thirty-six years, from 1764 to 1800. While chiefly remembered in the
romantic literature as the husband of the beautiful and talented Emma
Hamilton, mistress of Horatio Nelson, he was a superb archeologist for
his day. His collection of antiquities from the nearby ruins of Pompeii
(only recently rediscovered in 1748) was sold to the British Museum in
1772, and his researches led to the publication of several books on Etruscan, Greek, and Roman antiquities; these, in turn, had a tremendous
impact on Neo-classical taste in England and France.[200] In Joshua
Reynolds's portrait of him, he sits surrounded by his Greek vases; and his
collection served as the source of props for Emma's "Attitudes" (i.e.,
tableaux vivants). Hamilton had amassed more than one hundred gold
ornaments and three hundred examples of ancient glass in his first years
in Italy, bought in the main from the nascent Neapolitan market in ancient art supplied by farmers and clandestine diggers. Visiting him on
May 27, 1787, Goethe described the following scene:

> Everything was in a state of terrible confusion. Products of every epoch
> were thrown together at random: busts, torsos, vases, bronzes, paintings,
> and chance bargains of every sort; even a small chapel. Out of curiosity I
> pushed aside the lid of a long case on the floor; in it were two magnificent
> bronze candelabra. I caught Hackert's eye and asked him in a whisper if
> these were not very much like those in the museum at Portici. He silenced
> me with a look; no doubt they had strayed here from the cellars of Pompeii
> by a sideward path. Doubtless these and other lucky acquisitions are the
> reason why Sir William shows his hidden treasures only to the most inti-
> mate friends.[201]

But mention of Goethe and of Walpole brings out another antiquarian
ideal of the times, one that was contrary to the neo-classical style,
whether in its monarchical Roman or democratic Greek mode. This was
the Gothic style. It needs now to be discussed—and along with it another
(and entirely foreign) *anti-classical* style, "chinoiserie." For in these deliberate alternatives to the mainstream aesthetic, the classical rule of

taste, we find other important aspects (*archés*) of the mentality that underpins the modern conception and appreciation of the antique.

Horace Walpole's construction of Strawberry Hill (about 1750) is usually taken as the start of the Gothic Revival.[202] On the other hand, the Gothic had never really entirely disappeared from England (Kenneth Clark notes the existence of a "faint stream" of traditional Gothic continuing from the sixteenth century, especially in university and ecclesiastical contexts);[203] and the Gothic did not really achieve its full stride until, as part of the Romantic movement in the next century, it became the first of the Victorian eclectic revivalist styles, the Gothick.[204] Literary stimuli for the style appeared in Goethe's *Deutsche Baukunst* (1772), which extolled Strasbourg Cathedral,[205] and Richard Hurd's *Letters on Chivalry and Romance* (1762). Even though the structures depicted are classical, the widely published Roman engravings of Piranesi (1720–78) and Pannini (1691–1765), with their lushly overgrown ruins set in moldering landscapes, similarly evoke the Gothic mood; and these may be taken as contributing a visual stimulus.

But what was the aesthetic stimulus for the Gothic? First, it may be seen as a revolt against the "tyranny of regularity"[206] that the Augustan classicism required. But there were other reasons. It was, especially for the English, as *historical and national a past* as could legitimately be adopted. Consequently, for those who were building homes to be "the physical expression of the standing of their family and the tangible repository of its traditions"[207]—especially if that newly established family had no traditions—it legitimated the family tradition better than the trinkets obtained via the Grand Tour, for it was natively English. (Anglo-Saxon remains were rare; Norman ones not much more common, and French in origin anyway; the great cathedrals were gloriously English Gothic.) As Steegman notes, "many of these newer recruits to the privileged classes were anxious to make the homes on their recently bought estates look more nearly as if they had been built by founders of their line."[208]

Furthermore, in comparison with the classical, Gothic's lack of clarity and its asymmetricality (or perceived asymmetricality) had the effect of suggesting, on the one hand, mystery and religious associations and, on the other, ruination and decay. Many extant genuine Gothic examples (deserted abbeys and monasteries) were in ruins. This, in turn, suggested *distance*—both as a pastness with all its physical effects of agedness plainly in evidence and as a non-utilitarian otherworldliness. That "distance" of necessity disengaged the mind from its immediate workaday preoccupations and turned it toward metaphysical speculation, historical rumination, and, ultimately, aesthetic contemplation. The implications and consequences of the past "being like" (or simply "being") another country turn out to be multiple. But they stem from the same source: the fact that both the past and the alien are beyond our present pragmatic grasp. Confronted by artifacts enduring from the past or imported from abroad, our customary everyday moment-to-moment attention is disrupted; we are, consequently, required to attune ourselves to them in a mode different from (and thus altering) our quotidian habits of attention.

Moreover, in their decay, ruined Gothic structures also seemed to be returning to nature and its organic and biomorphic shapes (as opposed to the tectonic forms we expect in architecture), creating a dynamic tension between the structure's imagined pristine unity in the past and its present appearance to our senses in corrupted form. Such decay elicits an appreciation and awareness (even if only implicit and incipient) of the ineluctable mutability of all manmade objects that have endured and of the physical consequences of the passage of time.[209] From this perspective, what the Baroque of the seventeenth century did for art by way of embodying *temporality per se* in aesthetic experience of the artwork, the Gothic revival of the eighteenth (and nineteenth) century did by way of focusing aesthetic attention on the physical *endurance of the past* in the object. As Lowenthal (whose magisterial *The Past Is a Foreign Country* is essentially a "history of pastness" in Western consciousness) points out, "seeing the past as a different realm was no historical revolution, as it is termed, but a plant of slow growth nurtured by secularism, increasing scrutiny of evidence, and awareness of anachronism." He adds, "The past's alien character came to be widely recognized and accepted only near the [end of the nineteenth] century,"[210] for only when a culture has a complete enough and accurate enough idea of the past, of history, can it appreciate an object's pastness. Ruskin was later to assert that "rents or fractures or stains or vegetation assimilate the architecture with the work of nature" so that "the eye is delighted by injuries which are the work of time," and William Morris was to claim that "the natural weathering of a building is beautiful and its loss disastrous." These merely apply to the domain of architecture the aesthetic sensibility that Joseph Addison noted 130 years earlier in 1711 with regard to the medium of painting when he described Time as a craftsman perfecting every painting with mellowness.[211]

This taste for evidence of age was so strong that contemporary art dealers often smoked their paintings to make them more desirable.[212] Meanwhile, the Gothic's association with Nature and the biomorphic also combined well with another style that lingered on through the neo-classical—the Rococo—and the taste for the "grotto-esque," particularly as it was manifested in furniture and metalwork. It was in this mode that the Gothic was associated especially with what was called the "picturesque." And in this mode we can detect the first historical instance of the explicit and collective recognition and appreciation of the *pure aesthetic* effect of age on the beauty of the object. Uvedale Price, in his *Essay on the Picturesque* (1794), stated: "I do not mean to infer that an object to be Picturesque must be old and decayed, but that the most beautiful objects will become so from the effects of age and decay."[213] This way of speaking (like Addison's and Ruskin's noted above) suggests an appreciation of agedness as an aesthetic (rather than merely historical) phenomenon, and hence an appreciation that is quite different from the purely antiquarian and testimonial force of prior preferences for signs of age. It bespeaks an appreciation more emotive and associative (more Romantic) and less critical and cognitive (less classical).[214]

Finally, although we have mentioned the appeal of classicism for the new social and political ideals of the time, the Gothic had its own appropriate associations in this regard: the image of Medieval men and women living in communitarian conditions close to the soil and in harmony with nature, manifesting their virtue in honest labor that through ancient skills produced objects of enduring value. Ruskin and others took up the image in the Romanticism of the next century, and even Marx was not immune to this idyll, on which the general critique of the industrial revolution and its products and of capitalism and its social consequences was drawn.

This new aesthetic mentality required satisfaction. Since genuine Medieval Gothic with signs of ruin and decay did not exist in sufficient quantities to answer popular demand, new Gothic works were devised and aged. William Kent, the most famous landscape architect of the period, even planted a row of dead trees for a complementary landscaping project, though his preferred style of architecture was strictly neo-Palladian. And William Gilpin (along with Augustus Pugin the most important architect and designer of the Gothic revival in construction) advised how "to give the stone its moldering appearance—to make the widening chink run naturally through all the joints—to mutilate the ornaments—to peel the facing from the internal structure" and to "scatter heaps of ruin with negligence." But he added that the ruin must be put "at last into the hands of nature to adorn . . . [for] time alone . . . gives it perfect beauty."[215] Such were the various causes and consequences, the various presuppositions and conditions of the Gothic revival.

The other anti-classical style was called, collectively, "chinoiserie." Here, then, is the appearance of the "foreign country," the other form of "distancing," that by introducing alien elements (objects or motifs) into the present induces in the observer an aesthetic attunement to (rather than practical engagement with) the object. Today we would think of this as limited to Chinese style and distinguish it from, say, "japonism," but in the eighteenth century, "chinoiserie" encompassed all Far Eastern and Near or Middle Eastern art styles, including African, Indian, Persian, even Arab-Islamic motifs—all best typified by and culminating in that most eclectic of royal confections, George IV's Pavilion at Brighton, completed in 1818. Very few Englishmen or Frenchmen actually traveled to these foreign (i.e., non-European) regions in the eighteenth century— they were never part of the Grand Tour mentality—except for purposes of trade or conquest. Yet this conquest, and even more this trade, had its effect. Like the Gothic, but even more powerfully and more subtly, chinoiserie served as an antidote to the dominant contemporary style of the eighteenth century, the familiar straitjacket of neo-classicism. Unlike the Gothic, it could never be construed as a revived style or as a commemoration of the domestic past, even of the common European past. It was purely foreign. But for this very reason chinoiserie had yet another important consequence: it further culturally diversified and universalized the Western aesthetic sensibility.

Like the Gothic, chinoiserie combined well with the Rococo alternative to the Augustan neo-classical in England. And again, most often it manifested itself in the decorative arts such as furniture. In the 1750s designers such as Thomas Chippendale,

> seeing that imported Chinese wall papers were beginning to decorate some of the more advanced boudoires and bedrooms, forthwith introduced into the back of his chairs and galleries of his tables, that lattice work pattern that seems to form the balustrades of so many little bridges on porcelain or paper. With great dexterity he gave a Chinese flavour to some of his most intricate rococo work . . . [such as one sees in] those immense mirrors [surmounted by] a strange scene wherein macaws in palm branches hold pomegranates in their claws . . . or fight with herons among the arabesques of limewood.[216]

Several factors stimulated this taste. First was the economic one, the China trade that brought tea and silk and lacquerware and (most important in its consequences for the antique) Chinese porcelains directly to England. Chinoiserie also arrived in England via France through the importation of French decorative arts, especially silks and carpets. At the carpet manufactories at Aubusson in the second half of the eighteenth century fanciful designs of "butterflies tickling the noses of Europeans and pig-tailed cavaliers shooting centipedes with cannon" were mixed with traditional European motifs: Chinese shepherdesses à Watteau and pilgrims from Compostela complete with scallop shell.[217] It also arrived via France in the powerful influence of Watteau, whose transformative genius created through his paintings (such as *The Embarkation for Cythera*) a European analogue for "life's sweet taste" that mirrored the Chinese artistic mood of refined luxuries and delicate, peaceful amusements of the "scholar class."

And even more than the Gothic, chinoiserie was a sort of "guilty pleasure," a "private pleasure," in eighteenth-century England, providing an exotic world where one would prefer, at least for a brief time in the imagination, to live. As the very antidote to the real world (i.e., the common pragmatic workaday world), which was dominated by the rule of taste, the world of chinoiserie was deemed frivolous, not to say antinomian, in comparison. Thus, it was, up to the very end, given a subsidiary role in decoration. It governed a bizarre and unexpected world that existed privately behind a number of very English Georgian neo-classical façades. As Steegman comments, it was a world

> wherein mandarins, rajahs, and elephants wandered round the walls of boudoires, among weeping-willows and pagodas. While the dignified façades, the west fronts, the south fronts, the entrance halls and the State apartments continued according to the rule, somewhere, it was felt, in some anteroom or bed chamber, or some pavilion in the park, it might be permissible to be a little less English, and . . . experiment with something that was not included under the safe heading of "Good Taste." . . . [So] they lived among dragons and temple bells, and wore Oriental gowns over their hoops . . . often had themselves painted wearing a "Moorish" turban with a Chinese, or sometimes Turkish robe and Turkish slippers," and for a time preferred the employment of "Chinese house-boys to Negroes."[218]

We have already noted Watteau and the tapestries and carpets of Aubusson, but the etiology and role of chinoiserie in the French aesthetic experience (and its role in establishing the appreciation for the antique in the modern sense) was parallel to that of the English.[219] The only difference was the national form that the dominant rule of taste took. In France that rule was embodied in the three successive Louis styles. Chinoiserie was the exotic form—together with what we would call the Gothic, but to a lesser degree than in England—that was the antidote to these official

Louis styles (except when easily incorporated, as they sometimes were in
the Rococo of Louis XV but not in the Baroque of Louis XIV or the Neo-
classical of Louis XVI) until the Revolution of 1789. In France in the
eighteenth century, in fact, as Saisselin points out, the idea of "gothic"
was construed in such a "highly comprehensive manner"—by Mon-
tesquieu, for example—that the term included "the Egyptian, Chinese,
and Indian arts," and was thought of "not as the style of any particular
people, but rather as the style of the birth of art," that is, as a generic
term for naive or primitive art.[220] With the French Revolution, however,
the virtuous and earnest sobriety of neo-classicism in a new, "citizenly"
guise completely overwhelmed the "frivolousness" of chinoiserie/Gothic,
which, together with the Rococo with which it had been often combined,
was seen as part of the decadence of the ancien régime. The inhibition of
the Gothic in France was only temporary, of course, for in the next century it was revived with even greater vigor—for both Balzac and Thiers
were enamored of Gothic and in the mid-nineteenth century filled their
homes to overflowing with Limoges enamels and monstrances from
Rheims, while Viollet-le-Duc re-gothicized the decayed French architectural heritage throughout the nation. But during the Revolution itself, republican values required classicism, for classicism was both inherently
"native" and eternal.

We turn to the further consequences of this momentous revolutionary
event for antiques in a moment. But first we must summarize the archeological significance of the current subject. True, chinoiserie was not an
aesthetic mode that directly evoked the image of a world now past and
physically embodied agedness in signs of ruination, as did the Gothic in
its narrow sense. Yet following Descartes and Lowenthal, it has, in its exoticism, a similar *imaginary* force, insofar as the past is conceived as a
foreign country. Apart from this, there was in the use of chinoiserie a
playful and imaginative *mixing of styles* on a scale never before attempted. It was also, like the Gothic but even more powerfully, a means
of escape from the dominant aesthetic of the present as well as the concerns of the workaday world of the here and now.

But most important, chinoiserie (and to some degree Gothic revival)
was a stylistic mode that elevated the aesthetic status of even (and especially) quotidian objects, products of what would today be classified
as the decorative or applied arts in distinction from the fine arts. Chinoiserie appeared, after all, not in painting and sculpture (and certainly
not in literature), and only subordinately and usually derivatively
and privately in architecture, but in wallpaper, furniture, and the like.

Above all, it appeared in the Chinese ceramics that were being imported as cargo ballast in huge quantities. These were directly used, and in their use, imaginary and exotic worlds—past and foreign—were evoked.

Even more significantly, the best of these porcelains could be, and usually were, in accord with the French preference, given *bronze doré* mountings in the rococo mode that specifically elevated their status as objets d'art. Like the Medieval custom recounted above that revivified objects of the pagan classical past by resetting and incorporating them in new ecclesiastical objects, the French took not the object from the European past but the exotic foreign object (whether old or new—but even when new usually done in a traditional style) and remounted it for their own world. But we must note the important reversal. Medieval practice took what were originally art objects in the past (cameos, ivory carvings, etc.)—that is, objects of purely aesthetic appreciation—and turned them into objects for current use, usually a liturgical use. But the French of the eighteenth century took what were ordinary objects of use (bowls, cups, vases) in their native context and, by mounting them in expensive, convoluted, gilt-bronze frames that usually rendered their original function impossible or irrelevant, transformed them into objects of pure aesthetic contemplation, performing a transfiguration of the Asian commonplace object into the European art object.

It was the *marchands-merciers* who began this practice. These decorators/antiques dealers, whose shops tended to cluster around the rue Saint Honoré in Paris near the Louvre, were prohibited by law from producing *new* objects (thereby interfering with the charters and rights of the artisanal trades) but not from embellishing (*enjoliver*) old ones.[221] (In their dealings in secondhand goods, goods that they made enticing to customers by reference to their provenance and prior ownership, they engaged just another form of "embellishment.") In was in this same eighteenth-century context that the *bibelot*—the small object of beauty and rarity—came into its own. With the death of Louis XIV, the "old aristocracy gradually were obliged to sell the major works acquired by their ancestors," thereby establishing a "vogue for the lighter and less pompous styles" and smaller objects. Their lifestyles reduced in scale, they started moving into the large apartment houses of the Paris Faubourg, requiring a new and smaller type of decoration.[222]

The "embellished" exotic import, the ceramic vase or the painted lacquer panel from China, was thus consistent with (and useful to the practice of) this new taste in comfortable living for the affluent. Hence, we may extend Lowenthal's perceptive comment regarding knowledge of the *past* to knowledge of the *foreign*. Only when Western civilization had sufficient knowledge (in both quantitative and qualitative terms) of the exotic civilizations of the globe, their histories and culture, could the products of these civilizations take on the aura of an imaginative context rich enough to evoke a more or less coherent world for enjoyment, rather than remain merely what they had been in the preceding century—bizarre imported curiosities, *Wundersachen*.[223] Still, one should not imagine that this knowledge was "accurate" in the modern sense. And certainly the appreciation for the foreign was in no way based on the modern sense of respect (much less homage) due to all indigenous cultures of the world and their products (in some spirit of cultural diversity). Saisselin remarks on the

> hold Greco-Roman civilization still exercised on the minds of the educated classes [in the eighteenth century]. . . . In view of this why expect the Europeans to consider the arts of other civilizations seriously? . . . The discussions bearing on the relativity of taste were [therefore] academic. Taste was justified by the conviction of cultural superiority. . . . True art and its complement, true taste, were a European monopoly, its privileged possession, yet only in certain high moments of history [i.e., classical and neo-classical revivals]. Art was good insofar as it approached these ideal moments of perfection.[224]

Greater changes were to arrive with Romanticism in the next century. Still, one must consider the difference between the overt and conscious awareness and a more subtle, unconscious one. "To consider the arts of other civilizations seriously" in the sense of the rational calculation and critique of the relative worth of a civilization and its products has little actual effect on a purely aesthetic response to them. In the mid-eighteenth century the reaction (whether positive or negative) to Rousseau's critique of "civilization" per se (and the advancements it was supposed to have brought to humanity) shows how embedded the conscious idea of the inevitable progress of civilization through reason had become for mainstream thinking. The frivolity and anti-rationalism of chinoiserie, its antinomianism as much as its foreignness, coupled with the Gothic's elevation of a non-classical (indeed, an anti-classical) past, were simply aesthetic analogues of the rejection of this more "serious consideration." Meanwhile, the sheer volume of foreign objects' presence in the life and taste of the times, especially in the usages to which they were actually put, regardless of their status in the official hierarchy of taste, would soon have momentous consequences for the understanding of and appreciation of the antique in the wake of the revolutions to come.

2.6
Revolutions Romantic and Industrial:
The Nineteenth Century

We have already noted the tremendous impact that the French Revolution had on the availability of antiques. In France it encouraged that movement to the smaller and the quotidian object which was already in progress on native ground, while the grandest objects of Versailles were dispersed to foreign aristocracies elsewhere.[225]

But it is with the Age of Napoleon that we find the next stage in the development of the idea of the antique. Clausewitz's famous maxim that "war is the continuation of politics by other means" needs an extension. War is the continuation of trade by other means. As Marx so often argued and as even Plato observed in *The Republic*,[226] war is a consequence of the desire to obtain at any cost what is not available "at home" when the normal modes of international economic exchange fail. War is therefore also a continuation of intercultural awareness by other—more forceful and confrontational, more *extra*ordinary—means.[227] Of course, war is highly destructive of the products of civilization, even internally. Thus, French revolutionaries, thinking them representations of the kings of France, ordered destroyed the twenty-eight monumental figures ornamenting the West façade of Nôtre Dame. (They were in fact sculptures depicting the kings of Judea; and fortunately in this instance a pious collector secretly purchased and buried them, and they were eventually dug up in 1977.) But, destructive both internally and externally, war has its positive effects as well—for art, just as it has for other civilizational accomplishments. We noted very early in this history the effects of war and empire for the classical Roman consciousness of and taste for Greek antiques as objects of collection and connoisseurship. What were the effects of the Napoleonic Wars?

As Marx states in *The 18th Brumaire of Louis Bonaparte* (1852), "the revolution of 1789 to 1814 draped itself alternatively as the Roman Republic and the Roman Empire."[228] The democratic and imperial spirit each took on its own aesthetic formulation of the fundamental neoclassical style—the first Greek and light, in the pale blues and whites of the dying Rococo, the other Roman and heavy, in the red and gold of the emergent Empire. The period of transition between them (Marx's dates above are apt) also coincided with a curious tension between an inclusive universalism (or cosmopolitanism), expressed in Enlightenment-inspired tracts asserting the universal and inalienable rights of all humanity, and a chauvinistic nationalism, the French people as the vanguard of liberation and the bearers of a new world order. Cosmopolitan universalism, as opposed to national chauvinism, could take either the democratic guise (all men are equal and free citizens of a world of humanity) or an imperial form (the world needs an enlightened despot who knows how to unify the whole of mankind through imposing the universal laws of peace and justice). And with either form of universalism came the idea of a common human and universal heritage because, as Heidegger has noted, it was the Enlightenment that "elaborated for the first time in basic clarity the idea of universal history . . . above and beyond all nations."[229] Napoleon's wars began, after all, as war on behalf of an international ideal of "Humanity" based on eighteenth-century Enlightenment principles of the abstract rights of man, even if these wars soon became a function of national, French, indeed personal, imperialism.

As Jon King remarks regarding style and taste during the age of Napoleon, "furniture and decorative arts created during his rise, reign, and fall reflect the character and personality of his regime, and, at the same time, not unconsciously recall the grandeur of ancient Greece, Italy, and Egypt."[230] Thus, for example, the "Madeleine" Church begun by Pierre Vignon in 1807 for Napoleon as a "temple of glory" for his troops symbolically links Napoleon with Augustan Rome in its appearance. But it is only an appearance, a shell, encasing an interior capped with three domes of a form typical of Byzantine and Aquitanian Romanesque churches,[231] a Christian church "clothed in the costume of pagan Rome," as Helen Gardner remarks.[232] Similarly, Napoleon's desire to imitate Rome resulted in reenactments of Ancient Roman triumphs he ordered staged in Paris, where such works as the "Apollo Belvedere" (looted—or should one say "liberated"?—from the Vatican in the Italian campaign) were carried through the streets to celebrate "La Fête de la Liberté et des Arts." (It is interesting to note here the explicit connection between "liberty" and "art," as if the arts were seen as the natural adjunct of liberation.) One might view the looting of works by Napoleon in his campaigns as simply a "cultural rape" whereby the "victors declare their power by taking the art of the defeated as trophies"[233]—and one would likely be correct in this interpretation for many times and places in

earlier and subsequent history—but in this instance it was not so much a
rape of trophies as an *incorporation* or absorption of the achievements
of past civilizations because of respect and admiration for them (homage
to rather than contempt *for* them). In this we find a situation very similar
to the process we observed in ancient Rome itself vis-à-vis ancient
Greece. How like Verres was Napoleon, even early in his career, in carrying out the order of the Directoire to confiscate on behalf of the newly
created Musée Central great historical masterpieces of art as his armies
passed through the Mediterranean world (including Egypt and the Levant).[234] It demonstrated France's political victory, to be sure, but it also
demonstrated the culmination and preservation of human civilization in
and through this triumph, France's universalist "mission civilatrice."
Consequently, while it is in part true, as Arthur Danto puts it, that the
Musée Napoleon "gathered through conquest the highest artistic trophies of the nations conquered . . . [so that] the French citizens entering
the space of the museum [could] feel the power of the nation to which they
belonged,"[235] creating a sense of intense nationalism and self-pride, this
museum—like all the others shortly to follow—soon created in its atten-
dees not simply nationalist pride but rather a sense of awe and delight in
the divers achievements of human civilization. And the idea of the museum as institution moved from the concept of the trophy case to that of
an organization and institution devoted to universal scholarship and a
foundation housing objects for the aesthetic delectation of all persons.[236]

Besides the revival of the classical ideal at home in Imperial Roman
form, there was the serious study of antiquity beyond the perimeters of
Europe. This is especially so in the case of Egypt. Napoleon's encyclopedic *La description de l'Egypt* (printed in twenty-two huge volumes between 1809 and 1829) brought genuine scholarship to Egyptophile taste.
Earlier Egyptian *stylistic* references in European art and décor were
mainly fragmented quotes, mostly imaginary. And 99 percent of all references in art to Egypt as a *subject matter* (from Giotto to Raphael, and
Poussin to Rembrandt) were biblical in inspiration and function. Hence-
forth Egyptian motifs were (or *could* be) accurate and genuine rather
than fanciful. And ancient Egypt became a place and time with its own
self-subsistent culture and history, no longer having merely a borrowed
and adjunct existence or value.[237] And there were the objects of Egypt
themselves that could be acquired and brought back home. The Rosetta
Stone, found by Napoleon's troops, was in turn looted by the English
from the French as one of the truce conditions that permitted the French
to quit Egypt in peace after Nelson's victory at Abukir.

Of course most of the wars were fought in Europe. Steegman describes in detail the consequences of the Napoleonic Wars there for the antiques trade:

> As the French armies advanced through Piedmont or across the Alps into Lombardy and the Papal territories, or as the British armies advanced from Portugal into Spain and on towards the Pyrenees, they were followed by other armies, the armies of the collectors' agents and dealers in works of art; dwellers in the invaded areas, panic-stricken, were anxious to turn their goods into some more portable form of wealth, while at the same time victorious generals usually celebrated their victories by looting palaces of the vanquished, and of course it was always possible that the victors might in turn be defeated, and their booty again looted, or at the worst purchased very cheaply. Although these acquisitive camp-followers undoubtedly faced many real dangers, the prizes made any risk worth while, and shiploads of treasures found their way to England, for, though there was some risk of capture at sea, the English fleets were a very fair guarantee of safety. And since England was one of the few countries not invaded by the French; and since, therefore, there was no sudden dispersal of English capital; and since, thanks to the Industrial Revolution and de-spite our subsidising of most of our allies, there was a considerable amount of money in this country, England became the natural and obvious goal for most of what had been so advantageously secured by the campaigning dealers.[238]

What, then, were the consequences of the Napoleonic Wars for con-noisseurship and appreciation of antiques? In material and pragmatic terms they made available (as do all wars) a vast array of the objects of prior civilizations to new owners and did so on an international (i.e., extra-European) scale. They also fostered a serious scholarly concern to understand and a connoisseur-motivated passion to appreciate and value the achievements of the past of distant civilizations on their own terms—not just Greece and Rome, and not just "chinoiseries" by way of decora-tion and stylistic quotation. Egypt is the best example of this, inspiring what has been called an "Egyptomania" (recurring in the 1920s with the discovery of Tutankhamen's tomb by Carter), but Syria/Lebanon, Iran, and the Extreme Orient were not far behind.

The Napoleonic Wars also profoundly altered the conception of the past and of Western civilization's sensibility to it. "After the guillotine and Napoleon the previous world seemed irretrievably remote—hence to many doubly dear [as] industrialization and forced migration [uprooted] millions," Lowenthal remarks. And although it is not quite true, as Lowenthal claims, that "up to the 19th century those who gave any

thought to the historical past supposed it to be much like the present
[and therefore in no great need of preservation]—because as we have
seen this awareness of the past's *pastness* was already a feature of the Renaissance sensibility toward Antiquity—Lowenthal is correct in hs claim
that

> only in the late 18th century did Europeans begin to conceive of the past as
> a different realm, not just another country but a congeries of *foreign* lands
> endowed with unique histories and personalities. This new past . . . came
> to be cherished as a heritage that validated and exalted the present. And
> the new role heightened concern to save relics and restore monuments as
> emblems of communal identity, continuity, and aspiration. . . . It is now
> no longer the presence of the past that speaks to us, but its pastness.[239]

The mention of "industrialization" introduces another novel factor
into the conception of, sensibility for, and appreciation of the antique. It
was, after all, another revolution. Mass production of virtually identical
objects, many of which were poorly made and/or ugly in comparison
with their handmade predecessors (even if one discounts the reality of
planned obsolescence at this early stage of capitalism), soon further stimulated the preference for the past object, the antique.

As we have moved through this archeology of the antique, we have repeatedly found in the dominant art-historical style of each particular era
a clue to or facet of the contemporary development of the modern idea
and appreciation of the antique. It is to be expected that the archeology
of the antique is reflected in the art of an era and the general aesthetic
consciousness of (indeed within the entire weltanschauung of) a historical epoch. Hence, in the Medieval period we found the distancing of the
past, in the Renaissance the recapitulation of it in an attempt to retrieve
it, in Mannerism the appreciation of the stylistic possibilities of art itself
as the true subject matter of art, in the Baroque the beginnings of world-
expansiveness and world-incorporation, and so on. It is not surprising,
then, that the antique-relevant factors we have noted in the preceding
paragraphs readily find their reflection, intersection, and culmination in
the dominant art style at the beginning of the nineteenth century: Romanticism.

Romanticism espoused a new freedom from the classical ideal (in both
form and content) in the arts. In some respects Romanticism may also be
seen as a consequence of the failure of the Enlightenment's optimism. We
have already referred to Rousseau's critique of civilization. Reason's self-
assurance was deflated as it turned on itself and saw its own limits. The natural world exhibited a radical uniqueness of particulars and unexplained

and mysterious phenomena (wild, sublime) that were not rationalizable, systematizable, or classifiable; the human mind, too, seemed to escape rationalization, for its essence seemed at bottom an abyss of infinite longing, a thirst that only imagination, intuition, revelation could hope to satisfy. This led in turn to a skepticism regarding the future and the perfectibility of man. Let us note four of the consequences of these attitudes here for the purpose of establishing some further *archés* in the evolution of the idea of the antique.

(1) Romanticism exhibited a marked nostalgia for the past, but especially the ruin, the "gothic," the desolate and forever lost. In the decorative arts, this preference encouraged the recapitulation of past styles that we find in the Victorian era's successive revivals, a process that occupied the entire century up to around 1895 and the development of "Art Nouveau." Although at first this would seem merely a repetition of the Renaissance attempt to revive ancient Greece and Rome, it came now with at least two significant differences. First, Romanticism attempted not to reinvent or revivify the past but only to contemplate it, because what the robust and self-confident Renaissance eyed as a model for action, the Romantic era saw only in terms of quietist nostalgia. Second, Romanticism's sources went far beyond *one* past (the Classical era) and *one* place (Greece and Rome), which were the limits of the Renaissance's concern.

(2) Romanticism preferred the emotive, the sensual (the "aesthetic" in several senses), and the imaginative over the ratiocinative and the scientific observation of the here and now. "Sensitivity" became the primary receptive and productive capacity, and "genius" completely superseded "taste."

(3) Romanticism loved exoticism for its own sake—Egyptian, Moroccan, Indian (both senses), Chinese—and combined exotic forms with a self-conscious eclecticism never (or rarely) previously encountered.[240]

(4) Romanticism exalted the heroic ego—not merely as some particular personality of the past as a subject for emulation (Pericles, Caesar, Augustus, etc.), but the ego as the historical sum (a synthesis) of the world, a conception formalized in Hegelian philosophy and politically materialized in the imperialism of France and England.

In these separate but interconnected ways Romanticism further fostered and reflected, in its unique manner, the modern idea of the antique. The antique was a "natural" object of appreciation, collection, and connoisseurship for the Romantic mentality.

Of course, it was not always the case that in Romantic furnishings objects were required to be authentic originals and display their agedness.

Copies or reproductions in antique styles were accepted easily. Throughout the nineteenth century even most of the world's great museums displayed copies of celebrated paintings, plaster casts of famous sculptural and architectural antique originals.

A catalogue for the exhibition of French manufactures that was held in the Palais du Louvre in August and September 1823 lists by "M. Desnières . . . deux riches tables goût de siècle de Louis XIV, en bronze doré, pour M. le duc d'Hamilton." Who were Hamilton and Desnières? The Desnières (or, alternatively, Dénière) firm was founded in the late eighteenth century and lasted in the same family until 1903. For its entire existence it produced nothing but *reproduction furniture* in the styles of the eighteenth century—the three Louis styles—for its customers who wanted revivals of the past. The Duke of Hamilton furnished his estate wholly in this revivalist manner, as Ronald Freyberger notes, in which "virtually nothing was brand new, which should secure a major position for the tenth Duke's palace in the history of the Romantic interior."[241] Presumably, the pair of Desnières tables was an exception to his preference for genuine antiques, then, and was necessitated by the unavailability of originals to satisfy particular decorating requirements. The duke was hardly unique among his peers, and neither was the Desnières firm. Even before the Revolution, Parisian *ébénistes* (fine furniture makers) like Montigny in the time of Louis XVI made copies of André-Charles Boulle furniture constructed for Louis XIV in the Versailles Grande Baroque style of the preceding century and of furniture in the style Charles Cressent made for Louis XV in Régence-Rococo. These were primarily made for a French market seeking revivals of its own past—even before that past, in the form of the ancien régime, was forever extinguished by the Revolution.

After the Revolution and after Napoleon, the French taste was consistently revivalist. With Louis XVIII (1815–24) the main concern in the decorative arts was to outshine Napoleon. This required furnishings even more opulent, imperial, and monumental in scale; and they were fashioned by Dugoure, Demaltier, and Thomire. With Charles X (1824–30), during whose reign the Louvre was first opened as a museum to the public, the royal manufactory embraced full-fledged Gothic Revival.[242] Under Louis Philippe (1830–48) Renaissance Revival was in vogue, and the king redecorated his palaces in historical styles using both period and contemporary reproduction pieces. Under Napoleon III (1852–70) interior furnishing of the royal residences was simply more of the same again, with the addition of the Rococo revival.[243] The aristocracy and the haute bourgeoisie imitated as best they could.

The taste for the antique—whether as stylistic revival or actual objects—in this epoch was not limited to furnishings. As part of the "archeological" aspect of revivalist fashion, for example, Princess Canino (wife of Lucien Bonaparte) was famous for a suite of genuine Etruscan jewelry she wore in the 1830s. Where originals were unavailable or prohibitively expensive, contemporary Roman and Neapolitan jewelers made copies (in the form of reproductions, inspirational pastiches, or outright fakes). The most important of these jewelers were Fortunato Castellani (1793–1865) and his two sons, Alessandro and Augusto; and the most esteemed, an ex-Castellani workman, Carol Giuliano (1831–1918), who was especially good at "Etruscan."[244]

In *The Romantic Interior*, Clive Wainwright, discussing the homes of English gentry in the late eighteenth century, observes that "the style of these furnishings could have been neo-classical, Rococo, Chinese, or Gothic, but all newly manufactured and thus new in appearance." And James Fenton, commenting on Wainwright's book, notes that homes adopting the Romantic interior were "earlied up," that is, they "were conscious confections, exercises in style . . . [because] to fill a house with ancient furniture was a new idea, and a hard thing to achieve."[245] But to furnish a house with *genuine* antiques was something that at least some wanted to achieve and some (e.g., Walpole) did achieve. And it was something that more people wanted and actually did achieve in the nineteenth century. Thus, in the Romanticism of the nineteenth century, for many individuals reproductions in the style of the past were acceptable. But for those more historically conscious (because it included the pedigree or provenance), and for those more experientially sensitive or attuned to the material presence of the past in qualities of the object itself (because its agedness showed in its unique particularities), and for those fortunate enough or wealthy enough to acquire originals, the inclusion of genuine antiques and objects deriving from past civilizations of foreign lands was something to be preferred, lending a greater cachet to the collection and a greater stimulus for the romantic imagination.

Romanticism's rejection of neo-classicism and its rules thus had a liberating effect insofar as adherence to a particular era of European civilization (ancient Greece and Rome) was no longer required as the universal paradigm of excellence. Thus, aesthetic appreciation moved toward the view from the aspect of history rather than from the aspect of eternity and from the generic universal to the uniquely particular, for the eclecticism and revivalism of the mid-nineteenth century provided a vast historical and international repertoire of ornament as the basis of decoration. Stephen Calloway observes, "An even wider range of styles entered the canon of taste, whilst old furniture and objects and exotic and colorful pieces from the alien cultures of the Orient or the Middle East became much more widely admired and collected, having previously appealed only to a small minority."[246] The world exhibitions of 1851, 1862, 1867, 1873, and 1899 made available to the citizens of the Western world not only contemporary crafts and industrial novelties but also the variety of styles and objects produced in the material cultures of past civilizations. And such styles and objects were not limited to the select few but reached a large mass of the population.

The Romantic understanding that the essence of human nature is to be understood not through some classical and eternal abstraction but in a multiplicity of existential particulars dispersed around the world through history necessarily entailed the conclusion that all peoples and their cultural products are equally "natural" (i.e., that normative judgments are culturally conditioned) and therefore equally "good." Though the full consequences of this latter inference were yet to be realized, this was the ideological analogue of eclecticism, revivalism, and cosmopolitanism in art. It followed from the Romantic certainty that all great works are free creations of individuals of genius everywhere and at all times. The greatness of a work lies not in its conformity to the classical and ideal archetype (is not a relation to an objective standard of perfection) but in its subjective appeal to a universality of human susceptibility (sensibility) to beauty. This conception was first clearly articulated by Kant at the end of the eighteenth century, at the very beginning of the Romantic movement, in terms of a commonality of aesthetic sensibility (a *sensus communis*), based on what he called the "supersensible substrate of humanity." It was pithily rephrased by Oscar Wilde at the end of the nineteenth century in the maxim "All beautiful things belong to the same age."[247] Or as stated in these same years by Whistler: "The story of the beautiful is already complete in the marble of the Parthenon and embroidered with birds on the fan of Hokusai."[248]

A final characteristic of Romanticism's predilections which affected the appreciation of the antique is its acceptance of, even preference for, the fragment. The fragment is a touchstone, an epiphanic insight, a glimpse through a tiny window into another world.

The fragment has a quasi-religious side insofar as it functions as a *thanka* or an icon—a *relic*, in fact, a *reliquary* for the historical imagination. And indeed, Romanticism sometimes had a strong religious component. A wave of religious enthusiasm swept England between 1840 and 1880: the Oxford movement begun in 1833 attempted to revive certain Roman Catholic doctrines and rituals in the Anglican Church, while the

Pre-Raphaelite Brotherhood, founded in 1848 by Rossetti, Hunt, and Millais, and supported by Ruskin, Morris, and Burne-Jones, rejected the materialism of industrialized England and turned to what they took to be the naive innocence and simple sincerity of medieval and pre-Renaissance art and life. And this movement was itself inspired by a brotherhood of German painters, the Nazarenes, founded in Rome in 1810.[249]

But the primary relevance of the fragment to the antique per se is not its religious but its aesthetic conception and function. Because the fragment is only "a piece," the mind is enticed to complete it and complete the world in which it somewhere sometime "lived whole." The fragment thus becomes a magic feather for the flight of the imagination. As a piece of the past or a piece of another place it is both a residual of and a metaphor for the world it generates. Though we may find its art-historical precursor as early as the "vignette" in the Baroque era, the fragment as art object came into its own when Goethe published *Faust: A Fragment* (1808) as a complete work; and as Walter Kaufmann notes, "quickly, the German Romantics developed a predilection for fragments."[250] To be finished is to be perfect and to imply that time can be transcended to eternity. This is a classical, a Platonic, idea—that perfection is timeless and age is a blemish. Therefore, Romanticism rejected it and embraced the fragment, as it did the agedness of the past. Michelangelo's incomplete works, fragmentary not by any intention of his own, could now for the first time be appreciated for their fragmentary condition as an additional aesthetic characteristic; by the end of the century, Rodin's "fragments" were the result of his deliberate intentions and their "incompleteness" a primary condition of their aesthetic appeal.

This acceptance of the fragment, indeed the preference for it, affected profoundly the attitude toward restoration. On the one hand, Viollet-le-Duc (1814–79), the most prominent exponent of the Gothic revival in France, who was internationally celebrated for his publications extolling the organic wholeness of Gothic art, put his theory into practice by making whole what was in pieces. Beyond all others of his age he is famous (or infamous) for his massive restoration work on such historic French buildings as the cathedrals of Nôtre Dame de Paris, Chartres, Amiens, and Rheims and the entire city of Carcassone. He expressed thereby the age's commitment to preservation of the objects of the past—one wishes to preserve what one cherishes, after all. On the other hand, to restore, to bring back to life, to newness and to wholeness, what was through the accidents of time and fortune displaying age and ruination, was contrary to those other aspects of the Romantic mentality we have noted. Thus, the Society for the Protection of Ancient Buildings (one of whose founders was William Morris) had as a primary goal not just the preservation of Medieval churches in Great Britain against the ravages of time, but their protection from the overzealous restoration of architects like George Gilbert Scott, who, like Viollet-le-Duc in France, sought to "correct" the repairs and alterations made piecemeal over centuries and rebuild in accordance with the Victorian conception of "pure Medieval." This tension between restoration (understood as a return to original condition) and conservation (understood as keeping from further decay)—which is still with us today—was an aesthetic quandary first experienced in the Romantic era. *Nonrestoration* was a new aesthetic ideal, therefore, for until the mid-nineteenth century wholeness was generally required of art. Restorers had been repainting flaked glaze on ancient Greek vases and filling in missing arms and toes of ancient statues since the Renaissance. It was an early sign of the changing times that both Flaxman and Canova refused Lord Elgin's commission to restore the Parthenon marbles in the early decades of the century, thinking this proposal an act of hubris, if not sacrilege. Flaxman claimed that "few would set a higher value on a work of Phidias . . . with a modern head and modern arm than they would in their present state."[251]

Further developments in the understanding and appreciation of the antique had their roots in transformations in the economic and social structures of society in the nineteenth century, in particular the emergence of a large middle class of consumers and the appearance of the nuclear family. Both processes began in the eighteenth century and were completed by the end of the nineteenth. Before the Enlightenment and the Revolutions, the vast majority, the poor, could not afford to live in privacy, could consume and conserve little beyond the bare necessities of survival, and were thus unable to withdraw into the shell of the private home that encapsulated the physical and psychic comforts of today's nuclear family. On the other hand, the few, the wealthy, had been able to afford *not* to live in nuclear mode; for them their realm was their domain, their estate, their home. It was precisely during this eighteenth-century period that people (especially of the middle class) slowly turned to marriage and the private home to fulfill their closest emotional relationships. The closet of the home came to be viewed as a retreat into and a fulfillment of the self. The demonstrably affectionate, inward-directed, hothouse family unit was paralleled by a similar inward turning of self-consciousness, so that the "I" and the world (and the family and society at large) were seen in opposition.[252] Benjamin notes that "under the reign of Louis Philippe . . . the private individual makes his entry into history."[253] And Saisselin, speaking of mid-nineteenth-century Paris and the aesthetics of the flâneur, describes the bourgeois interior where "he gathered objects from remote places and the past to create the space of his dreams and secret longings."[254] Thus, after 1848 the climate of the West—with its political emphasis on equality and democracy, on individualism, autonomy, self-determination, and with its socioeconomic transformations in the movement of individuals to the big city for available employment and the creation of the insular family, rather than a previously predetermined mode of existence in the already established heritage of the small village, the commune, and the extended family—created the psychological conditions necessary for the eventual need of individuals deliberately to acquire a common heritage, even if only an imaginary one. By the end of the nineteenth century, in the final glow of the Victorian era, for a large middle class the ideal of self-realization became the "self-sufficient home celebrating its good fortune while marooned on its private island stuffed with acquisitions."[255] Indeed, our popular imagination of the High Victorian lifestyle derives from the excesses of this culture of materialism, as Egon Friedell characterizes it, a "padded and puffed-out world of cotton wool, cardboard, and tissue paper . . . [wherein] it is with the arts of adornment that the imagination is concerned: with the art of the upholsterer, the confectioner, the stucco decorator."[256] To what extent and in what sense this excess may be part of the so-called decadence at the end of the century we come to shortly.

It is in terms of the popular imagination that we must pursue the antique at mid-nineteenth century. Economically, the Industrial Revolution enriched many families, and the English Reform Bill of 1832 introduced compulsory education in the social sphere, enabling the many to read about past and distant civilizations, even about art. With this knowledge (and the imagination it could inspire), and with newly available capital as disposable income, many more could possess the past in the form of its antiques, and they avidly sought to do so. The situation in France was very similar to that in England vis-à-vis greater disposable wealth and a wider dispersion of education. Consequently, art criticism and appreciation by the mid-nineteenth century for the very first time became a subject matter for the *popular* press—either in the form of regular columns in magazines and newspapers or as independent, specialized magazines and journals—with articles written by Baudelaire, Dumesnil, Gautier, Charles Blanc, and the Goncourt brothers in France and by Palgrave, Ruskin, Morris, and Eastlake in England. It was also in the mid-nineteenth century that "art history" first established its legitimacy as an independent academic discipline. The new discipline permanently attached formal (not to say "official") determinations to all art objects of the past: they no longer could be merely "old and foreign" but were seen as instances of styles arising and perishing in cultures of precise locations and within established time frames.

Besides the more aristocratic art of painting, the craft object of the past was especially appealing to the rising bourgeoisie. Steegman observes, "Although the collecting of pictures and Old Master drawings was a long-established tradition among English connoisseurs, the collecting of *objets d'art*, and especially porcelain and bronzes, did not become a habit much before the middle of the century; during the 1850's, however, it developed very rapidly."[257] There were several reasons for the new trend. The materials of which craft objects were made were often of greater intrinsic value than canvas and paint, and the technical proficiency required in their production was more obvious to the unschooled eye and uninstructed intellect. Moreover, the quotidian object reflected the workaday world, in which, like the Dutch burgher of the seventeenth century, the middle class could easily imagine itself (and its ancestors) as having lived; and above all, it was more readily available for an affordable price. And price for this class was an important consideration.

As Rheims observes regarding the contemporary situation in France, "the golden age, or naïve period, of the trade in paintings and antiques began about 1825 . . . and came to full flower thirty years later under the Second Empire." He notes further that it was the bourgeois economy that "gave birth to the art expert. He made his entrance about 1850, when for a certain fraction of society whose chief interest was in making profits, the attraction of works of art was not due to their rarity and beauty alone but, in equal measure, to their financial value. Authentication was required for things."[258] Not that prior ages and collectors were indifferent to these matters. Even if prior ages did not much concern themselves with questions regarding the degree of an object's restoration, questions of provenance, authorship, and forgery were certainly not irrelevant, as we have seen from Ancient Rome to the Renaissance. But before the nineteenth century, "copies" had not quite the negative associations of today. Indeed, today's view of "the copy" had its origins in the mid-nineteenth century. Because authenticity guaranteed an artwork's economic value beyond all else, the French connoisseur-collector Ernest Cognac (founder of the La Samaritaine department store chain), for example, insisted that his Boucher and Fragonard purchases come with an invoice guaranteeing their authenticity.[259] Whenever financial considerations take precedence over aesthetic ones or whenever persons (for whatever reason) are unsure of their own judgment or "taste," paperwork guaranteeing the object is bound to take precedence over the

object itself. This was a further consequence of the bourgeois economy
and bourgeois mentality of the time—that the antique's authenticity (and
hence value) be determinable, verified by experts, and recorded in the appropriate document.[260]

Thoughts of the possibilities for the future of the arts and comparisons
of the art of the past with that of the present continually confronted mid-
Victorian aesthetic consciousness. We find, for example, that in recognizing the historical and international eclecticism that infused the successive
revivals (and subrevivals) of the century—Gothic, Celtic, Archeologi-
cal/Assyrio-Babylonian, Renaissance, Neo-Egyptian, Rococo—the Victorian aesthete often developed a genuine concern for the art production
of his own time, fearing that the possibilities for art had been exhausted.

On the one hand, this outlook can be seen as a recapitulation of the
beliefs recounted at earlier stages of this archeology—Xenocrates of
Athens' third-century B.C. claim that art had "stopped" in the generation of Lysippus, or Vasari's view which came into vogue in the High Renaissance that after Michelangelo and Raphael, art had reached its
"natural perfection." Wendell Garrett points to this stylistic uncertainty,
this sense of living in a period of transition—from something quite definite but without any sense of "whither to"—as the very intuition that
prompted the era's historicism: "in this atmosphere of uncertainty, the
Victorians exhibited an intense interest in the mirror of history."[261] Similarly, Steegman observes that "the progressive machine-making modern
of the mid-19th century contemplated the world of the past as soothing
contrast."[262] Many at the time may have been satisfied with contemporary achievements in the art of painting (though we likely would not
think very highly of many of its most popular practitioners today), but
all Victorian critics agreed "that [contemporary] architecture was in a
bad way and that the only chance of evolving a style worthy of the age
lay in an appeal to the past."[263] John Ruskin, the greatest critic of his
time and the first individual to hold the title "Professor of Art" at Oxford, in *The Seven Lamps of Architecture* explicitly describes modern architecture as little more than "a rattling of bones"—but then goes on to
aver that "we want no new style of architecture; the forms already
known are good enough for us."[264]

On the other hand, there is in the nineteenth century a new element
that needs to be considered, an additional cause of despair and discontent, a further impetus away from the arts of the contemporary world
and toward the objects of the past. Whether it was the global and historical consciousness of the era that caused the sense of the unworthi-
ness of contemporary production in the arts by comparison or whether

it was, on the contrary, a dissatisfaction with this production that turned the mid-Victorian toward distant times and places for inspiration and consolation—and consequently (and either way) encouraged the collection and appreciation of antiques—there is also the matter of the machine-made object.

Apart from the issue of *quality*—and not all mass-produced objects were of poor quality[265]—the new industrial production introduced a novel *distancing effect* between the object on the one hand and its creator and possessor on the other. Objects produced in multiple pre-need abundance and placed on view to the consumer arrayed on shelves—in "standing reserve," to use Heidegger's phrase—tended to have a certain anomie, a free-floating availability to anyone and at any time. They were impersonal. Before the Industrial Revolution, objects generally came into being on demand, uniquely, and passed directly into the possession of their owner-user-commissioner; in consequence, they were immediately experienced by other individuals as "already owned" and imprinted with a unique personality of their makers and their owner/commissioners. But the new mass-produced objects were indistinguishable "free radicals," with generic qualities appealing to the most common denominator among consumers.[266] Belonging to anybody, they belonged to nobody. Antiques, on the other hand, were exactly the sort of thing that was "already owned." They became desirable because they had of necessity already acquired a distinctive history and personality.

Similarly, as we noted in chapter 1, Benjamin speaks of the "aura" that had always accompanied the work of art of old which is "lost" in the age of mechanical reproduction because a personal and intersubjective one-on-one relationship between viewer and work is no longer possible. Not in the sense that the artwork is really itself a "subjective consciousness" that can behold the living viewer as the viewer himself beholds the work, but rather that only if the artwork is a unique and concrete historical production can the viewer confidently "invest" the work with the intentions (meanings, proposals) of its creator and its time, and thus can engage in an imaginative dialogue with its creator that is anchored in an authentic, an "owned," entity. The mass-produced object utters no appeal for connection. Just as one becomes indifferent and oblivious to the subjective minds composing the hordes at crowded airline terminals—what existentialists might call the "anomie of the 'They' "—so the mass-market object loses its attractiveness by repetitious impersonality. Through its multiple replication, almost always discernible as such, it suggests an indefinite proliferation that clutters the real world with excess baggage, with illusory existentiality. As J. M. Coetzee explains Benjamin here: "he makes loss of aura part of a wide historical development: the spread of a disenchanted awareness that uniqueness, including the uniqueness of the traditional artwork, has become a commodity like any other commodity."[267]

Of course, at the time, the mid-nineteenth century, this rather meta-physical perspective went unnoticed. Then the common criticism of the machine-made, the mechanical reproduction, was based usually on quality. Sir Francis Palgrave (1788–1861) excoriated the deadening effect of mass production on the applied arts generally by its creation of a "permanent glut of pseudo art."[268] The Pre-Raphaelites took the mass productions of the industrial age as the prime example of modern decadence.

Naturally there were those who took the opposite viewpoint. Charles Lock Eastlake, Librarian of the Royal Academy and later first director of the National Gallery, thought there was something vulgar and tasteless about antiques collecting, about the disparity in styles (of dates and places of origin) of objects inhabiting a single room, and was in general critical of unthinking and thrown-together historicism.[269] There were many other like-minded critics. We have already noted Friedell's characterization of the "padded, puffed-out world" of the late Victorian. The desire for environmental density—what may be called "accumulative eclectic"—combined with nostalgia for the past and longing to possess the residue of the entirety of the world may indeed be a sign of civilizational morbidity and personal spiritual vacuity. On the other hand, from the first-century Roman Empire to Victorian England to the last midcentury in America, the majority of noteworthy antiques connoisseur-collectors were hardly vapid or culturally disengaged personalities and the civilizations in which they lived were scarcely moribund.

Returning to the evidence of art history, we find that another force in the fine arts at the mid-nineteenth century provides insight into the archeology of the antique. It is the signal and seminal work of Manet, who is generally credited as one of the founders (if not *the* founder) of modern art. H. W. Janson in this connection speaks of Manet's "lifelong devotion to 'pure painting': to the belief that brushstrokes and color patches themselves—not what they stand for—are the artist's primary reality," of Manet's conviction that "a painted canvas is, above all, a material surface covered with pigments—that we must look *at* it, not *through* it."[270] Manet's works were also deliberately art-historical. However often it is said that the way a civilization sees things in the world affects the way it represents them in art, it is equally true (and more often forgotten) that the way things are represented in art affects the way things are seen in the world.[271] It is here that Manet's importance to art history and to the archeology of the antique arises. Manet's oeuvre calls attention to the *materiality* of the object of aesthetic experience, in this instance painting as a fine-art *object*, in a way that was historically original. But his work also calls attention to the history of art and its stylistic past. Both of these—our intense attention to the materiality of the object as object and our consciousness of the art-historical style in which it was created—are primary components of (if not necessary conditions for) the mentality that grounds our current aesthetic response to fine art and, all the more, to antiques.

Regarding the last point, Janson remarks that in such a painting as *Dejeuner sur l'herbe*, Manet pays tribute not only to his contemporary, Courbet, but also to Velázquez and Goya (and we may add Titian and Giorgione), so that "many of his canvases are, in fact, 'pictures of pictures': they translate into modern terms those older works."[272] We have seen this before in Mannerism's deliberate evocation of the past, where painting becomes self-consciously painting about painting. The primary purposes of historicism in Mannerism, however, were bravura (to outshine the past) and preciosity (the artifice of appealing to the connoisseur's taste for arcana). In Manet and, as a consequence of his work, in modern art throughout the twentieth century, the aesthetic uses of historicism were much expanded. Still more important than historicism, however, both for twentieth-century art and for the aesthetic of the antique, is Manet's devotion to the primacy of the medium.

Manet's *Bar au Follies Bergère* is instructive here. At first it appears in the manner of a Realist work of the era: it has no plot or message apart from being a contemporary moment or experience that has been arrested and captured in the optical event of standing at a bar. To the degree to which the then prevailing realist/naturalist perspective might be invoked as a basis for its interpretation, one might construe the meaning or message of its content as the observation that the barmaid is a heroine in the social saga of the impersonal forces that have rendered her alienated life inconsequential in her menial job. But if this is the message, the painting's "content" becomes the equivalent of a cell culture in a petri dish; it is a rather trivial subject matter. And one would have to ask, as critics of realism did at the time, why one would bother to deliver this message: the world is there already, and it is senseless to repeat it. One might as well step into the nearest bar rather than a painting gallery. In fact, however, the subject matter of the painting is much about itself, as a painting existing in its time and in a medium of paint and canvas. Our attention is directed away from *what* is represented to *that* and *how* it is represented—and perhaps *why*. Since Giotto in Western art, the viewer had been directed *through* the painting's surface as a window on a three-dimensional world "behind" (by which process he was informed about something). And from that stylistic viewpoint, from that conception of the art of painting, the "why" of the painting was obvious and the "that" and the "how" of the painting were—*theoretically*, but in all great works never *in fact* (and certainly not to connoisseurs)—meant to pass unnoticed. Manet's techniques work against this traditional viewpoint, for they encourage us to abandon "art as the illusion of reality." He calls attention to the **"that"**—the facticity of the painting, the flat surface of the canvas—*that* it is a flat plane covered with pigmented designs that cling to it. He calls attention to the technique of the painting whereby the brush-worked color patches (as in Velázquez) organize themselves into recognizable optical sensations for the eye. Manet does this by *un*doing what Raphael did, namely, by disintegrating the modeling, minimizing (or distorting beyond recognition) the effects of perspective and shadow (light sources), and the like. The "what" (the content) of Manet's paintings thus becomes a function of their "how" and their "that." It is not that he was the first artist to notice or to use the implicit relationships existing between the medium and the content of a work. All great artists do. It is not that he was the first to make this fact a *recognizable* component of the aesthetic experience or to do so with art-historical consciousness (already Mannerist and Baroque artists had achieved that). But he was the first to make this fact an *unavoidably explicit* component of the aesthetic experience of his works—indeed, a *necessary* condition of their aesthetic experience and for the peculiar aesthetic effect he was trying to achieve: illuminating the self-conscious artifacticity of the artwork, pointing to the physical presence of its unique construction and away from its role as an unobtrusive and generic piece of information-delivery equipment.

From this arises the essential historicism and the essential materiality (the fascination with medium) of his work. From this arises a shift in the view of what the art object is, or can be. From this arises a fuller awareness of the possibilities of the aesthetic experience, and in particular, the aesthetic preconditions for the mentality that easily embraces antiques as objects of aesthetic contemplation.

As I have argued at several places throughout this work and elsewhere,[273] the aesthetic experience of the art object derives not merely from what may be called its "content" (or whatever "meaning" or "significance" it may contain) but also from its "materialized form" (or the "material medium" in which the work is constructed and embodied).

"Fine art" and "craft," if they can be differentiated at all, can be differentiated only on the basis of the relation (or proportions) between these twin components: content (meaning) and form (material medium). As we saw in chapter 1.2.1's discussion of this distinction, to the extent that we tend to think at all legitimately of "craft" as a discrete category and of craft objects as forming the principal reference of the class of those things we "properly" call "antiques," and to the degree that it is precisely their sensuous materiality more than their "represented meaning" through which craft objects appeal to our attention as antiques, attending to the sensuous features of their medium as the primary component of the aesthetic experience becomes crucial to the ability to experience the antique *as antique*. Manet's work helped to bring about this change in perspective. Since this work was not codified in the doctrine of any of the major art-historical styles of the nineteenth century, his achievement remains to that extent unique. Manet is "located" by art historians somewhere amid Realism and Impressionism, and yet clearly neither category suits him. As we will see, it was to be Art Nouveau in the next century that gave priority to the "craft object" as an aesthetic object, calling deliberate and ineluctable attention to the physicality of (and the possibilities for) the medium of its creation. But Manet was the first to do this for painting as "fine art."

Romanticism stretched through Realism and Impressionism—and Manet—into the Expressionism of the fin de siècle. This art style provides a further clue—and our last nineteenth-century European one—in the discovery and development of the *archés* of the antique. Fin de siècle Expressionism was an artistic style or movement in which excess, moral inversion, death, and the fascination with the deformations of despair and the frightful juxtapositions of the nightmare took prime place. It increased the imaginative fascination with the past and the propensity to accumulate its most exotic relics in the most tangible and sensuous forms. In his *Decadence*, Richard Gilman suggests that this is decadence itself—that societies nostalgic for past virtues, "wishing to preserve what had been valued . . . in time found themselves valuing what had been preserved. . . . Value itself became the exclusive province of the past. . . . [and] in this steady accumulation of the past within all the spaces of the present . . . to live [became] in time *to have lived*."[274] Proust makes mementos of the past *the* touchstone for all interpretations of the present, and therefore the narrative of current life is permanently and perpetually infected with the residue of the past. Even more forcefully, in Huysmans's novel *A Rebours* we have a hyperbolic account of the aristocratic aesthete-decadent whose obsession with bizarre and extravagant furnishings of the greatest rarity and historical associations leads him to compulsive

excess—to replace life entirely with art. Huysmans's account of the furnishings of his fictional Château de Lourps was in part taken from the
actual furnishings in the home of Alexandre du Sommerand, whose collection of Medieval and Renaissance art later became the nucleus of the
Musée Cluny, and in part from the furnishings of the home of Robert,
comte de Montesquiou-Fezensac, on the rue Franklin, whose exotic contents were described to Huysmans by Mallarmé, who had visited there in
1883. Among the furnishings of Edmond de Goncourt's *Maison d'un
artiste* were a considerable number of exotic antiques about which this
tastemaker of French fashion at the end of the century waxed eloquent.
And the Paris apartment of Art Nouveau artist Alphonse Mucha ca.
1900 was later described by his son Jiri as a treasure trove of bizarre
luxury: the "small forest of articles which he had accumulated . . . had
become a veritable jungle. . . . Baroque furniture, antique brocades, costumes . . . *objets de vertu* jostled for space in an atmosphere . . . as a
'profane chapel.' "[275] Compulsive fascination with the accumulation of
the past through antiques collecting and connoisseurship was thus a major component of "aesthetic decadence" at the turn of the century.[276]

Here is not the place to engage in the psychoanalysis or critique of civilization at the turn of the twentieth century, however. And we must
move to our last section in the archeology: the American century.

2.7
The American Century

The subhead for this section suggests a forthcoming archeology of one
hundred years, but we terminate it several decades short of the end of
twentieth century. By that time all the *archés* of this archeology of the
antique will have been developed. Moreover, to detail all the permutations of the antique in the United States throughout the century would
require an account too vast to be included here. To compensate for our
truncation of the century, however, in moving to America we move
briefly back in time before the century began.

America was the New World. Its self-consciousness necessarily indicated a rejection of the old, especially the European Old. As Emerson put
it in the mid-nineteenth century in *Works and Days*, simply: "Whatever
is old is corrupt, and the past turns to snakes. The reverence for deeds of
our ancestors is a treacherous sentiment."[277] This conception, held by the
majority of Americans at the outset of the nineteenth century—the past is
bad, the future good—is consistently reconfirmed by the nearly contem-

porary observations of de Tocqueville's *Democracy in America* (1840), probably the most insightful account of the uniquely American consciousness of the time, and most likely for all time. Contempt for the past is not a sound basis for the development of the aesthetic of the antique. What were the consequences for aesthetics and the appreciation of the antique in such American assumptions in the first half of the nineteenth century?

In his 1841 essay "Art," Emerson provides another useful observation that reflects the American mentality:

> Pictures must not be too picturesque. Nothing astonishes men so much as common sense and plain dealing. All great actions have been simple, and all great pictures are. . . . Beauty will not . . . repeat in England or America its history in Greece. It will come, as always, unannounced, and spring up between the feet of brave and honest men. . . . It is in vain that we look for genius to reiterate its miracles in the old arts; it is its instinct to find beauty and holiness in new and necessary facts, in the field and roadside, in the shop and mill.[278]

Americans' sentiment or disposition toward themselves in relation to the past, and in particular *their own* past, was explained about thirty years later by Henry James as simply a function of youth—that America was at first bereft of tangible vestiges of the past of its own: "History as yet has left in the United States but so thin and impalpable a deposit that we very soon touch the hard substratum of nature."[279] Lowenthal has a much richer and deeper explanation:

> Many Americans conceived their country as exempt from decay because eternally youthful. Newly created by rational and blameless men, America lay outside the historical process. Providence had specifically spared it from history. . . . As the nation shook off the historical past, so its citizens divested themselves of family heritage. The ideal American became "an individual emancipated from history, happily bereft of ancestry, untouched and undefiled by the usual inheritances of family and race; an individual standing alone, self-reliant, self-propelling."[280]

Hence, the New World was marked at its outset with an obsession for the new, for the free radical fully competent to make its own destiny.

The idea that beauty needs to be found within the quotidian object of today rather than the "high art" of yesterday went conveniently along with this conception. With a profound trust in "honest plainness" and a Calvinistic (not to say Puritan) contempt for luxury, voluptuousness, extravagance, and conspicuous consumption, with preference for function over form, the useful over the decorative, the pragmatic over the stylistic, Americans looked to the present (and to the future) rather than the past to find themselves. So far this would seem an improbable culture in which to grow the seed of the antique. And there is further evidence.

We have noted that the evolution of the *archés* of the antique—and the mentality that supports the conception and appreciation of the antique—almost invariably finds reaffirmation and reflection in the dominant contemporary art style. In this regard we find corroboration of American attitudes in the portraiture of the period, roughly 1780 to 1860. For surely in representing themselves Americans betray their self-consciousness, and portraiture was the primary subject matter of painting during this period in the United States. Thus, Charles Bergengren characterizes American portraiture during this period as follows:

> The flatness and frontality, it turns out, are a result of social reticence in the presentation of self in egalitarian communities, rather than an unconscious abstraction resulting from, as previous assumptions held, either bold innovation or historical short cuts, nor yet from ineptitude. The paintings done at a period of rapid social change—the formative years of the republic—are as complicated as their era. The paintings are "ambivalent," that is, they display contradictory tensions. The portraits are poised between forces of modernization at the hands of an upwardly mobile bourgeoisie and forces of a conservative morality drawn from a Puritan egalitarianism.[281]

In English portraiture during this period (one may think of Reynolds and Gainsborough—or even Watteau and David in France) one finds subjects adopting formally aristocratic poses and purposeful gestures. In luxurious or historic settings, usually depicted in strong lighting and dramatic chiaroscuro, we discover the subject either amid a wild and unruly Nature toward whose elemental forces the subject shows sublime indifference or animatedly engaged at the center of the world-historical stage, on which their glorious deeds constitute the primary action. With painterly techniques codified in the academies, employing agitated and energetic brushwork to increase the sense of drama or the uniqueness, superiority, and individuality of the sitter, and the ephemeral yet momentous worth of the scene represented, this sort of portraiture was entirely unsuited to the American temper. The European legacy of Baroque, Rococo, Neo-classical, and Romantic portraiture was therefore rejected by American portraitists in favor of the simple and straightforward, the earnest and homespun, the egalitarian and restrained and workaday preoccupations of the Puritan ethos. Hence sitters are invariably "at home" (not in poses of classical statuary or amid the wilds of Nature or world-historically engaged), are shown centrally and (usually) frontally (almost never in three-quarters view or positioned off-center, which would imply greater drama and an "unstraightforwardness" of character),[282] with neutral lighting (no "shadiness" here), undifferentiated space, and a flatness that altogether downplay the aggressive presence of a personality at the center of momentous events and powerful forces, in favor of asserting stability and the assured comforts of homeliness.[283] What has such a mentality of plainness and simplicity, of reverence for the present and contempt for the past, to do with the appreciation and connoisseurship of antiques or the acquisition of physical residues of world civilizations?

These unlikely early predispositions represent collectively a mentality antithetical to the contemporary late-eighteenth- and early-nineteenth-century European one, and most certainly the antipode of the European fin de siècle "aesthetic decadence," whose preferences would undoubtedly have appeared indecent, if not immoral. Nevertheless, in the long run the United States, with minor shifts of emphasis, came to adopt and expand the idea of the antique that had already developed and matured in Europe, especially England and France.

The turning point had already been reached by the mid-nineteenth century. The United States had by then endured long enough to acquire a history and to accumulate relics of its own past. It had by then begun to develop a certain amount of "nostalgia for the past and a skepticism over urban life."[284] Even "by the fiftieth anniversary of the Declaration of Independence, Americans had created a significant body of nostalgia. This longing intensified throughout the 19th century."[285] America had already come to feel that its present and future were becoming unequal to the greatness of its past; and "even if that past was not long ago, Americans were exhorted to respect and preserve and protect the achievements of the Founding Fathers."[286] It experienced the similar cultural effects of the nineteenth-century revolutions—the industrial one and the Civil War—so that by the last third of the century America too (or at least some portion of it large enough to found the basis of antiques appreciation) was longing for its lost innocence and purity of youth as much as any Romantic poet pining for the rustic idyll of a long-lost love. But it was not merely its *own* past it craved. Above all, America had by that time acquired its own sense of a manifest destiny as the legatee of a universal heritage. Hence, Oliver Wendell Holmes in 1858 said of his fellow countrymen: "We are the Romans of the Modern World—the great assimilating people." And a decade earlier Herman Melville wrote: "We are not a nation so much as a world. For who is our father and our mother? Or can we point to any Romulus or Remus for our fathers? Our ancestry is lost in the universal patrimony, and Caesar and Alfred, Saint Paul and Luther, and Homer and Shakespeare are as much ours as Washington who is as much the world's as ours. We are the heirs of all time, and with all nations we divide our inheritance."[287]

Thus, as in Europe, it is not surprising that ancient non-Western civilizations left their mark on American aesthetic consciousness. Though overshadowed in importance by Greek and Roman patterning, the "Egyptian influence did exist [in America as well], and Egyptian motifs were understood and used with increasing archeological correctness between 1800 and 1850."[288] Even earlier, the huge China trade brought Chinese porcelains and chinoiserie into the American home, and in much greater abundance than they arrived on the shores of Europe. And again as in Europe, America in the nineteenth century went through the same sequence of revivals (usually five to ten years later) and the same appreciation and collection of antiques that spread from the aristocratic few to the bourgeois many. As Calloway observes, whereas "before 1850 [in the United States] there was very little collecting of what we call antiques—furniture, ceramics, silver, pewter, and other decorative arts"—in the second half of the century this "age of revivals brought with it new attitudes to the past and the art objects and artifacts which remained as testimonies of past styles. The collecting of what began more generally to be called 'antiques,' which had previously been the preserve of the scholarly antiquarian, became increasingly widespread, and we begin to recognize in England, and especially in America towards the end of the century, the origins of many of our own attitudes to historical houses and their furnishings."[289]

But the American appreciation of the antique began to show shifts in emphasis in the nineteenth century. Some are implicit in what we have already noted, and many showed their full consequences only in the following century. There was not at this time a well-developed appreciation (by any but a few connoisseurs) of either the formal character (such as art-historical significance) or the purely sensuous qualities (like agedness displayed in patina) of the antique object per se. Consequently, for the vast majority in the United States, these two *archés* of antiques appreciation remained relevant to a much lesser degree than in the *mentalités* of European nations, which were perhaps more world-historically sophisticated and educated and less affected by the Puritan or Calvinist contempt for (or at least reticence toward) sensuous experience. Rather, because of Americans' moral earnestness (not to say conservatism), combined just after midcentury with a sense of a loss of innocence vis-à-vis the Revolutionary Era, it was instead the object's historical associations—connections with persons of high moral esteem, places of national pride, and events of public curiosity and notoriety—that made the object of the past worthy of attention and appreciation. Thus, it was not the object in itself but what it could remind one of and what it could instruct one in that gave the antique its value. This is precisely that characteristic of the antique that it shares most closely with the artifact, the collectible, the trophy, and the memento—such as we have defined these terms and differentiated them from the "pure antique" in our earlier chapter (1.2). It is also a conception of the antique that is founded precisely on the attitude or mentality that construes the ordinary, everyday object of the past as an item of memorial or instructional use, and thus at best can elicit an "approbational response," rather than as a source of genuine "aesthetic pleasure." Emerson's "common sense" and "plain dealing" that finds beauty in the pragmatic object, "in the field and roadside, in the shop and mill," will be inherited by the collectibilia mentality (perhaps one might say "collectiphilia" or "collectimania") of the late twentieth century. Finally, precisely because the ancestral heritage of the United States is so diverse in its immigrant populations,[290] as remarked on by Holmes and Melville—and was becoming increasingly so in the decades after the Civil War—the young republic could a fortiori stake its claim to the cultural heritage of the entire world with greater credibility than other nations, and do so even before its historical moment of political empire fully arrived in the next century.

Let us now turn to some further instances illustrating these American peculiarities in the conception and appreciation of antiques in the first two-thirds of the nineteenth century. They complete the archeology and fill out more definitively the ten categories of collecting and connoisseurship in the next chapter. We remarked on the concern for the historical association. Almost magical benefits were believed to derive from an object's contagion with past greatness. There was interest in the educative properties of the object and a simple delight in the object's curiousness. So, for example, the Albany Army Relief Bazaar of 1864 exhibited George Washington's cane, pistol, and writing desk (along with a lock of his hair) as objects "of priceless value and great national interest." This fair also displayed Napoleon's garden chair, Voltaire's blanket, and nails from a Pompeiian house. In the same year, in Brooklyn, a "Sanitary Fair" exhibited a tablecloth that had arrived on the Mayflower and the dress of "a Nubian lady of quality" (according to its *Catalogue of Arts, Relics, and Curiosities*).[291] And at this same fair there appeared the first example of the "New England [read "Colonial"] Kitchen." The fair's coordinating committee set out its goals clearly in 1864:

> The idea is to present a faithful picture of New England farmhouse life of the last century. The grand old fireplace shall glow again—the spinning wheel shall whirl as of old—the quilting, the dancing . . . the dinner table, always set. . . . [The purpose of this being] to illustrate the domestic life and habits of the people to whose determined courage, sustained by their faith in God, we owe that government so dear to every loyal heart.[292]

This farmhouse with its colonial kitchen would establish an icon of American pride and evoke nostalgia for an imaginary idyll of the century past. (In the century to come, this imagery was consummated in the works of Norman Rockwell.) At a fair in New York in 1851 a chair made from the wood of a Mexican fort captured during the Mexican-American War of 1846–48 was displayed—a trophy and an item of national pride and commemoration. At the Centennial Celebration of Salem, Massachusetts (1875), there was on view a remarkable collection of antique colonial furniture and objects including clothes, books, silver, and glass, all lent by major Massachusetts aristocratic families (and early antiques dealers such as James Moulton and M. A. Stickney). But the exhibit also included "the last piece of jewelry worn by Louis XVI. While imprisoned he gave it to the jailer to buy files with, but was executed before he could liberate himself."[293] With such appeals to nostalgia, to curiosity, and to the moralistic story attached to the object, clearly these several instances do not suggest that the goal of these exhibits was to elicit aesthetic responses to form, craftsmanship, style, or signs of age in patina—as we would understand most of the important elements of a fully "aesthetic" response today—but rather to satisfy intellectual inquisitiveness in exotica, to stimulate patriotic sentiments, or to instill a moral virtue quickened by a longing for the simpler and purer life imagined to have existed in the Colonial and Revolutionary eras.[294]

But by the 1880s things began to change somewhat, and a more systematic and scholarly approach began to be adopted toward antiques and collectibles. These now slowly came to be appreciated not just as relics of past personalities and events but as aesthetic objects embodying stylistic and art-historically interpretable indices of the past and the peoples of an age. The works of English authors such as Henry Cole, Ruskin, and Morris in the Arts and Crafts movement began to take effect. Antique objects were not merely to be *looked at* in exhibitions but *lived with* at home. Eastlake's *Hints on Household Taste* (1872) went though eight editions and found an American equivalent in Clarence Cooke's *The House Beautiful* (1878).[295] Like Eastlake, Cooke advocated well-designed and well-crafted *contemporary* furnishings (whether furniture, porcelains, metalwork, etc.). But he adds:

> In the rage that has sprung up of late for "grandfathers" and "grandmothers"—a kind of thing till very lately ignored if not despised in the bumptious arrogance of our social youthfulness—it adds inestimably to the value of sideboards, andirons, and old china, if they have come to us by descent, and haven't had to be hunted up in a chaise. But everybody can't have a grandfather, nor things that come over on the "Mayflower," and those of us who have not drawn these prizes in life's lottery must do as best we can under the circumstances . . . and there is a feeling that in going back to its [the antique's] use, in collecting it, and saving it from dishonor, and putting it in safekeeping, we are bringing ourselves a little nearer in spirit to the old time.[296]

Twenty years later, in *The Decoration of Houses* (1897), another early discussion of interior decoration as a subject of serious aesthetic inquiry, Edith Wharton recommends the use of antiques for decoration because of "their suggestion of a mellower civilization"—provided only that they shall "be in scale with the room, and that the room shall not be overcrowded with them."[297]

All these authors also believed that as the life and character of a people is embodied and reflected in their arts, so, conversely, the arts have an impact on that life. And they feared that the contemporary public, confronted by graceless assembly-line products, were, in this assault on their aesthetic sensibilities by tasteless and shoddy objects, becoming spiritually and morally degraded.[298]

Unfortunately, a curious contradiction—or at least a tension between contradictory tendencies—arose. While Eastlake, Cooke, and many in the Arts and Crafts movement were trying to resurrect the ancient virtues of "art" in the revival of traditional *craftsmanship* that was visibly displayed in *new* works and in a *new* style, many found such newness per se contrary to their taste. The revived integrity (honesty, virtue) of the artisan and the creative act was not what they sought from the past. They wanted, rather, the age associations of the object that new objects, however well made and traditionally made, could not possibly provide, simply because they were, after all, new. At the other extreme, however, this connection to the past for many required only a *stylistic reference* of the object. And since by the 1890s having a personal connection to Colonial times (as Wharton says, having one's own "Mayflower grandmother") had become a status symbol representing an inheritance of right and privilege, and since this was not available (neither the family pedigree nor the hereditary objects) to the nouveau riche (and certainly not to the not-so-riche-bourgeoisie), beginning in the 1880s shoddily made Colonial Revival furniture was mass-produced to satisfy this desire. Thus, the arts-and-crafts call for the revival of the integrity of the artisan traditions of the past was, by those who wanted merely the appearance of or allusion to the past, derailed in favor of a proliferation of revivalist machine-reproduction objects in confused design and inferior materials that "harkened back" to the past.

This development did not fail to have its further consequences. Especially the Northeastern establishment simply eschewed the "Colonial" altogether and adopted a preference for the refinements and graceful forms of the Georgian taste (Chippendale furniture, Rococo silver, cut crystal) rather than the honest, sturdy simplicity of Puritan pewter and bread boards. This was a new trend, because before the end of the nineteenth century and the beginning of the twentieth, in fact, English furniture of the eighteenth century as a distinct category of antiques connoisseurship was not seriously appreciated at all, even in England.[299] At the American Centennial Exhibition of 1876, however, although more visitors probably came to see the new and improved labor-saving inventions of the modern world than to view the arts and crafts of the past, more "people of taste" were interested in the antique furnishings of Europe (especially England and France) than in either collecting Colonial antiques or purchasing 1880s reproductions of them (usually now referred to as "Centennial furniture").[300]

Another special preference of the Northeastern establishment, particularly in New England, was for the exotically mystical Far East, primarily Japan, though India and China were a close second and third. The desire of "Boston Brahmins" for objects of specifically aesthetic appreciation (rather than for intellectual curiosity or moral improvement), objects that embodied stylistic and art-historically interpretable indices of Japanese civilization, has been admirably recounted by Christopher Benfey in *The Great Wave: Gilded Age Misfits, Japanese Eccentrics, and the Opening of Old Japan*.[301] "Japan was the ultimate 'other,' a world arrested in the sleep of centuries, promising . . . something more courtly and stern, an island fortress impregnable and unbreached,"[302] he says. Only six years after Commodore Perry's breach of Japan's isolationism in 1854, the *New York Times* published an account of a parade of Japanese samurai down Broadway and included a poem by Walt Whitman characterizing the event as a "reversing" in the westward march of civilization.[303]

Many New Englanders went to Japan to experience and to collect; among the earliest was Edward Morse, who became the first Western expert in Japanese ceramics.[304] Henry Adams, arriving in Japan with his friend John LaFarge in July 1886 on an excursion to collect Japanese antiques, complained in a letter to John Hay (as quoted by Benfey): "Japan has been cleaned out. Kaikimonos are not to be got. . . . Fine old porcelain is rare and dear. Embroideries are absolutely introuvable. Even books seem scarce." And Benfey continues, "He failed to note the irony that one reason the market was so competitive was that Fenellosa and Bigelow, along with their friend Edward Morse, had already bought thousands of rare objects destined for the Museum of Fine Arts in Boston."[305] But in fact there were more than sufficient sources of Japanese ancient arts. With the fall of the Tokugawa Shogunate in 1868, the wearing of sword paraphernalia fell into disuse. The Japanese government therefore encouraged the export of such military items as *kokuza*, small knives (usually slotted through the samurai sword scabbard) with metal handles that were intricately wrought with scenes in combinations of different (so-called mixed) metals. These became quite popular in America. "The *kokuza* [handles] without blades became highly esteemed collectibles in the West," writes William P. Hood. And ultimately knife handles styled after *kokuza* were made in Japan specifically for export. In the late nineteenth century foreigners put *kokuza* to uses not originally envisioned by the Japanese—as handles for Western style dining implements.

> Among the first American silver manufacturers to do so was the Gorham Manufacturing Company . . . [whose archives for 1879 have uncovered] apparently genuine *kokuza* on a set of ornately engraved blades. . . . Dining implements with Japanese knife handles were also produced by Tiffany . . . each handle on [one such] twenty-four piece Tiffany set has a different motif. Twenty-two of the handles are genuine *kokuza* [and the remaining two, Tiffany's own matching facsimile versions of *kokuza*].[306]

In addition to this delight in the foreign and exotic (something we have seen frequently in our excursion through the archeology of the antique) there was another, a uniquely American, influence at work. Here it was not especially affirmative of the foreign at first, and it affected in particular those social orders lower than the "Brahmins." Due to the huge influx of non-English and/or non–northern European immigrants into the United States, primarily between 1890 and 1900, there arose the fear in the middle class of being inundated and dominated by "foreign" cultures. This fear led on the one hand to a popular contempt for their cultural achievements (and a supercilious ethnocentric mission to educate and assimilate these "wretched masses" in American virtue and taste) and therefore to a reemphasis on the priority of American antiques. On the other hand, the awareness that the very rich in America in fact lived among paintings, statuary, and other furnishings of European origin (even from such benighted places as Italy, Greece, and Spain—and now Japan, China, and India, too), whose cultures were older and more world-historically significant, argued against such cultural chauvinism—at least insofar as it was the ideal of the many to attain to the world and manners of the American aristocracy.

The newer immigrants from central and eastern Europe, meanwhile, could, after a respectable period of self-confidence-building as good citizens of their adopted land, opt for American antiques as their own, or for the antiques reflective of their various ethic origins, or both, or, as occurred eventually with some of their descendants, for the antiques of the entire world. Nevertheless, at first it was precisely in order to make of these newcomers good citizens, to assimilate them into the culture they had adopted, that the American establishment deliberately encouraged an indoctrination in American values through fostering an appreciation for American antiques.

Thus, for various reasons, after the 1880s, though American taste for the antique always had a special predilection for Americana as a kind of sociopolitical "default mode," this appreciation had reached beyond the American patriotic level and no longer required the justification of moral or civic improvement. Soon, too, in the last decades of the century, the influence of European "decadence" and what came to be called "aestheticism" crossed the ocean. Americans of wealth, fashion, and taste had to have their own rooms or "corners" furnished with Anglo-Japanese and Anglo-Indian motifs, in Near Eastern, Turkish, and other exotic styles, as exemplified by John D. Rockefeller's Moorish smoking room, now preserved in the Brooklyn Museum. Such influences were hardly stimuli for American chauvinism or any vision of moral betterment along traditional patriotic lines. In addition, a new literature of aesthetic appreciation appeared in the first decade of the twentieth century with books such as *Chats on Old Furniture*, *The Lure of the Antique*, *The Quest for the Quaint*, and *The Charm of the Antique*, along with connoisseur-collectors' associations such as the Walpole Society (founded 1910). In this way the appreciation of the antique in America during the 1890–1915 generation moved from the interest in antiques as mere curiosities and talismans with historical or cultural references (to persons or places or moral dispositions of note) to an appreciation of antiques as objects having peculiar artistic and aesthetic properties as well, objects that were evocative of the past and of the world of early America and also beyond America. And in the latter half of this period, because of the new societies and books, a more serious scholarship motivated American connoisseurs and collectors of antiques, who began to shun Victorian pastiches for "the real thing."

Of course there had always been collectors and connoisseurs of antiques in the most comprehensive modern sense in America, as we have noted, but they were exceptional. In a local newspaper story of 1870, the American collector Cummings Elsthan Davis (1816–96), of Concord, Massachusetts, is described this way: "His collection of antiques is worth several thousand dollars, and consists mostly of furniture, glassware, paintings, Indian relics, etc. . . . his pursuit holds him with the fascination of an invisible power. Rust and age have a weird influence over his heart. 'Whatever belongs to the remote past,' he says, 'has an unspeakable charm for me.' "[307] A similar and grander collection in Washington, D.C., was amassed by the founder of Washington's Gridiron Club, Ben Perley Poore (1820–87), who was inspired in his youth by a visit to Sir Walter Scott's Abbotsford to "create an American version of Abbotsford when he grew up." His "picturesque Gothic" confection of a mansion, made up (like the Hearst Castle later) of columns, staircases, paneling, fireplace mantels, and the like taken from stately homes of past notables of American history, also included antiquities from Egypt and the Holy Land as well as a replica of an old printer's shop containing Ben Franklin's original press.[308]

For the aristocracy of great wealth this type of collecting could be done on a colossal scale. In the 1880s George F. Harding Jr. tried to purchase an entire German castle and transport it to Chicago for use as his residence; only his refusal to make the expected payoffs to the mayor for permits prevented the transaction's completion.[309] For some, the private castle purchased from abroad reconstructed on American soil and packed with the antiques of the past was not enough. Really to acquire the glory of the past one had to do this where the past had actually been—abroad. Thus, William Waldorf Astor, seeking a higher sociocultural station than the United States could provide, purchased the country estate of Cliveden in England and had Sir Charles Barry (architect for the Houses of Parliament) rebuild it in Italian Palazzo style during the 1850s. To furnish it he had agents comb Europe for antiques. It soon had the best Italian Renaissance sculpture in private hands in England, as well as the best eighteenth-century French dining room (completely reassembled from a French chateau). His only serious competitors in this venue were the Rothschilds, who were also in need of a greater "establishment" amid the British nobility than their lineage provided. In architecture the French or Italian—or "Italianate"—seems to have been preferred. Hence, Isabella Stewart Gardner's Fenway Court was constructed on the marshy lands of the Boston fens as a Venetian palace, packed with masterpieces of European art and antiques, and was spectacularly revealed to Boston's haute monde on New Year's Eve 1902.[310]

Such efforts, often mocked, have been dubbed "steamboat gothic" or "robber baronial,"[311] but these ascriptions are usually unfair, at least insofar as they imply a lack of aesthetic discernment or concern merely with social status. Even the most exotic confections were usually carefully planned by these new multimillionaire collectors, who never would have considered "leaving it all to the decorator." This does not mean that decorators were not used, of course. Thus, it was said of the most prominent American decorator of the early 1910s, Elsie de Wolfe (who furnished Henry Clay Frick's Fifth Avenue mansion with much of the Parisian residue of the great Wallace Collection of antiques), that she "introduced Old French Furniture to New American Money."[312] Furthermore, just like the British in the eighteenth century vis-à-vis the Continent in the Grand Tour, many of America's new plutocrats in the latter half of the nineteenth century began to take extended trips abroad as a sort of senior seminar in culture; once back home, as Bruce Redford remarks, "the alumni of the Grand Tour designed galleries for their souvenirs."[313] Nancy Ruhling observes, "Indeed, Mark Twain wrote in his hilarious book *The Innocents Abroad* that in 1869 some 4,000 to 5,000 Americans per week were paying the then whopping sum of $1,250 to make the Grand Tour, and they were taking home everything that wasn't nailed down, and even trying to get a few things that were."[314]

The flow of antiques into the United States from Europe increased dramatically in 1909, when Congress eliminated American import duties (previously set at 20 percent of valuation) on all antiques, defined as works of art over one hundred years of age. This flow was further stimulated from Great Britain a year later when, through the efforts of David Lloyd George (then chancellor of the exchequer) and Winston Churchill (then president of the Board of Trade), "death duties" were imposed on all estates worth more than £1 million, permitting the art and antiques of great houses to be retained by family members only if they paid an inheritance tax of 25 percent, and thereby encouraging them to sell.

Cornelius Vanderbilt's mansion on Fifth Avenue in New York (at number 640, demolished in 1946) was designed and furnished in Victorian eclectic by J. Benooh and Christian Herter (with the assistance of Samuel

Avery, a major New York art and antiques dealer).[315] Vanderbilt was personally involved. According to William Baumgarten (assistant to Herter), "all designs were submitted to him from the first stone to the last piece of decoration or furniture. Mr. Vanderbilt was at our warerooms or at our shop almost every day."[316] As was similarly arranged in the case of the Duke of Hamilton and the Desnières firm, where genuine antique objects could not be found to suit the furnishing requirements, Herter meticulously designed new eclectic pieces in consultation with Vanderbilt; these pieces combined styles and motifs of the past and used the finest materials and most exacting standards of craftsmanship. But the Vanderbilt home contained many important genuine antiques, such as a malachite vase with French *bronze doré* mounts (made in 1819 for Count Michael Demidoff's Florence estate) which, at six feet tall and elevated on a four-foot plinth, dominated the center of the vestibule, whose walls were decorated in Pompeiian style and whose floors and ceiling were inlaid in Italian mosaic. The Vanderbilt *millefleur* Star Lattice Mughal carpet (made in Srinagar around 1700 and purchased by Vanderbilt in Venice in 1870) is another example.[317] The doors between the vestibule and grand hall were Barbedienne Foundry copies of Ghiberti's "Gates of Paradise." Chinese and Japanese silk embroideries were used lavishly, and cabinets in the dining room held collections of antique (eighteenth-century) continental porcelains. "Although the rooms did not look European, they drew on the historical culture of aristocratic Europe . . . the iconographic program of bounty and triumph that was carried throughout the house in a conscious allusion to Vanderbilt's fortune and power."[318] And Vanderbilt was quite self-conscious about what he was doing: he commissioned a four-volume work titled *Mr. Vanderbilt's House and Collection* (by E. Strahan) and, in imitation of the Louvre, made his picture gallery available to New Yorkers as a semi-public museum with a separate entrance and specified visiting hours.

Vanderbilt's "almost indiscriminate assemblage of styles" (to use his own words) was deliberately eclectic, just as his newly made Herter furniture was stylistically fusional. In the next decades, however, J. P. Morgan and Henry Clay Frick preferred to furnish their rooms in Old Masters and antique furniture in such a way as to allow each object its independent voice, rather than force it into a unified chorus of dazzling opulence. "Creating a more classical environment in their rooms than had been done in the homes of the Vanderbilts or Goulds—their Renaissance was not a Renaissance Revival, but more scholarly in spirit."[319] In accordance with the classical ideal, each part was to be appreciated in its own right, as well as appearing as an element within the whole.

In the first two decades of the twentieth century, a further change occurred. Whereas Morgan, Frick, Mellon, Gardner, Hartford, and their like pursued above all the genre of antique paintings (and some sculpture), acquiring antique furnishings as a quasi-functional (but essentially as an appropriate environmental) embellishment of the living space in which these artworks were to be enjoyed, Henry Ford and especially Henry du Pont pursued objects of the applied arts (furniture, ceramics, tapestries, glass and crystal, carpets, objets de vertu) for their own intrinsic aesthetic antique properties.

Where the aristocracy of wealth led, the less affluent followed. At American auctions by the time of the economic boom of the late 1920s, prices were realized for furnishings and decorative art objects that were not matched again until the 1960s. "During the 1928/29 auction season in New York City, the two largest auction houses reported a total of just over $9 million in sales . . . [and in March] 1929 some 37,000 people paid $1 each to attend the First International Antiques Exposition held at New York City's Commodore Hotel."[320] A healthy trade in antiques existed in major American cities even before the 1920s, but it was in that decade that for the first time there emerged a national (indeed international) continuity of shared knowledge and valuation. In 1922 the first issue of *The Magazine Antiques* appeared, followed by *The Antiquarian* the year after. They were so popular that in the case of the former "all January 1929 issues were gone within two days of printing." And "in 1928 nationwide directories of dealers were being published" for the first time.[321]

There were also apparent countervailing forces at the turn of the century. Art Nouveau, the dominant style of the 1895–1905 decade, was by its very name suggestive of novelty, liberation from tradition, radical breaks with the past, and youth over age.[322] Like the dominant artistic style of every epoch, Art Nouveau provides insights into the idea of the antique in its time. As a comprehensive stylistic movement founded in response to the exhaustion of revivals of traditional styles (and their eclectic amalgamations) and as a reaction to Victorian clutter generally, and deliberately using new techniques of production involving novel or nontraditional materials (glass, cement, tile, steel) in unusual ways and combinations, Art Nouveau would indicate a mentality antithetical to that which supports the antique.

Yet in two ways it uniquely fostered the appreciation of the antique. It was the first stylistic movement to disrupt the traditional hierarchy in the plastic arts wherein painting and sculpture (because they were "fine") held first rank. In the Art Nouveau style not only were the "decorative arts" or "crafts" given equal status, but in fact it was precisely in these "craft" forms and media that the Art Nouveau style most fully and pervasively expressed itself.[323] This emphasis supported the view of the "artfulness" and "aesthetic value"—even the "taste refinement" value—of the quotidian object that we encountered earlier in our discussion of the American preference for plainness and usefulness. Thus, in the first decade of the twentieth century, John Cotton Dana, founder of the Newark Museum, talked of "the undue reverence for oil paint" and even suggested that "oil painting has no such close relation to the development of good taste and the refinement as have countless objects of daily use."[324]

Second, with Art Nouveau's frank exhibition of the good craftsmanship of construction and its deliberate effort to make all materials, no matter how intractable, conform and submit to the peculiar imaginative designs of the artist (e.g., iron shaped as if it mere merely melted wax), Art Nouveau called attention to the sensuous physicality of medium above and beyond any content or message. This is important for three reasons. First, physicality is the special mark of the "craft" object we most often think of as the primary instance of "an antique" (rather than a painting, for example). Second, attention to medium is the uniquely modernist basis of the twentieth-century aesthetic response (beginning with Manet, as we have seen). Third, this forthright confrontation with the sensuous medium of the art object prepares us to respond aesthetically to the agedness of an antique's patina, immediately confronting us with its historicality.

In any case, by 1910 Art Nouveau was no longer "nouveau" but looked frightfully old-fashioned (many in the 1920s came to regard it with horror; Roger Frye, for example, characterized it as a mere "degraded modern analogue" of rococo).[325] And so again there was a turning away from the "deliberate and often tiresome novelty of the previous decade" to a taste for antiques: "period furniture was rediscovered to have charm, and old pieces of pleasing form and good patination began to be sought after. . . . Distinguished rooms were created which, whilst not seeking exactly to re-create the appearance of an earlier age . . . tried specifically to capture some essence of the past."[326] In America Edith Wharton and Elsie de Wolfe tended to favor French styles of the eighteenth century, and in Edwardian England the Sitwells promoted Italianate neo-Baroque. Meanwhile, throughout France and the Continent in the years preceding World War I, through the popularity of Diaghilev's Ballets Russes (with designs by Bakst and Benois), there was a craze for the Russo-Byzantine style in decor (even in Germany, where it competed with the nationally favored "Junker-Baronial cum Hunting-Lodge" style).

T. J. Jackson Lears nicely characterizes the entire situation in America
with regard to antiques:

> Throughout the later decades of the 19th century, the art fever rose
> steadily. It animated not only aesthetic pilgrimages abroad but also
> unprecedented institutional activity at home. The Metropolitan Museum
> of Art, the Boston Museum of Fine Arts, and the Corcoran Gallery in
> Washington, D.C., were all founded in 1870, the Chicago Art Institute in
> 1879. Private collections proliferated, their range widening as travelers
> added the Near East and Orient to their territories. Charles Langdon
> Freer, Denman Ross, and William Sturgis Bigelow assembled Japanese
> prints and porcelain; Isabel Stewart Gardner crowded her Boston home
> with oriental and medieval acquisitions; J. P. Morgan combined medieval
> and Egyptian enthusiasms in forming his huge collections [much of which
> later went to the Smithsonian and the National Gallery]; the sculptor
> George Gray Barnard spent years acquiring the paintings, sculpture, and
> stained glass for the Cloisters, which he opened in 1914. (The Metropoli-
> tan Museum bought the collection in 1925 with funds provided by John
> D. Rockefeller.) Earlier and more enthusiastically than their European
> counterparts, American collectors rescued Tukogawa pottery from mod-
> ernizing Japanese, unearthed twelfth-century Madonnas from roadside
> ditches, and in general tried to prevent the sacred relics of the past from
> becoming the detritus of the present.[327]

Lears observes that around the turn of the century there was a change
from the view of art as an instrument of instruction and/or moral edifi-
cation to a view "stressing that the aesthetic experience was primarily
psychological rather than moral." But he also notes that the psychological factor still had a moral connection (perhaps, we should better say, a
"pragmatic justification") in the sense that the aesthetic experience itself
was held to have therapeutic value ("like a good armchair in which to
rest from physical fatigue"), so that, being thus refreshed, one could return to more serious occupations. Alternatively, for those fortunate
enough to be unconstrained by serious occupations altogether, the art
object could derive its value entirely from being a means of freeing the
spirit from all mundane concerns. This was the view proposed by aestheticism as it crept across the Atlantic.

In this context, Lears also remarks on the connection between fashionable aestheticism and the appreciation specifically of antiques, citing the
example of Harvard at the turn of the century:

> The notion that art could provide release from bourgeois anxieties
> emerged most explicitly among young aesthetes who clustered at Harvard
> around the turn of the century. Scorning athleticism, a few students gathered

at the Stylus Club, where they quoted Huysmans and composed Wildean sonnets. For exemplars they looked to Santayana or Pierre Chaignon La Rose. . . . Like Santayana, they sought liberation from the "straightened spirit" of the late-Victorian bourgeoisie by tasting beauty in its many guises. Chalice and crucifix, Buddha and *Kakemono*, all became relics in the cult of the aesthetic experience. . . . The Harvard cult of aesthetic experience shared the psychic origins of the more general fascination with premodern [i.e., antique] forms. It also had some of the same results. Though they railed against modern culture's lack of "spirituality," the aesthetes detached pre-modern *objets d'art* [antiques] from any traditional religious meaning, creating a surrogate religion of taste well-suited to a secular culture of consumption.[328]

This last remark suggests an important contribution of aestheticism generally to the mentality of antiques collecting and connoisseurship. As we have seen, the medievals freed ancient objects from the contamination of the pagan Roman civilization that created them by resetting and reconfiguring them in Christian religious objects; the eighteenth-century French, by setting them in Rococo *bronze doré* mounts, took quotidian Chinese porcelain vases and bowls and both domesticated their foreignness and, defunctionalizing their use, transformed the commonplace object into the art object. So, by detaching objects from their traditional religious and social meanings through aestheticization, the mentality of the Stylus Club created a religion of taste that transferred to the object's peculiar objective properties all the priority in the aesthetic experience, and to the aesthetic experience alone the entirety of its objective worth. From this viewpoint, the experience has no purpose but its own enjoyment, just as the object has no function other than to be there for the experiencer. The object's past, its form and function, its qualities and categories are significant insofar as, and *only* insofar as, they provoke the aesthetic imagination to respond to it. For this reason, art museums at this time—now beginning to differentiate themselves from historical and commemorative museums—began selecting "objects on the basis of their rarity, authenticity, and aesthetic quality."[329]

But this aestheticism and hothouse exoticism did not long survive the First World War. (It is one of the prime characteristics of the modern century that styles and tastes changed with great rapidity.) As we noted above, the basic condition or default mode of antiques was always an *owned heritage*. Like "olde English" in Great Britain, in America "colonial" (or "olde English" [by adoption or presumptive inheritance] or, at least, "country kitchen") never died—even in the face of art deco and modernism in the decades to come. The extraordinary number of deliberate fakes of antique objects (particularly of the American Federal period) produced in major New England and midwestern cities in the 1920s merely confirms the demand for them.

The 1930s were in general not kind to antiques. The Depression deflated their monetary value, and since the aesthetic experience is a luxury in a world of basic needs unsatisfied, the collection and connoisseurship of antiques was again confined to the fortunate few.[330] In addition, the Bauhaus and International Modern encouraged a stylistic and furnishing austerity according to the maxim "more is less." Both were functional and "bare-bones-minimalist" versions of neo-classicism (a classicism not of Palladio but of Le Corbusier, Gropius, and Saarinen), classicism of the intellectual and astringent variety (like Schoenberg's music of the era). The preference, an intellectual Puritanism, for sparseness, the absence of color, the reliance on non-antique materials like sheets of clear glass and tubes of chrome, coincided with a deliberate avoidance of any hint of historicism. Actual antiques were often destroyed in the process of being made to conform to this new aesthetic mentality: antique furniture was peeled of its skin, its patina, and was "pickled" (bleached white like driftwood) or just painted white.

But there were "antiques-friendly" forces at work as well, especially by the late 1930s. Ralph Edwards, antiques connoisseur and curator of the Victoria and Albert Museum, argued in an influential piece in the magazine *Decoration* that whatever the benefits of modern style in terms of design and innovative use of materials, in terms of workmanship there were rarely to be found contemporary equals of antique furnishings.[331] There was also the discovery (or perhaps one should say the "invention") of "folk art," a category of aesthetic appreciation that one might describe as "adjacent" to antiques. As part of America's general reexamination of its political position in the world of nations and the reassessment of its Americanness, rooted in fast-disappearing "rural values," Holger Cahill, having "noticed" folk art in Maine in the summer of 1926, "discovered" it to the general public in 1932 with a catalogue and exhibition ("American Folk Art: The Art of the Common Man") at the Museum of Modern Art in New York.[332] And then there was the cinema, where historical epics were public favorites. In fact, the first large-scale American appreciation of the antiques of the Victorian era was the direct result of the national success of *Gone with the Wind*. The economy was sufficiently recovered by the end of the decade so that "a total of 100 small antiques shows occurred in America in 1939."[333]

Despite desperate attempts even into the next decade to make International Modern acceptable to the vast majority of Americans by such

luminaries as T. H. Robsjohn-Gibbings (the most influential designer/
theoretician of the period),[334] much of America continued to prefer the
past styles that antique furnishings provided as a more comfortable living
environment (even if for the majority this meant merely chintz and pastiches in mass-production replicas of antique or antique-like objects). The
economic and political effects of World War II further exposed American
culture to the civilizations of the globe (especially the Orient) and inspired
in it (as it had in France and England in the prior century) a self-
conception as liberator, inheritor, culminator of world civilization and its
history—and therefore the rightful heir, proprietor, and preserver of its
antiques.

After the 1960s just about every style was revived again, and all periods of antiques were collected and appreciated from around the world.
By then, Art Nouveau objects were old enough to be considered antiques, and that style was revived in new productions, their sensuous
curves and slightly decadent air blending well with the contemporary
hippie counterculture, which was soon absorbed into the aesthetic of the
mainstream culture. In the early 1970s, the "craftsman" and the art deco
of the 1920s were revived, and their productions became the new antiques; in the late 1970s objects of the International Modern became
antiques.

And it was in the 1970s also that art theory (in the writings of Arthur
Danto and others) caught up with much of what contemporary art had
been doing since the beginning of the century. Duchamp's *Fountain* of
1916 is, after all, the quintessential modern art object: an everyday object of use, a functional piece of equipment (a urinal) made dis-functional
by being spatio-temporally dislocated (in this case disconnected from
plumbing and placed in a museum) and, by being renamed or redefined,
presumptively transformed by the insight of the art world, for which it
was intellectually re-created from the commonplace object that it was
into the art object that it is (or that its art theory tells us it must be). Like
the Dadaists, the Surrealists were attracted to the displaced, the decontextualized, such as one would find in "the chance encounter of an um-
brella and a sewing machine on an operating table," in the famous and
oft-quoted phrase (of Isidore Ducasse a.k.a. "le Comte de Lautréa-
mont") meant to analogize the response to the ultimate Surrealist art object. Max Ernst described his art as "the coupling of two realities,
irreconcilable in appearance, upon a plane which apparently does not
suit them."[335] Such creations as Salvador Dali's fur-lined bathtub were
demonstrations of his belief that the art object should be "absolutely useless from the practical and rational point of view, created wholly for the

purpose of materializing in a fetishistic way (with the maximum of tangible reality) ideas and fantasies having a delirious character."[336] And as Benjamin has noted, the Surrealists were similarly attracted to objects displaced not only in space, in function, or in planes of reality but also in time: "objects that started to die . . . and fashionable places that had begun to lose their lustre."[337] Adding a further impetus to this new aesthetic appreciation was the appearance of "African art" (not just African "artifacts"). Already praised by Picasso for their geometric reductionism that "purified" forms and thus stimulated Cubism, African masks and sculptures—now uprooted from their original use-world and thus from their prior socioreligious function—were regarded by the Surrealists as "art," as transformed into art by their re-worlding in the contemporary art world.[338] Again, "another country" substituted for "the past."

Thus, in much twentieth-century theorizing about the nature of art itself, the object per se was set forth as a primary desideratum of the aesthetic experience. This is the object *in* its—and *entirely because of* its—purely decontextualized or "denatured" situation so as to bring out its heretofore unconsidered, "unnoticed" characteristics (whether these characteristics are perceived objectively as properties *of* or *in* the object or cognized theoretically as notions *about* the object).[339] In this way, the aesthetic consciousness of the twentieth century—as transformed by modern artists and interpreted by modern theories of art—was uniquely inclined and predisposed to the aesthetic encounter with the antique. Several interconnected factors demonstrate the consequences of modern art and its theories for our final set of *archés* for the evolution of the idea and appreciation of the antique.

First of all, the antique, decontextualized in time and culture, showing its age in its materiality, and forcing us to think about it in terms of its style and former use-world and its relation to history, confronts us much in the same manner as modern art does. Kasimir Malevich noticed this similarity in his 1928 essay "Suprematism":

> When we examine an antique column, we are no longer interested in the fitness of its construction to perform its technical task in the building but recognize in it the material expression of a pure feeling. We no longer see in it a structural necessity but view it as a work of art in its own right. . . . Antique works of art are kept in museums and carefully guarded, not to preserve them for practical use but in order that their eternal artistry may be enjoyed. The difference between the new, nonobjective ("useless") art and the art of the past lies in the fact that the full artistic value of the latter comes to light (becomes recognized) only after life, in search of some new

expedient, has forsaken it, whereas the unapplied artistic element of the new art outstrips life and shuts the door on "practical utility."[340]

Second, there was the final disintegration of traditional distinctions— not only of art vs. craft, but of ancient vs. modern, and art vs. non-art. This process began (as early as the late nineteenth century) with Modernism's subversion of the distinction between high and low culture and its consequent incorporation and transformation of the quotidian into what turned out to be a new elitist vision and thus in its own way elevated the mundane into an object of aesthetic contemplation and response. (Think of van Gogh's several paintings of peasant shoes.) After the 1980s every art-historical style had already been revived at least twice over and objects became antiques in a decade rather than a century. Every era and the antiques of every civilization became more or less equal in the estimation of connoisseur-collectors, and even a modicum of equality emerged between the "fine" and "not-so-fine" antique arts—with some examples of antique furniture reaching the $10 million mark at auction, thereby surpassing all but a handful of paintings. At this point Postmodernism reconstructed the concepts "revival" and "art" themselves.[341] On the theoretical level not only the traditional distinction between art and craft but the traditional categories separating "art objects" from "real things" collapsed (or at least became blurred): Brillo boxes and cartoons, stuffed goats, and excremental performances were proposed as art. Thus, modern art and modern art theory established the last *arché* in the archeology of the idea and aesthetic appreciation of antiques. If quotidian objects (the equipment of every usage—the urinal or the one-meter steel bar) can be aesthetically appreciated, how much more can antiques, whose beauty and untimeliness and decontextualization from the pragmatic use-world call on us (indeed require us) to notice them and attune to them as objects of aesthetic enjoyment.

In effect, twentieth-century artworks and their supporting theories have thus drawn our attention to quotidian objects—the objects of everyday use or encounter—in ways heretofore unimagined. It was in the 1950s that the theory first arose that art need not represent anything at all—not imitate, not express, not "be about," but simply "be," just as quotidian objects "simply are." Contemporary art has conditioned us to appreciate everyday objects, if only because it has (at least since Duchamp) proffered and proposed to us at least the possibility of appreciating anything aesthetically. Thus, whatever the ultimate consequence for "fine art" in general, the consequence of twentieth-century art for enabling and encouraging the aesthetic appreciation of antiques (which are normally thought of as exactly such everyday objects), for enhancing their potential for entry into the arena as "objects of aesthetic appreciation," has been beneficial—just as beneficial as the breakdown of the traditional distinction between the "fine arts" and those that are presumably "not so fine" (craft, decorative, applied arts).

Finally, on the practical level, contemporary art and its accompanying theories resulted in a public at a loss for obtaining genuine aesthetic enjoyment from "art." Since what art now was and how it could possibly be enjoyed were no longer easy questions to answer—or, if answered in theory, not easily achieved in practice—antiques filled much of this aesthetic void. Numerous artistically oriented and aesthetically sensitive individuals simply discovered in antiques many of the properties that contemporary art no longer afforded them, for they found it difficult to respond affectively to what was produced by a theoretical program.[342] For insofar as eliciting a purely cognitive response was the intention (or the only success) of many of these presumptive artworks— as a demonstration of some proposed truth or an instantiation of some theory—they were not (or were all the less) artworks in themselves, but at best, evidence for or instances of some assertion or set of assertions *about* art.[343]

And soon enough there arose a perceived shortage of an adequate supply of "real antiques" to meet the public demand. The market's need to supply objects of the past, coupled with the increase and/or blurring of categories formerly relevant to distinctions between fine and craft, art and reality, plebeian/ordinary and singular/extraordinary, led to the boom in collectibles (in origin a peculiarly American phenomenon).

Expansion (globalization and democratization) and rapidity of change (in categories and vogues) were the hallmarks of the last decades of the twentieth century. Indeed, globalization extended in every direction. Hence, many collectibles and antiques started leaving the Occident, where we have been tracing their arrival, and returning to their homes in the East; while others made new Far and Middle Eastern immigrants to the West feel at home there. In the 1980s Japanese collectors and dealers scoured American antiques malls for Disney-character cookie jars and at the same time repatriated to their homeland nineteenth-century Satsuma ceramics once thought too gaudy for native consumption and made only for sale abroad. In the 1990s expatriate Iranians living in Los Angeles sought out antique Persian miniatures, carpets, metalwork, and even glass waterpipes (all of the Kajar dynasty, which preceded the Pahlevis) to fill out their French Louis XVI decors and make themselves newly at home in the West. In the first decade of the twenty-first century we find new Chinese capitalists hunting down antique Chinese porcelains (even ones that once were considered worthy only for the export market) and new Russian industrialists repatriating Fabergé anything.[344]

2.8
Archeological Conclusions

Having sketched the latter part of the twentieth century only briefly, we bring this deconstructive archeology of the antique to a close at this point, for several reasons. First there is simply too much diversity of detail in the last half of the American century to be included in this summary of *archés* of the antique. The era needs its own independent history, its own book. This is due in large part to the era's greater openness in the *possibilities* of the antique, both in terms of the opening up *of* the category "antique" so as to be more inclusive of a wide range of objects (allowing for a greater overlapping with related categories such as collectibles, mementos, artifacts, and the like) and in terms of the opening up of the antique *to* a greater mass of appreciators. (Indeed, in many ways, the category "collectibles" has for a large number of people replaced or overshadowed "antiques.") Furthermore, this time frame (roughly from the 1960s to the present) is too close to us for "history," for we are still in the presence of this all-too-recent past. Nevertheless, for the purposes of this chapter—the fleshing out in history of the emergence and evolution of the idea and appreciation of the antique through its *archés*—all the essential elements of this concept as stated in the working definition have now been disclosed. We can, then, claim that we are up-to-date in terms of a "critical mass" of historical particulars to flesh out the skeletal definition. Still, we might want to have greater precision and detail regarding the objective makeup, the aspects, the components, of antiques and of our responses to them.

Consequently, we must now proceed to chapter 3 to render a comprehensive re-appraisal of the idea of the antique in schematic form, just as we found its formulaic summation in the definition of the antique in chapter 1. We will do this by setting out ten criteria for the idea and appreciation of the antique. This elaboration provides a final examination of the idea of the antique and of how we interpret it; and indirectly, it answers the question, what does connoisseurship of antiques amount to?

But as we leave this archeology, we may ask, what is *really new* in the perception and appreciation of the antique since the Imperial Roman era, when Pliny recounted his contemporaries' connoisseurship of antique Greek silver wine cups with their patinated surfaces? Certainly the kernel of the idea of the antique and the beginnings of aesthetic appreciation are already present in Pliny's Rome. The *range* has most definitely expanded since his time, along with the **types of objects** that are available for aesthetic appreciation of their antiqueness, and the number and **diversity of civilizations** whose "residue" antiques embody (the potential "world pool," one might call it) is greatly enlarged. What of the *appreciation* of the antique itself? On this issue it is difficult to say with certainty, for although archeologists may discover many heretofore unknown caches of objects treasured by lost civilizations (objects of yet further antiquity or exotic origin), we can never recover the subjective response—the comprehension, awareness, admiration, pleasure—of these peoples so removed from our own time frame. But the division between "fine art" and "craft," the elevation of the quotidian object to potential "art" or "aesthetic" object, the distinctions between the antique proper and other categories (the artifact, the collectible, the trophy, and such), the idea of civilization itself and the understanding of its embodiment in art and in an inheritance of artworks (i.e., the idea of art history, the development of the public art museum), and the transformation of the concept of time from cyclical to evolutionary—these developments all have undoubtedly enriched, advanced, and extended our sensibilities to these objects and thus deepened our aesthetic response to them. These developments are fruits of the passage of time and the discovery of the earth.

Is it possible that in setting forth the historical modalities of perspective, in seeing the applications and repetitions of different foci, and in examining mentalities that have fostered different ways of attending to and diverse modes of appreciating "objects with a past," our archeology may have delineated primarily matters of quantitative rather than qualitative change?

The idea of the antique, along with the development of a unique aesthetic response to it, seems to be a primordial component of advanced civilized life per se; and perhaps it is an indicator that civilization has indeed occurred wherever and whenever this idea and its accompanying appreciation arise, even as it has evolved over time across the globe. With each successive epoch or stage of development we have seen some "new" and "additional" features emerging to contribute to the totality of the concept "antique," so that one can talk sensibly about the steady and progressive *evolution* of the idea of the antique and its appreciation through its *archés* up to the present time—though in the Medieval period we found some losses (hence *devolution*) as well. We could also say that each period provides to a great degree only a cultural shift of viewpoint directed on *some* properties of *some* objects (rather than others) so that each epoch relights the same landscape for its own "objects with a past," reconfiguring a limited number of factors that collectively contribute to the meaningfulness of the term "antique" for that time. Thus, Ancient Rome, the Renaissance, and the nineteenth century each had in some sense an equally "adequate" concept of "antiques" even if this conception was not quite as rich and inclusive as the twenty-first century's idea of the antique. Consequently, we may assume that their aesthetic appreciation of antiques is unlikely to have been as comprehending or comprehensive as our own in the present time, though I would be as reluctant to insist that ours is always and in every respect an "improvement" on some earlier moment of this archeology as I would be to adopt the highly relativistic view that each epoch's conception is merely a reconfiguration or reformulation of its predecessor's or successor's conception and is never in any respect an "improvement" on it. In this light, the *archés* we have deconstructed in this archeological survey may be understood as expositions and interpretations of both the different portions of the definition of the antique that we proposed in the opening chapter and of the ten schematic categories of appreciation and evaluation of the antique that we will establish in chapter 3.

THREE

The Ten Criteria of Antiques

**Do antiques possess certain objective
traits that elicit the connoisseur's
aesthetic response to them?**

A s promised in chapter 1, I now propose ten $(3 \times 3 + 1)$ criteria for the connoisseurship and collecting of antiques. They have simply been extracted from the archeology of chapter 2 and are intended to amplify the definition of the antique given in chapter 1. Unlike our account there, which was concerned with meaning and interpretation, here we will emphasize and focus on pragmatics, on evaluative judgments and appraisals of antiques, making use of many concrete examples and counterexamples for understanding the issues to which these ten criteria give rise.

I have clustered these ten criteria in three groups of three, with a single criterion at the end:

Qualitative

1. Subject
2. Condition
3. Technical perfection

Quantitative

4. Rarity
5. Size
6. Completeness

Historical

7. Age

8. Authenticity
9. Provenance

Adventitious

10. Contextual

Let us now recall the definition given chapter 1: *an antique is a primarily handcrafted object of rarity and beauty that by means of its associated provenance and its agedness as recognized by means of its style and material endurance, has the capacity to generate and preserve for us the image of a world now past.* We may now note that the ten criteria are not collectively identical with the parts of the definition, in the sense of being able to be mapped one on one with each term or phrase of the definition. Thus, for example, "rarity," "beauty," and "age," which are terms used in the definition, now reappear among the ten criteria, for these are understood as essentially objective properties of the object—though not without a subjective aspect. But "generating and preserving for us an image of a world now past" does not reappear among the following ten, for this effect of generating and preserving is a primarily subjective aspect, namely, the individual's *response to* the antique's objective properties. Conversely, "authenticity" and "size" appear among the ten criteria, but they are not explicitly mentioned in the definition, though these matters certainly came into play in the preceding archeology's account. And some important characteristics of the antique appear explicitly neither in the definition nor in the ten categories above—"price," for example, which is especially relevant to authenticity but which will be separately discussed as part of the last of the ten criteria: *Adventitious,* "contextual." Let us explore these, and some additional reasons, further.

First, neither the terms and parts of the definition that characterize the antique in chapter 1 nor the ten criteria that follow here should be understood as stipulating the complete set of necessary and sufficient conditions for establishing the "antiqueness" of a thing. Rather, as stated earlier, the idea of the "antique" should be viewed as characterizing a family of similar things. If a sufficient number of the terms of the definition apply to a given object or if a sufficient number of the traits established by the ten criteria are experienced as objectively present in or relevant to the object—and *to the degree that they apply*, are present, or are relevant—then the term "antique" correctly attaches to the object in question. Rarity per se, for example, is neither a necessary nor sufficient condition for a thing's being an antique, though most antiques, *because they are antiques*, are indeed rare. Even age, which would, of all these criteria, appear to be a necessary condition (though certainly not a sufficient one, as we have noted), is a very loose requirement, simply because it is difficult to stipulate for all types of antiques that a specified precise number of years provides the requisite agedness for "age."[1] Hence a given object may properly be judged to be an antique and yet fail to satisfy one or more of the ten criteria to some degree. In fact, the degree to which it fails may itself depend on which criterion is being applied. But depending on the number of criteria and on its degree of failure to satisfy one or more criteria, in that respect a given object fails to be an antique.

Furthermore, second, we are considering these ten criteria for evaluation of the antique as part of the connoisseurship and collecting world, where in order for a thing to *be what it is*, it has to succeed in establishing its "right" to stake that claim. Hence, "authenticity" is not a part of the stated definition of the antique as given in chapter 1, simply because *in abstraction* we take it for granted that the definition will be correctly applied. But *in the practical world* of appraising and evaluating a particular object for its "antiqueness," authenticity is an appropriate consideration, and therefore is one of the ten criteria we propose. An object that fails to be authentic—or *authenticated* or *authenticatable*—will, to that degree, fail to be what it purports to be and fail to have the "capacity to evoke and preserve for us the image of a world now past" (or at least will fail to do so relative to another object that is otherwise similar and that has such authenticity), and thus, to that degree, it will fail to be an antique. Put another way, the definition was intended to specify what an antique is as an abstract universal category; the ten criteria are intended to function in the practical world of "more or less," of degrees, of estimations and judgments relative to a particular case.

A third reason why there can be no precise mapping of the terms of the definition on the ten criteria is simply that the terms of the definition affect differently the significance of some criteria (and vice versa) when applied to individual instances. Moreover, these criteria themselves are rarely *equally relevant in degree* for any particular case. That is, the terms of the definition and the criteria tend to overlap and reinforce one another, and one criterion may tend to render another more, or less, significant—or even irrelevant. A condition of the definition, "handcraftedness," for example, is relevant to such criteria as *technical perfection* and *condition* (which are qualitative criteria); but handcraftedness is equally relevant to identifiable persons who made the item in question and thus to *authenticity* and *provenance* (which are historical criteria). That the criteria themselves overlap and may imply one another also means that a deficiency in a given object with respect to one of these criteria may also affect (or be affected by) the object's satisfaction of another criterion. This occurs, for example, when we "forgive" an antique's unsatisfactory *condition* if the object is *very* old (an Ancient Greek vase) and especially if its *provenance* accounts for this condition (e.g., it survived a famous battle or natural catastrophe and has suffered this loss or deteriorated in this way precisely for that reason), or when we forgive the condition in certain *materials* that must necessarily show wear or physical degradation (a Coptic textile, the sun-bleached surface of wood) because of their fragility but may not forgive the condition so easily in other materials (an engraved carnelian or jade cameo).

Boulle furniture, for example, is inlaid with tiny pieces of wood, brass, and tortoise shell, and each of these materials has a different rate of expansion and contraction, making the piece inherently unstable; thus, after two hundred years of seasonal temperature and humidity changes we would expect problems with the condition of a Boulle piece. But we would be less inclined to forgive poor condition in another material, such as a "brilliant cut" crystal punch bowl that has cracked or been seriously chipped. More generally, we expect less of organic materials than inorganic ones vis-à-vis condition: the organic plasticity of a cracked chair leg gives less offense than the "crystallineity" of a fine porcelain or gem whose integrity has been compromised. Similarly, if the antique in question is constructed of many parts, we forgive damage to or loss of one of these parts more readily than damage to a thing that has no parts (i.e., is homogeneous). Again, some *historical* criteria, provenance and authenticity, for example, can be more significant than other historical criteria (e.g., age) and can trump all *qualitative* criteria combined—subject, condition, and technical perfection. This happens especially when a historically impressive provenance and certain authenticity combine with an extraordinary object's great rarity. Whereas, if an object is not terribly rare or is of unknown (or insignificant) provenance—which is usually the case for the vast majority of common antiques—then generally its age, condition, and beauty are extremely important.

The dialectic of age and provenance in relation to qualitative criteria is oftentimes peculiar, as can been seen in its effect on the price of similar antiques, and it is instructive to note how the permutations and interdependencies of these criteria play out in the contemporary antiques marketplace. Even if lacking in provenance, an early American eighteenth-century highboy (also called a "tall-boy" or "chest-on-chest"), for example, is worth ten times more than the English archetype on which it was modeled (even if the English one is older, better made by a known maker, and made of better materials). Similarly, a Confederate U.S. Civil

War sword, poorly made of poor materials, is worth more than the pre–Civil War U.S. Army regulation sword which it imitated (and which, again, was better made of better materials). A lesser-quality, smaller-size, poorer-condition silver spoon by Paul Revere is worth ten times the spoon by a silversmith who was his Boston contemporary (e.g., Ebenezer Moulton)—and this is so only by virtue of two accidents of history: Revere's famous "ride" that warned of the British arrival and, most of all, the celebration of this event in Longfellow's poem, which used to be memorized by generations of American schoolchildren. Hence, we must bear continually in mind the inherent instability, non-self-sufficiency, and interdependence of the ten criteria.

Recalling the ten criteria—*qualitative* (subject, condition, technical perfection), *quantitative* (rarity, size, completeness), *historical* (age, authenticity, provenance), and *adventitious* (contextual)—one might wonder why I have grouped them in three groups of three with a single criterion at the end. To this query I can offer no response other than this: that they seem to fall into these groupings and that it is easier to remember them this way.

Qualitative criteria are based on direct aesthetic appeal of the object due to its *perceptible excellence* in some respect.

1. Subject. In the case of antiques that are instances of the genres of painting, sculpture, and the like (such as the *nef* with which our story began) and that are therefore representational (and if they really are *antiques* in the genres of painting and sculpture they are unlikely to be *non*representational), then the subject matter depicted should be attractive and appealing, fascinating and enticing.[2] One thinks here especially of depictions of beautiful people or scenes, but even massacres and crucifixions, even certain "ugly" representations, can be fascinating and attractive.[3] Yet normally, "if [the painting] has lots of people, each doing something in a landscape, and if there is something both archetypical and individual about what is going on," and if the painting's subject or theme has been famously treated in some other genre (a celebrated play, poem, or novel, say), the subject matter is usually most attractive.[4]

But in antiques that are intrinsically nonrepresentational genres—what are usually referred to as crafts or decorative or applied arts and thus the usual sorts of things that are thought of as antiques—we cannot discuss beauty as it pertains to a subject matter within the work. Rather than attend to what I earlier called the "worked world *in* the work," as in representational art, we have here to attend only to the associated past "use-world *of* the object" in which the object did its work and which its "antiqueness" now evokes.[5] This use-world becomes a major part of its "subject." And in this instance it is the attractiveness of the object's function and its associations in its past world that matters, so that even apart from the materials from which they are made, chalices and chandeliers are normally preferred to chamber pots and cuspidors; and jewelry that can be associated with aristocratic or exotic or joyful events and functions is generally preferred to jewelry associated with daily, plebeian purposes or with mourning.[6]

In antiques that fall into the category of applied or decorative arts, because they have no internally worked world (and this because they exist more in terms of the "opacity of their media," as we have called it), the material of which the object is made usually plays a greater role than its past in the aesthetic experience. The material itself and its construction become almost as much the "subject" of the work as the past world to which it refers. Gold and ivory are generally preferred to terra cotta and wax, not simply because of their rarity or the monetary value of these materials, but because of the technical virtuosity that can be (must be) exhibited in their transformation from "mere stuff" into "art media." Even in paintings, where the inherent preciousness of the substances of which they are made (more often just canvas and oil paint rather than lapis lazuli and gold leaf) is generally not an issue, different material media have different consequences for the experience of the antique. That is why, all other considerations being equal, oil painting is preferred to watercolor is preferred to monochromatic drawing is preferred to etching is preferred to photographic print. Similarly, in sculpture, bronze is preferred to spelter (also called "Britannia"), and spelter is preferred to terra cotta, and terra cotta is preferred to plaster.

Some materials also age better than others, that is, while they show their age they do not make the object look "shabby" (for example, stone is generally better than plastic [think of the Pompidou Center in Paris]; statues if made of Britannia metal tend almost always to develop an unpleasant skin disease, whereas if made of bronze they develop a mellow darkened patina, unless exposed to saltwater). Some materials simply by their nature suggest an older age than others: bronze rather than brass rather than aluminum (though some early-twentieth-century uses of aluminum—for opera glasses, for instance—may make this a typical exception to the rule).

Hence, the subject, by its attractiveness—its appeal, its beauty, the materials of which it is made, what its functions were, and the world in which it functioned—entices, encourages us to evoke and image of the world now past.

2. *Condition.* Condition is a highly relative criterion. It is relative especially to age and material medium; it is also relative to rarity and provenance. As is the case in human physiology, there are two sources of an object's deterioration. The first is genetic: the material breaks down and slowly decomposes, especially in the case of organic materials (cloth, wood, oil paint). The second source of deterioration is accidental (traumatic): damage is by external forces such as wear, stain, breakage, and erosion. Furthermore, as we noted above, more or less is demanded of an antique's condition depending on its material medium and this medium's greater or lesser amenability to restoration. And again, more or less is demanded of an antique's condition depending on its genre. If, for example, we consider architectural instances of antique objects in disrepair (perhaps needing restoration or having already undergone restoration), we accept this deterioration in antique buildings fairly easily, whereas a cracked antique cameo would lose much of its value because of its poor condition (and probably the impossibility of its repair). Likewise, a marble statue without its head, though certainly less desirable than one without a finger, is more acceptable than a painting in which the portrait's head has been obliterated or cut out.[7] Probably more than anything, tolerance of poor condition is relative to age: generally, the older the work, the less we expect of its condition.

One wants the antique to be in good condition, complete and unrestored, but one usually also wants to see the signs of age not only in the work's style but also in the material medium—in the form of patina, for example, or showing the accidents of its passage through time and endurance into the present. This naturally affects condition if we understand this criterion to be measured in terms of a "falling away from" the work's original state.

How much damage (if indeed *any* change in the object from its original appearance is considered "damage") is to be tolerated (or even preferred) before the object is simply viewed as "in poor condition"? Sometimes both beauty and usefulness come into conflict with agedness in the context of condition. Often a small touch-up here or there does little to affect the appearance of age but vastly improves the antique's beauty and usefulness (since many antiques continue to be used for their original purposes) by improving its condition. Often, however, there is no middle ground, and one must either leave the object entirely as it is or go all the way. The antiques dealer especially finds himself in a quandary here: yes, shrinkage along the grain, patina, wear, even a bit of staining is acceptable, even nice to find, on an antique table's surface; but what is to be done when the surface is badly deteriorated—the varnish has not only fractured into an alligator pattern and has so far darkened that no wood grain can be seen below it at all and it has moreover been splattered with pink paint? What does one do with a set of antique silver spoons that someone has tied together with rubber bands that when removed have left black streaks all across the surface? Consider the case of the *nef* with which we opened this book. Should it be left with its added Victorian pin back; should it have been left without pendant pearls; should it have been left stuck in glue on the scrapbook?

The answer to these and similar problems of condition brings us to the further issue of restoration—and the related dispute concerning *conservation* (essentially keeping the object in its present deteriorated condition but preventing its further deterioration) as opposed to *restoration* (essentially bringing the object back to its original "pristine" condition). We cannot debate the relative merits of each preference, since this would take us too far from our present inquiry, but we should note the great variability in national predilections in this matter.

Until recently (when they came under the influence of Western taste in the antique), Asian cultures tended to restore by reconstructing anew. "The Chinese like the Japanese and other Asian nations have a tradition of conserving by copying, or rebuilding," comments Michele Cordaro, the director of Italy's Central Conservation Institute.[8] He attributes this difference to a different conception of time—a cyclical one, such that although each new dynasty restarted the calendar, the essentials of life remained the same: "in a world that was both eternal and ever-changing, rebuilding monuments made perfect sense." Copying was therefore seen not as a lack of originality but as an act of reverence; but copying only makes sense, he adds, "so long as you keep the artisan traditions intact."

There is also the British vs. Continental split. "An Englishman requires of his furniture a mellow faded patina produced by centuries of sunlight and layers of polished beeswax. For French furniture a quite different aesthetic is required: the furniture must look as it did the day it was made, and the preferred finish today is a very shiny French polish."[9] Indeed, modern British connoisseurs detest the brilliant red color of eighteenth-century mahogany English furniture—the color it was originally stained—and want only the faded shade it has acquired through oxidation and exposure to sunlight, just as we would shriek in horror at the sight of the Elgin Marbles painted in their original primary colors with original gilding and gold or *bronze doré*.[10] The British thinking vis-à-vis furniture rests not only on a visual preference for the subdued tone, but also on the sense that by being deprived of its signs of age, it has lost its some of its authenticity.[11] The United States tends to follow the British taste in this area.[12] (Similarly, antique sterling tea services need to avoid that "just brightly polished" look.)

Painted canvas and paper are other genres that have especially sparked the restoration/conservation controversy. All watercolors fade, and nothing can be done here by way of restoration; but they also get dirty, mildewed, "foxed"; and that damage can be reversed. All oil paintings tend to darken with time.[13] The darkening of oils is due in part to dirt and in part to the deterioration of varnishes, both of which can be removed. But there also occurs over time an irreversible change in the pigments themselves that makes it impossible to return any old oil painting to its pristine original condition. The first type of restoration reveals much. Rembrandt's famous painting usually called *The Night Watch*, after a recent cleaning, was surprisingly revealed to be a daytime scene! In 1995 a record price (to that date) for a marine painting was paid for Fitz Hugh Lane's *Sunset at Gloucester Harbor*. An art expert described it after the sale as an "extraordinary and world-class example of American Luminism which, among other tenets, displayed an almost mystical notion of light." However, the expert continued, regarding the widely appealing "golden light" of the painting's sky, "that yellow varnish you see in the painting is nicotine. I suspect the sky was really blue with a touch of pink." One wonders about the effect of an eventual cleaning on its "golden light" and whether the sunset would then appear quite so mystical. One then wonders: how much "cleaning" is "restoration" and can cleaning per se undermine a work's authenticity—either in terms of falsifying a particular antique's historical life or in terms of destabilizing the categories through which it is "seen" (i.e., understood and appreciated)?

The word "patina" comes from *patena*, the Italian word for dark varnish applied to shoes. As early as the seventeenth century it was added to paintings because it was considered by connoisseurs to be an enhancement of their beauty. But tastes change. Lowenthal remarks that "each epoch selects its own aesthetic and historical truths . . . the patina (*craquelure* and *pentimenti*) that modern restorers accept was distasteful to and concealed by 19th century connoisseurs, who instead enjoyed the 'golden tone' of antiquity now considered disfiguring and spurious."[14] Since it has been claimed that current preference is for strong colors and youth, radical restorers sometimes unconsciously transform the colors of antique paintings to "achieve more nearly the firm tones to which the modern eye is accustomed."[15] One need only recall the reaction to and debate surrounding the recent cleaning of the ceiling of the Sistine Chapel. (There was no problem of pigment deterioration in the restoration of Michelangelo's masterpiece, created in fresco, but there was the question whether he applied darkening shades *al secco* over the dried fresco, which would necessarily come off in cleaning.) Afterward it was remarked how wonderfully modern its bright colors were: as we marvel at their artificially induced youth and freshness, we are amazed to see how much they look like modern paintings.[16]

Of course no one would now suggest—as does an 1835 book, *On the Restoration of Paintings*—that "one remove varnish from paintings by rubbing them with sand, dousing them with carbonate of ammonia or nitric acid, or else—these failing—wetting down the surface of the canvass and leaving it outdoors on a frosty night."[17] But the alternative approach, doing nothing to restore but only to preserve, while avoiding the worst excesses of restoration zeal, may leave much to be desired in the object vis-à-vis its aesthetic appeal. Some have argued that museum curators cannot combat the essentially ongoing process of decay without affecting the appearance of the work and giving the object "the museum look."[18]

"Museum curators abhor cosmetic and speculative restoration. Their interest is in stabilizing a decaying work, in bringing out what is left of the original and at the most suggesting what was lost, never allowing the suggestion to pass for the original," observes G. Y. Dryanski in "Arts of the Restorer."[19] But what the curator calls "cosmetic" may be some essential element of what the work requires in order for the connoisseur to respond to its "beauty." The preeminent French restoration firm, La Maison d'André, according to its director, currently "restores in a visible way for museums, so there's no confusion. But for private customers, the [restoration] work is invisible. We reassure the eye, save the aesthetic appeal."[20] Choices usually have to be made. The traditional Asian approach to restoration—as opposed to making a new object altogether—in the case of a broken porcelain is to insert between the reassembled pieces a line of gold suspended in a bonding medium that fills in the seam of the repair. While it authenticates the act of restoration and brings out the object's accident of history, this makes the seam stand out strikingly and has the aesthetic effect of creating an entirely new art object—which in turn has the opportunity to be beautiful or not.[21] As a compromise, the Louvre currently has on display a restored seventeenth-century rock crystal vessel that looks complete. The fact that its missing handles have been replaced with Plexiglas replicas does not affect its aesthetic appeal; but under careful scrutiny they are a detectable restoration. Attempting to maintain or stabilize the work in its present form, however degraded its condition, so as to prevent its further deterioration surely has much to recommend it from the point of view of authenticity, which we consider later. The question here seems at first to be simply what takes precedence (assuming no neat compromise is practicable in a work that has significantly deteriorated): aesthetics and restoration or authenticity and conservation? One could argue that the aesthetic response itself entails authenticity and thus refuse the object's restoration; or on the contrary, one could argue that the object's authenticity entails aesthetic response and so demand restoration.

Perhaps any such stabilization or conservation is "inauthentic" in some sense regarding antiques because it tries to stop the painterly hand of time. Francis Sparshott argues against both restoration and conservation, against the idea that "works of art are not to be allowed to perish"; and claims that the "curatorial obsession that underpins talk of the rights of artworks threatens to convert the idea into a necropolis for dead masterpieces."[22] Kaufmann, in *Time Is an Artist*, similarly argues that conservers are "undertakers who refuse to countenance time, change, and death. They have no respect for age, for texture, for patina."[23] He believes this attitude derives from a classical—indeed Platonic—idea that perfection alone is timeless; and age, which brings blemishes, is a sign of change and a detriment to beauty.

Ultimately, whether restoration or conservation is meant when one speaks of "maintaining the condition of the artwork," it is a matter of highly variable and personal taste. In the long run, Etienne Gilson may be correct when he remarked, "There are two ways for a painting to perish: the one is for it to be restored; the other is for it not to be restored."[24]

As a matter of practice, much is left to the connoisseur/collectors in their given area to establish and maintain their own standards of "condition." For example, in antique machines of any kind, pristine condition (or at least minimal scratches or signs of use) without replacements is the ideal condition. In English furniture, as we have noted, this is not the case at all. There are abundant complexities and apparent contradictions; and these are merely part of the balancing act of applying the various overlapping and mutually affective criteria of antiques collecting and connoisseurship. As an additional complication, generally the older the repair or restoration itself is, the more "forgiven" it is.

And there are genre-specific peculiarities of taste. Among collector/connoisseurs of the tribal masks of Oceania, for example, a mask, *if cleaned*, is considered to be in "undesirable condition"—even if it was collected by nineteenth-century missionaries who on their return to Europe and America themselves had it washed before hanging it on a wall or placing it in a glass case where it has resided unmolested for one hundred years. But if one of these masks has been *entirely repainted in the twentieth century*, it is still considered to be in "good condition"—provided that the repainting was done by the tribe that made it and it is then used at least once in the ceremony for which it was created!

3. *Technical Perfection*. Technical perfection is an essential ingredient in an antique's qualitative excellence. Though affecting the object's beauty, this qualitative criterion of excellence is the "other side" of our first category (subject), for rather than being a concern of the "what," technical perfection is primarily a function of the "how" of the work. Technical perfection involves many elements. On the one hand, it concerns the questions of how (by what processes) the material medium has been formed (designed) and of whether or not the choice of materials in a given instance and the manner of conforming them to the design best embody the idea of the work. We also ask, conversely, does the idea best bring out the characteristics of the material? This aspect often is referred to as "truth to materials," which sometimes means allowing the materials the upper hand, giving them leeway to do what they most naturally tend to do (as when wood is left to show its grain and to dictate the shape and proportions of a table surface), but sometimes can mean allowing the idea and design to have the upper hand, forcing the materials to do that which by their nature they are disinclined to do (as when iron and glass are used in fashions contrary to their nature—in Art Nouveau constructions, for example). In either case, because of the design's relation to its material, it is extremely important that this evidence of *createdness*, of this *handcraftedness*, of this bravura of execution (what is referred to in Italian painting as "sprezzatura"), of the *how*, become evident and part of our encounter with the antique. Technical perfection is the cause of the experience that can only be captured by imagining that the work in presenting itself to us is saying, "Voilà!" Handcraftedness, which most clearly denotes a work's "createdness," is so important an element that Ruskin observed, "It is not the material, but the absence of human labor which makes the thing worthless; and a piece of terra cotta, or plaster of Paris, which has been wrought by the human hand, is worth all the stone in Carrara cut by machinery."[25]

This "how" of technical perfection is often discussed in terms of *style*, for the simple recognition of the usage of different styles usually provides us with the cue for determining what is to "count" as technical perfection in any given instance. One would not expect the same precision in the engraving of a Saxon cross as on a Fabergé snuffbox, for example. Style is the mode through which and by means of which the art object captures our attention, sets up a world, and directs us to attend to its contents or significance. What style is has been much discussed, and the interrelationship between one's awareness of the style of an object and one's ability to interpret the meaning of that object has been duly noted.[26] There are different loci of style, too—the style of the culture (ethos, nation), of the era,[27] and of the individual artist(s). There is no smallest or largest "unit" of style because almost any attribute of a work, however particular and small, is potentially an element of style. An object may display two different styles.[28] Styles also go "out of fashion," but some styles seem always to be "in fashion," and others "come back into fashion"— usually somewhat "refashioned." (Classical nude sculpture has to some degree been in fashion continuously since the Renaissance.)[29]

Style is a form of language, or perhaps a code, that enables us to interpret what the work is about by limiting and delimiting the way in which the work is seen. This point has often been made before. But *what* the meaning or idea of the work may be is inseparable from the *how* of it, for the experiencer must be prepared to recognize not only the world *in* and/or *of* the work, but the *how* of that wherein and of that whereof. For this reason, style recognition is the mechanism for determining that technical perfection has or has not been achieved in that work, as well as for recognizing the subject (significance, meaning) of the work.

Style connects with other criteria. In chapter 1 we saw that style is the first indicator of age and is the primary tool of establishing authenticity. Style also determines the relative importance of completeness and condition for aesthetic appreciation of the work—the classical style preferring a maximum of both characteristics, for example, the romantic style not so (as we noted in chapter 2's account of its predilection for the ruin and the fragment).

In terms of the antique's success in evoking for us an image of a world now past, technical perfection becomes especially important with regard to both handcraftedness and authenticity when these are connected with the inherent difficulties of working with certain recalcitrant materials. When we encounter a huge ancient Egyptian statue carved of diorite (an extremely hard granite stone), for example, its technical perfection—not just its beauty but its sheer achievement without the use of any modern machinery—powerfully bestirs the imagination to evoke this past world in all its splendor, often more forcefully than any historical narrative could achieve.

Quantitative criteria are based on considerations of *enumeration*: of how many exemplars of the class of antiques survive, how much of its original character remains (or how many of its original parts remain), and how measurably large or small it is.

4. *Rarity*. Rarity is a highly relative term and must always be understood in some context that provides the relationships in terms of which it

is measured. What one could call "general rarity" might be calculated on the basis of how many of this type of antique remain in existence relative to how many were originally made. One could also measure rarity relative to some specific time and place. Only a handful of life-size classical Greek bronze statues remain from the 5th century B.C., and they probably represent less than 1 percent of the total production. Only three artworks are known to exist from the more than one thousand pieces inventoried in the royal collection of Henry VII of England. "The whole remaining corpus of secular goldsmith's work from medieval France . . . contains about 50 items only."[30] Excluding Gothic cathedrals, only about 2 percent of all examples of European medieval decorative arts remain. The amount of red and black figured pottery remaining from Ancient Greece is not small, however—nor are Ancient Roman coins at all scarce—though they represent only a small fraction of the original production. The difference may be accounted for by the fact that in the first examples very few were made relative to the later ones. But there are other reasons, among which we may count the reusability of the material (bronze is melted down, marble winds up in lime kilns, but nothing much can be reused of a broken pottery piece). Another reason for rarity is the fragility of the material out of which the antique is made: paper versus stone, wax versus gold, cloth versus glass.

There is also the indifference or hostility of later generations. When in 1784, for example, a twenty-eight-foot statue of Saint Christopher, which was renowned at the time of its donation to Nôtre Dame in Paris, was accidentally damaged by construction work around the cathedral, it was ordered destroyed rather than repaired by the cathedral chapter. Six years later a 1791 guidebook approvingly refers to this destruction: "This ridiculous monument to the taste and devotion of our fathers has just been destroyed."[31] We may understand the discrepancy between 1784 indifference and 1791 hostility by noting the dates: the hostility was due to the anti-clerical and anti-religious zeal of French revolutionaries, the indifference was due merely to changes in taste and an apparent total absence of "the aesthetic of the antique" on the part of the cathedral authorities. Romanticism had not yet come into vogue, but as we saw in the preceding chapter, in another generation this indifference and hostility would turn into regret. The instance of this statue's destruction was not unique during the period. Rheims notes that being short of firewood during the Revolution, leaders of Paris districts were authorized to burn wooden statues from various churches and convents.[32]

But rarity is also occasioned by the opposite response: affection. We have referred to the looting of Europe's art objects by Napoleon (much the same occurred in Ancient Rome, as we saw in chapter 2.1, vis-à-vis the arts of Greece). He wrote home from his headquarters in Tolentino, "We now have all that is finest in Italy."[33] But the transportation of antiques, the dangers of travel, takes its toll on most antiques simply because of their fragility. Often antiques are much admired but for some perceived "defect" in later times, and consequently whole classes of antique objects get remodeled or transformed because of some new taste or new use. This also increases rarity. Drapery gets painted over nudes in painting, and fig leaves get attached to nude statuary. Consider how many fine Chinese porcelain vases were encased in writhing *bronze doré* mounts in the Rococo taste of eighteenth-century France.[34] Worse "desecrations" were to come in the twentieth century when such porcelains were drilled with a hole in the base for use as lamp bases.

Rarity may arise in other ways as well, as when certain antiques are not in themselves rare as a class or type, but some particular subclass has an especially rare aspect—being signed by its maker, being used for a special purpose, or being found in a particular collection. Thus, we see how its rarity is affected by an antique's being required to satisfy specific additional characteristics or criteria of authenticity or provenance. Often antiques become rare in the context of one of the other evaluative criteria we have specified; for example, there may be many individual survivors of a given sort of antique, but most quite ugly, or in bad condition, or small, or incomplete, so that a beautiful large complete exemplar in perfect condition becomes very rare. Another typical specific criterion of rarity relates categories of works to their makers in terms not merely of fewness in number but of fewness in a given genre; for example, a given artist has done few oils but many watercolors. Objects that are not in the least rare have little force to cause us even to notice them, much less occasion the evocation of a world now past.

5. *Size.* In purely aesthetic terms, an antique should be as big or as small as it needs to be to produce its own appropriate affect. Generally speaking, objects that are so very small that they require looking at through a magnifying glass will fail to produce the desired aesthetic effect, whereas objects that are so large as to be incapable of being experienced as a whole are too big. A small nail from a nineteenth-century chest of drawers, even apart from its failings with respect to the other categories, is not an antique; at best it is an antique fragment. Cities or even portions of them we would not refer to as "antiques."

Much about determinations of size depends on the material and the genre. Miniature paintings on ivory are small: they are made to be experienced by a single person at once and to be transported in a pouch or

worn as a pin or pendant. They also are small because ivory does not naturally occur in the sizes that wood or stone or glass or canvas comes in.

Size seems to become an important consideration in the judgment of
antique paintings especially on non-aesthetic grounds, namely, the possible current *uses* for this genre of antique. Thus, George M. Young remarks that "in a masterpiece, gigantic dimensions are a plus, but in
anything less than a masterpiece, the bigger the painting, the bigger the
headache. . . . A 30"×40" is about right. Much bigger than that, and
you cannot hang it in today's houses."[35] The same may be said of antique
furniture. Nevertheless, while this may negate an antique's suitability for
sale in the modern world, an antique's very size may stimulate the imagination toward the past world where its size was, for its own time and
place, "just right."

6. *Completeness.* The criterion of completeness may be understood as
a factor of "condition," such as when a statue is missing a hand or a
teapot a handle or a lid. Yet it becomes especially relevant when the antique object is a set of individual pieces forming a suite. In this case, on
the one hand, completeness may be determined by the number of pieces
in the original creation, but on the other, it may be determined by requirements of current use. The number itself is important. Generally,
odd numbers are less favored than even ones: a set of eight chairs is
preferable not only to a set of seven but also to a set of nine. The same is
true in sets of dinner china. There are exceptions, of course, for in many
Asian tea or chocolate sets the originals had five cups and saucers (according to the numerical preference of that tradition); and a suite of
paintings of the nine muses would certainly be deficient at eight and unexpected at ten.[36] Half a large set may be acceptable or even preferable in
current usage, as when a suite of twenty-four dining chairs is divided into
two sets of twelve, or an original suite of four Georgian sterling silver
candlesticks becomes two pairs.

Condition and authenticity also play an important role in the matter
of completeness. When, for example, a set of dining chairs numbers only
eleven, the owner either for his own use or for resale may have a modern
reproduction of the twelfth chair made. Alternatively (and often un-
scrupulously), small parts from some of the original eleven are removed
and replaced by new pieces; and these removed parts are then reassembled to make a twelfth chair. Since not enough pieces have been removed
from any one original chair for it to fail the "authenticity" or "condition" criteria (because in furniture minor repairs and replacements of
small parts are normal and expected over time), and no completely new
chair has been added to the original eleven, a complete set of twelve "an-

tique chairs" that are reasonably authentic and in reasonably good condition magically emerges from an incomplete set of eleven.

Historical criteria are all aspects of the essential fact about antiques with which we began this work: that they are objects with a *past*. That is why they have the capacity to generate and preserve for us the image of a world now past. Antiques can display their *agedness* either in their style or material condition or by the story (narrative) that attaches to them, which we call provenance.

7. *Age.* Most of what needs to be said about the criterion of age in antiques collecting and connoisseurship has already been said in chapter 1. The traditional age for antiques that was employed in most legal contexts is one hundred years, but this number is entirely arbitrary. As we pointed out earlier, for many years in the antiques trade, furniture had to be made before 1820 to be considered "antique" (in 1980, about when this stipulation was beginning to crumble, that meant a minimum of one hundred sixty years of age for furniture) whereas jewelry that was barely half a century old, specifically such items as Art Deco pieces by makers like Cartier, had already in the currency of the trade acquired the appellation "antique."[37]

Age is better understood as "agedness." This historical characteristic means that it clearly is made in a style that is no longer current and that it clearly shows material signs of aging (a condition-relevant question), but especially that it speaks for its age. That is, it is sufficiently exemplary of its past era to evoke for us an image of that world now gone. Age of course also attaches to the antique by virtue of its provenance, which we discuss below.

8. *Authenticity.* In speaking of "authenticity," we are actually introducing a meta-criterion. Generally and most commonly the word is used to denote a certified relation between the maker and the work, but it actually may be used in reference to most of the other nine criteria we have mentioned. If we ask, is it really a painting of General Washington, is it really an ice pail, is it made of gold or pinchbeck, is that the original finish, was it made in certain parts by machine, is it really different from others in its class, is that the original handle, the original mark, the correct mark, an altered mark, were there originally only four of them made, is it really eighteenth century, was it really part of Madame de Pompadour's toilette, is it the one referred to in the work called such-and-such by the author named so-and-so, was it part of the Rothschild collection?—all these are questions about the truth or falsity of *claims about the work in terms of the other criteria we have named*. That is why, I believe, "authenticity" is a meta-criterion and why, as I explained

above, the term does not appear in the definition proper but here where we ask what are the *practically relevant* factors for evaluating and appraising the antiqueness of an object.

In the public world, antiques usually appear along with descriptive accounts about them that constitute their "authentications"—certifications (stipulations, descriptions) that they satisfy the evaluative criteria in certain ways. These can be brief labels (such as one would find on a museum card or antique shop price tag, for example) or extensive analyses such as one would find in an auction sales catalogue.[38] As with the recognitions of style, we take them into account as part and parcel of our entire aesthetic experience of the work because, as narratives of the antique's historicality, authentications tell us all the particulars about the creation of the object and the life it has led that has brought it down to us.

The most commonly used sense of "authenticity" in the art world is one that relates the work to its possible, probable, or certain creator and the act of his creation.[39] This criterion can be of the greatest importance in the antiques and art market (especially at its "high end"), for it, more than anything else, seems to determine the price of a work. We pointed out in our fictional account of the *nef* in chapter 1, for instance, that its provenance would, more than anything else, count as a justification for its high pre-auction estimate. For the purpose of rendering a comprehensive account of the work as it satisfies the evaluative criteria, however, "maker" identifies only a detail in the range of factors determining a work's authenticity. Probably the most philosophically interesting and illuminating discussions of authenticity—as well as the ones most commonly encountered with the vast majority of antiques (for which the specification of a named individual creator is impossible or irrelevant)—arise in relation to the issues of restoration and of fakery, both already taken up in this book but not in relation to the criterion of authenticity proper.

Let us consider the restoration of the parts of the eleventh-century Romanesque church of Saint Sernin in Toulouse. It was stripped of much (not all) of its later Renaissance and Baroque architectural accretions and given a neo-Romanesque restoration by the famous architectural restorer Viollet-le-Duc in the mid-nineteenth century. His restorations have since been determined to be historically inaccurate in some respects. If we consider the criterion of authenticity and seek to understand it in this work, we must wonder what could relevantly be said of this church's authenticity or be done to further "restore" it authentically. One could remove Viollet-le-Duc's restorations and replace them with "the correct" Romanesque style. But this surely would affect the authenticity of the church: the new parts, however stylistically correct, would not be the original ones. Moreover, one could argue that the presence of Viollet-le-Duc's additions might be more effective at evoking for us an image of a world long past than if, alternatively, the church were stripped of all its historical additions down to its bare eleventh-century remains. Among other reasons, there might not then be enough of the original left to evoke much of anything. One could also argue that since more than a century and a half has passed, Viollet-le-Duc's alterations have become part of the church, and to remove them now would be to destroy a portion of the "antique" that the church has become over its last one hundred fifty years. Alternatively, one could restore the fifteenth- and sixteenth-century Renaissance accretions that he removed; they would be modern copies, but they could be accurate and would certainly be part of the authentic history of this church. But if one accepted these, one could not reject Viollet-le-Duc's Romanesque restorations—unless one made the questionable insistence on the priority of *new accuracies* (even if, in an attempt not to break the "aura of agedness," they were to be given fake wear and patina) over *naturally antiqued* and already antique *in*accuracies. Alternatively, one might come up with some arbitrary distinction and propose the following sort of argument: "the fifteenth- and sixteenth-century restorations were 'natural' and not deliberate 'restorations' for aesthetic or art-historical purposes but changes reflecting the daily and ordinary needs of the church at the time in accordance with the stylistic preferences of the era; hence restoring, but only as far back as the sixteenth century, is acceptable." But to this one could make the obvious counterargument: "restoring churches was part of the aesthetic needs of the nineteenth century (and perfectly 'natural' to it), and the restorations that century made were indicative of its knowledge and abilities and stylistic preferences at that time; hence, the church in displaying its old nineteenth-century restorations is showing its age."

What has occurred in this architectural example occurs with frequent regularity in jewelry (as we saw in our example of the *nef* with its pendant pearls) and in antique furniture, where nothing so much destroys the antiqueness of an antique table as its "refinishing." It is also common in antique metalwork, as when lamp bases made from candlesticks are "returned" (with a few blemishes) to their original state and function, or when old silver-plated objects, their plating mostly worn off in ugly ways, are replated. The situation with paintings is even more problematic, for as Eric Hebborn notes, "the borderline between what is restoration and what is simply repainting is not always clear." That is why, when we come to consider deliberate faking, we find that "the alteration of old pictures is a much more common practice than the making of old masters *ex novo*."[40]

One needs to decide, first of all, which is more "authentic": conserving the work in a completely unrestored condition (even if it has so deteriorated that it barely exists any longer—Leonardo's *Last Supper*, for example) or returning the work to its original condition through restoration. Surely, some might say, there can be no interest other than archeological curiosity in a total ruin. Before one decides on a preference, however, one must first answer two further questions: (1) must "authentic" *mean* "unchanged over time" and (2) can anyone be *certain* of the original condition?

One cannot simply justify "returning" the work to its original condition on leaving the artist's hands by an appeal to the artist's presumed intentions. Guido Reni (1575–1642), the great Baroque painter, claimed that "while the works of other painters lose something in the course of time, his own will, by yellowing, acquire a new luster, [and] the patina will bring out the mutual harmony of the colours."[41] Renoir (1841–1919) stated that a painting depends "not only on the elements of form and color but also on the element of time, for to speak of the patina of time is not an empty phrase. Yet the most important thing is that a work should support this patina, and only remarkable works can."[42] And Goya thought no painting could be restored in any case. In a letter regarding the work of a restorer, he wrote:

> In addition to the invariable fact that the more one retouches paintings on the pretext of preserving them the more they are destroyed, and that even the original artists, if they were alive now, could not retouch them perfectly because of the aged tone given the colors over time, who is also a painter. . . . It is not easy to retain the instantaneous and fleeting intent of the imagination and harmony of the whole that was attempted in the first painting.[43]

We know that Arts and Crafts furniture makers intended their wood to wear and their metal hinges, handles, and straps to develop appropriate patinas. In these cases, if restoration is impossible to achieve (or achieve with accuracy) or if it runs counter to the artist's original intent—and if these are relevant factors for the determination of authenticity—then restoration is entirely incompatible with a work's authenticity.

To resolve these difficulties it would appear to be essential to decide which is more authentic: a seriously deteriorated but untouched work or one that has been correctly restored (with or without the artist's intentions taken into account). But phrased in terms of authenticity, this first requires resolving a famous and long-standing metaphysical conundrum, that of *identity over time*. Aristotle has us imagine two ships, either of which (but not both of which) might be the ship named the *Argos*. The original *Argos* has been repaired over many years little by little until no part of it remains from the original, but the ship has all along retained the name *Argos*. Meanwhile, imagine that someone collects every one of the discarded pieces of the repaired ship and from them alone reconstructs anew the *Argos*. Which is the "authentic" *Argos*—the one that has undergone minute changes over time but has always remained and functioned as a ship and is pointed out as the *Argos* and yet contains no piece of the original, or the ship later reconstructed from all the original pieces? We do not attempt here to decide this metaphysical conundrum, but merely note its relevance to the questions of authenticity in antiques in relation to condition and restoration.

Consider another example of authenticity, one not involving restoration. No one doubts the aesthetic greatness of Titian's *Feast of the Gods* in Ferrara. But it is an overpainting job. The original work (visible under X-ray) is by Giovanni Bellini. Since it was considered by its then owner, Alfonso d'Este, to be too old-fashioned for his *studiolo*, Titian was commissioned to modernize it only a generation or so after its creation. This he did—pushing forward the scene by converting Bellini's grove of tree trunks into a green wall of leaves, undressing and voluptuating the nymphs, and introducing emblematic devices for the gods in keeping with the later stylistic preferences of Titian's time. Is there an authentic work here? It is no longer an authentic Bellini. But is it an "authentic Titian"? Certainly it has lived as an authentic Titian longer than as an authentic Bellini.

Consider also "original multiples"—not only in the case of prints, but even in sculpture and painting, for sculptors and painters since the Renaissance have produced several virtually identical versions of their works by their own hands. One might be tempted to say that any later work is a copy of the earlier. But if the later work is in any sense better or more complete, it would be just as reasonable to view the earlier one not as the authentic original but rather as the preliminary or trial effort for the subsequent masterpiece. We encounter here another metaphysical question, namely, the question concerning "the identity of indiscernibles." This subject is much debated in the philosophical literature,[44] and again it must remain an issue we cannot develop here. Suffice it to say that in the hypothetically ideal case of two works that are absolutely identical in every respect and to such a degree that nothing about the one (experienced or known, now or in the future) would not also be true of the other, the works are not *different* works and in fact there are not two works but only *one*. More interesting—and more real—are those cases in which at some point a minor difference appears. We say something more about this below.

But authenticity does somehow attach to the idea of originality and uniqueness. Perhaps the difference between the "amateur" and the "collector" appears most clearly here, though even for the amateur the knowledge of its uniqueness may certify an antique's authenticity and thus add to the totality of the aesthetic experience. Edith Wharton, in *The Decoration of Houses*, observes: "To the art lover, as distinguished from the collector, uniqueness *per se* can give no value to an inartistic object; but the distinction, the personal quality, of a beautiful object is certainly enhanced when it is known to be alone of its kind—as in the case of old bronzes made *à cire perdue*."[45]

In determinations of authenticity one must also consider the question of helpers. Throughout the world, it was common for student assistants to "finish" works by their masters. Rubens's huge studio of assistants enabled him to produce a prodigious quantity of work for which he was paid a price varying in accordance with the degree to which he himself worked on the work.[46] What can one make of "authenticity" in these circumstances?

But what about "authenticity" in relation to "forgery"? This issue too has been much discussed in the philosophical literature.[47] When the antiques trade finds an object's authenticity questionable, the traditional British way of putting it is: "It's not *right*." The French trade has an equivalent phrase derived from the usage of "respectable people" who are concerned about the virtue of a marriageable spinster: "Il y a un 'mais' " (There is a "however").

What is a "fake"? A "copy" is not necessarily a "fake." A *copy* is used in place of a lost or elsewhere-existing original. A postcard sent from Florence with a picture of a painting from the Uffizi is a copy but not a fake; so are large-format prints of these paintings not fakes. A subclass of the copy is the "replica." A replica is a reproduction of the original (located elsewhere) that copies all its important qualities—though it may be made of different materials or may be different in size. The four horses of St. Mark's presently on view above the entrance of the basilica are replicas; the originals are elsewhere (in the San Marco museum).

There is another sort of "copy." This is the kind of copy that is an act of homage. It is often seen in Chinese and Japanese art—in painting and ceramics especially—and even includes reproduced signatures of the originals. And there is yet another sort of copy that arises from the historical processes of stylistic and civilizational borrowings and so is also a form of homage. There is, for example, in the ceramics collection of the Victoria and Albert Museum a Chinese cup and saucer (ca. 1880) that is a copy (reproduction) of an earlier nineteenth-century Dresden copy of a Meissen eighteenth-century original cup and saucer; but this original Meissen cup and saucer's decoration is a clear borrowing of the Chinese "medallion style" of decoration (i.e., reserves of figures in genre scenes separated by "frames" of flowers and birds), which was itself originally developed (based on European engravings) by the Chinese expressly to suit the European taste. Now this V&A 1880 Chinese cup and saucer, which was a copy of a copy of a take-off of a deliberate borrowing, is in the early twenty-first century again being copied with reproductions from mainland China. Thus, we have a Chinese copy made for the Western market of a Chinese copy of a German copy of a German borrowing from a Chinese original made to suit European taste.

A fake is not quite the same as a copy. A fake is a "pretender" to originality, that is, a work deliberately intending to deceive; it is a form of fraud in that the forger passes his own work off as someone else's (thus the opposite of plagiarism).[48] As Nelson Goodman has defined it, a fake is "an object falsely purporting to have the history of the production requisite for the original of the work."[49] For our purposes regarding the antique in particular, we should add "and falsely purporting to have the provenance requisite for the original," because the work must also have undergone (endured) the history of the original *after* its creation.

But just as not all copies are fakes, so not all fakes are necessarily copies. The forger Van Meegeren never copied any of the existing works of Vermeer, nor did Eric Hebborn, who faked a wide variety of artists' works. They copied the *style* of Vermeer or Bruegel or Corot, used the same materials, and imitated the agedness of a work by simulating the effects of time on the materials—intending to deceive with "original" fakes. Most successful fakers of antiques make such original fakes.[50]

Style is, as we have noted, the first tool of detection of fakes—not only the generic style but, when known, the artist's personal style, his trademark "fingerprints" (e.g., he didn't use enough oil in mixing his paint, causing the cracks typical of his work; or he didn't often like to wipe his brush, causing messy drops of different colors).[51] There are also national (cultural) or historical clues arising from the production techniques of an antique (in their manner of construction, e.g., French locks turn twice, English only once; or in tool marks, e.g., no radial saw marks should appear on eighteenth-century furniture). Then there is the inspection of materials—did they exist then (with the same impurities), are they the typical ones for this sort of item, where were they obtained, in what proportions were they used? And finally, signs of age—is what I see real patina or is it the result of staining and smoking; are the abrasions indicative of real wear and not scratches artificially inflicted by sandpaper, and do they occur in the correct place for the actual use of the piece?[52]

It is often said that it is impossible for fakes to deceive for long—as we noted in chapter 1—because the style of the era in which they are made has a subtle but undetectable influence on them that eventually gets noticed only when that era has passed. Sometimes it is said that it is simply a matter of their beauty: Cellini stated that "all fakes are ridiculous."[53] But others, like Hebborn, have insisted this is simply not true, that fakes can be beautiful and can pass the test of time; and his successful fakes may prove his point. But of what consequence is the fake to the aesthetic experience itself?

We noted above the philosophical problem of the "identity of indiscernibles." Surely, in the hypothetical instance in which there is certain to be no way ever of distinguishing the "real" work from the deliberate "fake" that is its exact duplicate, there can be no difference between the works in the aesthetic experience. Yet the very idea—the information (something not perceived *in* but known *about*)—that one of them is a "fake" does itself alter the way either work is experienced.[54] Similarly, if we have not an exact duplicate but an original fake "in the style of," and even if we stipulated that it would never be possible to determine its authenticity, the sheer awareness that the work is a forgery would no doubt affect the experience of it. This demonstrates the importance of authenticity not only as a criterion but as an ingredient in the actual aesthetic response to the antique.

There remains also the issue of authenticity relative to contemporary expectations, an issue that brings us back to our earlier concern with authenticity as it relates to restoration. We have already considered the problem arising from the possibility of repainting classical Greek marble statuary. Most people would think it abhorrent. So, too, as Lowenthal observes, "those who equated classical beauty with the 'purity' of whiteness were appalled when Canova tinted statues according to actual practice. . . . And as recently as the 1950's, the copy of the Attalus Stoa erected by the American School of Classical Studies in Athens eschewed red and blue paint as *untrue*, not to the original but to the modern stereotype."[55] We encountered the same when a cleaned Sistine Chapel ceiling no longer conformed to the traditional art-historical conception of Michelangelo as a "stony," that is, architectural/sculptural, painter.

There is yet another relation of the criterion of authenticity to an antique, one that does not refer to either restoration or fakery. Here we would not mean by "authenticity" that the work is "certainly to be attributed to a particular maker and is not by another hand" or that "the work has not been altered" or that the work remains pretty much true to its original condition. Rather by "authenticity" here what we might mean is "being most true (because most *typical*)" of that maker's best or most art-historically significant works. By this sense of "authenticity," we would be asserting, for example, that paintings done by van Gogh in the last year of his life (and not his early Impressionist works) are the most "authentic" van Goghs. Similarly, the cubist paintings of Picasso and not his later ceramics; or views of the harbor at L'Estaque painted by Cézanne in the 1880s and not his portraits of the late 1860s and 1870s; glassware by René Lalique, not his furniture; *objets de vertu* by Fabergé and Cartier, and not objects done in some other genre of antiques—these are their most "authentic" works. In this sense, just as we would require authentic antiques to "speak for their age," so we here require them to "speak for their makers" and what most prominently comes to mind when we think of these makers. Thus, Souren Melikian, critiquing the auction sale of a rather ordinary van Gogh—one must assume the possibility of such things—states, "The name, the aura surrounding the Saint-Rémy period, the very fact that it is a self-portrait, are the three components of the magic potion, all external to art as such, that made it climb so high."[56] That is, in every respect, every way in which we would want "the real thing," this was a case in point. Just knowing we are encountering the genuine article inspires the imagination—just as a religious relic might—to leap from the ordinary world in which we presently lead our lives to the one from which the artwork comes and with which it puts us in contact.

9. *Provenance.* As David Hume observed in his *Treatise of Human Nature*,[57] it is only through continuity—from comprehending the evolution of something from the past to the present as the effect of a causal sequence of discrete events—that we can account for and give meaning to the things of the present. Provenance is the history of the antique as it has moved along a train of owners, uses, locations, associations, expositions, and explications from its creation to the present moment. More than any other of the aforementioned criteria, it distinguishes the antique from the art object generally by specifying the particulars of its passage through time. That is why our opening example, the *nef*, was a narrative of provenance. More than any of the criteria, it provides the aura of "contagion" to the antique, increasing its value by associating it

with human life (or a succession of lives) and often with fame. That is why provenance, even more than authenticity, is subject to the hype of the personality cult. Sales catalogues tend to wax eloquent about the importance of the owner (or owners) of the antique whose sale is imminent—in inverse proportion, it seems, to the significance, quality, or authenticity of the piece in question. Thus, a recent sale of Jacqueline Kennedy's fake pearl necklace—an object of machine-made costume jewelry of little value for its quality or age—achieved for that memento (more correctly, that "trophy") a sales price thousands of times higher than for a comparable fake pearl necklace of the same age and quality, and over ten times higher than what a *genuine* pearl necklace of *venerable age* would have brought.

Another characteristic of provenance that distinguishes it from all the other criteria (except perhaps rarity) is that it is not a quality perceptible *in* or *on* the object itself but a tale told *about* the object. Thus, it can easily be detached from and reattached to the object, as with our *nef* example. That is also why it is the most easily fabricated of all the antique's attributes. The typical antique that one comes across in an antiques shop is almost always without provenance. The typical antiques dealer, being asked the question that normally follows the question concerning price— "Where did you get it?"—is highly unlikely to be able say more about its provenance than where he bought it. Often he is reluctant be specific even about that fact. Since aura is what matters, so long as the antique in question is genuine (i.e., authentic in terms of the other criteria—age, material, place of origin, etc.), many dealers are less than scrupulous about the stories they attach to their antiques: "I picked it out of a trash bin" is hardly as "auramatic" as "It came from the estate of Countess de Brettville-Fflormont."[58]

Of course, when the provenance is genuine, who owned a particular item does affect, and justly so, how we experience it. At a recent Phillips sale in Edinburgh, a wooden cabinet that had been made from the elm tree under whose shade the Duke of Wellington commanded the Battle of Waterloo certainly had more historical significance and a more distinguished provenance than would another cabinet of similar make and materials of the same period, especially since other pieces of furniture made from this same elm were noted as being in the collection of the current queen of England. The rosary of black beads held in the hands of Mary Stuart (now on display in Arundel castle) at the moment when she was executed and as she proclaimed her belief—"I am settled in the ancient Catholic faith and mind to spend my blood in it"—would indeed have a veritable provenance. Provenance is also highly relative to public awareness and current fashion. Thus, again, in 1995, in an auction sale of silk robes, robes that actually belonged to the historical figure Lawrence of Arabia realized the same price as similar robes that were made for the actor Peter O'Toole, who played the role of Lawrence in the 1965 film.

Provenance does more than associate the antique with famous persons and historical events. It helps to authenticate it by citing vetted exhibitions or museum shows, or even former museum ownership in cases in which the item has been de-accessioned. As in our opening example of the *nef*, the mention of like objects elsewhere and the listing of printed works in which the item in question (or similar ones) has been discussed or photographed further authenticates the antique. Its quality, too, can be attested to in this manner, for often the former owners are noted connoisseurs. If they owned it, one reasons, it must be important. (As Hector Feliciano notes in *The Lost Museum*, during the Nazi looting of the French Rothschilds' collections during World War II, it was important that these collections be kept together—"selling them off piece by piece would have been unthinkable"—precisely because "these masterpieces could only have been intended for Hitler and Goering personally";[59] and these two collecting Nazis, of all people, valued the *Jewish Rothschild provenance* of the pieces!)

A break in the causal chain of provenance implies an existential discontinuity of the object and a sense of accidental survival. A break has the further effect of turning the antique into a mere "artifact." A continuity of provenance, on the other hand, implies a density of enrichments to the antique's life, a life that like a fine wine has mellowed and matured over the years. Moreover, continuity contributes to the work's unique character, for even antiques that are not unique on creation become so as a consequence of their aging, which provenance renders an account of. Aging brings transformation; transformations are accretions of experience that overlie what nature gives us at birth. A life itself has many stages, and provenance is the history of those stages in life; and in telling us of the lives of those with whom the antique has made contact, provenance accounts for what the object has become: why it has that stain, that dent, that hole. From the provenance of antiques we collect the evidence of their history. This is what we require from antiques, as André Malraux puts it: "the sense of life they impart, from the evidence of their struggle with time."[60]

   10. *Adventitious.* By "adventitious" is meant not merely "accidental," "fortuitous" or "chance," but, more precisely, "externally applied or applicable" criteria. They are criteria that come into play not so much in virtue of being unique characteristics of the object itself but in virtue of

the context in which the antique is encountered. This is essentially a catchall criterion for "environmental" factors that may affect the perception of antiques—their appreciation and valuation—but that are primarily attributable to extraneous causes. That is, this criterion relates to the antique in question only insofar as some particular individual at a given place and time and for a given purpose finds the antique especially enticing. This criterion therefore seems more relevant to such quasi-antique categories as the souvenir, trophy, artifact, and collectible. It also involves such matters as current fashion, locale, personal idiosyncrasies, price, and the like.

Thus, antiques in the Aesthetic Movement, Art Nouveau, Arts and Crafts, and Art Deco styles do not especially incite the historical consciousness or aesthetic imaginations of people in the southern United States. Consequently, in that locale they are not as appealing as they are on the East and West coasts. They certainly will not fetch the same price in Savannah, Georgia, as they will in New York. Antiques in the ancestral antebellum mid-nineteenth-century style (in New Orleans with French flourishes and associations attached) do.[61] In general, antiques are more valued in the locales where they were originally made and to the descendants (or would-be descendants) of those for whom they were made—not in the first or second or even third generations, but in those that follow.

Similarly, fashion—what is currently in vogue—plays an important role. Some have even seen a pattern of fashion cycles in antiques, particularly in the associated area of collectibles. Harry Rinker claims that collectible cycles often occur in twenty-year intervals, but that in the case of American folk art and antiques the run is fifty years (reflecting national celebrations of American Independence) or four years (for presidential memorabilia).[62]

Personal idiosyncrasies include decorating uses,[63] contribution to the completion of sets or collections, personal biographical connections or associations, investment programs, or simply competition. One prominent collector, when asked why he purchased the particular antiques he did, said that he used three criteria: "I like it, I can afford it, and I have a place to put it."[64]

This last criterion brings us to the issue of *price*. Although aesthetic purists would like to exclude this concern, it does enter into the totality of the experience of an antique. If the aesthetic appreciation of the antique is a desirable experience for those who enjoy such things or if collecting/connoisseurship is a desirable activity for those who engage in it, and if such experiences are not as freely available to the average person as going for a walk, then here (as elsewhere) they are things that have to be paid for in some manner. Price is simply the economic indicator or measure in the environment of the antique's availability of its desirability. The awareness of the high price of an antique brings to the experience of the object the aura of preciousness, a quality of rarity setting it apart from the ordinary sorts of objects.

There have been innumerable analyses of the prices of antiques, all usually taking into consideration in various ways the nine categories mentioned above. All also remark on the wide—and wild—fluctuation in prices for particular antiques.[65] The antiques world is currently awash in "price guides" to just about every category of antique, making every proud possessor of such a volume an instant connoisseur, or certainly an expert on the market price. As Rheims has observed, however, at least in the case of genuine antiques (rather than collectibles), "the concept of a 'market value' is pure fiction." Nevertheless, he calculates that in terms of "real money" there is little change over time in the prices paid for the "very best" in any category of antiques. What this means is that—perhaps surprisingly—whatever Louis XV may himself have paid for his writing desk is probably the equivalent in modern currency of what it would fetch on today's open market.[66]

We noted that antiques originally produced in a certain region of a nation or part of the world tend to command the highest prices in that same locale—assuming that the connoisseurship and collecting of antiques is currently practiced in that place. But price is highly relative not only to geography but to market level. If our opening account of the last few years in the life of the *nef* prior to its auction sale was illustrative of anything, it was that fact. Thus, there is the overall context of the sale (location, environment, demeanor of the salesperson): an antique sold in New York on Madison Avenue or in San Francisco in Jackson Square will sell for many times what the identical item will command in an antiques mall, a "mom and pop" shop, or a flea market in the same town. Finally, as participants in "The Antiques Roadshow" are often advised, the insurance value of their antique is always set much higher than its presumed retail value (insurers are notoriously committed to the position—generally true for most man-made objects—that older things are worth less than new, even when they know that the reverse is true in the case of antiques). Alternatively, "Roadshow" participants are often given two additional valuations: one for retail sale ("In my shop I would sell this for . . .") and another, much lower price for purchasing the antique oneself at some hypothetical auction. What these appraisers fail to mention explicitly is an altogether different price: that the average antiques dealer generally is unlikely to pay more than one-third of what he thinks he can sell the antique for—unless the dealer has a known and guaranteed client for a quick sale, or is himself looking for exactly this item to complete a set, or has just sold his last one, or has some other highly idiosyncratic reason of the sort mentioned above that makes him especially attached to this particular piece.

Having now offered these ten criteria as a comprehensive schematic account of the traits that make an antique "an antique," we turn to one final issue that constitutes our last, brief chapter. Given that we now know what an antique is and what to consider in granting (or refusing) it this status, and given that many people are not only aesthetically affected by antiques but seem to be almost consumed by the pursuit of them, what overarching benefit flows from these facts, and what does this all mean to humanity and civilization in general?

FOUR

Conclusion
Antiques and Civilization

It has often been asked: Where are the goods of the civilizations that
came before us, and where are the abundant riches known to have
existed among them? . . . It is civilization that through human labor
causes such goods to appear and can increase them or diminish
them . . . passed on by inheritance or transferred through trade or
war so that they moved from one to another, and from one dynasty
to another, in accordance with the purposes they were to serve and
the particular civilization that required them.
—IBN KHALDÛN, *The Muqaddimah* (V, 4)

Art is the highest metaphysical task of this life. . . . [It is] a
seduction, an overflow of blooming physically into the world of
images. . . . The aesthetic state possesses a superabundance of means
of communication together with an extreme receptivity for stimuli
and signs. It constitutes the highest point of communication and
transmission between living creatures.
—NIETZSCHE, *The Birth of Tragedy* and *The Will to Power*

This is not a work of cultural or philosophical anthropology but an
analysis and history of the idea of the antique; nevertheless, in the
preceding chapters we have continually referred to cultural matters
and to the evolution of civilization as a place where the idea of the antique
and the aesthetic response to the antique "matters." We have seen that a
civilization's conception of itself—of itself in its present as compared with
its past and of itself in comparison with other civilizations—plays an important role in establishing the idea of the antique and in grounding the
aesthetic response to the antique. In concluding this book, we cannot fail
to consider the reverse question: whether and to what extent the emergence of the idea of the antique and the aesthetic response to the antique
has affected not merely individuals but how a civilization sees itself and
sees others, and thus even affects how civilizations become what they are.

That is why we ended the previous chapter with a question: Given that we now know what an antique is and what to consider in granting (or refusing) some object this status, and given that many people are not only aesthetically affected by antiques but seem to be almost consumed by the pursuit of them, what benefit flows from these facts, and what does this all mean to humanity and civilization in general?

In answering this extremely far-ranging question, I am aware, as I said in my preface, that I offer more in the way of speculation here than in the preceding chapters, where I presented much empirical evidence and proposed philosophical arguments (sometimes extended at some length into the notes). Therefore, should the reader find this chapter less compelling than the earlier ones, I can submit only that it is briefer than they.

Much has been said of late about the cultivation of cosmopolitan, universalist, and humanist values, about whether and how they may serve to bridge gaps between cultures, about whether and how they may encourage or discourage the appreciation of cultural diversity, about whether and how they expand civilization.[1] Does the aesthetic response to the antique, which entails at least the admiration and preservation of the works of the past as the physically embodied residue of the totality of human cultural achievements and as the patrimony of humankind, provide the ground for establishing roots and continuity in a modern, rootless world that teems with discontinuities? Can it serve as an antidote to cultural chauvinism (which is, at its worst, the prelude to genocide)? Is there something special about the aesthetic appreciation of the antique that would allow us to recognize, understand, sympathize, tolerate, respect, appreciate, value, and attempt to preserve (perhaps in that sequence) one another—in both our commonality and our diversity?

I think the answer to these questions is affirmative. As I said in the preface, the antique becomes a tangible locus of preservation for the processes of civilization, enabling us to see the antique as a function of civilization (civilization "antiques" itself) and to see civilization as a function of the antique (the antique "civilizes"). Here I suggest why I think this is the case by reflecting and expanding on the history of the human sensibility to antiques as it relates to "humanism."

At the conclusion of chapter 1, as we considered the response to the antique in terms of evoking and preserving an image of the past, I mentioned in a note the double sense that the philosopher Martin Heidegger appeals to in his use of the German word *Wahrung* (the noun and also the related verb *bewähren*, which Heidegger deliberately conflates with *wahren* and *Wahrung*)—meaning both to "preserve" and to "hold true" and "authenticate"—when discussing our human understanding the

CONCLUSION: ANTIQUES AND CIVILIZATION 191

past. For Heidegger, all our understanding is a corollary of our "caring," especially of our caretaking, and especially of the past (in the face of the future). The mentality that appreciates the antique "preserves" the world it generates (the past and the foreign) and it also "holds" it "true," thereby authenticating, maintaining, saving, standing by, and in a sense "approving" it.

Recently, a frequent subject of debate has been the cultural domination of the world by the United States. Samuel P. Huntington, for example, attacks American foreign policy for its false belief that American culture represents the last (or best) form of Western civilization and that this culture and the values inherent in it are both universalizable and desirable for the whole world.[2] He argues that in default of a world empire and a common world culture the best chance for peace is in a world multiculturally divided and permanently separated into varyingly independent political spheres of influence. This is because at some point in globalization (which means Westernization, which means Americanization)—a point that always is reached, eventually, and a point at which we have now arrived—non-Western cultures become resistant to it and reassertive of their indigenous cultural traditions, traditions that were never really abandoned but merely held in abeyance. Non-Western societies feel this resistance is necessary because the modern Western cultural tradition has brought about internal contradictions, alienation, and anomie—and no doubt a permanent sense of inferiority in never being able to "catch up" to Westernization—for which their only alternative is a retreat into their own past. Such retreat usually takes the form of assertions of ethnic and/or cultural superiority and destiny, often supported by religious revival.[3] This, in turn, produces xenophobia, chauvinism, intolerance, bigotry, and sometimes armed combat. Whatever the accuracies of Huntington's diagnosis and prognosis, or the ultimate validity of his prescription for a cure, it seems to me that while isolationism and cultural chauvinism may bring temporary psychological satisfactions, insofar as this represents a retreat from the present (and any conceivable future) into the past and from reality into fantasy, the "mine-is-better-than-yours" stance of cultural chauvinism is doomed to failure. Alternative modes of embracing diversity within commonality (maintaining one's "own" within another's, and another's within one's own), employing the imagination as a means of connection within (rather than flight from) reality, and preserving the past as a source of (rather than a denial of) the present and future, must be found.

The capacity of art to achieve these ends—*and especially antiques, which as we have seen are imbued with cultural identity as confirmations of the continuity of the past into the present*—represents a potentiality usually overlooked. That is why the aesthetic response to antiques, objects that open windows onto worlds other than our own present, is a way of affirming the indigenous past, but without the evangelism of doctrine or chauvinist exclusivity. It is difficult, though admittedly not impossible, to despise or feel contempt for a civilization whose art and antiques one has come to understand and appreciate.[4]

Moreover, history has demonstrated that political domination does not always mean aesthetic domination, and political superiority does not necessarily entail cultural superiority. Indeed, it may be the mark of the superior civilization that it can adopt the art and cultural traits (and appreciate the historical productions) of another without fear for the survival of its own identity—simply because it sees itself as big enough, universal enough, to tolerate, to accept and include, even to embrace, differences.

That is why it has often also been noticed in the ebb and flow of civilizations that, over time, political victors may become the "cultural slaves" of the people they have conquered. The political victors—even when they have brought with them a new and successful religion—have often proved to be culturally too exclusive, too provincial, too spiritually small to dominate those they have overcome in other respects. One need only consider how often this reemergence of the former tradition occurred within the West with its successive revivals of classicism, or in Persia after the Arab conquest, or in China after the "eastern barbarians" who came to conquer it had become civilized (i.e., "sinicized"). Such cultural domination by the "foreign" and/or by the past may be a function of some temporary fashion or a permanent cultural susceptibility of a "lesser" to a "higher" culture. Even within dominant cultures, the styles and (sometimes values) of its subgroups, even subgroups that are generally considered weaker or oppressed, may become fashionable for the whole, suggesting a susceptibility—temporary or permanent—of the "higher" to the "lower" culture.[5] The susceptibility of a "high culture" to cultural diversity—internally or externally based—is not an aberration but the distinctive mark of the "superior civilization." It is the humanist historical sensibility of that civilization that makes this possible.

Joseph Alsop, in his monumental work *The Rare Art Traditions*, asks what the five "great traditions" (as he calls them) had in common to have developed and arrived at the same pattern of art-historical connoisseurship and collecting of art and antiques (with all the "by-products" of this cultural formation such as a complex market, fakery, museums, elevated valuation of the past, etc.), and to have arrived at the same level of appreciation for them, *besides* their common "imperialism" and "literacy." He concludes that it is their common "developed historical sense." Yet he cannot explain why this connection exists or what its components are.[6]

At least with respect to the antique, I have in the three preceding chapters tried to suggest what might provide the basis of such an explanation. It is a *care* for the uniqueness and irreplaceability of the particular—something we cannot fail to notice in the agedness and provenance of antiques—a particular that can be appreciated only in terms of the current civilization's relation to (and self-conception in comparison with) its own past and those of other civilizations. It is a relationship reflected and maintained in the mentality of its individual collectors and connoisseurs, who similarly construe themselves as the caretakers and preservers of the past for the present. Ultimately, theirs is an appreciation possible only in terms of the particular work's consideration under the idea of the common heritage of humanity, the civilization of humanity. It is a mentality and a sensibility that binds us to our own heritage and especially the antiques of other cultures, which provoke our awareness of our shared cultural inheritance and consequent sense of common humanity.

One might respond here that this sensitivity to the past and its continuity with the present through appreciation of antiques is merely wishful thinking of the most optimistic humanistic sort, and that for everyone who can respond to antiques in this way there are many more who see in them only their investment or monetary value; but I would argue that the facts "on the ground" indicate otherwise. Surely there are many who concern themselves with antiques—collectors and dealers, even connoisseurs—who do so only for monetary gain (especially among those who traffic in objects that are more properly called collectibles). But for the time and wisdom it requires to become acquainted with genuine antiques for this purpose, one would likely find it far more profitable to deal in stocks and bonds or in used batteries. There are better—easier, surer—ways to "make money."[7]

Hegel, in his *Lectures on the Philosophy of History*, observes that cultures become self-conscious only when they become conscious of themselves as developing out of their past. This self-consciousness manifests itself in language (which is the speaking and writing down of history) but also in concrete physical remains that are attestations *of* the past *for* a future.[8] This self-consciousness is the beginning of what he calls "freedom" because it is the "gathering together" of previously surpassed "spiritual shapes" to which the vagaries of human existence had been reduced.[9] Created in this gathering is a new interpretive form (shape) that includes them all.[10]

To say that an artwork is only meaningful in terms of some particular
culture that interprets it at some given moment is an obvious truth. To say
that its meaning is enhanced by taking into account the conceptions and
usages of the culture that produced it is equally obvious. To say it is *only*
meaningful for (or *only* meaningful in terms of) *one* of these to the exclusion of the other—*either* the current one *or* the past one—is ridiculous.

Kandinsky once wrote: "Every work of art is the child of its time. . . .
It follows that each period of culture produces an art of its own, which
cannot be repeated. Efforts to revive the art principles of the past at best
produce works of art that resemble a stillborn child."[11] Nevertheless, he
believes that there can exist a "similarity of 'inner mood' between one
period and another, the logical consequence [of which] will be a revival
of the external forms which served to express insights in the earlier age.
This may account partially for our sympathy and affinity with our comprehension of the work of primitives." But if this is true, as I think it is,
there is no reason to limit this "affinity" and "comprehension" to the
artworks of only primitives; and Kandinsky explicitly recognizes that
"an Egyptian carving moves us today more deeply than it did its contemporaries." It does so because, he claims, it embodies the "quintessence of
art," its "inner spirit," something that in itself seems to stand outside
time and space but that nevertheless "uses the external form of any particular period as a stepping stone to further development."[12] I have tried
to show that it is, in fact, the nature and existence of antiques, their enduring appeal, *as they are*, that on the one hand simply renders attempts
at "stylistic revival" otiose and on the other explains the affinity we feel
for the creations of the past and foreign.

Clive Bell, another famous interpreter of the history of aesthetic experience, similarly viewed art in terms of some core eternal spirit or truth,
which he called "expressive form." Bell also thought of this essential ingredient in all beautiful art as something to which particular cultural
considerations were irrelevant. He claimed that

> imperfect lovers bring to art and take away the ideas and emotions of their
> own age and civilization. In 12th century Europe, a man might have been
> greatly moved by a Romanesque church and found nothing in a T'ang pic-
> ture. To a man of a later age, Greek sculpture meant much and Mexican
> nothing, for only to the former could he bring a crowd of associated ideas
> to be the objects of familiar emotions. . . . It is the mark of great art that its
> appeal is universal and eternal.[13]

The truth of his claim does not entail, however (as he thinks it does),
that "to criticize a work of art historically is to play the science-besotted

fool." Nor is it true that to take into consideration the researches of art history ("besotted" or not) is to engage those discoveries merely for the purpose of seeing evolutionary progress in art so as to rate the later art better than the earlier: "no more disastrous theory ever issued from the brain of a charlatan than that of evolution in art. Giotto did not creep, a grub, that Titian might flaunt, a butterfly."[14] And consequently, though it is true that the mark of great art is its universal and its perpetual appeal (or at least the possibility of this appeal), it is false that this fact invalidates the appreciation of the connoisseur and the contributions and concerns of the historian. It is false, moreover, that as Bell would have it, the work's "provenance is irrelevant," that it must be "raised above the accidents of time and place," or that "the problems of" archeology, history, biography, or even of "subject matter" in regard to a work of art "are impertinent." Granting that the universal power of the work is the "mark of its greatness," we must also grant the "other side of the equation"—the work of the experiencer, who has attuned himself precisely to "the crowd of associative ideas" whereby the great art of any time and place can be capable of arousing an aesthetic response. Only the connoisseur of objects who knows the diversity of human creation and its past myriad cultural and stylistic possibilities can provide the conditions for a sufficient "crowd" of associated ideas that will bring to and take from the work the emotions of the present world as well as those of the past imaginatively evoked. And only the connoisseur can collectively unite these emotions with the perceptual and nonperceptual properties of the work in the present in such a way as to elicit from this experience the full aesthetic response.

Only this really makes us, to use Bell's same phrase to opposite purpose, "perfect lovers"—that we love the work for what it is in itself and what it does to us and what we can make of it, we love it for what it appears to be and for what we also know about it. And this entails, as I have tried to show, that we love it for what it presently is and also for what it was and how it came to be what it is—for the wrinkles and marks of age as well as the pristine youth of its former self. In appreciating the antique, one not only universalizes the care for the common humanity to which all art presumes to attune us but also sets this care in its historical context such that we can with tangible certainty bind ourselves to it in the present. The ideals of other people of other places and other times in the past are not severed from the present but preserved in the object; and because the object has itself been preserved and held true (*Wahrung*), its survival can be taken as an indication of its fitness for a universal human destiny.

Insofar as antique *objects* are concerned (those crafted quotidian productions enduring from the past that we normally think of as antiques), what is true of art generally in this regard is truer of them, for the latter have no interior worked world (whether this is understood as "subject matter" or "inner spirit"). Consequently, as historical artifacts imbued with the styles and marks of age, such antiques can refer us *only* to the worlds of the past, since they are expressive of (though not reducible to) the civilizations and epochs that made them. That is why we can care about them and care for them.

This is especially important for human life in the modern world, which is characterized by alienation in an environment where almost every object with which we deal is indistinguishable from a hundred thousand others and is immediately disposable. This is not news. But the relation of the antique to this situation needs to be elucidated.

What one might characterize as seeing the world "Wal-Mart-wise" has its theoretical roots ultimately in the seventeenth-century Cartesian conception of reality as a space/time picture in which things *have being* only insofar as they *occupy* space-time coordinates within the picture: they became what we called "free radicals," essentially identical, unowned objects with quantifiable primary properties that were the sole measure of that reality. This way of "seeing" the world and its objects found its social and political parallel in the uprooting of the "I" from its traditions and material conditions, an uprooting that was both the occasion for and occasioned by the revolutionary thinking of the eighteenth century: each person became a *citizen* with equal rights, equal liberties, equal possibilities, and by his own devices the arbiter of his own personal destiny.[15] And this way of seeing had its economic roots in the nineteenth-century Industrial Revolution, whereby the everyday objects we live with became reduced in their generic properties to their lowest (easiest) common denominator, became universally serviceable, infinitely interchangeable, disposable, and replaceable, and, being neither inherited by nor made by nor made expressly for anyone in particular, but rather, being available (for the posted price) to anyone at all, came to belong to no one in particular. The twentieth century saw the fruits of these successive abstractions and universalizations (with corresponding departicularizations) in the depersonalization of the self and its disconnection from the world. This disintegration of connection and continuity was enhanced by the inverse relations of persons and things to time's apparent ever-acceleration in the current century, so that people last twice as long (their life spans have doubled in a century) whereas objects last (much) less than half the time they once did.[16] It is to be expected in this sort of

CONCLUSION: ANTIQUES AND CIVILIZATION   197

world that we should cherish those things that have proved their endurance, that are imbued with provenance, that are unique, and that in their beauty call out to us for pause and attention. No longer solidly embedded in the material reality as a heritage that was "owned," we find in antiques the appearance of a salvation from an uncanny environment.[17]

That is why I am proposing that a foundation both for the diminution of human alienation and for the establishment of a humanistic basis for the peace of world civilization by its incorporation of diversity can be established through the nurturing of an appreciation of its antiques—by the function that antiques serve and by the very idea of the antique. The key to understanding this process can be found in the concept of *sensibility*, a concept first introduced into the discussion of human nature and nurture, and then into aesthetic theory, in the early eighteenth century. Some of the development and consequences of this notion were discussed in the archeology of chapter 2. But Gordon S. Wood provides a nice account in the following terms:

> There is no denying the extent to which scholars have come to regard sentiment and sensibility as the animating moral force of the 18th century. . . . Sensibility meant the receptivity of the senses, the capacity of people to receive impressions through their senses and thereby develop understanding and sensitivity. . . . Interest in this receptivity grew out of the sensationalist epistemology systematized by John Locke . . . that sense impressions gathered from the external world excited vibrations . . . and thus affected the character of people. Few revolutions in Western consciousness have been more important than the emergence of the culture of sensibility. . . . If only the impressions and sensations could be controlled . . . they might be able to create their own culture.[18]

In principle this meant two things. First, it meant that no one is bound *permanently* to any single culture and the conditions of experience it imposes. Rather like the "deep structure" of language that Noam Chomsky proposes as the basis for all human language acquisition and that, having been "switched on" in childhood and attuned to some particular language, makes possible the later acquisition of innumerable other languages, so an innate human sensibility to beauty, at first attaching only to objects stylistically/historically/geographically limited and familiar, can grow and expand so as to enable us to see and appreciate the divers forms that beauty has taken in different cultures at different times—to see how beauty is "civilized" and civilization "beautified" in manifold and reciprocal ways. While Mayan relief carvings may be, prima facie, as noncommutative (uncommunicative, unaesthetic) to a connoisseur of

Bernini as a speaker of Chinese would be to an average Irishman, still, one may learn and acquire the ability to "see" and aesthetically experience art styles just as one learns a language.[19] Antiques are uniquely suited to stimulate, to foster, a potentially universalist culture that is inclusive of our collective past. At the same time and by the same process, we can perhaps reverse the alienation that many experience in their relations with the objects of the world in which they live. And if unreserved and complete eclecticism is too much or too broad a range to expect for all to embrace, then encouraging each person to find and adopt that place and time whose style is most congenial to his nature and his own experience will enable him to ground himself in a past that is meaningfully present. If I "find myself" in Arts and Crafts lighting devices or in sixteenth-century Isnik ceramics, I may not likely find my equal home in Louis XV furniture or Meiji Restoration metalwork—but I *might* or *might come to.*

Second, this means that all humans, in sharing and actualizing the capacity of "sensibility," demonstrate and confirm to one another their common humanity. This notion was expanded at the end of the eighteenth century, especially by Kant. He argued that the aesthetic experience of natural beauty sharpened our sensitivity to a variety of stimuli that would, as he said, "set the cognitive powers into a harmonious free play" and produce the judgment of taste that is the recognition of the pleasure we feel in experiencing such beauty. Moreover, in the case of experiencing the beauty of the arts especially, Kant claimed that this experience not only freed up and enlivened the imagination but also encouraged and confirmed the existence of a common sympathetic understanding among all humans, a *sensus communis*, which, Kant held, made the judgment of taste "subjectively necessary."[20] It was this Enlightenment perspective on culture itself, supported by thinkers such as Kant, that established the basis of "humanism" in the modern sense, when this *commonality of sensibility* was extended across cultures and given a historical orientation.

Such is the credo of "humanism," as remarked by Lionel Trilling in passing in an incomplete essay on the teaching of Jane Austen:

> In its predilection for the . . . instructiveness of past cultures, humanism is resolute in the belief that there is very little in this transaction that is problematic; it is confident that the paradigms will be properly derived and that the judgments made on the basis they offer will be valid. Humanism takes for granted that any culture of the past out of which has come a work of art that commands our interest must be the product, and also, of course, the shaping condition, of minds which are essentially the same as our own.[21]

Beneath this lies an unstated but well-understood further assumption of all humanistic thinking about the process of coming to understand— to understand oneself, the world, and others. It is assumed that this process entails the dialectic of identity and difference, the essentially Socratic procedure of coming to know whereby the accepted (the given, the orthodox) is at every turn opposed by the heterodox, by altereity, so that when we get "home" we are certain that home is one we have made and comprehended as our own.

In art, especially the diversity of world-historical art, I can connect not only with others but with myself. Benedetto Croce once observed that, ideally, the activities and contents of the imagination in the process of creation and in the process of judgment are identical: both, the production and re-production, have an external objective existence in the analogue of the art object, "the product."[22] In the antique I can connect not only with the common present but also with the past present. Howard Mansfield similarly characterizes the emergence of this sensibility in the process of restoring antiques: "Good restoration is a two-way street, the object being mended in turn mends the worker. . . . The real value of the work lies in how this work restores and awakens us."[23] That is because not only can I empathize with the will and imagination that made it, but I can feel that I, too, had I the skill and will and imagination, would have made it just so—or that, in a certain sense, I wish I had, or had been able to—and now, in restoring it I am reanimating both it and its creator.

There is no "innocent eye," as we have remarked, quoting Nelson Goodman (quoting Ernst Gombrich): "the eye comes always ancient to its work, obsessed by its own past and by old and new insinuations. . . . The myths of the innocent eye and of the absolute given are unholy accomplices."[24] We also call the sophisticated way we see and create "style," and understand the way we have "aged in our eyes" as a progression (not to say evolution) of "styles." Connoisseurship that enables us to see and appreciate various styles—their connection to times and places—is the mark of civilization: and the greater the historical self-awareness, the greater the appreciation, and the greater the civilization.[25]

The insight that "nature imitates art"—together with the comparison of the sophisticated with the uninitiated and the historical with the atemporal—is instructive here. Hans-Georg Gadamer observes that the

aesthetic of natural beauty teaches us that, in a certain sense, this is an illusion and that in fact we can only see nature with the eyes of men experienced and educated in art. We remember, for example, how [before there emerged a stylistic vogue for the "English garden" and before the "land-scape" became pacified] the Alps were still described in European travel di-aries of the 18th century as terrifying mountain ranges whose ugly and fearful wildness was experienced as a denial of beauty, humanity, and the familiar security of existence.[26]

Going beyond Gadamer, one may well suspect that "beauty" itself never even arose as a possible way of seeing anything at all before the emergence of the idea of "art" on the earth—just as "antiques" remained unperceived until the emergence of our historical consciousness. In this sense civilization deprives us of an "innocence" that has made us blind.

We noted that only through diversity can one notice unity. Similarly, only through change can one notice history; and only through history can one "account for" change. Finally, it is through the awareness that history is not merely *of* the past but *in* the present that one can notice continuity in change. The primitivism of pre-Paleolithic peoples—"real" primitivism—is, like that found in natural species that have no freedom, no self-consciousness, but are determined only by their instinctual mech-anisms, always and everywhere pretty much alike. Primitive humans re-main timeless in their relationship with nature and in relation to their future and past generations. (That is why the Romantics thought they could find in them timeless truths.)[27] They may be "pure" and "inno-cent" and in some sense "perfect"; but like all such things, they have a tendency, like perfect circles, to quickly become boring. If there are no such "real" primitives (except in the fantasies of anthropologists) in fact, it is only because if we see their productions as in any way distinctive, we see them as having a style. To the degree that we can appreciate what is called "primitive art," however, we are seeing it as *not-primitive, not in-nocent* at all; and this is precisely what connoisseurs of primitive art try to call to our attention in the aesthetic experience of primitive art, namely, its *sophistication*. Hegel made us see that the eternity we mis-takenly thought to find in the primitive is nowhere to be found except in the historical and that the novelty so often prized in art is novel only in relation to the traditions from which it has sprung.

But if the future is only a creature of the past, does this pose a danger? Need we fear becoming "Egyptianized" (to use Nietzsche's term for civi-lizations that have become "mummified" through repetition)?[28] Will we stagnate and rot as the opening to the future is blocked by the debris, the detritus, of the past?

I think this unlikely. The modern mentality is so in thrall to the idea of evolution as an inevitable progressive improvement of our daily lives, and the modern world is so compelled by the force of technological development to face daily incommensurable, indigestible novelties—conditions envisioned in every science-fiction work we encounter[29]—that such fears of stagnation are a mere chimera.

Only if the artifactuals of the past are *seen as debris* is there a danger, for then their civilizing force has been ignored. Artworks especially do not block up space—whether in the world or in the mind. Rather, they open up. As Gadamer puts it, "every work leaves the person who responds to it a certain leeway, a space to be filled in by himself. . . . The identity of the work . . . is secured by the way in which we take the construction of the work upon ourselves as a task."[30] By "task" is meant not an onerous labor but the power of the work to nourish and inspire our imaginations. And to initiate play, as I have several times said above.[31]

Play is an essential aspect of aesthetic experience. It is also an essential aspect of civilization, and another mark of its achievement. For it is only when the tedious necessities of life have been provided for that one can luxuriate in the pleasures of caprice. This is the proper "use" of "free time" that makes artistic creativity (rather than the inventions of necessity) possible. The modern museum's chief role is to be the institutional memory and collector-connoisseur for society, but its original and primary purpose—the first one, the one in Alexandria—was the establishment of a locale for "musing," a place for housing texts and objects that incite the play of the imagination, for "amusement."

The role of play in civilization is not a new insight. It is merely often overlooked. Significantly, Plato and Aristotle mention it. Johan Huizinga, the most famous modern analyst of the role of play in our cultural life in general, concludes his *Homo Ludens*: "We have gradually become convinced that civilization is rooted in play and that, if it is to unfold in full dignity and style, it cannot afford to neglect this play-element."[32]

Huizinga quotes Plato in the *Laws*: "Man is God's plaything, and that is the best part of him. Therefore every man and woman should live life accordingly, and play the noblest games, and be of another mind from what they are at present."[33] Huizinga also points out that Plato "understood creativity as play."[34] Creation out of caprice, out of the spontaneous fullness of being, rather than out of the demands of necessity, is action in "imitation of the divine." Plato's key phrases here are "noblest" and "another mind from what they are." What they connote is, on the one hand, freedom to perform and, on the other, exemption and exception from the ordinary. Aristotle, similarly, discusses music as a form of mental recreation—as "idling" (i.e., being disengaged from the pragmatics of necessity)—for, he says, one must in life not only work well but also "idle well."[35] Huizinga notes that "this idleness or leisure is the principle of the universe for Aristotle . . . it is the aim (τέλος) of all work."[36] As liberation from toil, creative idleness is the very mark of the freeman, one who is a slave neither to nature nor to other men.[37] From this perspective, the necessary and the useful are not the only (much less the highest) concerns of humankind. As Aristotle says in speaking of his ideal state: "it is true that the citizens of our state must be able to lead a life of action and war but they must even more be able to lead a life of leisure and peace. It is true again that they must be able to do necessary and useful acts; but they must be even more able to do good acts."[38] He continues, "It is the power to use leisure rightly . . . which is the basis of all our life," because "to aim at utility everywhere is utterly unbecoming to high-minded and liberal spirits" (i.e., ones who are civilized, ones who are not barbarians and slaves). And hence, it is clear that by "play" Aristotle is not thinking of an activity that is merely a means to an end, a refreshing restorative pause that enables a return to work, but rather thinking of play as an end in itself: "we think of leisure here as having itself intrinsic pleasure, intrinsic happiness, intrinsic felicity. Happiness of that order does not belong to those who work but those who have leisure."[39] It is not leisure as "doing nothing," then, but leisure as "doing freely and creatively" that Aristotle thinks is best, for as he says, the end for which we live is a kind of activity, namely, that activity which most fully actualizes our most distinctive excellences, for this alone, he thinks, can bring us complete happiness.

In the foregoing I have attempted to lay the foundation for claiming an important role for antiques—particularly the appreciation of antiques—in civilization. Part of this role is, as we have said, the antique's function in the civilizing and humanizing of humanity. We have argued that it affirms, through the common sensibility it presupposes, the common humanity of humankind, absorbing diversity into unity and the past into the present; that it affirms self-identity and authenticity; that it bespeaks the fragility of the particular in its physical endurance through time and in its particularity, suggesting both its mortality and the preciousness that instills in us a care for its preservation.[40]

But in noting the relation of play to civilization, we bring to the fore another element in the connection between the antique and civilization. This element is the luxurious play with the beautiful object that imaginative engagement of the antique evokes. Insofar as it releases us from the toil of everyday constraints, aesthetic appreciation is a (if not *the*) primary mode of "freeing up our space." As such, the aesthetic appreciation of the antique is not merely a means toward civilization but an end of it and a form of it. Even if aesthetic playfulness is not (as both Plato and Nietzsche would have it) "the highest" task of life and man's most "god-like" occupation, surely the aesthetic dimension in human life is very dear. The appearance of art and the recognition of beauty are contemporaneous with the emergence of civilization. The appreciation of the antique seems to appear in civilizations that are—by all other gauges—civilizations at their height.

In the preceding chapters we have moved back and forth between the schematic—the various terms and concepts that delimit "the antique" (the definition and the ten evaluative criteria)—and the historical (the various stages in the evolution of the idea and appreciation of the antique in civilization). We have discussed the antique in its relation to craft and fine art and have attempted to interpret the aesthetic experience of the antique "as it appears" and has emerged and developed contextually through history.

Finally (and as a philosopher I suppose I am condemned to ask this question at some point), how shall we place the antique in the world of our experience in terms of its *reality*—as something genuinely to be reckoned on and reckoned with? Is there more to be said about the antique onto-logically, that is, more to be said about its being? This is to me perhaps the most interesting aspect of our aesthetic response to the antique.

Heidegger has demonstrated that at least since Plato, Being per se has always been associated most keenly with, and most certainly predicated of, that which *perdures*, that which *remains unaffected by time*. That is to say, that the being of a thing has been construed, measured, guaranteed in terms of time, so that the "realist" things have always been thought to be those that are eternal, simply because they "always are," or are not "subject to" time, or "are continually present."[41] With the historicization of Being in Hegel and the inversion of Plato by Nietzsche, time*li*ness has replaced time*less*ness as the indicator of genuine reality. In consequence, *endurance* as *changing in* time rather than *perdurance* as *unchanging throughout* time has become the mark of authenticity. Can we say, then, that the antique takes its justification for being, takes its "reality rights" (as it were), from this new insight—that its endurance (and the marks of its age that have transformed it and that now enable it to shine forth in the space it opens up to our imagination) makes it "realer" than either the mayflies of the present pragmatic moment or the essences inhabiting an eternal empyrean?

The identification of permanent presence with *real* being in the course of Western thought is not a historical accident or merely a prevailing theoretical hypothesis but is covertly grounded in humanity's dissemblance of its own mortality and finitude. The idea of the conquest of immortality through Beauty is as old as Plato's *Symposium*. The appreciation of antiques bespeaks a reverence for created things that have endured for a while (in the flux of things that come into being and pass away) and that show their earthliness in their signs of age. Antiques *are* what reality *becomes*. Perhaps this appreciation is an indication of the degree to which the classical ideal of perfection as the perdurance of eternal essences has been abandoned. The antique stamps the mark of Becoming on the heart of Being.

Notes

---

1. Preliminaries: Understanding Antiques

1 A earlier version of this section first appeared as a scholarly article, "The Aesthetic of the Antique," *Journal of Aesthetics and Art Criticism* 65, no. 4 (1987): 393–402. Extensive additions, deletions, and other substantive revisions have been made here.

2 Although I am aware that these remarks may strike some as unnecessarily evaluative and perhaps even carping in tone, I can only refer the reader to my article "The End of Art Theory," *Humanitas* 15, no. 1 (2002): 32–58, to engage my argument there for what I am claiming here. In brief, I believe one cannot separate a discussion of antiques from a discussion of art, and though I do not here propose to offer a full-fledged definition of art per se, I do not believe that evaluation or estimation can be eliminated from any definition of art any more than it can from the consideration of what makes an antique. That is, that one cannot entirely separate *whether* an object is to be classified as an "art" object from *how good* it is at being art or doing what it apparently purports to achieve. A normatively neutral description, definition, or classification of objects as "art"—as has been attempted by such philosophers as Arthur Danto and James Dickie, among others—is not possible. Thus, if a purported artwork is not in fact aesthetically satisfying, something I think art must be, either it is bad art or it isn't art at all. (And in some peculiar sense, simply by calling it "art" one has implicitly asserted it is "good," for especially in the contemporary art world, it is not always clear whether a given object is "bad" art or whether it is "not" art at all.) Rather, I believe, much of what passes for "good art" these days is not really *good art* at all and may not even be "*art*," but may well be good art criticism or good theorizing (philosophizing) *about* art that just happens to be appearing in the guise (thought the medium) of art. Philosophers and art critics and even artists are prone to forgetting that there is a difference between intellectual satisfaction (approval), which engages merely the cognitive faculties, and aesthetic satisfaction, which clearly involves sense perceptions and emotions. (But I will deal with these matters more fully later.)

As for my claim regarding the current preference by a major sector of the public for antiques over contemporary artworks, admittedly, I do not prove this—though it might be provable. I'd take odds, however, on the bet that there are more people who have aesthetic sensibilities (I'll not beg the issue by asserting that they have "taste"), who are ignorant neither of critical/philosophical theories of art nor of art history, who are not cultural Philistines and who like neither the "difficult" art styles of today nor the "easy" productions of artists like Thomas Kinkade, people who prefer to rummage through antiques shops for what they might discover rather than attend contemporary art galleries for the latest find—and who actually would buy such items for their living rooms—even if they live in New York City.

3 For example, as we will see in detail in the subsequent chapters, the fortitudinous consciousness generated in the Italian Renaissance by the reawakening of the classicism of Greece and Rome was not the same consciousness generated later by the revival of the classical past in the late eighteenth and early nineteenth centuries in England and France. The latter revival was characterized by *nostalgia* for the old and the past—the cult of the ruin, for example, and associations with the picturesque, perhaps foreshadowings of the Romantic temperament to come, which Hegel would identify not with "fortitude" but with what he called the "unhappy consciousness." Such reverences and revivals are not uniquely Western, of course. Ancient Egypt, primarily through reverence for its own heritage rather than through a subculture of antiquarianism, repeatedly produced renaissances and archaisms in its art. Japanese and Chinese instances also occur commonly.

4 Curiously, then, one might claim that whereas the idea of the antique has evolved over time, the reverse has happened quite late to the idea of "art," since, whereas once upon a time it was quite clear what sorts of things were to count as "art," now this is not so clear at all. What I mean is that just about anything might by some theory or person or institution be called "art" these days—and in consequence, anything and everything could be art. And in consequence of anything being art, nothing is especially art. This makes the term "art" entirely meaningless. Fortunately, we are in much better position with regard to a definition of "antiques," even if we are unable to stipulate its necessary and sufficient conditions.

5 And correlatively, if some set of assertions was proposed as a "theory" but made no sense cognitively, even though it might elicit an overwhelming sensuous aesthetic response, I would not call it a "theory."

6 See Arthur Danto, *Encounters and Reflections: Art in the Historical Present* (New York: Farrar, Straus and Giroux, 1990) and *The Transfiguration of the Commonplace* (Cambridge, Mass.: Harvard University Press, 1981). I use "entrenched" in his sense here to distinguish art from non-art objects. For Danto the art world has the power to transform entrenched into non-entrenched objects, a process he calls the "transfiguration of the commonplace," for which Marcel Duchamp's *Fountain* is the prime example: a urinal *discovered as art* in the world of the art gallery. Martin Heidegger might use the term "ready-to-hand" for "entrenched" (see *Being and Time*, trans. John Macquarrie and Edward Robinson [New York: Harper and Row, 1962], 80–104 primarily). Artworks are, by definition, not entrenched and not ready-to-hand. On the relevance of Heidegger's theories to art objects, especially to art-historical objects, and their possible connection to Danto's "entrenched/non-entrenched" objects, see my article "Heidegger's Aesthetics: The Art Object and History," *Studies in the Humanities* (June, 2008).

7 See my article "The Ontological Integrity of the Art Object from the Ludic Viewpoint," *Journal of Aesthetics and Art Criticism* 34, no. 3 (1976): 323–36. By "world" I do not mean some cosmological entity or spatio-temporal location, but rather, in Heidegger's sense, a realm of familiar phenomena in which an individual feels "at home" and "comfortable," a complex of meaningful patterns and pathways whereby we encounter and deal with things and people and in terms of which (through whose pre-established criteria and categories) we render these things and encounters intelligible—as when one speaks, for example, of the "world of the dance" or "sports world."

8 See my "Heidegger's Aesthetics" for a phenomenological grounding of this "ontological integrity."

9 It has been recently claimed by Larry Shiner, for example, that art—the *idea* of "art" itself—entered the consciousness of Western society only in the eighteenth century, particularly in and through German philosophical thought. Before then, there was just "craft." Not until (and precisely when) "art" arose, so too did a theory of it. (Though, perhaps, I might argue, it went the other way, the theory preceding the actuality of artistic fact.) Then, for the first time, a "fateful division occurred in the traditional concept of art," he says, so that *craft* was to be distinguished from *fine art* such that only instances of the latter, as works of inspiration and genius, were "meant to be enjoyed for themselves in moments of refined pleasure." (See Shiner, *The Invention of Art: A Cultural History* [Chicago: University of Chicago Press, 2001], 5.) Although I agree with Shiner that the psychological state of "disinterestedness" and the faculty of "taste" were *explicit* new developments in the eighteenth century, especially as advanced in Kant's notion of the beautiful as requiring "disinterested satisfaction," the actual distinction between art and craft per se was not entirely a new one. The distinction is implicit in Aristotle's *The Physics* 199a15–17. There Aristotle says that the constructive arts complete nature but that *mimetic* art "partly completes what nature cannot bring to finish and partly imitates her." I think it is both implicit and reasonable (given Aristotle's other claims, particularly in *The Poetics*) to interpret this to mean: "craft" only completes whereas "fine art" both completes and imitates nature. Or in the terminology I used above, craft objects *refer* to a world but fine artworks *also generate* (create and embody) one. Thus, the idea that fine art has an imitative content, "an about which," that comes packaged in the world it generates, whereas crafts only bring into being some kinds of things which add to the supply that nature provides, things that we can "use for" some purpose in the everyday world—this conception is indeed *implicit* in Aristotle's account. Neither is it, contrary to Shiner, entirely new to the eighteenth century to view art as having as its purpose pure contemplation or as having a therapeutic or curative effect on the soul, for these conceptions derive from Plato and (also) Aristotle and come down through early Medieval thinkers such as Plotinus and St. Augustine and St. Thomas, who ascribed such powers to beauty generally. The criterion of disinterested satisfaction and contemplation for "fine art" to which Shiner refers is certainly different from the *mimetic* one proposed by Aristotle—one that I have interpreted as "world-generating" rather than "world-referring." As a criterion for maintaining the "fine art"/"craft" distinction, the world-generating vs. world-referring duality can be understood as a characteristic (state, disposition) of the object, whereas the former, the "disinterested satisfaction," may be viewed as a disposition of the subject who experiences. Significantly, however, these two need not be treated as mutually exclusive. I believe that for a genuine aesthetic experience to transpire—whether for an artwork or for an antique—both conditions need to occur: the objective condition of the artwork (antique) itself which is translucently world-generating and the subjective condition of the experiencer who approaches the artwork as an object of disinterested satisfaction.

As for the categories of the fine arts themselves, Paul Oskar Kristeller, in his magisterial "The Modern System of the Arts: A Study in the History of Aesthetics," *Journal of the History of Ideas* 12 (1951): 496–527, and 13 (1952): 17–46, described in great detail how "the fine arts" (painting, poetry, music, sculpture, and literature)—a classification that

> underlies all modern aesthetics and is familiar to us all—is of comparatively recent origin and did not assume definite shape before the eighteenth century, although it has many ingredients which go back to classical, medieval, and Renaissance thought. . . . [But] the eighteenth century produced a type of literature in which the various arts were compared with each other and discussed on the basis of common

principles, whereas up to that period treatises on poetics and rhetoric, on painting, architecture, and on music had represented quite distinct branches of writing and were primarily concerned with technical precepts rather than with general ideas. (497–98)

See also Jerome Stolnitz, "On the Origins of 'Aesthetic Disinterestedness,'" *Journal of Aesthetics and Art Criticism* 20 (1961): 131–38. In any case, the traditional classification of the particular "fine arts" has nothing eternal and universal to recommend it—not the least because it fails to embrace modern art forms such as cinema and also art forms of past and non-Western civilizations, which, had they been asked which of their arts to include among the "fine," would certainly have mentioned calligraphy, carpet-weaving, metal-smithing, and stained-glass window making as readily as painting and sculpture.

Finally, regarding the craft vs. fine art distinction itself, one may ask: is either of the two criteria mentioned above—disinterested satisfaction (contemplation, "refined pleasure") or world-generation (imitativeness, "aboutness")—successful in maintaining the distinction? Or are there any other arguments in support of it?

Besides "world-generation" and "disinterested contemplation," to which I have already referred, there have been attempts to establish and preserve the fine art vs. craft distinction on the basis of "expressive power," "creativity/originality," and "medium." Let us briefly consider these three. (1) R. G. Collingwood is just one of many authors who claim that the difference between fine art and craft (and the superiority of fine art over craft) resides in its "power to express emotion." (Collingwood, *Principles of Art* [Oxford: Clarendon Press, 1938], 15–16.) Apart from the difficulty of ascertaining exactly what is meant by "expressive power" (emotional/intellectual impact, ability to communicate a message, sincerity?), it depends on which instances one picks, for surely *some* paintings and novels we have experienced in the course of our lives would do very poorly in the company of *certain* examples of craft (a Fabergé Imperial Easter egg, a Meissen porcelain dinner service, a Kashan carpet) on the basis of this criterion. As a generality, then, the claim is not very convincing. And finally, we should recall that painters themselves before, say, 1800 would never have imagined that "expressive power" was the indicator or the criterion of the "fineness" of their works, and that many a twentieth-century artist (e.g., Abstract Expressionists in the United States or Tachists in Europe) would consciously and explicitly deny expressive power as an aesthetic value of their artworks. (2) T. R. Martland, on the other hand, argues for creativity/originality: that "craft has no room for new relationships or new understandings" because it is "a service to categories which men have already completed." (Martland, "Art and Craft: The Distinction," *British Journal of Aesthetics* 14, no. 3 [1974]: 231–32.) That is, craft works within the realm of the familiar whereas art strives for creativity. Craft follows a formula and standard set by the trade, tending to repeat; and although craft may require "ingenuity," it does not require genius or imagination. There seems at first to be some merit to this claim; but again, it fails as a general criterion of distinction simply because it depends on the instances one picks, for there is much fine art that is not "original" or "creative" in the intended sense. Even instances of *great* fine art might fail this test (many a symphony by Haydn or painting by Corot or even, say, a later instance of Rembrandt's self-portraits). Furthermore, if true, it would make the first example of any craft (e.g., first pair of eyeglasses, first horse-shoe) "fine art" and all subsequent examples "craft." (3) Finally, some have proposed the material medium in which the work is produced as a criterion for distinguishing "fine art" from "craft." In the Hegelian scheme, for example, the five fine arts themselves are ranked by this criterion. It turns out for Hegel, then, that architecture is the least "spiritual" of the fine arts and poetry the most, poetry being the "highest" fine art simply because the sensuous element in that art genre is minimal and not "fettered in its realization to an externally sensuous material" whereas architecture requires the maximum of material for its embodiment. (Georg Wilhelm Friedrich Hegel, "Introduction to the Philosophy of Fine Art," in *Aesthetics: Lectures on Fine Art,* trans. T. M. Knox [Oxford: Clarendon, 1975], 1:82–89) But this claim, even if we buy into the Hegelian system, that its greater quantity of "physicality" or "materiality" or "sensuousness" is the criterion of craft (and among the fine arts the sign of lesser status), should certainly exclude architecture from being a fine art at all (placing it most definitely among "craft") while calligraphy and rug-weaving should certainly be "in" as fine art (as much "in" as, say, sculpture). To be sure, historically, as we see later, there was some undercurrent of socioeconomic prejudice in assigning "fineness" only to certain arts. Poets were always held in highest esteem, for they were almost never slaves, and, educated in the literary/religious tradition of the classical and medieval cultures in which they composed, poets "worked" only in words; whereas painters and sculptors performed manual labor for pay (or in servitude) under the command and instruction of the educated and wealthy (the state, the church, the patron); and it took the Renaissance and geniuses like Michelangelo to elevate "painting" and "sculpture" to the status of fine arts, the necessity to work a physical medium with one's hands being no longer a bar to this status. Thus, the "materiality" or "physicality" of painting and sculpture as the criterion of "fineness" is historically and culturally relative. The materiality of the medium as a criterion for the distinction is sometimes also made in reference to the two "noble senses"—sight and hearing. But this merely introduces yet another prejudice and would also render the special kinetic appeal of the architectural experience (walking through a Gothic cathedral or a church by Borromini) and the tactile appeal of sculpture insignificant, while certainly not excluding many crafts. (Besides, if one transferred the visually apprehended patterns and colors of a Kashan carpet into the medium of oil on canvas—or if *Guernica* or a section of the Sistine Chapel ceiling were faithfully transferred in every respect into a rug design or tile floor—we should then have succeeded, rather improbably, in transforming an instance of craft into a fine artwork and vice versa.) Apart from the accidents of history, socioeconomic prejudice against those who work with their hands, tradition-bound or arbitrary "quality" or "quantity" preferences for this or that medium, or a philosophically prejudiced preference for a minimalism of medium altogether, there can be no other basis for thinking one medium appropriate to fine art and another appropriate for craft.

The inadequacy of these three criteria leads us back to the two we began with: disinterested satisfaction (refined pleasure) and world-generativeness ("aboutness," "imitativeness"). "Disinterestedness" is sometimes contrasted with "usefulness," and then the distinction is presented simply as: "craft is useful, art useless." By this, it is usually meant that the crafts serve some external purpose or end in the routine of our daily lives, for which function alone they were created. Fine art serves only itself (it produces pleasure directly as an end in itself). This notion lies at the root of the famous epigram *ars gratia artis* (art for art's sake). Unfortunately, put in this simple form, the distinction cannot be consistently maintained. On the one hand, a diamond tiara by Cartier is not useful in the sense of being a kind of gear for warming the cranium. Its function is to please by being beautiful as much as any painting. On the other hand, the Parthenon of Phidias and Ictinus was certainly made for extra-artistic purposes insofar as it served functions religious, political, economic, and social. Again, the purpose of van Eyck's *Adoration of the Mystic Lamb* and of Bernini's *Ecstasy of St. Teresa* was primarily religious, i.e., to explain a religious dogma and evoke a religious experience. Finally, why would people purchase or pursue any art object unless it provided thereby some benefit (hence use) to them? Thus, crafts are not always useful, and fine artworks are not always useless—at least not as these terms are normally understood. Yet wouldn't what would normally be classified as a craft production simply *become available as* a work of fine art if, for example, it were constructed in such a fashion as to *not be useful* or if produced in materials rendering it *unusable* or if it were decontextualized or made for use in a world that was not presently available (because elsewhere or no longer existent)? Consider, for example, a monogram so intricately complex in its calligraphy that it became indecipherable or a water fountain made of papier-mâché (or Salvador Dali's fur-lined teacup and saucer) or an Art Nouveau wrought iron gate removed from the entryway to a long-demolished cemetery and hung on a wall. These may produce aesthetic pleasure as much as any fine art object. If we define "fine art" in such a way that it must have *always more than* "utility value" and define "craft" in such a way that it must *at least have usefulness,* this would not be unreasonable.

And this brings us back both to *disinterestedness,* with which we began this long note (as the basis of the "refined pleasure" that Shiner claims gave rise to the origin of the idea of fine art in the eighteenth century, and which we consider again in chapter 2), and to *world-generativeness.* "Mimesis" or "imitation" is probably the traditional and most "classical" formulation of this world-generativeness. It is the basis of Aristotle's distinction, for as we have already noted, the "productive sciences" or "constructive arts" function to "complete nature," whereas what we would call fine art "partly completes what nature cannot bring to finish and partly imitates her." But by "imitation" Aristotle does not mean simply "copy." Nor does he oppose "imitative" to the idea of "creative"; and indeed, he strongly suggests that certain "imitations" are most successfully "artistic" when they are most "creative"—they generate something—and are not mere repetitions of fact or historical recapitulations. (See Aristotle, *Poetics* 1447b14–22; 1451a1–10, 18–22, and also my "On Aristotle and Thought in the Drama," *Critical Inquiry* 3, no. 3 [1977]: 543–65; and "Re-thinking Aristotle's 'Thought,' " *Critical Inquiry* 4, no. 3 [1978]: 597–606.) There is much merit in his criterion of imitation for maintaining the fine art/craft distinction, in terms of the traditional, if rather simplistic, interpretation of "imitation." But it too is unsatisfactory, for it is hard to imagine in what sense architecture, for example, is "imitative" (no problem, of course, for Aristotle, because he did not conceive of architecture as "fine art"); it nowadays is almost as hard to imagine in what sense music is imitative (Aristotle thought it imitated our emotional states and hence our moral qualities or character types and called it the "most imitative" of the arts—see *Politics* 1339b11). It is harder still to imagine why, for example, an alabaster oil lamp carved in the shape of a lotus plant (such as the one found in Tutankhamen's tomb) would then (imitative merely by virtue of having this form) be not craft but fine art. And finally, and most seriously, it would be impossible to imagine how any nonrepresentational painting or sculpture—a good portion of the twentieth century's production—could then be "fine art."

But if we replace the simple idea of "imitative" or "representational" with the idea of "world-generativeness" or "aboutness," these difficulties disappear (or at least diminish substantially). C. B. Fethe, for example, puts his case for "fine art" vs. "craft" in Husserlian terms of the *Lebenswelt* (the "life"-world or "lived" world of daily experience). The judgment as to whether any particular object constitutes an instance of art or of craft should rest on the potential the object has to affect our experience of the life-world. A painting or sculpture should be considered a craft when we place it in an assigned role in the world of common events and reflect, for instance, on how it fits a room's décor or whether it captures the image of the subject; but it approaches the state of art when these questions vanish and the object introduces us to a new conception of reality. (See Fethe, "Craft and Art: A Phenomenological Distinction," *British Journal of Aesthetics* 17, no. 2 [1977]: 129–37.) It is in this sense that I have used the phrase "worked world" (in opposition to the everyday world of daily experience—the *Lebenswelt*) to denote the "facts" present in this "new conception of reality," facts generated and posited by the art object within its own structured and virtual world together with its own implied "explanations, purposes, laws, etc., which render a significant account of what is objectively given," as I have said (Rosenstein, "Ontological Integrity of the Art Object," 327). In the generated world, the worked world, of *Macbeth*, for example, ghosts and prophecies are as real as the given facts of death and drunkenness, while such notions as children, inheritance, and manhood/womanhood have become the "codes" or interpretive rules that render the actions within that play meaningful. To take an example from painting, in the worked world of van Gogh's *The Night Café*, the billiard table, clientele, and lamp are givens as contents of the worked world, and the peculiar combinations of color hues, brushstrokes, distorted perspective, figural poses and placement, etc., become the source of interpretation for (the "metaphysic" of) that world—a world in which (as van Gogh wrote to Theo) "one can ruin oneself, go mad or commit a crime . . . and all this in an atmosphere like a devil's furnace, of pale sulphur." (Quoted in Herschel B. Chipp, *Theories of Modern Art* [Berkeley: University of California Press, 1969], 37.) Thus the sort of distinction Fethe makes is reasonable.

The problem is that it turns out not to be a distinction between "fine art" and "craft" at all. Rather, Fethe's argument distinguishes between all *art objects* in general and all *non-art objects*. On this basis craft not only fails to be "fine" art; it fails even to be *any sort of "art"*—not decorative art, not constructive art, not applied art. Craft—which does not, like "the [fine] art object . . . negate the life-world in a radical way by presenting a possible substitute for it" but rather has as its "primary aim . . . to create objects which have an assigned place in the world of common activities" (Fethe, "Craft and Art," 134–35)—must on this basis be relegated to the non-art category altogether. But this categorization would be valid insofar as (and only insofar as) a given object failed to be "aesthetic" (i.e., failed to take us beyond our everyday preoccupations and occupation with it) to any degree. Craft objects would here be no different from instances of tools or equipment. But there are objects we would call examples of "craft"—a clay pot thrown and glazed by a great potter, say, or a Persian "polonaise" carpet, or a piece of jewelry by R. Lalique—which are in no way like the Tupperware pots we purchase for storage or the area rugs we buy at Home Depot or the earrings on cards we purchase at discount stores for a few dollars. These craft objects might well have the capacity to move us in some way besides using them for a practical purpose, even "introducing us to a new conception of reality." Hence, while one ought to abandon the *prejudice* that has separated fine art from craft, this does not mean that one must altogether abandon the *distinction*, even while recognizing that this distinction is not hard and fast and that there will always be matters of degree and dispute. Although one could more easily cite names of objects classified as "fine" that are in some sense "greater" than any craft object one could name, as we have already pointed out, one could just as easily imagine other instances to the contrary. Michelangelo's staircase for the Campidoglio in Rome or the great Imari charger with flying blue cranes by an unknown Japanese maker in the porcelain gallery of the Topkapi Palace Museum in Istanbul might both be viewed as either fine art or craft. Neither is inferior in any respect to the poems "By the Numbers" or "Once I Loved" by Rod McKuen or the oil painting *Naughty Kittens in the Knitting Basket* by Thelma Murphy Blitz, despite the traditional ranking of poetry and painting as the higher fine art genres. Thus, Fethe, who sees in the "new-world-generative-capacity" of fine art its distinctive criterion and mark of special advantage, does not in fact succeed in demonstrating the claim for the distinction between and superiority of fine art over craft, but only between art and non-art.

My view, which must wait for a fuller exposition in a later chapter, is simply that world-*reference* is a function of all objects. World-*generation* (or world-making or world-working) is a function of all aesthetic experience and all art. Art is art because it abandons at least in part the purpose of being a function of the everyday world (*Lebenswelt*) in order to set up its own "worked world." Insofar as man-made objects ("crafts" or whatever) remain within and must perforce continuously refer to *this* daily world, they are not art. But insofar as crafts contribute toward the generation of a different or alternative world, they are like art.

When it comes to antiques—whether understood as inclusive of the "fine" or as traditionally limited to "craft"—since they often cannot function within (refer to) the world of the present time, or cannot do so very well, their special world-reference is to a world past. But since this past world is no longer, their primary current function becomes to evoke (generate, create) for us an image of the past world, whether real or imagined. Thus, antiques, often originally "mere craft" productions, may be understood to have, through the loss or disappearance of their use-worlds over time, simply "fallen into" the condition of being "fine art," for they "re-create" the past world. That many of the types of things we usually call "fine" tend to do this sort of "world-making" (world-generating) more often or more readily than many of the types of things we usually call "craft" do is a consequence of our contextual habits and expectations and also of historical-cultural accident.

We may conclude, then, that although a distinction between "craft" and "fine art" may be maintained, it is a tenuous one—a distinction of degree and probability—having more to do with the extent of an object's world-reference vs. world-generation and with the regularity of an object's involvement with the everyday function of world-engagements than with any absolute disconnection that can be maintained on some criterion of usefulness, imitation, creativity, medium, or expressive power.

10 As for the question regarding the accuracy of the image evoked of the past, I need not resort to post-modernist critiques of the possibility of historical accuracy per se but refer the reader to the excellent work *The Invention of Tradition*, by Eric Hobsbawm and Terence Ranger (Cambridge: Cambridge University Press, 1983), where it is amply demonstrated that much of what we take to be a long-standing and indelible truth of "the past" is in reality a result of our own very recent (often idealized) invention.

11 Exceptions are possible. And sometimes artists deliberately intend to set one world in contrast with the other. If, for example, history had in fact shown Charles V to be a weak and pedestrian sort of fellow, these extra-artistic facts of the historical world and the painting's representation of his power, majesty, and glory in its worked world could have been deliberately juxtaposed so as to create ambiguous tension or contradiction; and this incongruity would have become a primary part of the painting's worked world, perhaps its theme and quintessence. We do find this contrast, this incongruity, for example, in some of Goya's portraits of the Spanish royal family and in Leonardo's *Lady with an Ermine*; and experience it to comical effect in the paintings of the modern (former Soviet) artist team of Komar and Melamid, who deliberately juxtapose, for good measure, art-historically incongruous iconography and protocols in their pseudo-Socialist-Realist paintings (e.g., their *Stalin and the Muses*).

12 Nevertheless, custom has normally reserved the term "antique" for works we would classify as "craft" rather than "fine art." Even while recognizing the "antique" qualities of a Titian painting, we generally have preferred to "notice" only its existence as a fine art object. (Titian's bed or chamber pot we might call "antiques"—*faute de mieux*, as it were.) We at least *seem* to have experienced *some* conflict in adjusting ourselves to the equal importance of the painting's "fine art objectness" on the one hand and its "antiqueness" on the other—or to the equal status or value of these different "modes of being" or "modes of perception" as the basis of aesthetic judgment. To set aside "antiqueness" in favor of "fine-art-ness" is of course a serious error, as pointed out earlier, for it deprives us of an important aspect of the total aesthetic experience of art objects such as Titian's paintings. If fine art objects exhibit properties that tell us they are *also* antiques, this tells us that they may and that they *should also* be experienced from that perspective. We would be fools to deny ourselves that pleasure simply from a prudish prejudice for "experiential purity," based, in turn, on the assumption that one condition or mode of being or perceiving of a thing has some sort of priority over another. As Nelson Goodman has correctly observed, rather, "the aesthetic properties of a picture plainly include not only those found by looking at it

but also those that determine how it is to be looked at." See Goodman, "Art and Authenticity," in *Forgery in Art*, ed. Dennis Dutton (Berkeley: University of California Press, 1983), 93–114.

13 Style is the formative strategy for composing the artwork and thus becomes the code for interpreting it. I will characterize its role more specifically in reference to antiques later in the text. But we need to understand how it functions more generally in any artwork; and especially to understand what has transpired with the usages of style in twentieth-century fine artworks..

One normally classifies "style" as a component of the **how** in the work, because once one starts talking about artworks in terms of two categories, form and content—the how and the what—one feels obliged to place "style" in one or the other category. And while the **what** may sometimes be some component of style (representations of "Achilles Lamenting Over the Dead Patroclos" are, for example, a common subject matter for Neo-classical but never Impressionist paintings), for the most part style is not normally thought of as being the **what** (except in those few contemporary artworks whose **what** has been reduced to their style—i.e., which have no reference, meaning, are about nothing but their style, whose style is their stylishness and this is all there is of their **what**) but must rather be part of the **how**. What I am here saying is that style must generally be understood as that part of the **how** that forms (informs) the artwork's physical materials in such a way as to adjust (conform, balance) them with its **what** (its meaning or content and the world it generates). This physical material is after all some form of matter with properties unique to its peculiar substance (rosewood, oil paint, bronze, lead crystal, wool); and yet matter or substance is never purely raw, for it must arrive together in some preconfigured allotment (ten inches— or bigger or smaller; cubic or spherical or rectangular; well polished and shiny or dull and jagged) before the artist chooses to design it. The style of any work must therefore be in accordance with (and create a concordance of) the requirements of the genre (e.g., architecture must "house"), the physical possibilities of the material (e.g., wood cannot be transparent), the fashions of the artist's time and place (e.g., late-eighteenth-century French Neo-classical), and the artist's personal preferences for the function it is to have in his world and for the interpretation he intends for the world within the work (if any).

14 On this issue and related matters, see Herbert Marcuse, *One-Dimensional Man* (Boston: Beacon Press, 1964), chap. 9, and *The Aesthetic Dimension of Man* (Boston: Beacon Press, 1978).

15 But I am not wedded to this term, and the phrase "aesthetic value" might just as well be substituted for "beauty," if this neutral phrase were in any way preferable. When I say that beauty would require *intensity*, I mean the object or experience must be "splendid" (it must "shine") and be revelatory and marvelous—"be epiphantical"—as in some of the older senses of "beauty" that essentially derive from the Platonic conception of beauty as "astounding," "most radiant," and "most enchanting." Beauty, this Platonic tradition says, is what, among all the things that become manifest in appearance, preeminently shines forth in and through sensible things with such affective force as to draw the soul up and away from the earth. *Intensity* in the experience of beauty is, I think, in the first instance supported by the characteristics and structure of the physical medium. These characteristics and this structure must occasion our delight by *fixing* our focus and *fascinating* our attention and make us respond approvingly and desire a continuation of the experience. This criterion alone would satisfy most of what would be required for a definition of "beauty in nature."

For beauty *in art* we need more, however. Hence, second, I would stipulate *integrity*. By this I mean coherence, unity, wholeness, completeness, that which in the object or experience makes it recoverable or retrievable after interruption. Integrity is partly a function of medium or form and partly a function of content and above all a function of the appropriate coalescence or coordination of medium, form, and content together, so that the object exhibits what I have elsewhere called "translucence." (Integrity is not reducible to mere symmetry or intelligibility, however, for a useful piece of equipment whose effective functioning engages our purposeful activity without much attention and without inspiring our imagination beyond everyday preoccupations may have these characteristics and yet only a limited integrity, and neither *intensity* nor *transcendence*.) The *integrity* of an object, as an aspect of the total experience, enables us to isolate it from everyday objects and engagements, from the "natural" order of things, whether these everyday things be the bare objects of nature or bits of useful "equipment" in terms of which our instrumental world is constructed. *Integrity* on the one hand provides a basis of "disinterestedness" and of "aesthetic distance" (we engage the object or its properties not in everyday terms or for everyday instrumental matters but "on its own," for it has self-substantiality). On the other hand, *integrity* forms the structure which makes possible notions that other philosophers have expressed when discussing beauty, such as "uniformity amidst variety" (Francis Hutcheson), "rapports" (Diderot), "consonantia" (Aquinas), and even Kant's "form of purposiveness without the representation of a definite purpose." Thus, integrity provides the self-referential and self-satisfying component in the experience of beauty so that it in some fashion supports (i.e., both justifies and feeds on) itself with its own criteria of meaning and worth.

Finally, I must call the third component of beauty, for lack of a better word, *transcendence*. By this I mean that whereas the beautiful or aesthetic object does not require us to engage it further in the daily round of commonplace activities (but rather, requires us to desist from our everyday practical concerns and attend to it, fascinated by what it presents to us), the object *does* stimulate our imagination and arouses us to move beyond what is immediately present to the senses. Another way to characterize this facet of the experience is to say it encourages "extra-perceptuality"—it stimulates our imagination and memory, even playful intellectual calculation, to inquire into what the work "is about"; it requires interpolations of and extrapolations from what is immediately and phenomenally present; it, in fact, proposes an alternative world and is, then, world-generative. The work takes us out of the immediate context of our instrumental life and yet relates us back to the whole of existence via a certain thread or cue. This transcendence or extra-perceptuality is what stimulates us to arrive at "interpretation," to complete the significance of the work by entering its world and then to make a place for it in our own. It is that aspect of the work which encourages what I have elsewhere ("Ontological Integrity of the Art Object") called its "play" and what Hans-Georg Gadamer calls "constructive accomplishment" (*The Relevance of the Beautiful*, trans. Nicholas Walker [Cambridge: Cambridge University Press, 1986], 27–28). Just as our first criterion, *intensity*, considered alone, allowed us to account for the beauty of nature (as well as art), so here *transcendence* as world-generative for the imagination may alone be adequate for the aesthetic encounter with the artifact, souvenir, trophy, religious relic, and collectible (as I define these terms shortly) and may be adequate for certain purported examples of contemporary art. Thus, I see all three as contributing to the entirety of "beauty."

To be sure, these three qualities of *intensity, integrity, and transcendence* interreact and support one another. Thus, for example, we have noted that integrity provides a basis for "aesthetic distance," but so does intensity. In fact, I am not certain to what degree a theory of aesthetic experience can separate these three components from the totality of their collective convergence and emergence in beauty. I hope this digression on three components for having an experience that is "aesthetic" or "beautiful" has clarified my meaning of the term as used in the definition of the antique, but I confess that I have not here defined "beauty" to my satisfaction. Nevertheless, unlike many of my colleagues in the philosophy of art, I am not reluctant to use the word. (This "callilogophobia"—if I may coin the term—is perhaps due to the fact that much of what they would like to be able to call "art" in contemporary production is not well suited for the application of this word; hence the fear and loathing of it—or at least their reticence to use it.)

16 Collecting criteria have become so stringent as to "grading" for valuation of collectibles that we now have not only the category "mint condition" but also "never removed from box." In this condition the object becomes an invisible icon "untouched by human hands." At this point it becomes clear that the qualities of the object itself have become irrelevant: no one sees it (or is ever likely to). Serge Tisseron, professor of psychology at the University of Nanterre, in an interview with the French antiques magazine *Aladin* (June 2007, 10), describes collectors in this way: "They are moved [not by physical touch or reality but] by 'information' and live in a virtual world. Many do not even open the packages they receive because the only important thing to them is having bought it" (my translation). Thus, nothing pertaining to the experience of the object itself plays any role in its desirability. *Acquisition*: that historical fact has become primary, and the object itself is merely a token verification or remainder of this fact. And it would seem such an object, of its "highest grade," insofar as it evoked for its owner an image of its past world at all, would necessarily propose a sad world indeed, for one might well imagine the likely circumstances surrounding the "unopening" of the box to have been tragic ones.

17 It is sometimes argued that the concerns motivating "connoisseurs" (literally, those who *know*) and "amateurs" (those who *love*) of antiques are quite different from those of the "collector." One may collect anything at all (things with no character and charm in themselves). One may do so out of some need merely to classify, making order and coherence out of chaos. Or one may collect to complete an incomplete set so as to finalize or accomplish groupings, employing one's historical, stylistic, and geographical knowledge to verify the accuracy of this process and for no further purpose than that. The connoisseur-amateur, it is said, is on the contrary concerned with the particular object, experiences its charms for what they are, has no concern for the completion of sets, and incorporates his knowledge of history, geography, and style into the *actual experience* of the object. Thus, Maurice Rheims states: "The art lover is very different from the collector. He seeks perfection through beauty and harmony, loving works of art not as a part of a series or historical sequence, but rather on account of their diversity, which corresponds to his own mentality, with its eclecticism and untidiness. Fashion, progress, the course of daily life, all things which hardly affect the true collector, concern the ordinary art lover who seeks a heightening of experience and sensation through art. He is prepared to respond to all art forms. . . . The art lover develops his powers [and range] of selection." (Rheims, *The Strange Life of Objects*, trans. David Pryce-Jones [New York: Atheneum, 1961], 5.) Rheims goes on to describe the "curio-hunter" (and we might add the "faddist" and the "souvenirist") as a hybrid form, as one without taste and concerned not with beauty and perfection in the object, but only with its rarity or its prestige and what is currently (or is shortly to be) fashionable.

18 On style, see note 13 above and Berel Lang, ed., *The Concept of Style* (Philadelphia: University of Pennsylvania Press, 1979); James S. Ackerman, "Style," in *Art and Archeology*, ed. J. S. Ackerman and S. Carpenter (Englewood Cliffs, N.J.: Prentice-Hall, 1963), 164–86; and Meyer Schapiro, "Style," in *Aesthetics Today*, ed. Morris Phillipson (Cleveland, Ohio: World Publishing, 1961), 137–71.

19 To be sure, van Gogh is classed as a "Post-Impressionist." But there is no "Post-Impressionist" style per se. Post-Impressionist masters like van Gogh perform stylistic riffs on Impressionism. If one thinks van Gogh too far advanced into a "Proto-Expressionist" camp to be classed as "Impressionist" at all, the same point can be made (using different characteristics of his medium, subjects, colors, brush technique, etc.) to distinguish Renoir (clearly in the Impressionist camp) from Monet.

20 Compare here the incongruity we now notice in the makeup and hairstyles of heroines in films of the 1960s playing nineteenth-century character roles in nineteenth-century costume.

21 See also Joseph Alsop's discussion in "The Faker's Art" (*New York Review of Books* 33, no. 16 [October 23, 1986], 30), which points out that we, as creatures of a self-consciously historical civilization, must adopt a purely aesthetic *and* a historical response to works of art; and that, in cases of proven inauthenticity (especially art fakery), the historical response "goes to war with" and "most often" subdues the aesthetic one.

22 I am not, of course, understanding "literary work" as "an individual manuscript," which could be a one-hundred-fifty-year-old autograph copy and hence "antique," but am thinking of the narrative *War and Peace*, for example, as it persists unaltered through hundreds of thousands of variable editions. One never asks, for example, "Is that the real (authentic) *War and Peace* on your bookshelf?" as one might ask "Is that the real *Mona Lisa* hanging in the Louvre?"

I am also thinking here primarily of the literary art of the West, of course. Chinese poetry that is traditionally tied to the calligraphy of the text is an obvious exception, as are some Japanese and Arab-Islamic literary works. See Simon Leys, "One More Art" (review of Jean François Billeter, *The Chinese Art of Writing* [New York: Skira / Rizzoli, 1990]), *New York Review of Books* 48, no. 7 (April 8, 1996), 28; Jan Stuart, "Beyond Paper: Chinese Calligraphy on Objects," *The Magazine Antiques*, October 1995, 502–13; and Robert Hughes's discussion of Japanese scrolls in *Time*, December 14, 1998, 97. See also my discussion in the following chapter (section 2.2), especially note 53.

23 John Ruskin, *Modern Painters* (London, n.d.), part II, sec. 1, chap. VI, p. 97.

24 Immanuel Kant, *Critique of Judgment*, "Aesthetic Judgment," sec. 22, trans. J. H. Bernard (New York: Hafner, 1951), 80.

25 Lionel Trilling, *The Liberal Imagination* (New York: Viking Press, 1953), 179.

26 I am indebted, for several of the ideas expressed in the above three paragraphs, to suggestions made by Yuriko Saito in the article, "Why Restore Works of Art?" *Journal of Aesthetics and Art Criticism* 64, no. 2 (1985): 141–55.

27 Walter Benjamin, "The Work of Art in the Age of Mechanical Reproduction," in *Illuminations*, ed. Hanna Arendt, trans. Harry Zohn (New York: Harcourt, Brace, and World, 1968; Fontana/Collins, 1973), 222–23.

28 Of course I am *not* saying that to appreciate the aesthetic of the antique one must actually have read these philosophers themselves. The "trickle down" theory always applies in the realm of ideas, even if it does not readily find such confirmation in economic life.

29 Richard Gilman, *Decadence* (New York: Farrar, Straus and Giroux, 1975), 82.

30 Let us again for a moment compare the antique and the fine art object in respect of the aesthetic pleasure the imagination affords in their contemplation. Even so "formalist" a philosopher of art as Kant admits that "while the judgment of taste by which something is declared beautiful must have no interest *as its determining ground* . . . it does not follow that, after it has been given as a pure aesthetical judgment, no interest (and consequently no other pleasure or response) can be combined with it." The pleasure that beautiful art inspires in us is *not merely a function of the immediately apprehended form* of the art object we perceive before us. On the contrary, Kant claims that the pleasure we take in beautiful art "must be derived from reflection," from "the reflective judgment and not from sensation." It is for this reason—viz., to undermine the presumed primacy of the immediate object of sensation—that he emphasizes the role of the active and productive imagination that reflective judgment requires. That is why he can define "beauty in general" as the "expression of aesthetical ideas" that are "representations of the imagination which occasion much thought, without any *definite* thought being capable of being adequate to it." It is therefore to reflection and to the "freedom and wealth" of the imagination that the primary roles in

aesthetic experience are assigned. Hence, Kant says, "the imagination (as a productive faculty of cognition) is very powerful in creating another nature, as it were, out of the material that actual nature gives it. We entertain ourselves with it when experience becomes too commonplace." And thus he notes the "very common play of our fancy, which attributes to lifeless things a spirit suitable to their form by which they speak to us." Kant, *Critique of Judgment* (trans. Bernard), secs. 45, 49, and 51.

31 I am here using "preserve" in Heidegger's double sense of "preserving" and "holding true"—*Wahrung*.

2. An Archeology of Antiques: A History of Antique Collecting and Connoisseurship

1 Francis Henry Taylor, *The Taste of Angels: A History of Art Collecting from Ramses to Napoleon* (Boston: Little, Brown, 1948); Joseph Alsop, *The Rare Art Traditions* (New York: Harper and Row, 1982). Francis Haskell, *History and Its Images: Art and the Interpretation of the Past* (New Haven: Yale University Press, 1993), and Maurice Rheims, *The Glorious Obsession* (New York: St. Martin's Press, 1980), are further excellent sources. I have relied heavily on these and other histories that range from the scholarly to the anecdotal. But even Alsop, who presents the elements of a pattern of "eight by-products of art" recurring within five great art traditions, never offers an explanatory theory of his categories, simply letting the matter lapse after a wonderful wealth of detail. The same is true of such works as David Lowenthal's *The Past Is a Foreign Country* (Cambridge: Cambridge University Press, 1985), which is not a history of collecting and connoisseurship per se but a *Geistesgeschichte* of the past and pastness, but without an interpretive theory that comprehends the process and explains the outcome.

2 I use the term "arché" (first principle) because it is included nicely in the word "archeology," although I mean the following analysis to uncover not only the principles that delimit and define our subject matter (the antique) but also the causes or explanations for the subject's coming into being (and thus might just as well have used the Greek word *aetia* [cause], calling this chapter "the aetiology of the antique").

3 Furthermore, insofar as this process reads backward through the text of history, our procedure of critique is properly a "deconstruction." This is so—to carry forth the "light" analogy—because of an interpretive "Doppler effect." That is, as the light providing the vision recedes in time from us, its collective colors themselves tend to distort, modifying the view they provide for us. It is for this reason that our interpretation must engage in a hermeneutic critique of "the historical record." It might be thought that history is no text for deconstruction—that since deconstruction is a critical process that applies to "texts" or similar forms of creative effort, it is an inappropriate procedure to apply to the subject of human history. This would be incorrect, however. Human history, as an interpretation of a people in their acts and creations in a time and place of appearance, is never a mere enumeration of data, a chronicle of atomic facts in temporal sequence. History is a text, an explanatory narrative, whatever else it may pose as. It is constructed by the historians of civilization and thus is an extended and incomplete text by an ongoing collaboration of authors. For this reason, the conceptual framework in terms of which civilization understands itself and its past ("the historical record") is never entirely neutral, never value-free, never even ontologically determinate. As Foucault and others have pointed out, our historically conditioned conceptions and our predetermined methods and terms of discourse are such that there cannot exist an absolute view from the aspect of eternity, namely, that degree of certitude that in any inquiry is usually construed as "objective truth." Moreover, the events of the past and the objects surviving from then into the present—*and the way they have*

survived for our present experience and appreciation—have no constant "nature." Not only the idea of an "antique" but the things that we would now classify as such—indeed, anything and everything that would or could be so classified—changes in the course of history. For these reasons we cannot even assume that what appear as antithetical experiences and conceptions of "the antique" have always been apprehended in this way or that we will always be capable of finding for these contradictions in particular instances a rational resolution in our current understanding. Consequently, the *deconstruction* of the history of antique connoisseurship and collecting presented here must be understood as an engagement of the hermeneutic circle.

4 See I. Nagy, "Remarques sur le souci d'archaïsme en Egypt à l'époque saïte," *Acta Antiqua Academiae Scientiarum Hungaricae* (1973): 53–63.

5 See Taylor, *Taste of Angels*, 5.

6 As for another aspect and adjunct of the modern mentality conducive to antiques collecting and connoisseurship—namely, the delight in foreign objects and appreciation of foreign styles, both for themselves and in their eclectic reflection and reconstruction in the artistic taste of the present—the first clear example on a broad scale may be found in Achaemenid Persia. Thus, Herodotus tells us that the Persians "borrow the fashions of foreigners more than all other men; they dress like them and find their costumes more beautiful than their own" (see his *Persian Wars*; this quotation from André Godard, *The Art of Iran*, trans. and ed. Michael Heron [New York: Praeger, 1965], 157). And it was not merely a matter of fashion in costume. André Godard, in *The Art of Iran*, says: "Variety is one of the special charms of Achaemenid sculpture. It made full use of exotic shapes in its decoration by looking to them as so many souvenirs of countries which Persia conquered or, to put it another way, as a collaboration of all those countries in the task of aggrandizing the Achaemenids. . . . But what could have been no more than a hotch-potch, a discordant harlequinade, obeys the taste of the constructor; it becomes harmonious and assumes a picturesque and imaginative character" (118). Finally, Donald N. Wilber, discussing the ruins of the so-called Treasury at Persepolis (whose walls are covered with reliefs of tribute-bearing ambassadors from twenty-eight subject nations), observes: "What emerges from a study of the artifacts recovered is that the Treasury was an imperial museum . . . some items were gifts from the subject lands, as depicted on the stairways of the Apadana. . . . [This would suggest an understanding of] kings as preservers of the remains of other cultures, and, in a sense, as the legitimate heirs of those cultures." (*Persepolis: The Archeology of Parsa*, rev. ed. [Princeton, N.J.: Darwin Press, 1989], 64–66.) Nevertheless, it seems unlikely that anything like what is currently meant by connoisseurship of foreign antiques was present in ancient Persia. But clearly several of the components of the mentality that is a precondition for this consciousness were then present in Persian culture, at least at the royal level.

7 Pierre Grimal, *Hellenism and the Rise of Rome*, trans. A. M. Sheridan Smith (New York: Delacorte Press, 1968), 185.

8 Roughly from the Persian Wars to the arrival of Alexander the Great.

9 Having just observed that the cement sidewalk outside my home bears the name of its contractor—"J. Hooker, 1936"—I am not as certain of this last claim as I once was.

10 On this and several of the particulars that follow, see Rudolf Wittkower and Margot Wittkower, *Born under Saturn: The Character and Conduct of Artists* (New York: Norton, 1963).

11 Pliny the Elder, *Historia naturalis*, 34.55.

12 *Poetics* 1149a15.

13 Wittkower and Wittkower, *Born under Saturn*, 4.

14 The English word "beauty" itself derives via the French from a late Latin root suggesting emotional attachment and affectionate approval, for the Latin *bellus* (meaning

"handsome," "fine," "pretty") is a diminutive form of the root *deu*, which in its original and primary Greek and Latin forms means "able to perform," hence "useful, worthy, good."

15 Not to mention the occurrence of beauty as an important issue throughout such other works as the *Hippias major*, the *Republic*, the conclusion of the *Philebus*, and book II of the *Laws*.

16 See *Republic*, bks. III and X.

17 Seneca later explicitly denied a place for painting among the liberal arts (*Epistulae morales* 88.13), and Plutarch remarked that "no wellborn youth would want to be Phidias or Polycleitus however much he may admire their art" (Wittkower and Wittkower, *Born under Saturn*, 6).

18 Aristotle, *Nicomachean Ethics* 1140a1–15, *Physics* 199a15–17, *Metaphysics* 1070a5–10 and 1046b2–25, and *Poetics* 1447a–b, trans. Ingram Bywater, in *The Basic Works of Aristotle*, ed. Richard McKeon (New York: Random House, 1941).

19 Aristotle, *Poetics* 1450b1–13, 1453a36, 1453b11–12.

20 Paul Oskar Kristeller, "The Modern System of the Arts: A Study in the History of Aesthetics," *Journal of the History of Ideas* 12 (1951): 496–527, and 13 (1952): 17–46; this quotation, 12 (1951): 506.

21 Taylor, *Taste of Angels*, 15.

22 Alexander the Great kept his copy of Homer in a gold box ornamented in pearls and precious stones which was looted from Darius's tent. Surely, he could have had a Greek one made in the latest fashion if he had so desired. Was it just a souvenir, a trophy? Or was there in this choice some intercultural-historical consciousness mingled with a political conception of world empire that combined in such a way as to provoke an aesthetic appreciation of an unusual sort for his time? See preceding two notes.

23 See Pliny the Elder, *Historia naturalis*, 35.60 and 36.24; also Pausanias, *Descriptio Graecae* 9.35.6.

24 Plutarch, *Lives*, "Marcellus," 21.

25 Pliny, *Historia*, 37.81–82.

26 Pliny, *Historia*, 34.8; Strabo, *Geography* 8.6.23.

27 Taylor, *Taste of Angels*, 22.

28 Pliny, *Historia*, 34.62.

29 *Epistolae* 7.23.

30 Rheims, *Glorious Obsession*, 8–10.

31 Pliny, *Historia*, 35.

32 Rheims, *Glorious Obsession*, 8–10.

33 Robert Adams, *The Lost Museum: Glimpses of Vanished Originals* (New York: Viking Press, 1980), 40. Thirteen centuries later, the Byzantine scholar Nicetas Acoinatus thought enough of these Greek art objects that had been transferred to the new imperial capital of Constantinople to list in a separate volume the statues destroyed in 1204 by the Fourth Crusade, which pillaged that city.

34 Pliny, *Historia*, 35.127.

35 Ibid., 35.18.

36 Taylor, *Taste of Angels*, 27.

37 Averil Cameron, "Before the Fall," *New York Review of Books* 42, no. 11 (July 22, 1995), 58.

38 Ibid.

39 Having finally won Egypt from Anthony and Cleopatra for the empire and, specifically, for the Julio-Claudian dynasty, Augustus (through the same sorts of fabricated associations whereby Vergil's *Aeneid* linked Rome and Julius Caesar with Greece, Troy, and Venus) tried in this and other ways to create historical and cultural linkages between his family and the Ptolemies, between Rome and Alexandria, and between Jupiter and Amon-Re-Serapis.

40 Pliny, *Historia*, 36.58.

41 See Phaedrus, *Fabulae*, prologue to bk. 5, 4–9.

42 *Pliny the Younger, Letters*, trans. and ed. William Melmoth (London: Heinemann, 1915), 2:205.

43 Statius, *Silvae*, 4.4.29 and 59–98.

44 *Historia*, 36.6.

45 See Gisela M. A. Richter, *The Furniture of the Greeks, Etruscans, and Romans* (London: Phaidon, 1966); and Alsop, *Rare Art Traditions*, 202.

46 *Historia*, 33.157.

47 *Epigrammata*, 8.6, 34, and 51.

48 The first great American connoisseur and collector of Italian Primitives was James Jackson Jarves, a follower of Ruskin. That he was *ahead* of his time is evident from the fact that he was so unsuccessful in selling his collection that he finally gave it all (this in an age before the income tax deduction) to Yale University, where it can still be found. See Edith Wharton, *False Dawn* (New York: D. Appleton, 1924); and Rémy Saisselin, *The Bourgeois and the Bibelot* (New Brunswick, N.J.: Rutgers University Press, 1984), 93.

49 Alsop, *Rare Art Traditions*, 202.

50 See Cyril Mango, ed., *The Art of the Byzantine Empire, 315–1453* (Englewood Cliffs, N.J.: Prentice Hall, 1972), 58; and Alsop, *Rare Art Traditions*, 209–10.

51 Edith Wharton and Ogden Codman Jr., *The Decoration of Houses* (New York: Scribner's, 1914), 188–89.

52 See Alsop, *Rare Art Traditions*.

53 Simon Leys describes the Chinese art of calligraphy in general:

> Like painting (which, being born of the same brush, is its younger brother rather than its twin), Chinese calligraphy addresses the eye and is an art of space; like music, it unfolds in time; like dance, it develops a dynamic sequence of movements, pulsating in rhythm. It is an art that radiates such physical presence and sensuous power that it virtually defies photographic reproduction—at times, its execution can verge on the athletic performance; yet its abstract and erudite character has special appeal for intellectuals and scholars who adopted it as their favorite pursuit. . . . [Its appreciation derives not only from its contents as literature] but in an imaginative communion with the dynamics of the brushwork; what the viewer needs is not to read a text, but to retrace in his mind the original dance of the brush and to relive its rhythmic progress.

See "One More Art" (review of Jean François Billeter, *The Chinese Art of Writing* [New York: Skira / Rizzoli, 1990]), *New York Review of Books*, vol. 48, no. 7 (April 8, 1996), 28.

Leys perhaps overstates the role of "physical communion" with the medium and understates the import of the intellectual effect of meaning, but this apt characterization of the total aesthetic response to this art beautifully communicates to us the fact that a Chinese poem is appreciated in aesthetic fullness not only in the intellectual contents and imagistic metaphors it contains, which are understood by reading, but in the very ideograms in whose written characters these ideas are embodied, which are appreciated by seeing. And this aesthetic fullness not only is a function of the ideogram itself, which is after all duplicable many times over in many fashions so as to be read by any literate person, but also is a function of the unique visual mode that the ideograms take, i.e., in the actual writing style of the artist-calligrapher who has executed the characters—their size, shape, placement on the page, and, above all, the individual sensitivity that the calligrapher displays in his "invention" on *the given* (i.e., the predetermined number, the fixed sequence, and the pattern of brushstrokes permitted for the execution of his ideogram). Finally, and even more uniquely, it is a function of the physical page itself, which displays signs of age and the seals and notes of its successive owners, its provenance as an antique. Thus, there are four interlocking sources of its "beauty": (1) the idea or set of concepts communicated, (2) the picto-ideographic representation of those concepts visually, i.e., the text (using, indeed, one of eight possible script forms), (3) the unique writing style of the particular calligrapher who executed the work together with his choices in the arrangement and conformation of figures (whether as on a page of paper together with some scene or filling a contoured band across a bronze vessel, for example, where elongated strokes adjust the ideograms to the vessel's shape), and (4) signs of provenance and agedness attaching to the object.

Moreover, it should be emphasized that this calligraphy—literally "beautiful writing"—while normally done on paper or silk, may be placed on various sorts of materials. When placed on any object whatever, it elevates the metaphysical and aesthetic status of that object. The inner dynamism and rhythmic cadence of an assemblage of ideograms on a page or vessel—said to resemble at its best "ascending dragons and soaring phoenixes"—are, in principle, inseparable from either the message communicated or the form (or medium) the object possesses. Thus, for example, on a Chinese porcelain teapot, an imagistic representation of people drinking tea in a springtime garden together with an ideographic text embodying a poem alluding to the purity and refreshing nature of tea in such a way that "the sketchy execution of the bamboo [in the scene depicted] matches the exuberance of the calligraphy, and the words wrap around the vessel to flow into the leafy branches," where even the choice of the bamboo plant (emblematic of spring and hence rejuvenation) conjoins with the object's function and the poem's message (and where, moreover, the teapot manifests in its form and style the era of its creation and in the aged condition of its physical body its provenance and use over time by generations of precisely such contented tea drinkers)—such an integration represents the acme of the union of word and image (and historicality) in the object, when, as in the present example, the object of aesthetic appreciation is an antique Chinese porcelain teapot. (For the quotations and some of the particulars here, see Jan Stuart, "Beyond Paper: Chinese Calligraphy on Objects," *The Magazine Antiques*, October 1995, 502–13.)

The same situation occurs in Japanese scroll paintings, where both a poetic text and the visual scene it "illustrates" unite in aesthetic fusion. Thus, Robert Hughes, commenting on an Ogata Kenzan scroll called *The Eight-fold Bride*, describes it as "an illustration of a poem with the poem itself written into it—the planks of the bridge briskly indicated, the calligraphy mingling with the broadly brushed leaves of the water iris as if it too were part of the reed growth of the pond . . . the whole image has an iron control within its spontaneity." (*Time*, December 14, 1998, 97.)

54 Patrick Pacheco, "The Splendors of Imperial China," *Art and Antiques*, April 1996, 46. This more recent view must supersede the claims of Alsop, *Rare Art Traditions*, and R. C. Rudolph, "Preliminary Notes on Sung Archeology," *Journal of Asian Studies* 22 (February 1963): 173–75, that *objects per se*—as opposed to calligraphic works on scrolls—were not appreciated until the Song dynasty.

55 Alsop, *Rare Art Traditions*, 157.

56 In W. R. B. Acker, *Some T'ang and Pre-T'ang Texts* (Westport, Conn.: Hyperion Press, 1979), 199–200.

57 Rudolph, "Preliminary Notes on Sung Archeology." See also Chang Lin-Sheng, "Li Kung-Lin and the Study of Antiquity in the Sung Dynasty," *Arts of Asia* 30, no. 3 (May–June 2000): 123–30.

58 As Michael Sullivan puts it: "Bronze vessels [of the Shang dynasty] have been treasured by Chinese connoisseurs for centuries: that great collector and savant, the Sung

emperor Hui-tsung (1101–1125), is even said to have sent agents to the Anyang region to search out specimens for his collection." (*The Arts of China*, 3rd ed. [Berkeley: University of California Press, 1984], 22.) That is, in modern parlance, he was engaged in archeological pilfering of antiques—or grave-robbing—for connoisseur/aesthetic purposes from a dead Chinese capital city (Anyang, destroyed by the then barbarian Chou dynasty, a city whose great period of bronzes lasted from 1300 B.C. to 1028 B.C.). See also Percival David, *Chinese Connoisseurship* (translation of *Ko Ku Yao Lun*—*The Essential Criteria of Antiques*, 1388; London: Farber and Farber, 1971), and Willem van Hensden, *Ancient Chinese Bronzes of the Shang and Chou Dynasties* (Tokyo, 1952).

59 *Ko Ku Yao Lun*, 141.

60 See J. M. Addis, *Chinese Ceramics from Datable Tombs* (London: Philip Wilson, 1978).

61 Chu-Tsing Li, "The Artistic Theories of the Literati," in *The Chinese Scholar's Studio: Artistic Life in the Late Ming Period*, Catalogue of an Exhibition from the Shanghai Museum, ed. Chu-Tsing Li and James C. Y. Watt (New York: Thames and Hudson / The Asia Society, 1987), 37.

62 Ibid., 15–16.

63 This scroll was included in the exhibition "Splendors of Imperial China: Treasures from the National Museum, Taipei," shown at the Metropolitan Museum of Art, New York, March 19 to May 19, 1996.

64 Ibid.

65 Alison Beckett, "An Emperor's Ransom," *Antique Collector* 66, no. 5 (May 1995).

66 Alsop, *Rare Art Traditions*, 156–57.

67 J. C. Harles, *The Art and Architecture of the Indian Subcontinent* (New York: Penguin, 1986), 81. These artifacts, through the great diligence, sacrifice, and personal risks of their museum curators, managed to survive the recent purges of such "Satanic objects" committed by the Taliban.

68 Richard Krautheimer, *Rome: Profile of a City, 312–1308* (Princeton, N.J.: Princeton University Press, 1980), 200.

69 Quoted in W. S. Heckscher, "Relics of Pagan Antiquities in Medieval Settings," *Journal of the Warburg Institute* 1 (1937–38): 208.

70 Krautheimer, *Rome*, 198–99. Heckscher believes that this tract, which forms part of a larger work, the *Graphia aureae urbis Romae*, was issued for political reasons on behalf of the "popular party" that in 1143 overthrew the papal/aristocratic control of the city, in its stead reestablishing the "Senate and the People of Rome" in imitation of the Roman Republic of antiquity. See Heckscher, "Relics," 206.

71 Heckscher, "Relics," 205.

72 *City of God*, XIX.11.

73 In accordance with St. Jerome's *Commentary on Daniel*, ii.37 and vii.3 ff.

74 Heckscher, "Relics," 205.

75 See Emma Amadei, *Le Torri di Roma* (Rome, 1932), 113–18.

76 Krautheimer, *Rome*, 189. Henry was not unique in his response, even among English Medieval travelers. Two centuries after Henry, another Englishman, one Master Gregorius, who visited Rome in the thirteenth century, describes a statue of Venus: "The image is made from Parian marble with such wonderful and intricate skill that she seems more like a living creature than a statue; indeed she seems to blush in her nakedness. . . . Because of this wonderful image, and perhaps magic spell that I am unaware of, I was drawn back there three times to look at it despite the fact that it was two stades distant from my inn." From Master Gregorius, *The Marvels of Rome*; see *Journal of Roman Studies* 9 (1919): 26; cited in James Fenton, "On Statues," *New York Review of Books* 43, no. 2 (February 1, 1996).

77 See Edwin Panofsky, "Abbot Suger and St. Denis," in *Meaning in the Visual Arts* (Chicago: University of Chicago Press, 1982), 108–45.

78 See Edwin Panofsky, ed. and trans., *Abbot Suger on the Abbey of St. Denis and the Art Treasure* (Princeton, N.J.: Princeton University Press).

79 Heckscher, "Relics," 216–17. See A. Lecoy de La Marche, *Oeuvres complètes de Suger* (Paris, 1867), XXXIV, 208. Heckscher remarks in a note: "Sometimes a whole species of pagan relics received a new glamour from becoming associated with a biblical name. Beautiful jugs of late Roman origin became known as "vases of Cana," Arabo-Sicilian vases and ancient jewels as "Opera Salomonis.""

80 Heckscher, "Relics," 215.

81 See Richard Lightbown, "The Migration Period and the Middle Ages," in *The History of Silver*, ed. Claude Blair (New York: Ballantine, 1987), 38–43.

82 Heckscher, "Relics," 210–11.

83 Ibid., 211–12.

84 Umberto Eco, *Art and Beauty in the Middle Ages* (New Haven, Conn.: Yale University Press, 1986), 14.

85 Jean Longren, introduction to *The "Très Riches Heures" of Jean, Duke of Berry* (New York: Braziller, 1969), 15.

86 Eco, *Art and Beauty*, 14.

87 Taylor, *Taste of Angels*, 43.

88 See Watson, "Mounted Porcelain," International Antique Dealers Show Exhibition Catalogue, New York, October 6–10, 1990, 42. In two hundred years' time, the difference is immense. Philip II of Spain possessed no fewer than four thousand pieces of Chinese porcelain.

89 Heckscher, "Relics," 209.

90 Alsop, *Rare Art Traditions*, 342. The taste for antiques in Byzantium is a topic as yet barely investigated, but we know it existed in persons other than Chrysorlas. Zoe, co-empress of Byzantium with her sister Theodora in the mid-eleventh century, had the connoisseur antiquarian's passion and "daily gloated over her collection of *darics*, for which she had bronze coffers made." Michael Psellus, *Fourteen Byzantine Rulers*, trans. E. R. A. Sewters (London: Penguin, 1966), 186.

91 Roberto Weiss, *The Renaissance Discovery of Classical Antiquity* (Oxford: Oxford University Press, 1964), 28.

92 Alsop, *Rare Art Traditions*, 322–36.

93 Ibid., 322–36 and 356–58.

94 The first complete account at this time of the collector's passion for books is documented in the great tribute to bibliomania, *The Philobiblon*, a twenty-three-chapter "confession of a hopelessly intoxicated spirit," written by Richard de Bury (1237–1345), bishop of Durham and adviser to King Edward III.

95 See Wittkower and Wittkower, *Born under Saturn*.

96 Artists per se did not even have their own unions. Thus, in Medieval Florence painters were members of the Society of St. Luke, a guild including wood and metal workers as well, while in Venice they were part of the guild of gilders, case makers, and harness makers. But see Wittkower and Wittkower, *Born under Saturn*.

97 See Charles Hope, "In Lorenzo's Garden," *New York Review of Books* 46, no. 11 (June 24, 1999), 65–68.

98 See the accounts of the lives of Michelangelo and Titian provided by the artist and biographer Giorgio Vasari (1511–1574) in his *The Lives of the Artists*, which is available in many translations and editions. Citations here are from the George Bull translation, vol. 1 (London: Penguin Books, 1965).

99 Vasari, *Lives*, 1:233.

100 For further details, see E. Müntz, *Les arts à la cour des papes* (Paris, 1878).

101 Piero Ligurio, a contemporary of Michelangelo, was an antiquarian who thought of ancient civilization as a vast machine that had been destroyed, its fragments scattered throughout the contemporary world as ruins. He endeavored from these fragments imaginatively to reconstruct as in a jigsaw puzzle the physical form of the ancient world, seeing this world in the shape of its last unity, Rome. As the designer of the Villa d'Este gardens, he later had the opportunity to embody this vision in stone and water. This connoisseurship and artistry did not prevent him from also being—indeed, it enabled him to be—as Charles Mitchell characterizes him, "the blackest name of the calendar of Renaissance forgers." See Sándor Radnóti, *The Fake*, trans. Ervin Dunai (Lanham, Md.: Rowman and Littlefield, 1999), 29 n. 31, and Charles Mitchell, "Archeology and Romance in Renaissance Italy," in *Italian Renaissance Studies*, ed. E. F. Jacob (London: Faber, 1960), 458.

102 Properly speaking, I should refer to the period between 1300 and 1420 as "proto-Renaissance." It is only around 1420 that one may find on a broad and sustained basis all the elements that constitute the Renaissance world-view.

103 Ingrid Rowland, *The Culture of the High Renaissance* (Cambridge: Cambridge University Press, 1998); Anthony Grafton, "Remaking the Renaissance," *New York Review of Books* 46, no. 4 (March 4, 1999), 34–36. See also Thomas D. Kaufmann, *The Mastery of Nature: Aspects of Art, Science, and Humanism in the Renaissance* (Princeton, N.J.: Princeton University Press, 1993); Elizabeth Cropper, Giovanna Perini, and Francesco Solinas, *Documentary Culture: Florence and Rome from Grand Duke Ferdinand I to Pope Alexander VII* (Bologna: Nuova Alfa Editoriale, 1992); and Paul Findlen, "Possessing the Past: The Material World of the Italian Renaissance," *American Historical Review* 103 (1998): 83–114.

104 Taylor, *Taste of Angels*, 89–90.

105 Quoted in Christopher Hibbet, *Rome: The Biography of a City* (New York: Norton, 1987), 115.

106 Ibid.

107 Ibid.

108 Ibid., 116.

109 Alberti, *On Painting* (1436), II, ¶25.

110 Martin Wackernagel, *Der Lebensraum des Künstlers in der Florentinishen Renaissance* (Leipzig, 1938), 234 (my translation).

111 Filarete, *Treatise on Architecture*, I, 320.

112 Alsop, *Rare Art Traditions*, 407. Alsop remarks further: "The standard in almost all early 16th century Italian art collections was a mixture of as many classical works of art as the collector could afford and a miscellany of later Renaissance work plus occasional paintings from the Low Countries."

113 Taylor, *Taste of Angels*, 111. What Lorenzo did not get, the Gonzaga cardinal from Mantua did, thus greatly augmenting that ducal collection until it was sold to Charles I of England. For a detailed inventory of Lorenzo's estate with valuations, see Eugene Müntz, *Les collections des Médicis au XVe siècle* (Paris, 1888), although unfortunately Müntz omits what would be classified broadly as "furniture." Much of Lorenzo's collection was later discovered to have been plundered during the Savonarola period when Cosimo I (grand duke 1519–74), awaiting a reconstruction of his Pitti Palace, had the collections of his great predecessor assembled at the Palazzo Vecchio for inventory by Vasari and Bronzino. Ferdinand, fourth son of Cosimo I, became head of the Medici clan and grand duke in 1587. He systematically pursued the scattered treasures of his family, "which were slowly cropping up in the attics and cellars of Florentine houses, whither they had gone after the looting of Lorenzo's palace in 1494" by Savonarola's followers. (Taylor, *Taste of Angels*, 113.) But Ferdinand himself was hardly destitute of artworks in his own collection.

Before returning to Florence to receive the dukedom, Ferdinand had lived for thirteen years in Rome. While there he had purchased the Villa Medici (now the French Academy in Rome) on the Picino and filled it with such masterpieces as the "Medici Venus" (from Hadrian's villa at Tivoli), the "Dancing Faun," and "Niobe and Her Children" (from the Porta San Paulo). Ferdinand's grandsons, Ferdinand II and Giovanni Carlo, brought to completion the final Medici collections as we have them in the Uffizi and Pitti galleries today. The whole was given to the city of Florence by their grand-niece, Anna Maria Ludovica, last of the Medici (d. 1743), with the stipulation that "none of these collections should be removed from Florence and that they should be for the benefit of the public of all nations."

114 Taylor, *Taste of Angels*, 100–101.

115 Ibid., 96.

116 Ibid., 107–8.

117 See Rowland, *Culture of the High Renaissance*.

118 See Charles Hope, "The Myth of Florence," *New York Review of Books* 43, no. 17 (October 31, 1996), 56. Lowenthal observes: "The Renaissance was the first epoch to see itself as 'modern,' as distinct from both the immediate past it discredited and the remote past it idolized." (*Past*, 86.)

119 Although it is never necessary or sufficient to rely on such analysis alone, to understand the consciousness of a given epoch—in our particular program focusing on its connoisseurship of antiques—I find it helpful to consider the political and psycho-social substructures on which this consciousness or mentality or vision rests. The Late Renaissance art-historical epoch is called the *maniera*—"of or pertaining to manners," "manners" themselves, or indeed "*the* mannered." This refers to the representation of the world in forms that from the realistic (and classical) viewpoint appear contorted, contrived, and arcane—images spatially, coloristically, intellectually, geographically "stretched." In the negative sense, *maniera* characterized a vision *précieux* and effete; in a positive sense, complex, subtle, precocious, sophisticated, self-consciously elegant, and displaying capricious virtuosity (*sprezzatura*). Whatever else it was, it was *not* a vision clear, precise, calm, symmetrical, or direct.

It was therefore not High Renaissance. And only in the last century has *maniera* been appreciated on its own terms and not as merely a decadent form of High Renaissance neo-classicism. On the traditional assumption that the vision expressed by artists derives from the world as comprehended by them, art historians have engaged in a theoretical analysis of the culture of this era, an analysis that tries to tie this vision to the discovery of new worlds (geographic, astronomic, microscopic), the Protestant attack on the universal Church of Rome and the sack of the city of Rome in 1527 by the troops of Charles of Anjou, and the introduction of so many new intellectual possibilities for thinking about reality. Simply being able to collect and coordinate (not to say reconcile) the assorted and divers parts and pieces of a reality now in the *maniera*'s view required an intellectual sophistication and technical bravura unattempted and unsuspected in the High Renaissance. In the end, it was said, the Baroque era to follow (after ca. 1620) "overcame" *maniera*'s intellectual acrobatics and visual contortions and disproportions, restoring art's harmony in a new clarity and higher synthesis.

120 See E. H. Gombrich, *The Story of Art* (London: Phaidon, 1950), 265.

121 Alsop, *Rare Art Traditions*, 421. Castiglione also notes as a reason for collecting the "pleasure from ornamenting their rooms." Thus, decorative elegance of the living environment was always an important factor in the enterprise.

122 It is not until the Baroque era that we find many like Fra Carlo Lodoli (Venice, 1690–1761), who collected things "very different from others," things that he bought from "rag-pickers and Jews who dealt in anything which had been discarded by others." See

Andrea Memmo, *Elementi d'architettura lodoliana* . . . (1786), cited by Alsop in *Rare Art Traditions*, 116. It turns out that these "very different things" included not only drawings and unfinished sketches but also "Greek paintings" (i.e., Byzantine icons) and proto-Renaissance masters.

123 See, e.g., Jean Adhémar, "La collection de François 1er" in *Gazette des Beaux-Arts*, July 1946.

124 The world discoveries of the Atlantic seaboard empires naturally had an effect on Mediterranean Italy, and this effect only increased in the Baroque Age. Bernini's "Fountain of the Four Rivers," with its Egyptian obelisk centerpiece in the Piazza Navona, is a good example of this consciousness reflected in art, for it not only combines the themes of world geography and world history, but also, and perhaps not so unconsciously or strangely, borrows from a similar Imperial Roman model of sixteen hundred years earlier in which statues of the Nile and Tiber (the latter encrusted with *putti*) were conjoined in multicultural harmony in the great Temple of Isis, whose ruined precincts were excavated in Bernini's day. In the next generation in Italy, we will have the immense rococo ceiling frescoes of Tiepolo (1696–1770), wherein the painter sees the great events and epochs of history as one vast carnival in which he indiscriminately brings together people from all nations: the universe is a colossal repository of stage props, with people, gods, and animals as players and with Tiepolo as its director.

125 The example of Fra Lodoli mentioned in note 122 is one.

126 Inheriting that sobriquet from the last empire entitled to it—the Holy Roman Empire of Charles V in the sixteenth century.

127 Quoted in Taylor, *Taste of Angels*, 132–33. Geza von Habsburg notes that a "teatro mundi" that contained specimens of the animal world was created for Francisco de' Medici, but this type of collection was not common in Italy. "European Princely Families: The Passionate Collectors," lecture delivered October 29, 1994, at the San Francisco Fall Antiques Show, Festival Pavilion, Fort Mason Center, San Francisco.

128 Alsop, *Rare Art Traditions*, 7.

129 Lauran Toorians, "The Earliest Inventory of Mexican Objects in Munich, 1572," *Journal of the History of Collections* 6, no. 1 (1994): 59–67.

130 Taylor, *Taste of Angels*, 163. Most of these artworks were later acquired by Queen Christina of Sweden.

131 See Leon Rosenstein, "Dresden: Rococo Miracle of Augustus the Strong," *The Quest: Newsletter of the Classical Alliance of the Western States* 25, no. 3 (April 1993).

132 Von Habsburg, "European Princely Families."

133 "A Collector's Cabinet," exhibition shown at the National Gallery, Washington, D.C., May 17 to November 1, 1998; catalogue by Arthur Wheelock, published by the National Gallery. See also Ellinoor Bergvelt et al., *Verzamelen: van Rariteitenkabinet tot Kunstmuseum* (Heerlen Gaade Uitgevers, Netherlands: Open Universiteit, 1993).

134 *Works of Francis Bacon*, ed. James Spedding, Robert Ellis, and Douglas Heath, 15 vols. (Cambridge, 1863), 5:398.

135 *Discourse on Method*, part 1.

136 See Wheelock, National Gallery exhibition catalogue, "A Collector's Cabinet."

137 Louis Auchincloss, *Richelieu* (New York: Viking, 1972), 205.

138 It was at Mazarin's direction that the Académie des Beaux Arts was founded by Colbert in 1648, thus formally institutionalizing French art just as his predecessor, Richelieu, had formally institutionalized French letters. With Le Brun as its first director, this institution established the artistic despotism of the "grand style" according to rules of ideal perfection, which was to dominate French taste for the next two hundred fifty years.

139 "The Fronde" (1648–53) refers to a period in French history when the Parlement of Paris in collaboration with ambitious nobles and an impoverished populace tried to limit

the growing authority of the Crown. It may be seen in part as a struggle for power between king and parliament paralleling the contemporary one in England, but with opposite consequences (or with similar consequences—just delayed for more than one hundred thirty years).

140 The agent was the dealer Alfonso López, who claimed to be descended from the Moors of Granada and who was dubbed by Richelieu (who had previously engaged him) "le Seigneur Hébreu."

141 See E. Bonnaffé, *Dictionnaire des amateurs français au dix-septième siècle* (Paris, 1884), and le duc d'Aumale, *Les richesses du Palais Mazarin* (Paris, 1877).

142 Taylor, *Taste of Angels*, 308. This is my own translation from the French text cited by Taylor. The phrase in brackets, *petits tableaux*, might also simply be translated as "paintings."

143 See Taylor, Taste of *Angels*, 350.

144 It was not merely the contents of Versailles that fell to the auction block and thus fostered the trade in antiques. On November 2, 1789, the properties (tangible and real) of the Church were "mise à la disposition de la Nation." And between 1811 and 1813—as the forfeit property of "émigrés"—more than seven hundred fifty aristocratic houses were emptied of their contents.

145 Adams, *Lost Museum*, 173.

146 Maurice Rheims, *The Strange Life of Objects*, trans. David Pryce-Jones (New York: Atheneum, 1961), 18.

147 Adam Nicholson, *God's Secretaries* (New York: Harper/Collins, 2003), 107.

148 Wolfgang Schivelbusch, *Tastes of Paradise*, trans. D. Jacobson (New York: Pantheon, 1992). Schivelbusch interprets this unprecedented interest in beautiful and exotic objects as a function of social class elevation, and believes that, like the origin of the objects themselves, the East motivated not just the economy but the culture of Europeans, just as today oil embargoes and Coca-Cola work their economic *and* cultural influences on the civilizations that are ready to absorb them or are destined to submit to them, willingly or not.

149 Gordon S. Wood, "The American Love Boat," *New York Review of Books* 46, no. 15 (October 7, 1999), 40. In re-creating their image of the exotic world, they were *playing at* being there. I return to role of play in civilization in chapter 4.

150 Initiated by Charles Perrault with his poem "Le siècle de Louis le Grand" (1687), followed by his famous *Parallèle des anciens et des modernes* (1688).

151 Rémy Saisselin, "Critical Reflections on the Origin of Modern Aesthetics," *British Journal of Aesthetics* 4, no. 1 (1964): 7–21.

152 L. Tatarkiewicz, "L'Esthétique associationniste au XVIIIe siècle," *Revue d'Esthétique* 13, no. 3 (1960): 287–92.

153 Saisselin, "Critical Reflections," 19.

154 Richard Woodfield, "On the Emergence of Aesthetics," *British Journal of Aesthetics* 18, no. 3 (Summer 1978): 217–27. The art-historical examples are my own.

155 See Richard F. Jones, "The Background of [Swift's] *Battle of the Books*," in John B. Bury, *The Idea of Progress* (London: Macmillan, 1920).

156 Alsop, *Rare Art Traditions*, 459.

157 Ibid., 148.

158 "Il était bien fait, beau de visage; il avait l'âme grande . . . il avait tous ses trésors à dépener, et toutes les pierreries de la Couronne d'Angleterre à se parer." Taylor, *Taste of Angels*, 219.

159 The Ottoman Empire.

160 Taylor, *Taste of Angels*, 229–31.

161 Ibid., 229.

162 Nys's predecessor as British ambassador to Venice was Sir Dudley Carleton. When Rubens saw his collection of antique marbles, he gave Carleton some of his paintings in

exchange. Most of these paintings Carleton later sold to Charles I, and Rubens later sold the marbles to Buckingham.

163 Among its many classical works was Michelangelo's fake antique "sleeping cupid," noted earlier. It helps us understand how such an antique "traveled" at the time to trace its history. When Cardinal Riario discovered it was a fake, it went via Cesare Borgia to the Duke of Urbino, Guidobaldo de Montefeltro, with whom Cesare was trying to form an alliance. When later, in 1502, Cesare reversed policy and attacked and captured Urbino, Guidobaldo and his wife, Elisabetta Gonzaga, fled to the court of Mantua and the protection of Elisabetta's good friend and sister-in-law, Isabella d'Este, Marchioness of Mantua. Isabella was herself a passionate and ruthless collector, however, and had all the perseverance of the "exquisite materialist" (Taylor, *Taste of Angels*, 80). She "made herself a burning glass for art," according to her contemporary, Niccolò da Coreggio, and waited barely three days before getting the cupid from her sister-in-law. It would have been improper to demand it openly from the Montefeltro as the price of their sanctuary, of course. So she wrote to her brother, Cardinal Ippolito d'Este, in Rome, asking him to intercede for her with Cesare, who now had possession of the work along with the rest of the Urbino collection and who himself (so she wrote) had "little taste for antiquities" (ibid.). She was successful, and despite the restoration of the Montefeltro to Urbino shortly thereafter, Isabella flatly refused to return the cupid. (According to another version of the story—and there are several—the "cupid fell into the hand of Duke Valentino, who gave it to the Marchioness of Mantua." See Vasari, *Lives*, 1:478.)

When the Gonzaga sale at Mantua took place in 1627, the dealer, Nys, failed in his attempt to quietly keep the cupid back for himself, and thus it wound up in Charles's collection at Whitehall, the main royal residence at the time. If it remained at Whitehall, then, as Taylor apparently believes (ibid., 83n), it perished in the fire of 1698. If, as was more likely, it wound up in the Commonwealth Sale of Charles's collection in 1651, then it could have been one of several cupid sculptures mentioned in the inventories and sold to one of four dealer syndicates to be shipped abroad, since Puritan England at the time did not generally provide a good market for such things. (A contemporary account of the art destruction during the Civil War describes a Puritan crowd that barged into Canterbury Cathedral in 1642 and "giant-like began a fight with God himself," venting "their malice upon the hangings in the choir, representing the whole story of our savior; wherein observing divers figures of Christ [I tremble to express their blasphemies] one said, 'here is Christ,' and swore that he would stab him: another said, 'here is Christ,' and swore that he would rip up his bowels: which they accordingly did, so far as the figures were capable thereof, besides many other villanies" [quoted in Margaret Aston: *England's Iconoclasts: Laws against Images* (Oxford: Oxford University Press, 1988), 73–74]. Not surprisingly, when the city of York finally capitulated to the iconoclastic Puritan forces in 1644, it surrendered with the special provision that the medieval stained glass of its minster would be unharmed. In the following year, however, the Puritanical zeal of the July 23 Act of Parliament declared that any pictures representing the second person of the Trinity or the Virgin Mary be burned.)

If shipped abroad, the cupid likely wound up in Amsterdam, then the center of the European market for art and antiquities auctions. Rembrandt often frequented them. His irrepressible passion for fine textiles, antique busts, weapons, and curiosities from the Orient and the New World finally bankrupted him. The inventory of his estate prior to his bankruptcy sale in 1656 in fact lists a "kinder van Michel Angelo Bonalotti." If true, this mention is the last known reference to the whereabouts of the cupid, and it is now considered by most art historians a lost work. (See Charles de Tolnay, *The Youth of Michelangelo* [Princeton, N.J.: Princeton University Press, 1947], 24 ff. and 201 ff., and Paul Norton, "The Lost *Sleeping Cupid* of Michelangelo," *Art Bulletin* 39, no. 1 [1957]: 251 ff.) It may, of course, reappear at any moment! Another cupid, long attributed to Michelangelo, has turned out to be an authentic antique work that was restored in the Renaissance and given a Michelangelo-styled head. (See John Pope-Hennessy, "Michelangelo's *Cupid*: The End of a Chapter," *Essays in Italian Sculpture* [London: Phaidon, 1968], 111 ff.) And recently, yet another Michelangelo cupid has resurfaced as a decorative object in the French Embassy in New York, after nearly a century of disappearance following its sale at Christie's in London, 1902 (see Kathleen-Weil-Garris Brandt, "A Marble in Manhattan" *Burlington Magazine* 138 [October 1996]: 644–59)—if it really is a Michelangelo (see Laurie Attlas, "Less Than Meets the Eye: Louvre Symposium," *Art News* 95 [May 1996]: 75; Ann Landi, "Michelangelo/Not Michelangelo," *Art News* 95 [April 1996]: 104–6; and Michael Daley, "Drawbacks with Cupid," *Art Review* 51 [March 1999]: 60–64).

164 Alsop, *Rare Art Traditions*, 453–57.

165 "The most minuscule prices." Taylor, *Taste of Angels*, 236.

166 Ibid., 208–9. His heir, living in France during the twenty-year interruption in the monarchy, was restored as Charles II in May 1660. In the month preceding his return to England, Charles II purchased a collection of seventy-two Old Master paintings from the dealer William Frizell in Breda.

As for his father's former collection, the Convention Parliament, on the day following Charles's official restoration, appointed a committee of eight lords to "consider and receive information where any of the King's goods, jewels, or pictures are; and to advise of some course how the same may be restored for his Majesty." Within the week the House of Lords issued a proclamation that all persons with goods of the former King Charles I return them within seven days, and this order for return was repeated three months later on pain of forfeiture and seizure. Many of the paintings had already been sold, as we noted, to Mazarin and Philip II. Almost all the silver plate and gold regalia had been melted down. What remained in England had been purchased by both aristocrats and commoners. The aristocrats generally failed to comply with the order, but in the end made a show of making returns look like gifts. Since return was without indemnification, it was more of a hardship for some of the commoners, who were not men of means and had been paid with the king's goods by the Commonwealth for services or as creditors or who had bought them on speculation or as a safe investment opportunity. See Stephen Gleissner, "Reassembling a Royal Art Collection for the Restored King of Great Britain," *Journal of the History of Collections* 6, no. 1 (1994): 103–15.

167 Strange as this may seem to us today.

168 Taylor, *Taste of Angels*, 254.

169 Rheims, *Strange Life of Objects*, 102. For a superb account of the Dutch world at this time, see Simon Schama, *The Embarrassment of Riches: An Interpretation of Dutch Culture in the Golden Age* (New York: Knopf, 1987).

170 For a further and purely philosophical discussion of this subject grounded on a Heideggerian ontology, see my article "Heidegger's Aesthetics: The Art Object and History," *Studies in the Humanities* (June 2008).

171 John Steegman, *The Rule of Taste: From George I to George IV* (London: Century Hutchinson, 1986), 36–37.

172 Quoted in Anthony Chrichton-Stuart, "The *Grand Tour* and 18th Century Italian View Painting," *Christie's International Magazine*, January–February 1996, 18.

173 R. W. B. Lewis, *The City of Florence* (New York: Henry Holt, 1995), 181.

174 Louise Lippincott, *Selling Art in Georgian London* (New Haven, Conn.: Yale University Press, 1983).

175 Quoted by Erika Langmuir, *The National Gallery Guide* (London: National Gallery; New Haven, Conn.: Yale University Press, 1994), 197–98.

176 Lippincott, *Selling Art in Georgian London*, 100; see also Lesley Lewis, *Connoisseurs and Secret Agents in Eighteenth Century Rome* (London: Chatto and Windus, 1961).

177 Jonathan Richardson, *Two Discourses* (London, 1719), 141–52.

178 Steegman, *Rule of Taste*, xiii.

179 I should perhaps say "separated attention," for Shaftesbury's analysis deals in part with beauty in the arts *as such*, i.e., without discussion of the moral improvement it might provide.

180 Or "reintroduce," since we have perhaps a suggestion of it already in Thomas Aquinas, who, though he says that beauty is what pleases the eye—"pulchra dicantur quae visa placent"—is referring not to sensuous enjoyment but rather to something that is brilliant and glorious and shines forth in a striking way to capture the attention of our minds. *Summa theologiae* Ia.5.4as.1 and a.39.8. In addition to this quality of *claritas* (radiance/brightness), Aquinas proposes *consonantia* (harmony/symmetry) and *integritas* (unity/wholeness) as characteristics of beauty. See my discussion of beauty and disinterestedness in the preceding chapter, note 15. See also Jacques Maritain, *Art and Scholasticism*, trans. Joseph W. Evans (Notre Dame, Ind.: Notre Dame University Press, 1974), 161, and Joseph G. Brennan, *The Meaning of Philosophy* (New York: Harper and Row, 1967), 404. Moreover, as the eminent philologist and medieval historian Umberto Eco has noted (*The Aesthetics of Thomas Aquinas*, trans. Hugh Bredin [Cambridge, Mass.: Harvard University Press, 1988]), there is in Aquinas's conception of "visio" the sense of "disinterested knowledge," which has to do not with sensuous rapture and mystical communion but indeed with a "disinterested pleasure," for as Aquinas states, "It pertains to the notion of the beautiful that in seeing or knowing it the appetite comes to rest." *Summa theologiae* I–II.27.lad.3. So it is perhaps here that we should look for the first account of "disinterestedness" in aesthetic judgment.

181 That does not mean that such moralizing of aesthetics and in aesthetics ever came to an end, even in the first decade of the twenty-first century. It seems often to have returned with a vengeance so that the very idea of contemplating or discussing art "disinterestedly" is considered to be "elitist"—this last term construed derogatorily.

182 Larry Shiner, *The Invention of Art: A Cultural History* (Chicago: University of Chicago Press, 2001).

183 Again, as we see below, though I would agree with Shiner that the psychological state of "disinterestedness" and the faculty of "taste" were explicit new developments in the eighteenth century, they were not entirely without precedent. Neither is it, contrary to Shiner, entirely new to the eighteenth century to view art as having as its purpose pure contemplation or as having a therapeutic or curative effect on the soul, for these conceptions derive from Plato and Aristotle and come down through early Medieval thinkers such as Plotinus and St. Augustine, who ascribed such powers to beauty generally. The subsequent chapters of Shiner's book (following chapter 1) are well documented and do much reinforce the evidence and arguments I advance hereafter.

184 Shiner, *Invention of Art*, 5.

185 Quoted in ibid., 6, from Abrams, *Doing Things with Texts* (New York: Norton, 1989).

186 The distinction between art and craft is implicit in Aristotle, *Physics* 199a15–17. There Aristotle says that art "partly completes what nature cannot bring to finish and partly imitates her." I think it is both implicit and reasonable (given Aristotle's other claims, particularly in *The Poetics*) to interpret this to mean that "craft" only completes whereas "fine art" both completes and imitates nature. When one crafts a basket, one increases the types of objects that inhabit the earth (one completes Nature, which doesn't supply us with baskets); but when one writes a play or paints a painting of Oedipus and the Sphinx, for example, one not only increases the sorts of things that inhabit the earth (paintings and plays now do) but also "imitates," i.e., one takes objects of nature—Oedipus and the Sphinx and their story—as a subject matter for imitation. Thus, when Shiner says in

Invention of Art that Aristotle does not separate "in their *procedures*" the fine arts of painting or tragedy from crafts like shoemaking or medicine, and quotes several authorities to support this view (Pollitt, Roochnik, Havelock), I would agree that this distinction is not developed *explicitly*. But the idea that fine art has an imitative content, "an about which," whereas crafts only bring into being something more than nature provides, something that we can "use for," is indeed *implicit* in Aristotle's account. Some support for my view may be found in Paolo Moreno, "Painters and Society," in *The Dictionary of Art*, 34 vols., ed. Jane Turner (New York: Grove's Dictionaries, 1996), 13:548–53. Furthermore, while Shiner is at pains to argue that Aristotle's *poein*, the verb form of "poetizing," "means simply 'to make' with none of our overtones of romantic creativity," he fails to note Aristotle's claim that poetry is not history: it doesn't merely restate particulars (e.g., making one basket after another) but offers general interpretations of them, speaking of things in universals (hence being creative and imaginatively reconstructive and interpretive), somewhat as philosophy does. Surely basket weaving and shoemaking do not do this—i.e., "represent" in the form of universals—for there is nothing "about" which they "speak." See Shiner, *Invention of Art*, 21–22; and Aristotle, *Poetics* 1451b5–7. Still, it must be agreed that Aristotle provides "no doctrine of an autonomous aesthetic pleasure" (Shiner, *Invention of Art*, 25, quoting Stephen Halliwell, "Aristotle's Poetics," in *The Cambridge History of Literary Criticism*, vol. 1, ed. George A. Kennedy [Cambridge: Cambridge University Press, 1989], 162). But see my "The Last Word on 'Catharsis,' " *Annales d'Esthétique* 23–24 (1984–85): 29–57. Lessing's *Laocoön* (1776) is possibly even derived from Aristotle's account, for it analyzes the important relationship between the medium of the art form (its physical substance) and the content (the subject matter it refers to). Lessing argues that the particular physical medium of a given art genre (poetry constructed from words, the usage of which "take time," as compared to paintings constructed of paint on canvas, the usage of which "takes space") places constraints and limitations on the type of subject matter that the genre can contain (i.e., represent), such that the medium is not "innocent" or "inert" but something that has the power to permit or exclude certain subject matters as more or less appropriate for representation in that medium.

187 *The Poetics* is limited to the discussion of the principles governing tragic and epic poetry, but these could, with some effort, be generalized to produce a comprehensive theory of art. See also my "Last Word on 'Catharsis.' "

188 Shiner seems to be unaware also of Aquinas's notion, which we also referred to earlier, that in the contemplation of beauty "the appetite comes to rest."

189 "Fine art" is generally taken to be Kant's "schönen Künste" in German. See the discussion of the arts at ¶¶51–53 of *Critique of Judgment*. In the translation by J. H. Bernard, "schönen Künste" is given literally as "beautiful arts" (New York: Hafner, 1951), 164. My point here is that even if it was Kant in the late eighteenth century who enshrined the doctrine of "disinterestedness" as a requirement for aesthetic experience, this does not entail "uselessness" on the part of the object experienced; and hence uselessness does not entail the "craft/fine" art distinction. It is *the way* in which the object *is experienced* by the perceiving consciousness and not the actual or intended function of the object itself that determines the possibility of the aesthetic response. If one looks at a painting as a good investment, it is "useful" for one's investment portfolio and one would be "interested" in it as an object of purchase. So long as one views the painting in this way, its traditional status as "fine art" cannot make it an object of aesthetic satisfaction. That is why, for Kant, furniture (normally located in the "craft" category) can be an object of aesthetic appreciation—even though its use would tend to "limit" (*eingeshränkt*) the experience. The craft/fine distinction has enjoyed perhaps a two-hundred-year period of favor and clearly only a Western one, since Persian carpets to much of Middle East and writing (calligraphy) in the Far East have always been among the highest (finest) arts of those cultures.

190 See Kristeller, "Modern System of the Arts." Kristeller was the first to note that the "fine arts"—painting, poetry, music, sculpture, and literature—a classification that "underlies all modern aesthetics and is familiar to us all, is of comparatively recent origin and did not assume definite shape before the eighteenth century, although it has many ingredients which go back to classical, medieval, and Renaissance thought." Ibid., 12 (1951): 498.

191 Finally, Diderot's *Encyclopedia* (1752), by its prestige and wide dissemination, further modified Batteux's system. Diderot replaced with "architecture" Batteux's "dance" as one of the five "fine" arts, presumably because he no longer thought "fine" art had to be tied to the imitative principle and dance was imitative. Furthermore, Diderot's article "Beau" (volume 2) formulated what was surely the most seminal definition of beauty to be expressed in that century: that which arouses the mind to the pleasure of contemplating relations ("rapports") between things real or imagined and between parts and wholes.

192 That the man of taste could find only the works of dead masters admirable was repeatedly ridiculed by Hogarth, who showed his resentment in a painting he displayed at the 1761 Exhibit of the Society of Artists in which this ideal "man of taste" is depicted as an ape dressed as a fop watering three dead plants.

193 Steegman, *Rule of Taste*, 8–10, 22, 81.

194 H. J. Habakkuk, "England," in *The European Nobility in the 18th Century*, ed. Albert Goodwin (London: Adam and Charles Black, 1953), 1–21. Burlington's tastes were quite broad. He even included Chinese and Gothic motifs, which were peculiar to fashion in the pure Classicism of the eighteenth century's first few decades until Walpole and Beckford at midcentury, as we discuss later.

195 Alsop, *Rare Art Traditions*, 159. "Rarely" would be more accurate than "never."

196 Quoted in Nancy Ruhling, "They Came, They Saw, They Shopped," *Art and Antiques*, September 1997, 101. See also Bruce Redford, *Venice and the Grand Tour* (New Haven, Conn.: Yale University Press, 1996).

197 Quoted in Ruhling, "They Came, They Saw."

198 Taylor, *Taste of Angels*, 204.

199 Quoted in *Italian Journal* 9, no. 1 (April 1995); see Jane Martineau and Andrew Robison, eds., *The Glory of Venice: Art in the 18th Century* (National Gallery of Art exhibition catalogue; New Haven, Conn.: Yale University Press, 1994). Where local Italian painters were not purchased, contemporary French masters (or, better, French masters of the *preceding* century such as Poussin or Claude Lorrain) who painted the countryside and ruins of Italy could be had. In consequence, much English Derby porcelain of the second half of the eighteenth century is painted in these French styles with famous continental scenes for its English customers.

200 Hamilton's most influential publication was the 1791 *Collection of Engravings from Ancient Vases*, dedicated to the Earl of Leicester, president of the Society of Antiquaries. Hamilton was one of the first—along with Winckelmann–to recognize that these vases were not in fact "Etruscan" but Greek. By the late 1790s, Greece rather than Rome was considered to have a higher aesthetic value (perhaps one should say cachet) by true men of taste. Josiah Wedgwood, who had established his ceramics factory in 1770, named it "Etruria," but "in time Wedgwood too came to regard Greece as a worthier source of inspiration than Etruria . . . [and this perception and preference] came to dominate the aesthetic temper of the age and not just aesthetically but politically" (Steegman, *Rule of Taste*, 140). This was because by the last quarter of the eighteenth century in the spirit of the Enlightenment and its nascent revolutionary mood—the successful new republic in North America was admired by many, and the French experiment was nothing if not stimulating—the image of the Greek city-states with their presumptive democratic ideals was preferred over that of Imperial Rome, which was the political and artistic prototype of the Augustan, the antipopulist, the monarchical and aristocratic. See Steegman, *Rule of Taste*, 154.

201 Johann Wolfgang von Goethe, *Italian Journey, 1786–1788*, trans. W. H. Auden and Elizabeth Mayer (San Francisco: North Point, 1982). Jacob Hackert (1737–1807), a German landscape painter and a friend of Goethe, was living in Naples at the time and introduced Goethe to Hamilton. Goethe published a biography of Hackert in 1811.

202 There was also William Beckford's Fonthill Abbey, whose collection was sold in 1822; the contents of Strawberry Hill were auctioned off in 1842.

203 Kenneth Clark, *The Gothic Revival* (New York: Harper and Row, 1974).

204 The terminal "k" is generally used to denote the Victorianized revivalist Gothic confections of the nineteenth century that quote and commingle a variety of styles and forms rather than revive pure Gothic. Walpole was dedicated to historical accuracy and would not have tolerated the Victorian anachronisms and stylistic Frankensteins of the later Gothick.

205 Goethe was not the only enthusiast. In 1788 a Mr. Lloyd of Conduit Street in London purchased from John Berry, a local glazier and secondhand dealer, the stained glass from the windows of Salisbury Cathedral which restorer James Wyatt was demolishing at the time. Berry writes to his customer: "Sir, this day I have sent you a Box full of old Stained & Painted glass, as you desired me to due, which I hope will sute your Purpos, it his the best I can get at Present. But I expect to Beate to Peceais a great deal very soon, as it his of now use to me, and we do it for the lead." See Adams, *Lost Museum*, 87.

206 Steegman, *Rule of Taste*, 49.

207 Ibid., 56.

208 Ibid., 81. Of course, they weren't built by the founders, and the "line" went back a generation or two perhaps.

209 Vasari mentions that in the sixteenth century at Pesaro a house was constructed for the Duke of Urbino in the classical style (*Lives*, 3:263–64). Lowenthal remarks, "Only since the 16th century has the look of age been widely appreciated" (*Past*, xxii). We have seen that this would be to ignore the classical world. We have also noted that "the look of age" may refer to several different things and in each case may inspire several different sorts of appreciation.

210 Lowenthal, *Past*, 232–33.

211 See John Ruskin, *Modern Painters* (Boston: Dana Estes, 1873), I, part 2, sec. 1, chap. 7, paragraph 26; and his *The Seven Lamps of Architecture* (1849; New York: Noonday, 1961), 183; William Morris, "The Beauty of Life," in *Labour and Pleasure versus Labour and Sorrow* (Birmingham: Cund Bros., 1880), reprinted as *The Beauty of Life*, abridged ed. (London: Bentham Press, 1974); and Joseph Addison's *Spectator*, no. 83, June 5, 1711. Presumably this taste would be doubly satisfied by a well-aged painting depicting ruined Gothic architecture as its subject.

212 Hogarth naturally mocked the practice of artificial aging and the notion that agedness could be appreciated as an aesthetic component of beauty in his painting *Time Smoking a Picture*.

213 Quoted in Steegman, *Rule of Taste*, 64. See also Uvedale Price, *A Dialogue on the Distinct Characters of the Picturesque and the Beautiful* (Whitefish, Mont.: Kessinger, 2008), which is Price's 1801 response to objections to his *An Essay on the Picturesque, as Compared with the Sublime and the Beautiful* (1794; reprinted in 3 vols., London: J. Mawman, 1810).

214 This is not to say that the older, more typically Renaissance view did not continue to find expression in the eighteenth century. Thus, Francesco Algarotti, in his *Essay on Painting* (1769), states, "By giving testimony to their antiquity [the patina of time] renders them proportionably beautiful in the superstitious eye of the learned." Quoted in Lowenthal, *Past*, 149.

215 Cited in Lowenthal, *Past*, 157. See also Augustus W. N. Pugin's *Contrasts* (New York: Humanities Press, 1969).

216 Steegman, *Rule of Taste*, 41.

217 Ibid., 43. Chinoiserie was usually a fantastic mélange of styles, but it could maintain standards of cultural accuracy. At the Pagodenburg near Munich the king took his tea amid genuine and consistent Chinese decor and objects. But the combinative forms of what might best be called "fantasy chinoiserie" were far more congenial to English taste. The English architect William Halfpenny, for example, wrote *New Designs for Chinese Temples* in 1749 and *Chinese and Gothic Architecture Properly Ornamental* in 1752. Both are rather far from manifesting concern for stylistic purism.

218 Steegman, *Rule of Taste*, 38–40. Thus, the neo-classical rule was never overthrown. As Steegman notes, "Sir William Chambers' attempt in the 1750's to effect a revolution in favour of the Chinese was . . . unsuccessful in the face of the Palladian formality of the school of Wren and the grandeur of Le Nôtre" (114).

219 Only one of many influential and typical works—in this instance offering designs for silk manufacture—was Jean Pillement's *Cahier de douze barques et chariots chinois* (Paris, 1770).

220 Rémy Saisselin, *Taste in Eighteenth Century France* (Syracuse, N.Y.: Syracuse University Press, 1965), 88.

221 See Robert Fox and Anthony Turner, eds., *Luxury Trades and Consumerism in Ancien Régime Paris* (Brookfield, Vt.: Ashgate Publishing, 1998).

222 Taylor, *Taste of Angels*, 353. The causes of this change were not only political but economic as well. It was not simply that with the death of the Sun King the nobility were released from the boring life of their country estates and the court etiquette of Versailles; the bursting of "John Law's Bubble" in 1720 caused a market crash and crisis that required the move to Paris. Similarly, in England, as John Brewer has shown in several works (*The Pleasures of the Imagination: English Culture in the Eighteenth Century* [New York: Farrar, Straus and Giroux, 1997], *The Consumption of Culture* [London: Routledge, 1997], and *The Birth of a Consumer Society* [Bloomington: Indiana University Press, 1982]), the traditional conception of the Victorian period as being the first in which middle-class consumers went about shopping for goods in well-stocked stores is mistaken; such consumerism is really a phenomenon that began in the eighteenth century.

223 In addition to the Far East, there was the exotic style of Egypt. Its first influence on eighteenth-century European taste can be traced to Giambattista Piranesi's publication of a number of Egyptian ornamental designs in *Diversi maniere di adornare i cammini* in 1769, which followed shortly on the fresco paintings he did for the new English Café (Caffè degli Inglesi) in Rome between 1765 and 1767. These designs—with mummies, scarabs, bulls, falcons, and fake hieroglyphs—were hardly accurate. Furthermore, unlike the Gothic and chinoiserie, Egyptian design did not conform well to the prevalent undulating late Rococo aesthetic, but it did combine rather well with the Palladian and Greco-Roman. Certainly it was by no means as powerful or pervasive an influence on cultural taste in the eighteenth century as was the "Tutcraze" revival in the 1920s and 1930s, when "Egyptian" blended marvelously with the linear and flat Art Deco style—or even as it was to become after 1802 when Dominique-Vivant Denon (an archeologist and engraver who accompanied Napoleon's savants as head of the archeological team in Egypt) published his lavishly illustrated *Voyage dans la basse et haute Egypte* in both London and Paris. "Egyptian" was at its height in the first decade of the nineteenth century in France, when Egyptian-motif furnishings were made for Napoleon's private apartments in the Tuileries. The famous *passages couvertes* of Paris (the contextual subject of Walter Benjamin's *The Arcades Project* [see n. 242], which discusses the flâneur and, especially for our concern, the collector) were inspired by the covered souks encountered by the French in Napoleon's Middle East campaigns. One of the first passages (built in 1799 by Percier and Fontaine, architects of the emperor) was called the Passage du Caire. It sported obelisks and pyramids, rows of giant

masks of the Egyptian goddess Hathor, and a fountain designed by David representing "Nature" as an ancient Egyptian woman posed between two lions. (One begins to suspect again that the reduced and recombinant confections of contemporary Las Vegas are nothing new!) In England in 1805–15 Egyptian motifs can be found in the work of Thomas Sheraton, Thomas Hope, and Chippendale the Younger. Still, that these Egyptian motifs even appear, and that they appeal at all to late eighteenth-century aesthetic sensibilities, says much about the capacity of Europeans to appreciate and incorporate this ancient and exotic style.

224 Saisselin, *Taste*, 88–89.

225 Some are still moving about; others have been restored to their original homes. Thus, a marquetry commode by Jean-Henri Riesener made in 1778 for Louis XVI and sold off in 1794 during the French Revolution for 1,600 livres (about one-quarter of what the piece cost Louis)—eventually making its way to William Beckford's Fonthill Abbey, thence via Hamilton Palace in Scotland to a book dealer, before becoming a Rothschild piece—has recently been restored to Versailles (at $10.98 million at Christie's Auction the most expensive piece of French furniture ever sold). See *Maine Antique Digest*, September 1999, 2D. But it was not only the royal contents of Versailles that were dispersed. The duc d'Orleans sold his collection in Paris in 1792 (via M. Le Borde) to a Mr. Jeremiah Harman for £40,000, and Harman in turn sold it to an English syndicate composed of two dukes and one earl. They retained the cream of the collection and sold the residue in London during 1799 for £80,000. See John Steegman, *Victorian Taste* (London: Nelson's University Paperbacks, 1970), 56. Regarding the sale of the contents of Versailles, some of the particulars are illuminating. After the linens were sent off to hospitals and a few paintings sent to the Louvre, there were 17,182 items remaining to be listed in the catalogue. The sale, beginning September 30, 1793 (eight months after Louis's execution) at 10 a.m. in the Cour des Princes, lasted about a year. Most of the crowned heads of continental Europe stayed away (as they or their agents had not, as we noted, from the English king Charles I's sale), but British aristocrats and bourgeois collectors and merchants did not–nor did nonroyal continentals abstain. Prices were low. Foreigners exporting pieces bearing royal coats of arms were exempt from taxes. Many of the craftsmen (like Riesener) who had originally been commissioned to produce pieces now bought back their own. In the twentieth century the French government, trying to refurnish Versailles with original pieces, has paid up to four hundred times the original sale price of the item at auction—the Riesener/Rothschild piece noted above being one.

226 *Republic* 373e.

227 To take the most striking contemporary instance of this intercultural consciousness-raising: how many Americans ever were aware of the two largest denominations of Islam—*Sunni* and *Shiite*—before the present war in Iraq?

228 Quoted in *Gardner's Art through the Ages*, 10th ed., vol. 2, ed. R. Tansey and F. Kleiner (Fort Worth, Texas: Harcourt Brace, 1996), 932.

229 Martin Heidegger, "Phaenomenologie und Transzendentale Wertphilosophie," *Zur Bestimmung der Philosophie, Gesamtausgabe* 55–56 (1987): 133–34.

230 "Furniture and Style under Napoleon," *Art and Antiques* 6, no. 1 (November–December 1988): 101.

231 In the same manner, we find incongruence between styles and structure in Nash's Royal Pavilion at Brighton. On the exterior it looks like an Indo-Islamic palace (often referred to as "Indian Gothic") with its Taj Mahal domes, and on the interior it sports columns in the form of palm trees with leaping Chinese dragons. Both its interior and exterior actually hang on an armature (or endoskeleton) made of cast iron.

232 *Gardner's Art through the Ages*, 2:932.

233 Arthur Danto, "Art and the Discourse of Nations," in *Philosophizing Art* (Berkeley: University of California Press, 1999), 257.

234 See Juan Cole, *Napoleon's Egypt* (New York: Palgrave / Macmillan, 2007). After its fall to Napoleon in 1797, Venice, the thousand-year-old Most Serene Republic, was also looted of its art. Much was taken away to Paris. Much was destroyed, some wantonly, most for more practical ends: for example, "ecclesiastical equipment" in gold and silver weighing a total of 535 kg (valued at 29,223 ducats at the time) was melted down for coinage. When Napoleon fell in 1814 and Venice came under Austrian rule, the enlightened Austrian emperor Francis I, showing a greater historical sensibility, had the treasury of San Marco inventoried. In 1820 he asked for a valuation of the objects it contained, specifying that in addition to the rare and precious materials of which these objects were made the valuation "should be determined in relation to a large number of events during the course of time, and the historical origins of the objects, taking into account the state of the arts in the various periods when they were made." Guido Perocco, "A History of the Treasury," in *The Treasury of San Marco*, ed. David Buckton, LACMA exhibition catalogue (Milan: Olivetti, 1984), 68.

235 Arthur Danto, "Postmodern Art and Concrete Selves," in *Philosophizing Art*, 132–33.

236 This is not to ignore the Bonapartist lust for "la gloire," as if absorbing the past of the world through its magical incorporation in the treasuries of the empire guaranteed Napoleon's immortality as something destined for all time—as if God at the moment of creation had made the world for him alone. Interestingly, the Prado in Madrid was established by Joseph Bonaparte and the Rijksmuseum in Amsterdam by Louis Bonaparte.

237 One may see the change in music as well. Compare the representation of Egypt in Mozart's *Magic Flute* (1791) with its representation in Verdi's *Aïda* (1869)—the latter's story suggested by August Mariette, Egypt's first Keeper of Antiquities.

238 Steegman, *Rule of Taste*, 156–57.

239 Lowenthal, *Past*, xvi–xvii.

240 One might think of ancient Iran, whose example was noted at the outset of this chapter, or of Egyptian (Alexandrian) art during the Roman period; but even if these were self-conscious international eclecticisms, they were not the part of the nostalgic historical consciousness we find in Romanticism.

241 Ronald Freyberger, "The Duke of Hamilton's Porphyry Tables," *The Magazine Antiques* 144, no. 3 (September 1993): 351.

242 Walter Benjamin quotes E. Lavasseur's *Histoire des classes ouvrières et de l'industrie en France, de 1789 à 1870* [(Paris, 1904), 2:206–7]: " 'All of a sudden,' says a reporter on the exhibition of 1834, 'there is boundless enthusiasm for strangely shaped furniture. From old châteaux, from furniture warehouses and junk shops, it has been dragged out to embellish the salons, which in every other respect are modern. . . .' Feeling inspired, furniture manufacturers have been prodigal with their 'ogives and machiolations.' You see beds and armoires bristling with battlements, like thirteenth-century citadels." *The Arcades Project*, trans. Howard Eiland and Kevin McLaughlin (Cambridge, Mass.: Harvard University Press, Belknap Press, 1999), 212.

243 See the catalogue "The Golden Age of Decorative Arts (1814–1848)," for an exhibition shown in Paris at the Grand Palais, December 1991.

244 In France the best of these revivalist jewelers included Eugène Fontenay (1828–87); in England, Robert Phillips (1810–81).

245 James Fenton, "An Ardor for Armor," *New York Review of Books* 46, no. 7 (April 22, 1999): 57–58.

246 Stephen Calloway, *Twentieth Century Decoration* (London: Weidenfeld and Nicholson, 1988), 11. Betjeman and Osborne Lancaster satirized this taste at the time with such epithets as "Stockbroker's Tudor" and "Curzon Street Baroque."

247 Kant, *Critique of Judgment* (1790), secs. 40 and 57; Oscar Wilde, "Pen, Pencil, and Poison" (1891), in *Intentions* (London: Unicorn Press, 1948).

248 James Whistler, "Ten O'Clock Lecture," in *Mr. Whistler's Ten O'Clock Lecture* (London: Chatto and Windus, 1888).

249 We cannot delve into the details of the religious connection here. Much of the appeal—especially of Romanist traditions and ritual—to otherwise good Protestant Germans and Britons was based on the powerful aesthetic and historical associations of Roman Catholicism. But see Charles Harvey and Jon Press, *William Morris: Design and Enterprise in Victorian Britain* (Manchester: Manchester University Press, 1991). The Nazarenes began as German art students expelled for disobedience to new regulations of the Art Academy in Vienna in 1803 and who came to occupy the grounds of the derelict convent of St. Isidore near Trinità dei Monte; calling themselves the Brotherhood of St. Luke, they spent the mornings in simple household chores and devoted the afternoons to painting, using Early Renaissance works (especially Perugino and Dürer) as models. There were also revivalist societies of a purely aestheticist and art-historical bent—the Arundel Society, for example, founded by Alex Lindsey with Ruskin, Layard, and others—whose stated purpose was to preserve and diffuse the knowledge of early Italian painting (especially frescoes) by publishing chromolithographic illustrations of these works through subscription. E. H. Gombrich, in a review of Francis Haskell's *History and Its Images: Art and the Interpretation of the Past* (New Haven, Conn.: Yale University Press, 1993), quotes Haskell as saying, "By the 1840's it had become almost conventional to assert that the arts of a country could give a more reliable impression of its true character than those more usual yardsticks . . . which had hitherto been made use of by historians." See Gombrich, "What Art Tells Us," *New York Review of Books* 40, no. 17 (October 21, 1993), 60. Coincident with this view, Gombrich claims, was the historical contextualization of the experience of art: "No wonder art collectors and museums had begun even in Goethe's time to arrange their treasures historically and to give the visitor a vicarious experience of the passage of time" (61).

250 Walter Kaufmann, *Time Is an Artist* (New York: Reader's Digest Press, 1978), 62.

251 Lowenthal, *Past*, 171.

252 "Romantic" love, the sentimentalization of children, and the marked decrease in the public display of affection and emotion between men are all further features of this transformation.

253 Benjamin, *Arcades Project*, 8.

254 Saisselin, *Bourgeois and the Bibelot*, 29.

255 Todd Gitlin, "The Medium," in *Seeing through the Movies*, ed. Mark Crispin Miller (New York: Pantheon), 20.

256 Egon Friedell, *A Cultural History of the Modern Age*, 3 vols., trans. Charles Francis Atkinson (New York: Knopf, 1930), 3:299.

257 Steegman, *Victorian Taste*, 253.

258 Rheims, *Glorious Obsession*, 243 and 274.

259 Ibid., 243.

260 Today's proliferation of "price guides" to every conceivable field of collecting is merely an historical elephantiasis. What antiques shopper hasn't heard the seller's refrain: "It's listed in the book at . . ."? In this way the document becomes a facsimile of the object, a false but alternative life form of it.

261 Wendell Garrett, editorial, *The Magazine Antiques* 133, no. 6 (June 1988): 1343.

262 Steegman, *Rule of Taste*, 74.

263 Steegman, *Victorian Taste*, 79.

264 Ibid., 88.

265 E.g., Wedgwood's "jasperware" and many mechanical objects such as clocks.

266 Just as in the seventeenth century the *object per se* was liberated in science from its "equipmentality" by Galileo and Descartes—its final end always having been a function of personal ownership so that it was "made for Mr. Vance to do his toilet in"—so

the industrial revolution of the nineteenth century replicated things in multiplicity such that all simulacra were equal, like the "free agents" who were the citizens of the political revolutions in the preceding two generations. Thus, industrially manufactured objects became "free ions" that were able to be latched onto by collectors and embedded into their complex molecular selves, like free workers available for any employment.

267 J. M. Coetzee, "The Marvels of Walter Benjamin," *New York Review of Books* 48, no. 1 (January 11, 2001): 30. Benjamin himself quotes Otto Rühle's book on Karl Marx: "With price tag affixed, the commodity comes to the market. Its material quality and individuality are merely an incentive for buying and selling. . . . Once escaped from the hand of the producer and divested of its real particularity, it ceases to be a product ruled over by human beings. It has acquired a 'ghostly objectivity' and leads a life of its own." *Arcades Project*, 181.

268 See *Quarterly Review* 66 (1840): 324 ff.

269 See Steegman, *Victorian Taste*. It is hard to say how much is too much clutter. Cecil Beaton, in *The Glass of Fashion* (Garden City, N.Y.: Doubleday, 1954), once remarked that in interior decoration one must avoid "the Scylla of antiques and the Charybdis of an operating room sterility."

270 H. W. Janson, *History of Art*, 5th ed., 2 vols. (New York: Prentice Hall / Harry Abrams, 1995), 2:704-5.

271 No one has ever given a wittier account of this, I think, than Oscar Wilde, in his essay "The Decay of Lying."

272 Janson, *History of Art*, 704.

273 In my discussion of the aesthetic experience per se and my discussion of art vs. craft in the preceding chapter and in several articles: "The Ontological Integrity of the Art Object," *Journal of Aesthetics and Art Criticism* 34, no. 3 (1976): 323-36; "The End of Art Theory," *Humanitas* 15, no. 1 (2002): 32-58; "The Aesthetic of the Antique," *Journal of Aesthetics and Art Criticism* 65, no. 4 (1987): 393-402; and "Heidegger's Aesthetics: The Art Object and History," *Studies in the Humanities* (Spring 2008).

274 Richard Gilman, *Decadence* (New York: Farrar, Straus and Giroux, 1975), 52.

275 Calloway, *Twentieth Century Decoration*, 46.

276 Artists were especially prone to it—and not just in France, as our current text might suggest. Thus, e.g., Lord Leighton, "Prince of Aesthetes," in England, and Frederick Church in the Hudson River Valley, to name only two, were similar connoisseur-collectors. It should be noted that in using the phrase "aesthetic decadence," I refer to a category of style. "Aesthetic decadence" is therefore not to be confused with "decadent aesthetic."

As J. W. Burrow notes regarding decadence in *The Crisis of Reason: European Thought, 1848-1914* (New Haven, Conn.: Yale University Press, 2000), "world-weariness, a sense of a world grown old and of belonging to a prematurely exhausted, post-Romantic generation" (16), was a common theme of European thought in the latter half of the nineteenth century. This world-view was often coupled, he says, with a "tormenting self-consciousness, precluding action or commitment," and arose from the sense of a personal "failure to translate the idea of freedom from political rhetoric to an inner autonomy" (148). Marx, Ruskin, Wagner, Nietzsche all decried the modern predicament—its mechanization and commercialism, its alienation and its aimless stagnation—which they all referred to as "decadence." They (except Marx) called for cultural redemption through art, Ruskin and Wagner looking for models in the medieval world and Nietzsche in the ancient Greek world. Russian literature of the nineteenth century (Turgenev, Tolstoy, Dostoyevsky, Chekhov) took this same aimlessness and weakness of will—the typical indicators of decadence—as one of its major themes.

277 Ralph Waldo Emerson, *Works and Days* (1870), in *Complete Works*, vol. 7 (Boston: Houghton Mifflin, 1904-12), 177.

278 From *Essays: First Series, 1841*, quoted by Wendell Garrett in *The Magazine Antiques* 148, no. 2 (August 1995). Presumably, then, Raphael's *School of Athens* or Michelangelo's *Last Judgment*—not to mention the picturesque horrors of Rubens's entire oeuvre, from portraits, to religious, to mythological works—would not appeal to modern "brave" and "plain-dealing" men.

279 Henry James, *Hawthorne* (London: Macmillan, 1897), 12–13.

280 Lowenthal, *Past*, 109–10. The internal citation is from R. W. B. Lewis.

281 Charles Bergengren, " 'Finished to the Utmost Nicety': Plain Portraits in America, 1780–1860," in *Folk Art in America*, ed. John Michael Vlach and Simon J. Brenner (Ann Arbor, Mich.: UMI Research, 1983), 85.

282 Like contemporary primitives who "straighten up" for "The Photographer."

283 Bergengren ("Finished," 85) observes that such stylistic preferences are revivals of a modality of painting not seen since Medieval times and thus American portraiture of this period appears "almost iconic." Early American portraiture that attempts to imitate the European style—representing the apotheosis of George Washington, as seen on the Capitol dome, for example—is usually inadvertently hilarious.

284 Wendell Garrett, editorial, *The Magazine Antiques* 133, no. 5 (May 1988): 1111.

285 Howard Mansfield, *The Same Ax Twice* (Hanover, N.H.: University Press of New England, 2000), 165. Speaking of Samuel Woodworth's poem "The Old Oaken Bucket," he adds, "Americans have sung about losing their hometowns almost as long as they have had hometowns."

286 Lowenthal, *Past*, 117–19. He believes this change can be detected in American culture as early as 1820, but one can find even earlier examples. Thomas Jefferson "when resident in Paris from 1784–89 had 86 packing crates of furniture shipped home to the U.S." Elspeth Montcrief, "Ebénistes Extraordinaires," *Antique Collector* 61 (September 1990): 69. Although one has no way of knowing precisely which among these shipped items were *antiques at the time* rather than contemporary pieces, since the *marchands-merciers* from whom Jefferson purchased them sold both old and new furnishings, Garry Wills, in his account of Jefferson's buying spree in Paris, itemizes "seven busts by Houdon, forty-eight formal chairs, Sèvres table sculptures of biscuit, damask hangings, four full-length mirrors in gilt frames, four marble-topped tables, 120 porcelain plates"; he adds that "some Sèvres work made for Louis XVI (it is unknown how he got it)" was among these imports, and notes that Jefferson "spent years in the quest for a silver replica of a pot found at Pompeii." Wills, "The Aesthete," *New York Review of Books* 40, no. 14 (August 12, 1993): 6–10. Although these facts are insufficient to demonstrate that Jefferson was a connoisseur of antiques in the modern sense, much of the preconditional mental attitude was there. And there is more. Back in Monticello, which Wills calls "the complex masterpiece that he lived in and used and contemplated," he furnished his entry hall ("my Indian hall") with painted buffalo robes, headdresses, moccasins, and warrior apparel. He spoke of himself as "acquiring artifacts for the improvement of national taste" and, according to Wills, "had a sense that his belongings would become relics from a sacred era." On the other hand, one might well argue that Jefferson was operating under a primarily European mentality anyway or that he was, as in many other ways, a man well ahead of his time and thus not typical of the American mentality. During the Revolution, Colonel James Swan, who was employed by the French Revolutionary Commission of Supplies to send over one hundred ships of wheat, leather, furs, and other goods from the United States to France, loaded these ships for their return voyage with French furniture and porcelain for auction. These ancien régime items did not sell well here. See Howard C. Rice, "James Swan: Agent of the French Republic, 1794–1796," *New England Quarterly* (September 1937): 467–76.

But there were other, more positive, examples. The Reverend William Bentley (1759–1819) of Salem, Mass., collected antiques of every kind and on a worldwide basis. He valued them both as relics with historical associations and as evidence of lost craft skills and local customs. He wrote: "I grieved to see the connection between the past and the present century so entirely lost. . . . There is something agreeable, if not great, in the primitive manners . . . everything in its own manners, and away, far away from present fashion." Elizabeth Stillinger, *The Antiquers* (New York: Knopf, 1980), 17–18. The first Medieval stained-glass windows arrived in America in 1803, purchased from La Sainte Chapelle by the Philadelphia merchant William Poyntell; and about the same time, Medieval manuscripts were avidly collected in Baltimore by Robert Gilmore Jr. Peale's Museum in Philadelphia owned a mail shirt as early as the eighteenth century. See Elizabeth Bradford Smith, "The Earliest Private Collectors," in *Medieval Art in America: Patterns of Collecting, 1800–1940* (University Park: Palmer Museum of Art / Pennsylvania State University Press, 1996).

287 The Melville citation is from his *Redburn* (1849). Both Melville and Holmes are quoted by Wendell Garrett in his editorial for *The Magazine Antiques* 132, no. 1 (1987): 119.

288 George Smith, Upholsterer to His Majesty, *Collection of Designs for Household Furniture and Interior Design* (1808; reprint, New York: Praeger, 1970).

289 Calloway, *Twentieth Century Decoration*, xi and 33.

290 Whether one cares to think of this diversity in terms of the contemporary metaphors of the "melting pot" or the "salad."

291 See Stillinger, *Antiquers*, xii.

292 Quoted in *The History of the Brooklyn and Long Island Fair, February 22, 1864* (Brooklyn, N.Y., 1864), 73, and Stillinger, *Antiquers*, 8–9.

293 See *Catalogue of Antique Articles on Exhibition at Plummer Hall*, Salem, Mass., 1875 (Press of the Salem Gazette, 1875).

294 See Stillinger, *Antiquers*, xii. Thus, today, by this measure—which derives from the same attitude as Emerson's love for the humble object of the roadside—Hitler's personal pair of binoculars or the gloves alleged to have been worn by O. J. Simpson have greater "beauty" for many than a magisterial proto-Renaissance painting of unknown provenance and authorship. "Beauty" aside, the former examples would certainly have greater appeal to the mentality concerned with the relic, the memento, the collectible, and the trophy.

295 The tangible achievements of Morris and the Pre-Raphaelites of England inspired U.S. artists and taste as much as the doctrines of Eastlake. Eastlake influenced American furniture in the person of Gustav Stickley. Morris inspired Elbert Hubbard, who in 1895 established the Roycrofters, a community of craftsmen in East Aurora, New York, which in turn influenced Frank Lloyd Wright, who was a founding member of the Chicago Society of Arts and Crafts. The austerity and simplicity of structural forms, the truth to material, the linear and plain surface decoration of their products contrasted sharply with the frills of Victoriana. In some ways it paralleled but in others it was inconsistent with the contemporary artisans of the "Art Nouveau" movement (especially those like L. C. Tiffany, who preferred the subtly shimmering and glowing surface and organic and curvilinear forms, having much in common with the Rococo).

296 Quoted in Stillinger, *Antiquers*, 58–60. Thoreau said much the same: "How much more agreeable it is to sit in the midst of old furniture like Minott's clock, and secretary and looking-glass, which have come down from other generations, than amid that which was just brought from the cabinetmaker's, smelling of varnish, like a coffin! To sit under the face of an old clock that has been ticking one hundred and fifty years—there is something mortal, not to say immortal, about it; a clock that began to tick when Massachusetts was a province." Quoted in Stillinger, *Antiquers*, 7.

297 Wharton and Codman, *Decoration of Houses*, 187–89.

298 This is an argument familiar to readers since the beginning of art criticism. See Plato, *Republic* 402–403.

299 Perry Macquiod's four-volume *History of English Furniture*, the first comprehensive study of the subject, appeared in 1904.

300 Wharton herself recommended the preference for classical French antiques.

301 As early as the 1840s Emerson and Thoreau looked to Hinduism and Buddhism for inspiration. In 1883 the Reverend Phillips Brooks (rector of Boston's Trinity Church), on a trek to the temple at Bodh-gaya (where the Buddha attained enlightenment), wrote home, "In these days, when a large part of Boston [he meant the Lodges, Adamses, and Cabots and the artists and intellectuals of his congregation] prefers to consider itself Buddhist rather than Christian . . . I consider this pilgrimage to be the duty of a minister who preaches to Bostonians." Quoted in Christopher Benfey, *The Great Wave: Gilded Age Misfits, Japanese Eccentrics, and the Opening of Old Japan* (New York: Random House, 2003), xii.

302 Benfey, *Great Wave*, 19.

303 Ibid., 38.

304 In 1879 Edward Sylvester Morse, who was then employed as professor of zoology at the Imperial University in Tokyo, expanded his interest in seashells to include the collecting and appreciation of antique Japanese pottery, as Benfey (*Great Wave*) notes: "Through the tea ceremony, Morse discovered in turn the whole aesthetic world of 'tea taste,' with its emphasis on rustic simplicity, irregularity, muted colors, and contrasts of rough and smooth. This is the *wabi* aesthetic associated with sixteenth-century tea master Sen no Rikyo." After delivering a series of lectures on Japanese folkways at the Lowell Institute in Boston, he returned to Japan in 1882 on a final journey "as a collector, pure and simple," with the express purpose of preserving Old Japan (already abandoning its ancient practices and objects for their Western counterparts) from imminent extinction. (This concern on the part of Westerners to preserve the ancient arts and artifacts of foreign civilizations, and to do so despite pressure from the locals to overcome or ignore—even to despise and destroy—their own heritage, is mirrored throughout the world of Morse's contemporaries: one thinks especially of the French, Italians, and British in Egypt.) On his return to Boston, Morse wrote *Japanese Homes*, a book that "became a pattern book for American builders of Victorian houses" (and later inspired the likes of Frank Lloyd Wright), and left his collection of Japanese pottery to the Museum of Fine Arts in Boston. See Benfey, *Great Wave*, 63–70. It was Morse who brought Ernest Fenellosa to Japan to teach the works of Hegel and Emerson, but soon the direction of education reversed, and Fenellosa learned and spread the traditions of Japanese culture to the West.

I believe the late nineteenth century marks the transition from *japonaiserie* to *japonism* in the West. What the difference in terminology connotes is this: "japonaiserie" is a characterization of subject matter (generally referring to *what* is depicted) whereas "japonism" is a term referring to manner whereby and foundation wherefrom (materials, techniques, proportions, and the like) the work is constructed (the *how*). That is, in the prior period Japan was the source for "quotations" and decorative motifs (fans, cherry blossoms) whose exotic qualities aroused the imagination to wishful fantasies, but thereafter Japan became the source of primary stylistic structural devices (such as unconventional perspective in painting and unusual angles and planes in architecture) that more fundamentally underlie and create the Japanese aesthetic. These stylistic devices came to be exploited in the avant-garde artistic creations of the West in the late nineteenth and early twentieth centuries.

305 Benfey, *Great Wave*, 143.

306 William P. Hood Jr., "Western Dining Implements with Japanese Kokuza and Kokuza Style Handles," *The Magazine Antiques* 165, no. 1 (January 2004): 142–49.

307 Stillinger, *Antiquers*, 25.

308 Ibid., 28.

309 See Smith, "Earliest Private Collectors."

310 See the full account in Alpine B. Saarinen, *The Proud Possessors* (New York: Random House, 1958), 27–55.

311 Barrymore Laurence Scherer, "Robber Baronial," *Art and Auction*, May 1995, 116–21.

312 Calloway, *Twentieth Century Decoration*, 62.

313 Ruhling, "They Came, They Saw," 101–2.

314 Ibid., 102.

315 As Scherer describes the situation: "New York City had the greatest concentration of tycoons . . . and Fifth Avenue was *their* street, nearly two miles of mock-Renaissance and medieval palazzi, châteaux and fortresses along the verdant expanse of Central Park. Here lived the Haights, Goulds, Belmonts, Astors and other plutocrats in regal style. . . . With their humble origins a mere generation behind them—if that—the Carnegies, Rockefellers, Haggins and Fricks sought to conquer the heights of social position by buying the trappings of an aristocratic heritage." "Robber Baronial," 117.

316 Alice Cooney Frelinghuysen, "Christian Herter's Decoration of the W. H. Vanderbilt House in New York City," *The Magazine Antiques* 147, no. 3 (March 1995): 408–17.

317 The carpet, also used in "The Breakers," was sold at Christie's in 1989 for a then record sum for an oriental carpet of $720,000. See *Christie's International Magazine*, March–April 1995, 12.

318 Frelinghuysen, "Herter's Decoration."

319 Scherer, "Robber Baronial," 120.

320 David Hewett, "Antiques and the Great Depression," *Maine Antiques Digest*, June 1999, 32–33-C. See Stillinger, *Antiquers*, and also Gerald Reitlinger, *The Economics of Taste: The Rise and Fall of the Objets d'Art Market since 1750* (New York: Holt, Rinehart, and Winston, 1963), for additional details.

321 Hewett, "Antiques," 32-C.

322 These terms are derived from the alternate names for this movement as it appeared in different countries: "Art Nouveau" in France, "stile liberty" in Italy (admittedly derived from the name of a bookshop), "Jugendstil" in Germany, "Secessionismus" in Austria, and, peculiarly, "Yachting style" by the Goncourts.

323 Its attack on mass production and appeal to the medieval craftsman ideal also connected it with the "Arts and Crafts" movement.

324 Quoted in Edward P. Alexander, *Museum Masters* (Nashville, Tenn.: American Association for State and Local History, 1983), 87.

325 Roger Frye, *Transformations* (1926; Garden City, N.Y.: Doubleday, Anchor Books, 1956), 166.

326 Calloway, *Twentieth Century Decoration*, 60.

327 T. J. Jackson Lears, *No Place of Grace: Antimodernism and the Transformation of American Culture, 1880–1920* (New York: Pantheon, 1981), 186–87.

328 Ibid., 191–92. Lears goes on: "The emergence of art as a religious surrogate posed a significant dilemma for liberal Protestants. Traditionally hostile toward graven images, they nevertheless increasingly felt the emotional power of Catholic art and symbolism. . . . The problem became acute as Protestant congregations built Gothic churches, decorated their interiors, and elaborated their services with music and ritual."

329 Lears, *No Place of Grace*, 188.

330 The New York auction figure for 1938, which included the huge collection of William Randolph Hearst, was only a third of the 1928–29 sales totals. See Hewett, "Antiques," 33-C.

331 Ralph Edwards, *Decoration* (1936).

332 See also Allen Eaton, *Immigrant Gifts to American Life* (New York: Russell Sage, 1932), which describes various ethnic and folk art exhibitions in America between 1919 and 1932.

333 Hewett, "Antiques," 33-C.

334 See his *Goodbye Mr. Chippendale* (New York: Knopf, 1944) and *Homes of the Brave* (New York: Knopf, 1954). Later in life Robsjohn-Gibbings became obsessed with the study of the furnishings and decor of the ancient world and retired to an apartment in Athens with a view of the Acropolis.

335 Max Ernst, "What Is the Mechanism of Collage?" (1936), in *Theories of Modern Art*, ed. Herschel B. Chipp (Berkeley: University of California Press, 1969), 427.

336 Salvador Dali, "The Object as Revealed in Surrealist Experiment" (1931), in Chipp, *Theories of Modern Art*, 417–27.

337 Walter Benjamin, "The Work of Art in the Mechanical Age of Reproduction," in *Illuminations*, ed. Hannah Arendt, trans. Harry Zohn (New York: Harcourt, Brace, and World, 1968; reprint, Glasgow: Fontana / Collins, 1973), 219-53. Andrew Hussey similarly notes, "The Surrealists were obsessed with images and objects that were just about to become out of date and lose their original meaning or function." *Paris: The Secret History* (New York: Bloomsbury, 2006), 333.

338 The leader of the Surrealists, André Breton, was an avid collector of African masks, as was the Dadaist's primary spokesman, Tristan Tzara. The Surrealists opposed colonialism on the grounds that no civilization is inherently superior to another and thus all their art productions are of equal worth.

339 See Arthur C. Danto, *The Transfiguration of the Commonplace* (Cambridge, Mass.: Harvard University Press, 1981). See also Danto, "The End of Art," in *The Death of Art*, ed. Berel Lang (New York: Haven, 1984); "Art after the End of Art," in *Embodied Meanings* (New York: Farrar, Straus and Giroux, 1994); *The Philosophical Disenfranchisement of Art* (New York: Columbia University Press, 1986); *Philosophizing Art* (Berkeley: University of California Press, 1999); and *Beyond the Brillo Box* (New York: Farrar, Straus and Giroux, 1992). See also my "End of Art Theory."

340 Kasimir Malevich, "Suprematism," (from *The Non-objective World*), in Chipp, *Theories of Modern Art*, 344.

341 See especially the works of Danto (note 339) and my "End of Art Theory."

342 A century earlier Nietzsche had described the artists of his time as "the sons of a scholarly, tormented, and reflective generation—a thousand miles removed from the old masters, who did not read and only thought of feasting their eyes." Friedrich Nietzsche, *The Will to Power*, trans. W. Kaufmann and R. J. Hollingdale (New York: Random House, 1967), 437.

343 And being "evidence for" or "an instance of" is not a felicitous status or basis for an object's being able to elicit an affective response.

344 To cite one extraordinary instance: Sotheby's announced in January 2004 that it would auction off the entire Malcolm Forbes collection of Imperial Russian Easter Eggs in April of that year. By February it was announced that the auction would not occur. Rather, Sotheby's had brokered a private sale between the Forbes family and Viktor Vekselberg (one of the new Russia's super-rich) for the entire collection. The sales price was never officially disclosed, but experts in the field assume it to have been $100 million. Sotheby's had predicted that the collection at auction would achieve a minimum of $90 million. See articles by Carol Vogel, *New York Times*, January 9 and February 5, 2004.

3. The Ten Criteria of Antiques

1 We have also noted that the "foreignness" that decontextualizes (un-worlds) the object may sometimes "substitute" for pastness, if only in the sense of eliciting a similar aesthetic response. Moreover, some objects (archelogical artifacts) may be *too old* to be antiques.

2 When we consider "quality," naturally the idea of "beauty" comes to mind. This concept we have already dealt with in the first chapter as best we could. In a nutshell, the

object must "shine forth" in its world situation with sufficient power and internal unity or coherence to be able to refer us to something beyond itself (transcendence) and thus must create its own world (distracting us from the everyday one)—either the world interior to (generated by) the work or the one in which the work originally functioned and to which we are referred by the work, or both.

3 Although we cannot pursue the issue here, the aesthetic categories of the "ugly" and the "grotesque" have often been analyzed and debated in the philosophy of art and art criticism. For example, Theodor W. Adorno's discussion of the "categories of the ugly" in his *Aesthetic Theory*, trans. Robert Hullot-Kentor (Minneapolis: University of Minnesota Press, 1996).

4 Quoted from George M. Young, "A Box Score for Quality," *Maine Antique Digest*, April 1995, 20-B. Young proceeds to rank in precise detail and descending order of appeal other subjects that are generally and inherently less and less attractive in paintings: elegantly dressed women enjoying themselves in sumptuous surroundings is ranked next (i.e., second), followed by exotic persons (foreign, ethnic), landscapes with small figures and animals, then harbor scenes, followed by ordinary objects extraordinarily painted, followed by religious themes, a "nude with body hair, hanging dead fish, a racially or ethnically insensitive caricature, [and finally] a big abstract thing if being sold more than 80 miles from New York" coming in last. His ranking is, admittedly, really more a matter of salability than of attractiveness or beauty—but the connection is not accidental.

5 This is also true of the fine art object, though as explained above, this past and use-world is rarely attended to, so that old paintings, for example, are usually—and incorrectly—not thought of as "antiques."

6 Of course, there are collectors and connoisseurs of all these categories.

7 This, I suspect, is due to that fact that the sculpture is a three-dimensional embodiment of a three-dimensional subject, whereas the painting is a two-dimensional surface creating the illusion of a three-dimensional object; and therefore the imagination has to do more "filling in" of the missing part in the latter instance.

8 Quoted by Alexander Stille, "Faking It," *New Yorker*, June 15, 1998, 36–37. The Japanese shrine at Ise is deliberately destroyed and rebuilt exactly the same at regular intervals.

9 Elspeth Moncrief, "Ebénistes Extraordinaire," *Antique Collector* 61 (September 1990): 69.

10 Indeed, modern taste so far expects sculpture in the classical style as a genre to show age through damage that it has even been suggested that the reason Thorvaldsen's (1770–1844) neo-classical statues are, for all their excellence in other respects, unpopular is that being in that style and genre they *should* show signs of age too—but do not. See Robert Adams, *The Lost Museum: Glimpses of Vanished Originals* (New York: Viking Press, 1980), 226. Worse still, such original ancient Greek statues as were dug up in the sixteenth through eighteenth centuries and that did not confirm to the presumed classical ideal of the time (based on such already canonical works as the "Apollo Belvedere") were not only "skinned" for cleaning but recut to conform to that false ideal, thereby destroying more than the patina of age. It is only since the end of the nineteenth century that a small fragment of a fifth-century B.C. Attic statue in its "as found" condition has been deemed preferable to a large and perfect Roman copy; and no one now would think of adding a missing arm to a broken original—Greek or Roman. See Joseph Alsop, *The Rare Art Traditions* (New York: Harper and Row), 8–10.

11 See C. K. Binns, "The Importance of Patina on Old English Furniture," *Antique Collector* 42 (1970): 58–64. On patination of bronzes, see Phoebe D. Weil, "A Review of the History and Practice of Patination," in *Corrosion and Metal Artifacts*, ed. B. Floyd Brown et al. (Washington, D.C.: U.S. Department of Commerce, 1977), and R. J. Gettins,

"Patina: Noble and Vile," in *Art and Technology: A Symposium on Classical Bronzes*, ed. Susannah Doeringer, David Gordon Mitten, and Arthur Steinberg (Cambridge, Mass.: MIT Press, 1970).

12 There are two contemporary watchdog agencies that try to combat restoration, Art Watch International and the Association pour le Respect de l'Integrité du Patrimonie Artistique. But the resistance to restoration is not a purely twenty-first-century phenomenon. The English counterpart to Viollet-le-Duc in the nineteenth century was James Wyatt, known by the nickname "the Destroyer" by his purist foes Ruskin and Pugin.

13 This does not mean that necessarily stone endures while paper or canvas does not: descriptions and drawings of destroyed monuments have sometimes long outlasted their famous subjects. A preliminary sketch by Titian for a great series of paintings of the Twelve Caesars has outlasted the original set, destroyed by an Alcazar fire in 1734, and Michelangelo's sketch of a figure from Masaccio's fresco "La Sagra del Carmine" (completed in the 1420s) has survived but the fresco was destroyed in the 1590s.

14 David Lowenthal, *The Past Is a Foreign Country* (Cambridge: Cambridge University Press, 1985), 161.

15 René Huyghe, "The Louvre Museum and the Problem of the Cleaning of Old Paintings," *Museum* 3 (1950): 191–206.

16 Lowenthal (*Past*, 163) quotes an observer of the restored paintings in New York's Frick Collection: they all "look, he said, as though they had been painted by the same artist, probably an impressionist!" Richard Boston, "The Lady Varnishes," *The Guardian*, September 25, 1981, 11.

17 See Adams, *Lost Museum*, 223.

18 Howard Mansfield, in *The Same Ax, Twice* (Hanover, N.H.: University Press of New England, 2000), speaks of the museum's "epoxy-essence" that freezes the object in time, and argues for a restoration that contains "its opposite: going away, softening, decay. Even the most meticulously preserved object, all glittering and pristine, should hint of its fate" (53, 273). He goes even further: "Curators are condemned to live on a planet where the fingertips of earthlings leave behind acid that tarnishes silver, where bronze and pewter are prone to 'diseases' and dust can defeat a suit of medieval armor. . . . Sunlight, air, and water sustain us and destroy us. Life consumes all we wish to save" (53).

19 G. Y. Dryanski, "Arts of the Restorer," *Connoisseur*, April 1988, 108–13.

20 The current director, Mme André, quoted in ibid.

21 See Sandra Andacht, *Oriental Antiques and Art* (Greensboro, N.C.: Wallace/Homestead, 1989), 414–15.

22 Francis Sparshott, "Why Artworks Have No Right to Have Rights," *Journal of Aesthetics and Art Criticism* 42, no. 1 (1983): 13. As an interesting side note, in 1719 the pope had to decree that all excavation in Rome must cease; so excessive were the depredations caused by Romans' random excavation for antiques in their own city that they risked reducing it again to ruins.

23 Walter Kaufmann, *Time Is an Artist* (New York: Reader's Digest Press, 1978), 28.

24 Etienne Gilson, *Painting and Reality* (London: Routledge and Kegan Paul, 1957), 99.

25 Quoted by Wendell Garrett in *The Magazine Antiques* 150, no. 3 (September 1996): 315.

26 I have already discussed style but offer the following gloss on the preceding definition: style is the ensemble of distinguishable and distinctive characteristics (of both form and content) of a given work which, due to their relative repetition and stability, makes that work comparable with others and which has resulted from the various choices (both conscious and unconscious) made by its creator from among the variable strategies available within (1) the laws (i.e., the invariable parameters) of the genre and (2) the taste (the variable cultural-historical preferences) of his time, place, and culture. This is a definition

derived from Kendall L. Walton, "Style and the Processes of Art," in *The Concept of Style*, ed. Berel Lang (Ithaca: Cornell University Press, 1987), 72–103. That the recognition of the stylistic features of a work and the recognition of its aesthetic significance (meaning) are *mutually interdependent* activities, however, is well demonstrated by Jenefer M. Robinson, "Style and Significance in Art History and Art Criticism," in *The Philosophy of the Visual Arts*, ed. Philip Alperson (New York: Oxford University Press, 1992), 481–89.

27 Peter Thornton claims that there is a "period eye" that understands style as a "measure of the degree of emptiness or clutter, or of plainness or embellishment, in interiors which people seem to find pleasing at a particular time." Quoted in Stephen Calloway, *Twentieth Century Decoration* (London: Weidenfeld and Nicholson, 1988), 12.

28 There is the even more perplexing question, why do styles change? Is it that people invariably in different times and places and over varying durations get tired of "the same old"? Is it that influences extrinsic to art—technical advances, or sudden archeological discoveries, or economic, social, and political transformations, or the vicissitudes of war and trade, of science and wealth—bring about stylistic change? Or is it that the possibilities inherent in any style are not infinite and that consequently after a considerable number of possibilities have been worked out and all the interesting ones realized, the style somehow dialectically generates its own overcoming into the "next" style?

For example, after the discovery of Pompeii in 1748 there was a neo-classical revival that lasted for about eighty years. Did the archeological find *cause* this or was it simply that the rococo had died out, that people wanted something different, even antipodal (and classical is about as far as one can get stylistically from rococo), or that classical was due for another of its cyclical renewals? Style may (or may not) be separable from fashion, which seems more like a subcategory of style. Just before the French Revolution, Parisian ladies of fashion wore fantastic white hairstyles in the shape of a ship to commemorate the sinking of *La Belle Poule* in 1778. During the Revolution they took to wearing thin red ribbons around their necks, a style called, aptly but somewhat gruesomely, "à la guillotine." Shortly thereafter, on the restoration under Charles X, the monarch being presented with the gift of a giraffe by the khedive of Egypt, for the next few years the social and economic success of everything depended on its being "à la giraffe."

29 But such sculpture is refashioned and often curtailed by current taste. A huge nude marble figure of Napoleon decorates the entryway to Apsley House, a gift to Wellington from the British Parliament in gratitude for his defeat of *L'Empereur*. Could we imagine a comparable nude statue of Saddam Hussein given by the U.S. Congress to General Sanchez or President Bush?

30 James Fenton, "On Statues," *New York Review of Books* 43, no. 2 (February 1, 1996): 38.

31 Ibid.

32 Maurice Rheims, *The Strange Life of Objects*, trans. David Pryce-Jones (New York: Atheneum, 1961), 115.

33 Rheims, *Strange Life of Objects*, 117. Rheims goes on to note that Napoleon's loot from Spain was so massive that the roads were clogged for a year with transports crossing the border, and crates were still being delayed in Bayonne when the emperor was forced to abdicate.

34 Sir William Walton, formerly director of the Wallace Collection in London, recounts how when he opened the first exhibition ever held that had as its theme these European-mounted Chinese porcelains at the Chinese Institute of America, he began his welcoming speech, "I imagine most of you here this evening think I have organized an exhibition of desecrated Chinese porcelain." No one in the assembled company uttered any "audible sounds of dissent." Sir Francis J. B. Walton, "Mounted Oriental Porcelain," in *The International Antique Dealers Show Exhibition Catalogue, New York, October*

6–10, 1990 (New York: National Art and Antique Dealers' Association of America, 1990), 42–47.

35 Young, "Box Score for Quality," 20-B.

36 It is true that nine was fixed for the number of muses rather late in antiquity. Were one to find another number of them, either the antique in question would be very ancient indeed and this divergence would be good evidence for that belief (though not likely for a set of paintings, which unless in some medium other than canvas would have long since deteriorated) or it would be simply a quirk or mistake on the part of their maker—though without other independent evidence for the latter alternative, it would rather count against the set, making it *in*complete.

37 A colleague in the antiques trade has suggested to me "pre-barcode label" as the cut-off date.

38 Auction sales catalogues often rival the most scholarly studies of objects in their authentications. They are also as prone to puffery and hype as the enticements of the sleaziest salesperson.

39 Walter Benjamin defines "authenticity": "The authenticity of a thing is the essence of all that is transmissible from its beginning, ranging from its substantive duration to its testimony to the history which it has experienced." *Illuminations*, ed. Hannah Arendt, trans. Harry Zohn (Glasgow: Fontana / Collins, 1973), 223. But as we see below, it is not as helpful in practice as it is reasonable in theory.

40 Eric Hebborn, *Drawn to Trouble: Confessions of a Master Forger* (New York: Random House, 1991), 115.

41 Quoted in Ernst Gombrich, "Dark Varnishes," in *Art and Illusion* (Princeton, N.J.: Princeton University Press, 1969), 58.

42 Quoted in Otto Kurz, "Time the Painter," *Burlington Magazine* (1963), 96.

43 Quoted in Kaufmann, *Time Is an Artist*, 65.

44 See especially Dennis Dutton, ed., *The Forger's Art* (Berkeley: University of California Press, 1983); Sarah Walden, *The Ravished Image* (London: Weidenfeld and Nicholson, 1985); and the work of Nelson Goodman, e.g., "Art and Authenticity," in Dutton, *Forger's Art*, 93–114.

45 With Ogden Codman Jr., *The Decoration of Houses* (New York: Scribner's, 1914), 191.

46 Rubens's correspondence with his clients shows three prices. The highest price was demanded for canvases painted entirely by himself. A lower price was charged for works he did in outline or sketch and to which he added the final touches after his assistants did the oil painting. The lowest price was for works from his studio that he had no part in creating except, perhaps, for offering advice and certifying the finished product.

47 See Dutton, *Forger's Art*.

48 See Sándor Radnóti, *The Fake*, trans. Ervin Dunai (Lanham, Md.: Rowman and Littlefield, 1999), 109.

49 Nelson Goodman, *Languages of Art*, 2nd ed. (Indianapolis, Ind.: Hackett, 1976).

50 The greatest forger of the early twentieth century was one Icilio Federico Joni, whose career is brilliantly recorded in his autobiography, *Affairs of a Painter* (Siena: Protagon, 2004 [text in English and Italian]), and whose successful sales to Bernard Berenson still grace the walls of the Villa I Tatti. In the nineteenth and early twentieth centuries the great forgers were Bastianini (1830–68) and Dossena (1878–1937). Italy seems to be the favored locale for the world's great fakers, and has been since the Renaissance. The Venetian Marco Boschini in his 1660 satirical poem on the art world of his city warned of contemporary art faking, which included "smoking" to age and "elaborately gilded" frames to entice the unwary. But there are innumerable others and extensive histories of their "achievements."

51 Examples of generic style: sentimental children's portraits are typical of the nineteenth but not the eighteenth century; if the eyes of the gilded bronze caryatids on the purported

eighteenth-century French *bureau plat* look a bit narrow and tilted, it may be a twentieth-century Thai or Taiwanese or Chinese fake.

52 The determination is not always easy. It is generally assumed that a piece of furniture made in France before the Revolution should be significantly different from one made under Charles X or Napoleon III. But suppose a cabinet maker who was 25 years old in 1789 was asked in 1830 at the age of 65 by new amateurs of the style of the ancien régime to create a piece in the Louis XIV style; or suppose his son continued in the same shop, working in the same way with the same tools, and in 1880 by new amateurs of this same style was asked to produce a similar piece. We would likely have a whole century of uncertainty for establishing the authenticity of the piece. See Maurice Rheims, *The Glorious Obsession* (New York: St. Martin's Press, 1980), 275.

53 Ann Headington, "The Great Cellini," *Connoisseur*, September 1986, 98–103.

54 See Goodman, *Languages of Art*.

55 Lowenthal, *Past*, 344 and n. 278. Italics mine.

56 Souren Melikian, "Lure of the Instant Image," *Art and Auction*, January 11, 1999, 24.

57 Bk. I, pt. 4, sec. 6.

58 I would guess that there are as many antiques purporting to be from the Warhole Estate, the Garbo Estate, or the Liberace Estate as there are splinters in European reliquaries purporting to be fragments of the True Cross.

59 Hector Feliciano, *The Lost Museum: The Nazi Conspiracy to Steal the World's Greatest Works of Art* (New York: Basic Books, 1997), 51.

60 André Malraux, *The Voices of Silence* (London: Stecker and Warburg, 1954), 635.

61 And probably this is further due to the fact that anything which the genteel classes could not have afforded after (and as a consequence of) the Civil War appears nouveau riche and foreign.

62 Harry Rinker, *How to Make the Most of Your Investments in Antiques and Collectibles* (New York: Morrow, Avon Books, 1988).

63 Gaylord Dillingham has noted: "The antiques bought for our homes are by and large a reflection of fashion and popular appeal, not educated taste . . . [so that] antiques are, often, too good for the people who own them." "Letter from London," *Antiques West*, October 1988, 40.

64 Quoted of an "antiques collector of considerable taste" by Brian Morgan, president of the British Antique Dealers Association.

65 See especially Gerald Reitlinger, *The Economics of Taste* (New York: Holt, Rinehart, and Winston, 1963), and Wendy Smith, "Art and Finance," *Art and Antiques*, February 1986, 83–84.

66 Rheims, *Glorious Obsession*, 45.

4. Conclusion: Antiques and Civilization

1 See Samuel P. Huntington, *The Clash of Civilizations and the Remaking of the Modern World Order* (New York: Simon and Schuster, 1996); Martha Nussbaum, *For Love of Country* (Boston: Beacon Press, 1996); and T. M. Scanlon, *What We Owe to Each Other* (Cambridge, Mass.: Harvard University Press, Belknap Press, 1999).

2 Huntington, *Clash of Civilizations*.

3 We could note associated forms of resistance: the "purification" of national languages from the pollutions of English, the refusal to wear the standard business attire of the West (adopting instead a traditional costume or keeping the basic Western mode with some significant deletion—the Western businessman's tie, for example).

4 The converse is well known: in order to despise another people or civilization, one disinherits it, destroying its achievements and obliterating its history. Even within one's *own* civilization, revolutions always begin by blowing up the past "to make room for the future"—at least they start out that way.

5 Consider the currently fashionable "prisoner look."

6 Joseph Alsop, *The Rare Art Traditions* (New York: Harper and Row, 1980), especially 31–32 and 294–97.

7 Even if true, this objection does not disprove the general claim regarding the civilizational benefit of antiques for the rest—those who *do* have this awareness and sensitivity, regardless of any money to be made. (I might also note, by way of analogy, that even if many people are delighted to take a tax deduction for charitable contributions on their income tax forms, this does not mean that charity per se, even among those who gladly take the deduction, does not exist or would cease to exist if the monetary benefit disappeared.) In any case, however unhistorically sophisticated some antiques dealers may be compared with the world's great connoisseur-collectors, and however concerned with the monetary values of their antiques they may really be, I have never personally known one who furnished his home with Ikea.

8 See G. W. F. Hegel, *Lectures on the Philosophy of History*, trans. H. B. Nisbet (Cambridge: Cambridge University Press, 1975), 135–37.

9 This gathering produces what Hegel calls the "Aufhebung des Daseins"—the "sublation of existence."

10 See also G. W. F. Hegel, *Phenomenology of Mind*, trans. J. B. Baillie (London: Allen and Unwin, 1961), for a complete account of this "gathering." Avoiding the necessity of Hegel's dialectic and the reductionist form of his philosophy, one could agree that civilization per se is a "collection" of the achievements of all cultures. Hegel was not the first to say this about civilizations. Giovanni Battista Vico, in his *Scienza Nuova* (1744), asserted that all cultural epochs must recapitulate or revive their pasts in order to discover themselves. Nor was Hegel the last philosopher of civilization to make the point.

11 Perhaps this is another reason, besides the fact that they show no material marks of aging, that Thorvaldsen's sculptures appear to many to be "soulless Greek." The quotation in the text is from Wassily Kandinsky, *Concerning the Spiritual in Art*, portions of which are reprinted in *The Philosophy of the Visual Arts*, ed. Philip Alperson (New York: Oxford University Press, 1992), 129–45.

12 Ibid., 135–36. This is a rather Hegelian view, in the long run, and one that makes us wonder what Kandinsky thinks there is in the work and/or in humanity that enables this "inner mood" to endure through time and to revive or produce such "affinities" among different civilizations and generations of later times. It cannot be the "inner spirit" itself—for this, according to Kandinsky, is a matter entirely of the formal and timeless properties of the medium, viz., it appears only in terms of the necessary effects of choices regarding the use of specific colors and shapes, as he explains.

13 See Clive Bell's *Art*, excerpted in Alperson, *Philosophy of the Visual Arts*, 126.

14 Clive Bell, *Art* (New York: Putnam, Capricorn Books, 1958), 75.

15 The "I" that the nuclear family, cocooned (marooned) in its home, has barely managed to sustain.

16 Think of cars, computers, toasters, clothes—whose obsolescence need no longer even be deliberately preplanned because their materials and construction techniques (e.g., the plastic screws used in car interiors, the gigabytes of our computers) make them disintegrate or otherwise incompetent; in fact, their rapid disutility through obsolescence (e.g., cell phones) even precedes their material disintegration.

17 I use the phrase "uncanny environment" as a poor equivalent of what would appear in German as *unheimliche Umwelt*—a surrounding world from which we feel estranged

and in which we are uncomfortably ill at ease, un-at-home. It is a world in which we find nothing in which we can recognize our unique selves, but where we find things belonging anywhere or to anyone else.

18 See Gordon S. Wood, "The American Love Boat," a review of *Sentimental Democracy*, by Andrew Burstein, in *New York Review of Books* 46, no. 15 (October 7, 1999). The relevance of "sensibility" for the aesthetic theories of Shaftesbury and Kant is noted in chapters 1 and 2.

19 There are fundamental universals. In all languages there are metaphors, puns, alliterations—just as in all human experience there are sorrows for life lost and joy for hope regained.

20 Immanuel Kant, *Critique of Judgment*, §§1–60. Within the context of his whole system of philosophy Kant went further in his appeal to the consequences of these claims. Beauty, he thought, confirms that there are subjectively sufficient grounds for the belief in freedom and thus affirms the human community of moral agents who collectively constitute civilization. To use Kant's own terminology, if autonomy is a regulative principle, its subjective justification may be found in the aesthetic feeling provided by two other regulative principles: the *sensus communis* and the "purposiveness" to be found in those representations that we call beautiful. That is, perhaps the very possibility of being motivated by the moral law is based on the possibility of the human agent's being able to imagine the factual success of his will (and all wills like his) appearing within the world of experience, an appearance whose "symbolic" representation is beauty. The beautiful then provides the possibility of (or assurance for, even if no "proof of") this moral motivation.

21 From *The Moral Obligation to Be Intelligent: Selected Essays*, ed. Leon Wieseltier (New York: Farrar, Straus and Giroux, 2000), as quoted by Andrew Delbanco, "Night Vision," *New York Review of Books* 48, no. 1 (January 11, 2001), 41.

22 See Benedetto Croce, *The Aesthetic as the Science of Expression and of the Linguistic in General*, trans. Colin Lyas (Cambridge: Cambridge University Press, 1992), 57.

23 Howard Mansfield, *The Same Ax Twice* (Hanover, N.H.: University Press of New England, 2000), 273.

24 Nelson Goodman, *Languages of Art*, quoted in Alperson, *Philosophy of the Visual Arts*, 89.

25 Were the terms not so loaded one would be tempted to modify "civilization" with "modern" or "advanced."

26 Hans-Georg Gadamer, *The Relevance of the Beautiful, and Other Essays*, ed. Robert Bernasconi, trans. N. Walker (Cambridge: Cambridge University Press, 1986), 30.

27 The predilection for the primitive as the opposite to or alternative of the antique has been noticed. Whereas the antique is supposed to burden us with the stultifying weight of tradition, the primitive art object "restores the spontaneity of youth" (see Jacques Barzun, *The Use and Abuse of Art* [Princeton, N.J.: Princeton University Press, 1974], 80–81). In its ahistoricality, it is supposed to speak with a voice eternally valid (perhaps an echo of Freud's "what is primitive in man is ineradicable") and, in its absence of elitism (specialization, academicism, and other hierarchies of the "art world"), to bespeak the moral superiority of a utopian democratic egalitarianism. It has been argued that prior to Romanticism, no one could have appreciated New World art for its purely aesthetic qualities. Thus, Christian F. Feest claims that Albrecht Dürer was impressed only by its value, exoticism, and craftsmanship: see his "The Arrival of Tribal Objects in the West," in *Primitivism in Modern Art*, vol. 1, ed. William Rubin (New York: Museum of Modern Art), 85. (But, as I have quoted his actual words earlier, I do not think this is true.) Besides primitivism, a similar predilection has been noted for novelty among living artists in cultures that have developed the aesthetic of the antique. Praxiteles' novel realism ca. 350 B.C. (the culmination of a rapid development in Greek sculpture over barely a century) may have provoked his

contemporary Plato to offer conservative praise for Egyptian sculpture (see *Sophist* 235e–236a and *Laws* 656d–e). Plato also noted (*Republic* 560–64) the curious affinity of the democratic temper for extreme novelty along with its anxious discontent with the present. He would no doubt find in the spirit of modernity—its rejection of traditional values along with its unbridled pursuit of new pleasures of infinite variety—a contemporary analogue of the "democratic soul."

28 Nietzsche also used the metaphor of "more Chinese" (see *The Genealogy of Morality*, ¶12).

29 Though not without a hint of uneasiness, a certain piquant fear for the unforeseeable consequence, soothed by a correlative comforting faith in the innate power of "the best in the species" to overcome any and all adversity.

30 Gadamer, *Relevance of the Beautiful*, 26–28.

31 As Shakespeare wrote in *Midsummer Night's Dream*: "imagination bodies forth the forms of things unknown . . . and gives to airy nothing a local habitation and a name." Act V, scene 1, lines 14, 15.

32 Johan Huizinga, *Homo Ludens: A Study of the Play-Element in Culture* (Boston: Beacon Press, 1955), 210.

33 Plato, *Laws* 803–4 and 685.

34 Huizinga, *Homo Ludens*, 162.

35 Aristotle, *Politics* 1339a29. The Greek says: σχολάζειν δύναθι καλώς.

36 Huizinga, *Homo Ludens*, 161.

37 In this sense civilization is liberating. Sigmund Freud in *Civilization and Its Discontents* defines civilization as the sum of achievements and regulations that protect us from nature and adjust our mutual relations (James Strachey, trans. and ed. [New York: W. W. Norton, 1962], 42). Insofar, however, as he sees it as the principal force constraining the direct satisfaction of our primary instincts, civilization is also constrictive.

38 The "good" is clearly here distinguished from the useful and necessary; the good is the fine, the beautiful.

39 See *Politics* 1333b, 1338a–b.

40 In an interesting recent article on whether or not libraries containing actual printed books should be maintained now that the promise (if not quite the actuality) of digitizing them "all" has arrived, with Google undertaking the task of putting them online, among the several arguments advanced by Robert Darnton for preserving the physical objects themselves is that digitization fails to "capture crucial aspects of a book," among which he names size, feel, printing and paper quality, binding, signs of peculiar techniques of printers and pressmen, use by past readers, and even smell: "According to a recent survey of French students, 43 percent consider smell to be one of the most important qualities of printed books—so important that they resist buying odorless electronic books." Darnton, "The Library in the New Age," *New York Review of Books* 55, no. 10 (June 12, 2008): 79.

41 For the medieval theologians, what made God's being "supreme" over all others was the fact that the "whatness" and the "thatness" of God were coextensive.

Index

Hearst, William Randolph, collection of, 242n330
Hebborn, Eric, 181–82
Hecksher, W. S., 61, 62–63, 63–64
Hegel, Georg Wilhelm Friedrich, 249n12; and classification of arts, 208–9n9; and historical consciousness, 35, 76, 118, 193, 200, 203; *Lectures on the Philosophy of History*, 193; on Romantic temperament, 206n3
Heidegger, Martin, 114, 127, 203, 206n6, 229n170; *Wahrung*, 190–91, 217n31
Henry VII, collection of, 172
Henry, bishop of Winchester, 61–62, 71
Herodotus, 218n6
Herold, Johann, 30
Herter, Christian, 144–45
Hildebert of Lavardin, 60
Hippolytus (Euripides), 27
Historia naturalis (Pliny the Elder), 44
history, deconstruction of, 217–18n3
History of English Furniture (Macquiod), 241n299
Hobsbawm, Eric, 212n10
Hogarth, William, 102; *Time Smoking a Picture*, 233n212
Holbein, Hans, 28
Holmes, Oliver Wendell, 135, 137
Hood, William P., 141
Hope, Thomas, 235n223
Horace, 50
Hubbard, Elbert, 240n295
Hughes, Robert, 221n53
Huizinga, Johan, *Homo Ludens*, 201–2
humanism, 190, 192, 193, 198–99; in Renaissance, 66, 68
Hume, David, *Treatise of Human Nature*, 183
Huntington, Samuel P., 191
Hurd, Richard, 105
Hussey, Andrew, 243n337
Hutcheson, Francis, 99, 101, 214n15
Huysmans, Joris-Karl, 131–32, 149

Ictinus, 44, 209n9
immigrants to United States, and antiques, 137, 141–42
Impressionism, 28, 131, 183, 213n13, 215n19
India, collecting in, 59
individualism, 35, 123–24, 196
Industrial Revolution, 107, 116, 117, 124, 127, 196; and United States, 135

integrity of artworks, 15–16, 22
intensity, as aspect of beauty, 22
International Modern, 150–51
Isabella d'Este, Marchioness of Mantua, 228n163

James I, 90–91
James, Henry, 133
Janson, H. W., 128–29
Japan, 57; art of, and United States, 140–42, 145, 148; copies in, 166, 180; porcelain of, 96, 141, 148, 211n9; revivals in, 206n3; scroll paintings of, 221n53. *See also* japonaiserie; japonism; porcelain: Oriental
japonaiserie, 241n304
japonism, 97, 108, 241n304
Jarves, James Jackson, 220n48
Jefferson, Thomas, collection of, 239n286
Jerusalem, pilgrims in, 65; Temple of, 24, 50
jewelry, 120; Cartier, 26, 209n9
Johnson, Samuel, 97
Joni, Icilio Federico, 247n50
Jonson, Ben, 85

Kandinsky, Wassily, 194
Kant, Immanuel: on aesthetics, 100–101, 121, 198, 231n189; on art vs. craft, 101; on beauty, 32–33, 121, 207n9, 214n15, 216–17n30, 250n20; on classification of arts, 101
Kaufmann, Walter, 122, 169
Kennedy, Jacqueline, 184
Kent, William, 107
King, Jon, 114
Ko Ku Yao Lum, 57
kokuza, 141
Komar and Melamid, *Stalin and the Muses*, 212n11
Krautheimer, Richard, 61–62
Kristeller, Paul Oskar, 47, 207–8n9, 232n190
Kunstkammer, 79–81

Lady with an Ermine (Leonardo), 212n11
Lalique, René, 183, 211n9
Lane, Fitz Hugh, *Sunset at Gloucester Harbor*, 167
Larsus, 55
L'art pour l'art, 36, 46
Last Judgment (Michelangelo), 239n278
Last Supper (Leonardo), 178
Lawrence of Arabia, 185

INDEX

261

Poussin, Nicolas, 28
Praxiteles, 53, 67, 77, 250n27
pre-Columbian artifacts, 80, 85
Pre-Raphaelite Brotherhood, 122, 128, 240n295
Price, Uvedale, 107
price, 186–88, 243n344; in contemporary marketplace, 160, 162, 187; guides to, 11, 187, 237n260; record, 153, 235n225, 242n317; of Rubens's works, 247n46
primitive art, 200; vs. antiques, 250n27
Proust, Marcel, 131
provenance, 9; and aesthetic response, 7, 33–34; continuity of, 185; as criterion of antiques, 162, 183–85; fake, 8, 184; and trophies, 24
Pugin, Augustus, 107, 245n12
Puritanism, 133–34, 136, 150, 228n163

Querelle, 87–89, 99, 101. *See also* "Battle of the Ancients and the Moderns"
Quintilian, 54
quotidian object, 86, 96, 196; aesthetic appeal of, 110–11; American view of, 133, 137–38; and Art Nouveau, 147; as art object, 14, 156; and bourgeoisie, 125; and contemporary art, 13–14, 153–54

Racine, Jean, *Phèdre*, 27–28
Ranger, Terence, 212n10
Raphael, 28, 76–77, 93; *School of Athens*, 239n278
Rare Art Traditions, The (Alsop), 192–93
rarity, 8, 160, 171–73, 187; and beauty, 22, 26
Redford, Bruce, 144
Reisener, Jean-Henri, 235n225
relic, religious, vs. antique, 22, 24, 62, 68, 183, 214n15, 240n294
Rembrandt, 93, 208n9; collection of, 96, 228n163; *The Night Watch*, 167
Renaissance: appreciation for antiques in, 34, 66–78, 94; conception of past in, 74–77, 89–90, 97, 117, 118, 225n118
renaissances. *See* revivalism
Reni, Guido, 178
Renoir, Auguste, 28, 178
Republic (Plato), 113, 240n298
restoration, 33, 122–23, 199; and authenticity, 176–79; vs. conservation, 123, 166–69, 245n12; Medieval conception of, 64, 66

Revere, Paul, 163
revivalism, 11, 105, 126, 153, 192; and Romanticism, 119–21; in United States, 136
Reynolds, Joshua, 104
Rheims, Maurice, 50, 96, 125, 172, 187, 215n17
Ribera, José, 28
Richard II, collection of, 90
Richardson, Jonathan, 98–99
Richelieu, duc de (cardinal), 226n138, 227n140; collection of, 83
Rinker, Harry, 186
Robinson, Jenefer M., 246n26
Robsjohn-Gibbings, T. H., 151
Rockefeller, John D., 142, 148
Rockwell, Norman, 138
Rococo, 114, 119, 234n223, 240n295, 246n28; and Baroque, 36; and chinoiserie, 108, 110, 111, 149, 173; and eclecticism, 120, 126; and Gothic, 107; and interest in world, 77, 85
Rodin, Auguste, 122
Roman Catholicism, and art, 82, 121, 237n249, 242n328
Romanticism, 107, 117–18; and antiques, 35–36, 118–23, 172, 206n3; conception of past in, 118; and primitivism, 200
Rome: appreciation for antiques in, 34, 48–56, 68–74, 155–56; and Egyptian art, 52, 53; and Greek art, 34, 49–52, 53–54, 173; pilgrims in, 60, 72
Rosetta Stone, 115
Rothschild collection, 2, 5, 143–44, 185, 235n225
Rousseau, Jean-Jacques, 35, 112, 117
Royal Pavilion, 108, 235n231
Roycrofters, 240n295
Rubens, Peter Paul, 69, 180, 239n278, 247n46; collection of, 91, 227–28n162
Rudolph II (emperor), 81, 94
Ruhling, Nancy, 144
ruin: cult of, 35, 105–7, 110, 118, 206n3; in Medieval thought, 64
Ruskin, John, 124, 126, 138, 220n48, 237n249, 245n12; on agedness, 32, 106; on handcraftedness, 170; on medieval ideal, 107, 122, 238n276; *Seven Lamps of Architecture*, 126

Saint Sernin, church of, 176–77
Saisselin, Rémy, 87–88, 110, 112, 123–24
Salutati, Coluccio, 67–68